What to Look for in Winter: A Memoir in Blindness

What
to Look
for in
Winter:
A Memoir
in
Blindness

Candia
McWilliam

HARPER

An Imprint of HarperCollins*Publishers*
www.harpercollins.com

HarperCollins books may be purchased for educational, business, or sales promotional use. For information, please write: Special Markets Department, HarperCollins Publishers, 10 East 53rd Street, New York, NY 10022.

Grateful acknowledgment is made for permission to reproduce from the following:

"One Art," taken from *Collected Poems*, © the Estate of Elizabeth Bishop and reprinted by permission of Farrar, Straus and Giroux Ltd.

"The Waste Land," taken from *The Waste Land and Other Poems*, © the Estate of T. S. Eliot and reprinted by permission of Faber and Faber Ltd.

"The Trees," taken from *Collected Poems of Philip Larkin*, © 1988, 2003 the Estate of Philip Larkin and reprinted by permission of Faber and Faber Ltd. and Farrar, Straus and Giroux LLC.

"The More Loving One," taken from *Collected Poems*, © 1957, 1991 W. H. Auden and reprinted by permission of The Wylie Agency LLC.

First published in slightly different form in Great Britain in 2010 by Jonathan Cape.

FIRST U.S. EDITION PUBLISHED 2012

Library of Congress Cataloging-in-Publication Data has been applied for.

ISBN: 978-0-06-209450-6

12 13 14 15 16 QRK/RRD 10 9 8 7 6 5 4 3 2 1

TO

OLLY

CLEM

&

MINOO

The art of losing isn't hard to master;
so many things seem filled with the intent
to be lost that their loss is no disaster.

Lose something every day. Accept the fluster
of lost door keys, the hour badly spent.
The art of losing isn't hard to master.

Then practice losing farther, losing faster:
places, and names, and where it was you meant
to travel. None of these will bring disaster.

I lost my mother's watch. And look! my last, or
next-to-last, of three loved houses went.
The art of losing isn't hard to master.

I lost two cities, lovely ones. And, vaster,
some realms I owned, two rivers, a continent.
I miss them, but it wasn't a disaster.

— Even losing you (the joking voice, a gesture
I love) I shan't have lied. It's evident
the art of losing's not too hard to master
though it may look like (Write it!) like disaster.

One Art by Elizabeth Bishop

Be as thou wast wont to be;
See as thou wast wont to see;

Oberon to Titania
A Midsummer Night's Dream by William Shakespeare

Femme qui boit du vin
Fille qui parle latin
Soleil levé trop matin
Dieu sait quelle sera leur triste fin

French Proverb

Contents

CONTENTS

A Paper Umbrella

One of the last things my mother gave me was a paper umbrella; it must have been from Japan. Its wooden spars were webbed with an oily paper that smelled of pine resin and fish. When you put the umbrella up, the paper separated from itself with a faint disgustingness of sound, unidentifiable as yet to a child of eight, that would later reveal itself to be that of flesh separating from flesh or the frozen surface of a lake beginning to shiver apart.

My paper umbrella was of little use in Edinburgh, a city with some call for the kind of umbrella that keeps off not the glare of the sun but the fall of the rain. Nonetheless, I loved it. My mother was a woman with too many superstitions, a trait I have inherited, so she didn't like the umbrella to be put up inside the house. I didn't want to upset her, so I would stand just outside the house, on the stone step, under my orange paper umbrella, whirling it and looking up through its oily sections, listening to the seagulls mewing over our street.

My mother shook silver in her pocket under the new moon, avoided looking at that moon through glass, said she wouldn't have hawthorn or peacock feathers in the house, and telephoned on our party line regularly to St Anthony of Padua when she lost things. Or she tried to keep to these strictures. In fact, she seldom had silver in her pocket, the moon went where it wanted to go, and she found herself surprisingly often arranging the hawthorn in vases or making fancy-dress outfits for me with glittering many-eyed peacock feathers she had stolen from the Zoo. St Anthony I cannot speak for. So, she knew what to avoid, but did not quite do it.

Hers was a compressed life, folded back down into itself only shortly after it had apparently emerged into some kind of light. Nonetheless in its shade other lives have grown up, my own and those of my three children. I have the instinct too that she had many friends, though I do not know this, and that people who met her remembered having done so. But that might be wishful thinking of the sort we scatter on the young dead.

Tomorrow this book of mine, which is greatly hers, goes to the printer. It is an account of many kinds of light denied. It is also the account of how certain forms of shade are rich if you are fortunate enough to stay sufficiently long to read them. I have already lived for eighteen years longer than my mother did.

Wanting to surprise her when I was about five, I tried to make purple ice cubes, using violet ink. We had only recently become a family with a refrigerator. Before that, we had had a meat-safe, a sort of individualised Iron Maiden. I took the burning cold ice tray, with its square eyebaths for the water, held in tight form by a metal grid, like the letters in my printing set. Each one I filled with the dense swarming ink and water mixture, black until you spilled it, when it flowered kingly purple. I was acutely conscious that I must be quick as I dosed the small moulds. No shoogling. It occasioned the sort of rapt guilt that making sentences can to a child taught only of the primacy of fact; I was lucky not to be born such a child, though later events were to change that. The private nature of what I was doing was blissful as was the idea that my actions were exactly aimed to delight someone I loved. I closed the ice compartment upon my inky tray of socketed dark water.

I returned to my drawing at the kitchen table and waited for my mother. The tact required from her must have been great. Purple hands covered her small new fridge. She went about her kitchen tasks until such time as it would have been natural to open it, perhaps to get some milk, or some anchovy paste, of which, and smoked cod roe, she was fond (I often wonder whether she and I are really part-time seals). Inside, the shelves and contents of her newly acquired zone of hygiene and modernity were drenched imperially with violet ink.

She took in what I had intended, rather than what I had achieved. She told me that it might be fun – next time – to use food colouring not ink, so that no one would be poisoned. And we could put in some grapes too, or flowers.

So, a short life, but one in which she took time to pay close attention to the ideas of others. She had little, but was much.

This book is the merely paper umbrella that I have been able slowly to erect against the usual human weathers and one surprising cloud – my blindness – over several years. Sometimes as I have variously spoken it or tapped it out, I have felt as though an umbrella of skin held between bones were forcing itself through my person. Why umbrella? Again I have returned to that paper umbrella; shade is the most one can ask, shade from which to see with some kind of truth, neither hectic with sunlight nor sodden to blackness.

The world of addiction and recovery from it is full of necessarily approximate language. Plenty of aesthetically snooty addicts hang offshore from sobriety, unwilling to accept the slogans on offer. I know several. I have been one. It's too easy, though, to go clever against the pat sayings that offer you some handhold as you fall: 'I came'; 'I came to'; 'I came to see'; 'Let go and let God'. You have to open up to the possibility that your private pain is not to be held furled and weapon-like, but to be opened out as you fall, parachute not ferrule, so that it may protect another, a collective shelter from a fearful rain.

While we are on weather, observant readers may notice that I have made at least one compass error of grave consequence. That I can think of these errors in any way that might be useful is due to those I love who are here described and to what I have read. The work of Sybille Bedford is seldom far away. My then husband and I had supper with her once. She was formidable and cross. He reminded me of that long gone evening in the winter of this year, 2010, when he had first read this book. He said that it was hard to convey how much I had once had – he was not speaking materially – and how much I did not now have; it is indeed like a cautionary tale or a minatory melodrama. I know that this will not be lost on certain schools of comment. I recall a friend telling me of how she had seen someone look at a photograph of me surrounded by dolls in a magazine and say, 'Look at *her*; her life's so perfect even her wretched children *look like dolls.*'

PART ONE: SPECTACLES

Earpiece I

W hy don't you write your memoirs?' I've been asked, or, worse, 'Why don't you write your life story? No one would believe it.'

Well, that's why.

My friend Allan Massie wrote to me in 1996 that I was, as a novelist, 'insufficiently prolific'. But for one thin book of stories, I am exactly as unprolific now as I was then.

My last novel was published in 1994, my last book of short stories in 1996. It's not that I'm not writing, or it wasn't, but rather that I had taken a wrong turning and got stuck. I saw this baulk reflected back to me in every face I met. It got so bad that I could not bear the glare.

That unbearable glare has in the last years taken on an entirely new meaning for me.

Friends who knew me better than the ones who simply asked about a memoir, said, 'You really must write something about Scotland; it's changed so much since when you were a child.'

In the new millennium, I attended a rehabilitation clinic for alcoholism. When the press discovered this, for a whole day I couldn't walk through my native city without being stopped for I was that day's page three and four girl; double spread, as it were, 'my alcoholic hell by Scots writer'. I had my youngest child Minoo with me. His reaction was phlegmatic: 'People who believe that angle believe that angle,' he said. I telephoned the other children. One was in a pub in Caithness; I worried that he would be hurt. 'Nonsense,' he said, 'I'm up here with a few of the boys carrying on your tradition. Seriously, Mummy, it's fine.' My daughter had left a long soothing message on every telephone in Scotland that might pertain to me about the nature of truth and corruption and how dreadful it must be – and she's right – for really famous people.

Nonetheless all three children lived the painful truth of having an alcoholic mother. When it came to be known by certain publishers that this was the case, just one feeler came out to me. Would I write a misery memoir: 'Middle-class, middle-aged woman at War Hotel spills all', sort of thing? 'War Hotel' is the term used to describe rehab when you want to big it up.

My reply to this was the worst possible and constituted the last drink I've had to this day. It lasted a fortnight, I think. One drink being too many and a thousand not enough.

In the rehabilitation centre, which was set in a house about whose architecture and inhabitants, The Souls, I had once, long ago, written a review, several of the counsellors, themselves mostly 'in recovery', asked me if I would write about the experience. I was surprised because confidentiality is one of the tenets of all twelve-step programmes of recovery from addiction. They said, 'No, yours would be different; it could help people.'

To one of my temperament, to be of use to others is an irresistible spur. Even my last child was an attempt to please my mother-in-law who had said bitterly, 'I expect I'll get a book a year instead of a grandchild.'

Still, I wrote no memoir, but I was thinking it. Towards what end I did not know, but I'm glimpsing now.

I didn't see it coming, but in this spring of 2008, I've had to close down on my other addiction, far more serious than the drink, that was lifelong, beautiful, consolatory, solitary and terminal: reading.

For it appears that I am gone blind.

———◆◆◆◆———

Blindness, and I gather that this is so for many who cannot see, is not a solid or unmodulated blackness such as one might imagine comes over the head of a hawk when you put on its hood. In addition my blindness could be termed illegitimate, since it is not so that my eyes cannot see.

It is simply the case that my brain has chosen to close them. For twenty-two hours every day I am unable to open them.

That is the reason why I'm writing a book more full of 'I's than I'm temperamentally moved, or perhaps even equipped, to. When you imagine a writer writing what do you see in your mind's eye? I'm not talking about those pictures of writers' studies in lifestyle sections. I'm talking about the thing itself, the solitary maker of what you read.

Unthink it now, perhaps, for I am not actually writing at all, but dictating, pacing a room sixteen of my paces long and fourteen wide and having my spoken words typed by a fine-featured young woman with the auspicious name of Liv Stones. I am marching blindly to and fro with my Diet Coke, carrying my pointless spectacles and trying to think aloud in sentences and paragraphs, I hope for your benefit, or, better, your pleasure.

Before I went blind, I would if forced to choose my most beloved author have said Henry James. He has been joined by Tolstoy and Proust. But he is still my great love and here it is irresistible to put in his tribute to Miss Theodora Bosanquet, his last, near-telepathic amanuensis.
James wrote to his brother William:

A new excellent amanuensis, a young boyish Miss Bosanquet, who is worth all the other (females) that I have had put together and who confirms to me in the perception afresh – after eight months without such an agent – that for certain, for most, kinds of diligence and production, the intervention of the agent is, to my perverse constitution, an intense aid and a true economy! There is no comparison.

I managed to read about the first twelve words of that aloud to Liv, by holding my eyelids open with my fingers, but it got too sore and if I waste sight this early in the day I will be bumping into things like a bumblebee by elevenses. I fall over a lot and am covered with the sort of bruises that worry social workers. Last week I had a pretty black eye that I wanted to keep for longer; I came by it walking into the bough of a pollarded wisteria in Radnor Walk. Since the blindness really took hold, I have hardly worn eye make-up and I had forgotten what an enjoyable, if minute, recreation the painting of one's own eyes is. I feel like a Greek fishing boat without its painted eyes. Without my sparkle I can't seem to see my way. In India mothers put kohl on babies' eyes to ward off blindness. My black shiner was a beautiful mix of colours: navy, rose, ochre, olive, ultramarine. It returned one of my eyes to me in definition at least, for they feel as though they have fallen in and dried out like deserted eggs, or like painful stones behind crisped, gluey lids. It is to be hoped that together Liv and I may either lift, or bring life to, those stones.

Why call this chapter 'Earpiece'? Because I have to accept that I cannot read through my eyes and must listen (I still can't call it reading) through my ears. I held out pridefully, typically, self-punishingly, until 10 July 2007, when a friend got me to listen to *On Chesil Beach* by Ian McEwan on her iPod. The iPod was on speakers because I still cannot bear to block another sense by putting things in my ears and stopping up two more holes in my head like Odysseus as he avoids the Sirens' song.

You can't hide in a talking book, and with my iPod problem I can't 'read' in company. But that's lucky, in a way, as I am almost always alone.

I do not live with my husband. I left him more than ten years ago. We are legally separated but not divorced. It was a mistake. He said to me when I went blind, ' Perhaps you have had to lose everything to return to yourself and your art', and it's a thought, though rather too grand for me, who have always put on a clean, ironed, white apron in order to sit down to write. It's the sort of thing you can say about dead people. I do feel dead sometimes. I feel like a fat ghost.

What's the difference between the old way of reading and this new listening? Partly that is what this book will be about. In practical terms, there are the questions of the machines and the vital question of the reader, or actor, of the book. Machines first: I like tapes, even though they go wrong and are soon to become obsolete; CDs, with their wafery holographic smoothness, just don't say 'words' to me. But I consume both in inordinate quantities. Part of whatever it is that has gone wrong in my brain involves broken sleep and where I would once have turned to a book I click on the merciful munching tape or set the CD spinning.

There is pleasure, and I really doubted that there would be, in re-listening, just as there is delight in rereading. It is a very different pleasure, and one of which I might not have, in the purist old days, approved. I have always deprecated the habit of reading simply for plot, for the solving of the puzzle. It is the texture of the text, the touch of the writer's thinking upon my own thought, the intimacy of interinanimation that I loved and that had accompanied me all my conscious life.

I confess I haven't had even one jolt of this quality of delight since becoming a listener, though there have been many moments when I clumsily tried to stop the machine *there – just there –* and catch the words again, in order to make, as I'm afraid I would have done before, a note in the margin, or on a bit of paper. I find these notes now next to my bed where I do most of my listening, but of course I can't read them; it's like darning a black sock trying to read my writing now. The sort of reading that I used to love, reading several books simultaneously, is not now possible. I used to do it when I felt a novel brewing, that time when the unconscious is bulging, sticky and collecting with a view to its unknown quarry; in those conditions the strangest books forged relationships with one another and something new would be born. Books, even alone in a room, have that quality; they breathe; they can even, somehow, parthenogenetically, reproduce.

Somehow? I know perfectly well how in my case. I buy them. It's silly and I buy fewer than I did when I read or when I had some idea that I could or would read them, but I buy them to have them handy by me, to have their breath in my air, their breathing mixing with my own. I miss them.

❦

Just how hard this is to express came home to me only yesterday when, after Liv's first morning typing for me, a young friend of my daughter's visited. He had told me last week that he was going to spend the bank holiday weekend, among other, ice-creamier things, reading *Timon of Athens* in order to ready himself to read A.D. Nuttall's *Shakespeare the Thinker* on *Timon*. Never would I have thought that the intensest pleasure of my fifty-third year would be brought by being read aloud to from this generous, precise, thrilling book. It is the most intimate experience of my year so far and that intimacy was with the text and the ideas within the text and the modesty, breadth and quiddity of an, alas now posthumous, scholarly voice.

So far, in my experience, this hasn't happened with talking books, but they are marvellous things nonetheless. I have the addict's tooth-grinding shakes when I'm running out of talking books. I know that I can turn to Proust again, but I like to have a fresh stash hidden somewhere about the place. There are, for example, three box-fresh sets of CDs (Plutarch's *Lives*, Aristotle and *A Guide to Ancient Greek Philosophy*) hidden in this room, and every room in the flat has a similar hoard. It is exactly like keeping vodka in your steam iron. Any alcoholic, set the task of finding my hidden tapes and CDs, 'just for emergencies', you understand, would be through with the hunt in five minutes, easy as finding a bottle in a gumboot.

The medical term used for my type of blindness is 'functional'. The topsy-turvy logic of this is that I function hardly at all and can do very little for myself. I carry a fold-up-able white stick when I leave the house, which is seldom, and then mainly to visit doctors. You buy these white sticks from a website set up by the RNIB where all sorts of gadgets may be found, including talking microwaves. I've been fighting off microwaves since first they began and people started saying things like, 'You can reheat your nasty cold coffee.' I really don't want a chatty microwave, but of course I see the point.

It is a new world and I'd best take it as the adventure it is, generously, as though it were a gift. It is in a way a new way of seeing, not to see.

Here I must advert to, and then we can each forget, or absorb, the saturation of our language with metaphors to do with sight.

One of the unlooked-for benefits of this functional blindness was that I simply gave up cooking as too extreme a sport; sadly, the new lot of drugs they are trying on me have made of the new, thinner, me the old, fatter, me.

Functional blindness is not a pest merely for its possessors. The state and its bureaucracy don't much like it either, and in the past eighteen months I have spent much time with well-meaning personages assessing such grey areas as my 'toileting ability'.

As things stand, I was advised by the state that I must apply for a Disability Living Allowance, since without this I cannot register as blind which I must do before I can be considered for a guide dog. This allowance has just skyrocketed 65 pence per week. But my short career as a benefits scrounger will, as far as I can see, be terminated at the next Budget, when, if New Labour are still in, I shall be reassessed and, putatively, retrained to do a job more suited to my capacity or rather, as they say, 'ability', meaning the opposite.

Back to that word 'functional'. Perhaps it is my Scottishness, but I can't see a way of writing this book without wanting it to be of some use. The privilege, as I understood it, of being a novelist was to touch the imagination of others with one's own and to establish a contact more real than many other forms of encounter. It was my task, I thought, to convey the truth of what it is to be alive, to feel, and to think, to catch both differentness and connection in narratives that shed light on the secret human heart. So, perhaps, this exercise that intimidates me, on account of its going so deeply against my grain, may touch your synapses with my own as I give some account of what it has been to have lived, to have felt and to have thought within my head before and since it closed down its main route to, and means of, interpreting the world, my eyes.

I shall affix this spoken earpiece to the coming, first, dark lens of my account that follows. I wrote it before I knew how blind I was to become. After the central chapter named 'Bridge', the words are again spoken not written with that last stub of sight I had.

But first a few compass bearings:

I have three children each with a different last name.

I have been married twice.

In one sense I still am.

My children have two fathers.

My name is Candia. It is not Candida. When I meet people, they often say, 'Don't you mean Candida?' not even, 'Do you mean Candida?' My nickname, which is complicated for reasons that will become clear, is Claude. My name is not Claudia. It is Candia. Greek, not Latin.

I have called five people Mum, Mummy or Mama.

The Partition of India and Pakistan in 1947 contributed much to the splitting of my second marriage.

My second husband, Fram, lives with someone else.

Her name is Claudia.

Fram and Claudia live together with her twins, whom I love, and their father, Toby Buxton.

I love my two husbands' two partners.

Among the words that make me most frustrated are 'Candia McWilliam's swallowed the dictionary'. I heard them first in the sandpit, where I had just said 'avocado'. I was three. It strikes me now that the accuser must have done some pretty heavy swallowing too. The sneers recurred a lot in reviews of my stuff; what annoyed me was the implication that women had better stay within lexical limits.

That said, I last heard these words, or their equivalent, only a few months ago in the mouth of a prodigiously educated Cognitive Behavioural Therapist at Guy's Hospital. How ingenious of him at once to have found me out. I was, very nearly, angry.

------◆◆◆◆------

The following things are also true:

I am six foot tall and afraid of small people.

I am a Scot.

I am an alcoholic.

There is nothing wrong with my eyes.

I am blind.

I cannot lose my temper though I am being helped to, as you see above.

I exude marriedness and I am alone.

This book is, among very many other things, an attempt to find that temper in order that I may lose it, and in losing it, perhaps, find my lost eyes.

LENS I: Chapter 1

I have conducted my conscious life for as long as I can remember by suppression, and so this is, or threatens to be, the sort of book which I am not temperamentally suited to write, an account of a life lived, not transmuted into fiction. For me the fiction had carried the deep truths behind which I had felt able to retire, and to carry on weaving it.

Some writers, from Henry Green to Hilary Mantel, can manage this poetically veracious memoir-writing naturally. I read the best of them with pleasure and fascination. They illuminate without glare and delineate privacy without harming it. The memoirs I shrink from are accounts of profitable suffering; no, profitable accounts of suffering.

I can't imagine that this book will be profitable in a pecuniary sense. Yet I know that any suffering in my life – 'suffering' may be too extreme, too official, too martial, above all too tragic a word for whatever has happened to me, though maybe not for what I have brought about – might be of some use to someone. I am porous to the pain of others, but just of late have got stuck. I am fogged up. Here's why.

It has been brewing since I was five, I know it now. I found that the way to distance oneself from discomfort was to trap it in not spoken but written words, and that, similarly, the way to hold fast to the good was to try – much less easy – to do the same. I was greatly helped in my project by being a fat child. I was good at sitting still because I wasn't any good at moving. It was my good fortune to have two parents who never stopped making marks on paper and the richest part of whose lives were led in her imagination in one case and his intellect in the other. I copied them.

◆•••◆

Why start on this now? In 2006, anxious about money and aware that I was about to start out aged fifty on a life alone, in Oxford, a city in which I had taken twenty years not to feel at home, I accepted an invitation to become a judge of the Man Booker Prize for Fiction. I was a sedulous, note-taking, reader of contemporary fiction as well as a lot of other stuff, and I thought I might as well harness my habit. I liked either the actuality of or the sound of the other judges. I wasn't wrong to.

The entire process of judging fiction is difficult to defend or articulate and painful even – especially? – for any 'winner' of tender conscience but, insofar as it is possible, we remained pure. Early on, the Chair of the judges' committee had given me a fine piece of advice: 'If you fall in love with one book you will be setting yourself up for heartbreak,' she said. I took prophylactic measures, and fell in love with three or four.

After the first judges' meeting, which took place in the solid surroundings of the Athenaeum, I went to visit a friend with whom I had been at school after I was sent away from home in Scotland. We have known one another since we were twelve. 'What is wrong with your face?' she asked, and offered to balance teabags on my eyes, which did indeed feel wonky, despite the soothing light of a grey spring day in St James's Square. My eyes juddered in their sockets as though they were coming loose and they were hot and couldn't settle unless I told them to. So the implicit pact between intellect and eyes, eyes and reading heart, had to be declared and had already begun to involve willpower instead of consolation and ease.

I had noticed that I was having difficulty holding the gaze of anyone who was talking to me, but had, characteristically, ascribed this to even more reading than usual and an unadmitted struggle with sleeping, especially through the hours between two and four in the morning, the time when suicide suggests itself and addicts give in.

I kept on reading, of course. Twice, I visited GPs, who each prescribed eye drops. I was aware that I couldn't deal as well with people as I had been used to, because I couldn't hold their gaze. I wondered if this was a late-onset affectation, like a fake stammer to imply an engaging tentativeness. But I couldn't employ my will over my eyes, couldn't respond or beam or seek or console as I had always – I realised – been used to doing.

My stint as secretary of one of the Alcoholics Anonymous meetings came to an end and I was relieved, as I had relied upon my intensity of gaze, my peripheral vision and my attunedness in order to intuit who needed to speak when and for how long.

From my father I have inherited the characteristic that I am irresistible to panhandlers. University towns are rich in such people and I have all my life felt that I *am* one. There's no gap to mind. Most of the beggars in Oxford know my name, or a version of it. My chief heckling bridesmaid at the time was a rather cross, sometimes violent, highly intelligent alcoholic, named Man. By the cashpoint one day he said, 'Ere, Candice, what *is* wrong with your eyes?'

I visited an ophthalmologist who laughed handsomely at the amount of reading I reported myself as doing. I found that odd, in Oxford. I doubt that I was reading as much as, for example, many dons, or my neighbour the Reverend Professor Sir Henry Chadwick, whose elegant figure might be seen daily as he got into the car on the way to the library in order to set about the Early Church with grace and vigour; and he, after all, was rising to the challenge of manuscript with eyes that had been working for all but a half century longer than my own.

I was reading those soft options, novels, printed (one might have thought) in typefaces congenial to the eye, faces confected to encourage and reward the process of reading.

I got more drops.

I took seventy or so books home to the Hebrides, where part of me had been a child. I rented a wee cottage down the drive from my adopted family, so that I might work. My family visited on a generously formal basis. There were painful family events occurring, than which any passing funny business with my eyes was far less harrowing. Also, my sisters, who are not really my sisters, each noticed, with her own fine eyes, that things had got better with those bad peepers since I had 'come home'. That was so. The air in the Western Isles is cleaner than it is in Oxford. Certain stresses were removed. I read around seven hundred pages a day, took notes, wrote letters. For the first time since late childhood, I did not accompany my family as they walked around the island. If I had done I might have fallen off it, but I didn't say that to anyone. A heron came each morning and stood in the burn among the reeds, his small knees like knots.

I went across to Edinburgh, leaving the island on my own for the first time in my life. I cried when I left as the sea widened between the ferry and the island. I do not often cry, but crying has proved to be one of the few things that wash clear my sight, however briefly. I've been trying to take it up more.

I watched the island go, and the other islands pass: Jura, Islay, Mull, the Grey Dogs, the Isles of the Sea.

I went through, as the process of crossing Scotland's waist is called, to Edinburgh, did a reading over breakfast of a short story or two to an audience in the mirrored tent at the Book Festival, which has been a kind of annual transfusion for me in the many years during which I have read more than I have written (which is not hard), and then bolted for a train down to London for another meeting of the Man Booker Prize judges.

I'd been going to fly, but a terrorist incident had grounded all planes and put the nation on its guard against, among other things, carriers of lipstick, scent or fountain pens. Guilty on all counts, I packed my longish frame and a 900-page novel into the vestibule, as the greased-up hinge between carriages of a passenger train is fabulously designated, of a southbound train, and settled to some hours' standing room only.

I minded even more than usual being photographed, as we all were, for the long list press meeting. It wasn't – only – vanity, it was an acute sense that I couldn't open my eyes. But when making a point or really engaging with the other judges, I could momentarily see into their faces. I realised that this peeled state of being was mind-altering and, while quite useful for an indentured servant of fiction, and a state desirable if it might be useful to the artist in one, not much good in a mother or a friend.

I returned to the North, relieved to be leaving the Quaker club where I had been staying in a bed off whose end I hung. In the night I had met polite dressing-gowned ghosts of either sex in the corridors, between fire doors, up in Town for a play or to clock the City churches. In each room at the club is a list of local things worth visiting which reads like a list of my great-aunts' enthusiasms, those penurious educated lonely accomplished women. I could feel the fulcrum tipping as I passed into my own past and with some relief felt young no more.

LENS I: Chapter 2

In Edinburgh, as always happens, I took a lease of life and shared it with my younger son. We had a happy few days listening to authors, a really peculiar thing to enjoy doing, but we do. I continued to see jokes and architectural detail, two things that keep me going, though only as it were in stroboscopic clatters of vision.

My son returned to school and autumn was upon us.

Opposite me in Oxford lived two neurologists. The wife was slight, pretty, part-Chinese. By now, if I did have friends to visit, I was experimenting with wearing a green hat indoors to see whether this soothed my sight. I had accommodated to the difficulty of combining walking with seeing by capping the reclusion I had been working on for a decade with completely hermetic habits. I had stopped attending all meetings, including AA, save those for the Man Booker Prize for Fiction 2006.

I visited the GP once more and met a new doctor, young, surrounded by books; on his wall – I saw! – was my favourite *New Yorker* cartoon, showing a snail in love with a Sellotape dispenser. I told him what had happened, that my world had narrowed quite and that I found it difficult to open my eyes.

He used a word that made complete sense, a direct lift from the Greek. It was very rare, he said, but it did exist. The word was blepharospasm. *Blepharon* comes up a lot in Homer, and is the Greek for eyelid. Spasm was it.

I was relieved that I had not been making all this up.

My neighbour the pretty part-Chinese neurologist knocked at my door one dusk in September. I wasn't actually wearing my green hat, as I had been alone. Nor was I wearing sunglasses. I could manage by, as I had come to think of it, 'striving' with my neck and chin, to focus a bit and gather from her outline who she might be, and I could smell that she had quinces about her person.

'Can you not see me?' she asked.

'No, not really very well.'

'I've got some quinces from our tree,' she said, 'and you have blepharospasm.'

And so I do. My eyes are fine, my vision acute, but my eyelids will not open.

In order to gain sight, I grimace, stretch, peer and above all hold taut and high my already rather camel-like head with the result that I look, if I do go out, like the caricature of a snob. Mainly I take steps so as not to emerge from my tall thin house whose many and irregular stairs fill me with a reinforcement of the dread of falling to my death downstairs that I have had all my life; my parents' house in Edinburgh had sustained such a death down its stone stairs, I had always gathered self-propelled; that was part of the reason they could afford it, I think.

I now have the elastic-braced white stick with which I hope to dispel the impression of a monstrous dowager with Tourettian facial tics and the creep-and-lurch gait of a not sufficiently surreptitious drunk. Also, of course, I don't want to embarrass people, or to oblige them to ask if it is getting better. It doesn't.

In some cases it can be alleviated by the injection of botulinum toxin, which hauls me up for my ugly pride in declaring that I'd never have facial 'work', as puritanical fans of plastic surgery call it. I clamoured for the injections now. In Scotland we call them jags and I had four jags in each eye, always praying while the needle goes in that I am somehow buying off Fate for my children and those I love, a dangerous deal and foolish, the worse and worst always offering themselves to the inward eye of a parent.

And as my eyes have closed, so I have learned perforce a number of things, some of which may even be passed on or rendered down, as those quinces were, into something useful or reminiscent or nourishing or maybe merely scented with something that reminds you of something else. It was as if my deep brain was telling me that I, with my lucky and unlucky life, have seen enough and that I really am for the dark. I must catch the light and offer it around, like those quinces and that insight from my generous diagnostic neighbour.

And of course it is not telling you a secret if I confess that I am blindly hoping by hunting down the light, the past, those lost places and people, to lift at any rate some of the stone that has rolled across the mouth of my cave.

My youngest child asked me, 'It is a vulgar question, but, may I ask, do any of your other senses compensate yet?'

One of my sisters who are not my sisters declared, and it comforted me about her decided unchangeability, 'Well, we always said we'd rather go blind than deaf.'

How dared we?

How lazily I have assured dying friends that they look well, how idly nodded when people mentioned the unerring ear of the blind piano tuner. Now is the time for me at any rate to pay attention and look hard, close, even if only upon what has been.

This might be as good a point as any to say that none of the treatments described in this book was covered by private health insurance. I did not have it.

Books have been throughout my life very much more than mere consolation and escape, but I cannot deny that they have, and the act of reading itself has, been that too. I now read with a certain amount of difficulty, and can do about a paragraph at a time. Reading in bed is not the bower it was. I cannot at the same time both lie and read, as I have, in the prone not mendacious usage, done lifelong. Reading is tiring which it has never before been. I have all my life eaten books, walked and run and done all I cannot actually in person do among, within and around books, and now am trudging and lagging. Nothing however that insists upon concentration, as this limitation does, is all bad. Memory grows less swooning, more muscular, recall more instructable, like a messenger, and as potent and alarming.

Most things had I thought gone wrong in my life by 2006, but there was always reading. Well, is there? Not in the old sense, the wandering, greedy sense, no. But, even if, in the worst case, I am left no longer able to read, reading will of course remain within me. I used to think, when I was five or six, at night in my nursery, that I would certainly die for books, for Greek and Latin, for words (of course I didn't think of it then as freedom of speech); I know I would surely give up my own sight of them for these things' sake.

I peg up my thinning eyelids with my left-hand thumb and little finger, wearing them through. This is called by doctors 'the sensory geste' and it's a sure sign of blepharospasm. There are gadgets, of some of which I am afraid, most especially the metal loops, called Lundy Loops, that clamp open the perusing eye that then must be moistened with specially measured sterile artificial tears. The unfortunate echo of Belloc's tearful Lord Lundy – 'Gracious, how Lord Lundy cried!' – seems all too apt. It all feels too metaphorical and too true. I have always felt people's eye stories in my own eyes, cannot watch enacted scenes of blinding, the cloud crossing the moon, or even, truly, the cutting into a fried egg; I fear to read of Odysseus grinding the hot tree trunk into the Cyclops' only eye.

The already challenging narrative of 2006 folded symmetrically closed, the judging eyes upon and against the judging dark, and the truth, had I even known it, could not, in the little pond of the 'book world', have been told. The hilariousness of a blind judge for a literary prize already buffeted by vulgar attention might have done an indignity to the prize or its sponsors. Before the actual dinner at the Guildhall in the City of London, I had to tell the public relations people for Man Booker, Colman Getty, that I was 'functionally blind'. They were jolly nice about it and sat me with clever, tactful (and dashing) friends. They agreed that it must not be known and asked that I not wear dark glasses, which can offer relief from the juddering and facial tics. Later that week my daughter told me that someone, a literary editor, had told a newspaper gossip column that he had been on a deadly dull table. The columnist noted that this was my table.

I had bumped into the chap who had me down as deadly dull afterwards, as I slipped off (a system agreed with the publicity firm) before the sorrows-drowning, gossip and commerce began in earnest. What I couldn't tell him, as I no doubt hurt his feelings by not recognising him, and hurt his pride by bumping into him and towering over him, was that I couldn't see him. I'm sorry I bored him that night at dinner. I couldn't think of any way of letting him know that did not let him know too much.

So now let me try.

LENS I: Chapter 3

The City of Edinburgh, heated, when it was, by coal and coke and paraffin, had not yet been cleaned. Its grave beauties were still black. Snow fell in the May before I was born. Black-and-white pictures display it all pretty much exactly as the city looked in colour. Scotland, East Coast Scotland, after the war, was cold, dirty, architecturally grand and architecturally ravaged, sumptuarily poor. Ladies over a certain age wore hats indoors. The smells in the street were of wool of stone of coal and, at home in Puddocky (which means: 'The home of frogs', fit for frogs only), of the pong of hops and yeast from the brewery at Canonmills, down by the Water of Leith, where the flour for the church's canons had once been ground. We lived just a stone wall from the river, which was prone to flood. Our house smelt of wet washing, polish, joss sticks, my mother's *Je Reviens*, and cats and their requirements. Our whole street had been condemned.

My mother boiled ox-lights for the cats. These enormous organs arrived full of air and redness from the butcher, Mr Wilson, and then clopped down, frothing in her jam-making pan, to chewy brown boxing gloves, under the meaty scum. She deflated them further – they hissed – into manageable chunks with kitchen scissors that I have now, sent down south to me thirty years later by my stepmother in a consignment including my toy box and a Fru-Grains tin, all transported by the Aberdeen Shore Porters, the world's oldest removals firm, established more than five hundred years ago to move fish at the harbourside in that silver city.

The kitchen scissors were for kitchen jobs only, the sewing scissors for thread and cloth, and the paper scissors for paper alone. The pinking shears were so heavy and specific that they lived in a holster in the sewing chest with the button box, the cotton reels and the Kwik-unpik, a natty hook for the slashing open of stitches in order mainly to 'let things down', or to 'let things out', terms perhaps now unknown outwith the psychotherapeutic context. There were few rules in my childhood under the dispensation of my mother, but the scissor rule was set. Paper blunted the sewing scissors and kitchen work dirtied the paper scissors. And as for the grapes – they were a luxury to eat (or was it drink, so wet was their taste and so otherwise seductive?) and to look at, so at all times blunt silver grape scissors must be used, like a little flat bird skeleton with a toothed beak, so as to keep the bunch groomed and uncorrupt. I would take grapes with my fingers and leave behind the damp pippy stublet; mould then might spread through the bunch. It seemed I was always found out. If I was caught mid-theft, I would rush to blind whichever parent it was had found me with kisses so that they would not see that I had been greedy and failed to use the scissors. So kisses were connected with distraction and misdeeds – and, it's true, stealing fruit. This book will be a struggle to find that Eden when they were both about, my oddly paired parents, both, incidentally, lovers of pears, and each devoted to a separate means of paring pears. She made slivers, he made hoops.

Another firm rule was that you must never – ever – write on nor fold down the pages of books. I have not obeyed this rule at all thoroughly and as a child was even worse, for I ate the corners of the pages, gouging out soft thumbsful of paper at the corner, chewing it, and collecting a ball. I was making paper, I suppose. An owlish child's pellets.

It is hard to convey to a young reader the frustrations of my mother's life. She was of a generation of women so much less free than my own, as mine is, I hope, less free, or more unrealistic, than my daughter's. I am a poor example of any kind of liberation. 'Are you a feminist?' I was asked in my middle thirties with I knew not what kind of weight. The questioner was a colonial tycoon. I was nibbling at the sort of lunch thought suitable for reasonably attractive married women at that time in history, when the man was paying.

I replied, unforgivably, I think now, with a sort of, 'Let's assume that it's been more widely achieved than that' gesture. This man later went on to murder his wife. There's no conclusion.

It is hard for my daughter to imagine the life of her grandmother, a woman of intelligence, allure and independent mind, who disappointed her father, her mother, and husband by being too much of all of it, too tall, too original, too keen to be the little woman, too anxious to conform. Me she did not disappoint, save by disappearing too soon.

✦

My parents' marriage was a practical disaster, as I felt it. It commenced in passion and was rooted at any rate emotionally and artistically, though only for brief times geographically, in Italy, a place which was in those days even more of a state of mind than it is now. I felt these undertow loves under my parents' more ragged love. My parents often spoke Italian to one another. She was Scots-Irish and he was Irish-Scots. Both were anglicised, that is they spoke with what we would now call old-fashioned upper-middle-class English accents. He corrected her pronunciation of the word 'orchestra'. She, like the mother in *The Prime of Miss Jean Brodie*, did not call people 'dear' like Scots mothers, but 'darling', and sometimes even 'dulling'. Of course it was embarrassing. I do it too.

They didn't want more of me, and I have been told they didn't even want me. It's an odd little thing for someone to pass on to me, and I'm not at all sure that they felt like that. They were worried all the time about money and they fought about it. They both hit one another. It almost certainly hurt each more than it hurt the other. I pretended to want brothers and sisters; I don't expect I did. I knew things were desperate between them and it is one of my fervent and impure occasions for relief that I haven't any whole siblings. Impure, because that way I have my mother to myself, I suppose, and I'm not proud of that.

I did have many dolls whose names, characteristics and academic records I kept in my ledger; any dolls not at the front of that day's routine or drama lived on my nursery chaise longue, which was called 'the chaise longue', just as the tall bookcase, where the *Petit Larousse* I had for my fifth birthday was kept, was called the 'secretaire'; my father used the correct words for things, my mother not always, though she could taste words exactly despite not being almost painfully good at pitch as my father was in music as well as in language. My dolls were ranked by strict precedence related to length of tenure. After my father's remarriage they went to live in a box at the top of the stone stairs known as 'the coffin'.

My mother took the contraceptive pill in an early form, I think. We visited a family whose father was a sculptor one weekend in Kinross-shire and there was a dash to hospital after the youngest child ate the medical contents of my mother's handbag. I don't know whether the tranquillisers were in there yet with the Pan Drops and the hanky that she used to scrub at my face with lick like Tom Kitten's mother in the picture, and the lipstick that smelt of wax roses and the Consulate cigarettes and her dark glasses with the pussycat slant and her copy of *The Turn of the Screw*, or whatever it was she was reading at the time, but that's one I remember.

She left over fifty lipsticks at her death and I used them up in a furious winter of drawing nothing but sunsets. What else was there to do with those lipsticks than make sunsets? My mouth was big enough for all those lipsticks to go on in candy stripes but I was nine; and anyhow she had left a lot of blank paper that needed covering by some means. I still have rolls of it that came south with the Shore Porters in the nineteen-nineties.

The cats were too plural in that crammed house in the Crescent. Before I was born the tortoiseshell Nancy Mitford, who enjoyed Dundee cake, had died. My mother's passion for *The Pursuit of Love*, which she read aloud to me, lasted all her life. I think that she was, although so differently extracted, like sad adored Linda Radlett, and

knew it; the same affection for Labradors and the same instinct for
rotters. My father was not a rotter. Among the cats there remained
grey Godfrey Winn with his small lopsided moustache, Peter Quint
who was my mother's fat-footed grey plush familiar, and Lady Teazle,
a sealpoint Siamese of the pansy-faced, silk-stockinged sort, whom
my mother took shopping on a lead.

This in the days when tradesmen in Edinburgh wore different-
coloured cotton overalls, like indoor coats in cotton drill, the shade
according to the trade, the tobacconist Mr MacDonald the only
one who wore an uncovered suit. Mr Cockburn, the ironmonger,
wore a cotton coat in grey, Mr King the grocer in royal blue, Mr
Dundas the greengrocer, who kissed my mother one year under the
mistletoe, in green of course, Mr (Charles) Wilson in pure butcher's
white.

Later, she added to the household. In the background there were
as many make-believe horses as you can fit imaginatively into a
crumbling house belonging to an ascetic bibliophile who doesn't
care for animals and an insecure hoarder with a menagerie habit,
and the solitary child they bred.

My mother was horsey, to look at and by temperament; she would
go out to the suburb of Liberton to a stables to ride a horse called
Lady Gay. I rode the arms of the burst Regency sofa in the drawing
room, perfectly happy with picking at the horsehair stuffing and
keeping any actual animal content as remote as that. She loved all
horses and waged a campaign to get blinkers removed from the dray
horses which brought milk from Murchies dairy, where they still
patted the butter and stamped it with a thistle, and from the giant
Clydesdales who rumbled along with beer barrels to the pubs or
loads of bluish-sheered coal under the tarps. The horse would stand
at a massive mincing halt in the road outside the house while the
coalmen hove sacks on to rests of greasy hopsack on their shoulders and chuted the noisy coals down into what Edinburgh folk
call the 'area', then shovelled it into the cellar where the Indian lady

lodger saw the black rat and where years later I put kohl on my eyes before the Scout dance at St Cuthbert's church, aged thirteen, for make-up was not allowed. I was six feet tall already then and they were right about the make-up. I looked like a caricature without underlining any of it.

LENS I: Chapter 4

My father died quite young. My mother died very young. After my father died, I was asked to give a lecture in his memory. I called it 'Living with an Eye'. At the time, I considered this both a kind of gentle joke of the sort at which my elegant father shone – the kick against grammar's apparent rule – and a gainsaying of egotism, since my father, whose eye was wonderful, a plain fact to which his writing and his memory attest, was not an egoist. This was what I believed at the time I wrote my lecture.

I believe it differently now, having discovered that the sort of egoist he was not was not easy for either of them when combined with the sort of egoist my mother was not, and their issue is me, who can hardly bear to write the word 'I'.

But I had best crack on and do it, or my children could be cast adrift as I was by unassertion. Thank God their fathers are fully furnished with a good I in each strong head.

Three meetings jolted the long-laid reason to start digging for my life. I met myself in a published diary and feared the loose half-life of what I found there. I met my father in a memoir and saw him as a boy. And I met my daughter's notion of the Queen as a being without meaning, and I thought that if I did not at least try to re-enthrone the monarch in my female child's head I hadn't a hope of sharing my imaginative life with her, or of consoling her, no matter how much I madden her now, after my death.

The person I met in the diary was referred to as 'the beautiful bolter'. It was like being sicked up. I couldn't get the smell of it from me, because I was made of the vomit. Of course, part of having any kind of publicity, which is now a wretchedly essential part of selling books, carries an afterwash, but this was in the diary of someone I had loved and respected, to whom I had sent the only frequentative

Valentine cards of my life, apart from those to my children. The adjective disquieted me as much as the noun in Jim Lees-Milne's phrase. And in those pages I met Fram, Minoo's father, damaged, and that by me.

My father as a boy I met in the autobiography of Frederic Raphael. The author had ascribed to Daddy the wrong first initial 'F', turning him into the sculptor F.E. McWilliam, but he meant my father Colin Edgar. Boys of that time had not much use for one another's first names. I had known that my father was a committed socialist and enraged by injustice, but I hadn't quite known how lifelong this lay. He appeared in these pages as defender of the small Raphael against anti-Semitism at Charterhouse. It also seemed that he had been the dux classical scholar in the school and on account of this (there could have been no other reason; he hated authority and loathed punishment, though he was perforce to mete it out to me) head boy of the school.

I knew nothing of this. It is unusual for public school men of my father's generation not to allow their children to understand to what it is they are expected to rise. My father was not of this type. He terribly disliked male institutions, large groups of men, or men at all of a certain bullish type. He was a sophisticated man reflexively prejudiced against his own class, unless some mutual architectural or artistic enthusiasm would allow him to forget what they had in common in those unutterable ways.

I was astonished to learn of my father's rank at school, for his dislike of authority was complete and mischievous all the time I knew him. He was sceptical even of the Brownies, an organisation he couldn't quite agree was not crypto-Nazi at some level. Later, in a long and kind letter, Frederic Raphael tried to recall for me this tall gentle senior boy, 'a kind of demigod to a new boy' at the school. To my surprise, he remembered my father showing off a scarf that he had purchased for his 'Popsy' one Christmas. Popsy was the word used; I could hear it.

All his life my father was irresistible to women. He was handsome and fragile, funny and fundamentally, I think, rather cold, or cool. Catnip. I had always assumed that he had had a relationship involving what he called 'the usual thing' (for which Simon was expelled from Charterhouse) with his friend Simon Raven at school. I used to think that that was why Simon liked me, but now I think that they were simply friends, and anyhow I'm not sure how much Simon did like me; I was simply an experimental frog, though a frog he was once able in my twenties consciously to rescue from a nasty admirer by being fantastically rude to him over tea in the Stafford Hotel.

My father, not wholly a fiction man, loved Simon's *Alms for Oblivion* sequence of novels; I think their classical heartlessness confirmed something for him, and he enjoyed the long tease on his boyhood bugbear William Rees-Mogg. Always, for a clever and subtle man, surprisingly willing to embrace prejudice were it against a Tory, my father was nonetheless open-hearted always about the boy, and the man, James Prior, another contemporary at Charterhouse.

Then: 'Why do you like the Queen, Mummy?', my undergraduate daughter, who, as it happens has had far more actual contact with the royal family than I have, asked in the car on the way to the eightieth-birthday gathering of the man who is not my father, but whom I address, as do his six blood children and their children, and my children, as 'Papa'. And then I knew I had to write this book to tell her.

I like the Queen because she isn't dead. I like her because she defers, as far as one can see, most gratification. I like her because she was there and is here, because she puts duty before sensation, because my father carried me to see her on Princes Street when she was a new Queen, because going to the cinema is connected with her dreary but durable anthem, because she is happy in Scotland, because she is the Duke of Lancaster and a woman, because she has found a way of looking and looks it, has found a way of being and is it, because she is absolutely not stupid but not intellectual, because she is not me, not even the best of me, but she is my times, and shelters my life. In the car I tried to say this.

'I like the Queen because I loved my parents,' I said, trying again. It stuck like a granny-knot, instead of flying like the standard I had intended.

'But Grandpa was a republican.'

He was a contrarian, of course, a formalist and an anarchist, a patrician flincher away from all unfairness, a detester of privilege who knew great houses more intimately than some of their owners. He had that eye, yet was not, unlike me (until this closing of my eyes), a voyeur.

Now though, I am more a voyeur of what is coming back to me out of the past than of what offers itself to my closing eyes. They are becoming like lychees, jelly with a stone and a thin rind lid. And over it all still reigns the reigning Queen.

'Like' is too passionless a word for what I feel for her. The Queen is an emblem and carrier of memory, as rock music for my daughter perhaps.

Then again, as bores say, just as one thinks one can make a bolt – that word! – for it, then again, the Queen is like my own mother in one single way. She is safest, we imagine, among creatures. Where the Queen has her mystery and her awesome power of patronage, pure in itself but corrupting for the corrupt, to defend, my mother had her horribly vulnerable person; my mother was eaten up by other people wanting a bit of her. She was made of sex appeal, sweetness and unconfidence.

Two things I have said, in attempt at self-definition, for years. I've not believed them as I said them, but I was impersonating the solid sort of person who might be heard to say such things.

One is, 'I don't trust the sort of woman who prefers the company of animals to the company of humans.'

The other (which I haven't said for about twenty-two years,

prevented by some prefiguring shadow maybe) is, 'I cannot stand a woman drunk.'

The first is Mummy.

The second, who might as well have modified her statement's punctuation to, 'I cannot stand, a woman drunk', is, of course, me.

LENS I: Chapter 5

The sort of unpopularity that I enjoyed during my first period of schooling was regrettable mainly for the sort of popularity it set up later. I was unpopular because I was odd and then popular for the same reason. This made an unsound base for the dreadful glamour that visited later, attendant upon my mother's death and the passive allure of my widowed father.

◆►◆◆◄◆

Today, when I am writing this, is a Monday. Monday is washing day; I do the big wash on Monday, which is right. I know this because

> They that wash on Monday
> Have all week to dry,
> They that wash on Tuesday
> Are not so much awry,
> They that wash on Wednesday
> Are not so much to blame,
> They that wash on Thursday
> Wash for shame,
> They that wash on Friday
> Wash in need,
> But they that wash on Saturday,
> Oh! They're sluts indeed.

My godfather Francis Gordon of Cairness gave me for my first birthday, 1 July 1956, the book from which this jingle comes, an airily laid out nursery rhyme collection called *Lavender's Blue*, compiled by Kathleen Lines and pictured by (these are the terms used) Harold Jones. I enjoyed that crossed wire of nomenclature, as soon as I could read the poems for myself, that it was actually Harold Jones who did the lines. His is a line-led relaxed style, not fussy but full of detail and shading. He makes the human figure architectural, though not massive, as in a frieze, and architectural detail, such as that of London Bridge as it falls down, dances along the page. The rhymes, proverbs and nostrums are placed handsomely within each page. Print and its layout drew me very soon; I loved lettering, but I remember being churlishly resistant to my godfather's encouragements to learn calligraphy, the exercise sheets, the nibs, the black Indian ink that shone coppery if you spilled it on anything hard and non-absorbent. I had an ugly hand till I was about eleven, and after that a self-forced Italic that was over-decorative and built, thanks to that early shirking, on an insufficiently Roman armature.

Fram writes a good Italic hand. His was inherited from Wilfrid Blunt, brother of Anthony, who had taught that hand to many generations of boys at his school. I taught myself mine in order to have an accomplishment with which to win book tokens. I used regularly to win a handwriting prize sponsored by Brooke Bond tea.

⟡

Much of my childhood was to do with line and the materials used for making, drawing, following, understanding lines – pens, pencils, crayons, T-squares, protractors, chisels. My parents drew lines but hardly ever drew the line, save in matters of moral taste. After one outing with another family, I used an expression to which my father objected. If I think of it now I taste earth in my mouth. It was 'little Jew'. I copied it from a father who was describing another father. My own daddy took me out of our house and walked me through the old streets. He sat me down with a book, with those photographs, the heaps of legs and deep-shadowed eyes, the shoes, the spectacles. I do not know where the book was kept in our house as I had found every other book that might be mined for prurience or horror by the time I was eight. I felt none of the sense that this was a world to come, that I felt when I poked about in *Gray's Anatomy* or *Fanny Hill.*

I felt that this was it. This was the world from which the destroyed worlds of my night-time fears had come, that people could do this to other people. It was not a nightmare; it was the truth. It was not a private horror but a filthy fact. The next time we visited friends, the man of whom had been in Auschwitz, he got me to look at the number on his arm and to sit and listen. He gave me a maths tutorial immediately after the talk of how it had been in the camp, which no doubt he watered down. Never had mathematics been so welcome, so consolatory. I counted the white hairs in his beard with delight as though they were shoots coming through. Time looked valuable suddenly.

My father had that certainty, that racial or religious discrimination of any sort was evil. He had been raised in a household where everyone, including the servants, attended – Anglican – family prayers every morning. He hated that and was mortified though seldom mentioned it since the source of the piety was his mother and he was never in my hearing disrespectful of her, very likely never was so in his life. He was a choral scholar at the Pilgrims' School, which supplies the choir for Winchester Cathedral, as were his brothers, Ormiston and Clement. Clement went on to become the organist at St George's Chapel in Windsor Castle, then at Winchester Cathedral. My father loved the liturgy all his life, attended church, and sang, but I'm not sure what he believed. He loathed the Pilgrims' School and its School Hymn, into which he would insert the word 'not', as in

> He who would valiant be
> 'Gainst all disaster
> Let him in constancy
> Follow the Master
> There's no discouragement

Shall make him once relent
His first, avowed intent
NOT to be a pilgrim.

It was a hymn at my first wedding, an occasion it is too late now to ask my father about. Was he wretched or relieved that another man gave me away? What had happened to make this possible?

At the time of taking me out into the streets to tell me about the Holocaust, to shake me out of my sleep of reason, my careless imitation and failure to listen or hear, I think that he may already have lost any faith he had, and that he was an intelligent sceptic with anarcho-Anglican leanings, and knew he was lucky to live in a country that allowed all these contradictions to be lived by, lived through, lived out even. He was idealistic about line, and the Labour Party, which embodied, then, post-war socialism. It is hard to explain to my children the simplicity of his belief, when he was so complicated. Labour was for the working man and was the natural party for making good the ruin of the war. Men like my father, classically educated modernists who believed in conserving what was good and beautiful about the past, thought that all this was possible. They thought, because so many they loved had died in war, as had my McWilliam grandfather, that there had to be a reason for all that loss, that things could be made good, that something new and fair was possible. It is extraordinary that these thoughts have come in three generations to sound so naïve as to be alien, swivelled and uprooted and shaken aside by the advance of consumption, save where, perhaps, they are subjecting themselves to smart repackaging.

By the end of his life I think he felt the public world was all chaos. For a subtle man he enjoyed hating rather much. I think that he felt such rage about Mrs Thatcher, whose virtues he was incapable of seeing, although his wife was not, that his outrage really did all but kill him.

When I was going through a holy stage, after my mother's death, I asked my father to listen to my prayers at night. He reasonably replied that he could not offer me that certainty. He was deeply thoroughly self-subvertingly principled. He could not bear the appearance of emotion for fear that it be inauthentic.

Nonetheless it is clear to me as I live that he felt it, hid it, and suffered from its burial.

◆━◆◆◆━◆

I have come back just now from a trip into the centre of Oxford, the town in which I don't feel I live but where actually I have for twenty years. I took my white stick and held my head up in the way that makes it possible to see the crevice through which I negotiate myself. I was going to collect a prescription. I get so many of these at the moment that the surgery calls to say, 'Your script is ready.' 'Script' is the junkie word, not the straight-world word. There are elaborate courtesies extended at the rear of the old-fashioned department store where I collect my drugs and the methadone-dependent collect theirs. The pharmacists are bilingual. They are as charming and responsive and chatty to those of us who say, 'Mustn't grumble' when asked how we are as to those of us who reply, 'In fucking bits, mate, kicking off all over the place.'

The drugs I'm collecting at the moment constitute a sort of capitulation, but I'm trying to think of them as a contribution to a process that collaborates with hope and with my writing all this stuff I swore I would not write, ever. They are antidepressants, which I fought off for a good while, since I don't think that I am depressed at all; I am sad.

Many things combine to induce that sadness and it seems a rational state in which to find myself at this point of my bewildering life. Indeed I think that to be not sad would be to be dim, or to use a similarly sight-suggesting word, unenlightened. But I agreed to take chemical help because something needed to change even if its terminus was not, quite, sight, or not the sort of sight that I had so greedily enjoyed. So, I caved in to these drugs and asked for their, as I saw it, only fair counterparts, which was something to close me down at night against the racing thoughts in the double dark, though we blepharospastics often see better at night, I am told; I haven't yet met another 'functionally blind' person, as I feel that attending Alcoholics Anonymous is already a great enough adventure in fellow feeling, and I can't face more, but must conserve it in order to invent characters in fiction, and put them through suffering. I have not written a novel for thirteen years, though short stories have come out of me like sprits from a forgotten potato.

I was in town on my drug run just now and I garnered two ribald jeers and a couple of flinches from people I recognised and who, in their shyness at what they registered as my catastrophic change, twisted their eyebeams away and moved swiftly on. One brave acquaintance spoke to me. The consolatory hyper-observant me was absent from this tame safari into Oxford. Even at my shyest and most reclusive, I've been visually fed by people in the street. By fascination with how they present themselves, how they sound, when that is compared with, or added to, how they appear; all those things. Because I couldn't garner any human interaction and haven't been able to for a while, I went into the clothes shop Zara, which I find can top me up. It's something to do with its being Spanish, perhaps. The girls don't snip at a blind woman holding up the garments to feast off their detail, and the smell is good, which is extra important. The cottons smell like cotton, the lurex has a foily taint. The wool is sheepish and soft. I harvested Zara and came home, passing a woman who smelt of lily of the valley and a group of people who smelt like synthetic bananas; is that the smell of poppers?

There are a number of medical people who have given advice on my present blindness, which does feel as though some dreadful thing, a sight-burglar, maybe, or another childhood terror from the dark, such as one of the Cauliflowers, the monsters who lived in my brocade nursery wallpaper, were sitting on my own head, my own deep brain's poor florets. These expert eye doctors are of the firm, committed and explicit opinion that to seek relief from my affliction by any means other than sternly physiological would be deluded and even self-indulgent. Two other medical people believe that there are certainly psychological causes – they maintain that it's hard for me to face life as it is at the moment conformed, with the result that I have taken refuge in my blindness.

I am not sure which is the case, but suspect a category error in any hard and fast distinction. All I know is that I am falling through the dark and that utterance feels like the only available light. I'm entirely unsure what stone, even what sort of stone, it is that I am looking for, as I sieve and pan the past, in order to lift the blinding weight off the seeing part of my brain.

In town groups of boys or girls catcalled. I look odd and slow and vulnerable. I creep along and hold my eyes up in their itching sockets as people hold spilling glasses of drink above a throng – as though the drinks with their precious realised meniscuses are threatened, and must be protected with an exaggerated care. I have also started to make involuntary noises and pre-emptive twitches and sallies with my head, which aches even by the end of a morning as if weighted with lead beans at the back as I hold it up as though trying to read the world with my chin. I saw (actually saw: she was sitting for some reason on the ground and I can at the moment see the pavement) a child with a rucksack in the shape of a teddy. He had sewn-on felt crosses on the blanks of his eyes and I knew how he felt.

Fram's girlfriend, Claudia, very reasonably suggested that maybe I had seen enough in my life. I have for sure been lucky in what, and in how and with whom I have seen.

LENS I: Chapter 6

Elegance of posture was a great thing for my Henderson grandmother, my mother's mother, the opera singer. She held up her noble head right till the end in her nineties. Her silver hair streamed down her back. She could sit on her hair, as could my mother and I once, and my daughter. Each of us has had it chopped at some point. My grandmother shingled hers in the twenties to irk her ferocious pa. My mother did it to manage her hair and I suppose her life just before she died; women change their style at important moments in their lives, we are told.

My stepmother did the only sensible thing after Mummy died and had mine cut off. It was a weighty reminder of my mother, a great pest to maintain, a personality in its own right and attached to one already disobliging; it also encouraged nits. For years after I had my long heavy striped brown plait (the Scots word is pleat) in a box; then I lost it after I went away to school in England. My daughter has lovelier hair than mine; it is fine and silver and grey-gold, and thick as fairytale hair. It weighed down her small head dreadfully I now sometimes guiltily think. She made a practical teenaged choice to have a lot of it cut off. It was the right thing to do. People had asked her about it before asking her about herself, as though she were a unicorn or a mermaid and it, the massive silky rope, her horn or her tail; it was a natural feature too much emphasised. Her hair is so thick that it has to be thinned in summer. It is miraculous stuff, glistening and falling with a kind of lunge of health. Mine I cannot bear to cut. I'm getting like my grandmother Clara Nella Henderson, the tines of whose silver plait fell to nearly her waist on the last day of her life, when she told me a great white bird was at her window and I thought in relief, 'Oh, she *has* got some faith at last in her bitter life and at the bitter end.' It wasn't an angel. It wasn't the Holy

Spirit. It was a herring gull driven inland to eat from the refuse bins of Reading General Hospital by that Christmas weather. She died in the night before Boxing Day. I want to think that we were reconciled. She thought that last day that I was her daughter, my mother, Margaret, whom she hadn't found easy either.

I am growing increasingly like my grandmother. When she was getting infirm and failing to eat (I believe that she starved herself to death), I looked at 'places' for her to go. She fought against it. I took her to one. Most I had visited had been too upsetting to contemplate for her, but this one seemed 'nice', whatever such hell can be. There was a real room, and a real view; the nurses were, seemed to be, kind countrywomen. I smelled no fear nor piss nor shit.

My grandmother, whom I called Nana, was at over ninety still as tall as I and had been taller. She was very thin. Her lovely legs were sticking out of a garment taken from a hospital pool of such shapeless clothes. At home in her bungalow on the estate in Reading hung and lay her immaculately cared for frocks and cardigans, her evening gowns, her treed shoes, her gloves. She was, as the dying often are, terrified of disgracing herself, of having an 'accident'. She did what any sensible child would have done in these circumstances. Terrified, about to be alone, as she felt it, maybe about to be abandoned by her own flesh and blood, she made herself, although she had little in her stomach, violently sick. The nurses were not kind, not understanding. We left, my imperious beautiful grandmother holding a grey cardboard kidney bowl aswim with bile and mucus. My grandmother carried the day, all her own teeth in her head, her gracious smile of triumph and relief as we left transforming her proud stony sad face for close to the last time.

I am growing more like her now, afraid of the powerlessness my body is forcing me towards, scared stiff of being disposed of, tidied away, thinking I maybe should do it for myself. I'm just over half the age she was when she gave in, and even then she forced herself to do so by refusing food and water. She was a far stronger character than

I and I do not actually want to die. I find notes that I have written to myself and they remind me of my grandmother's diaries that I dare not read. They're engagement diaries, only, but it is enough.

She had been alone from the night when her husband, my grandfather, tried to murder us both in the drawing room of the house he himself had built, The Folly, West Drive, Sonning-on-Thames, Berkshire. He was a strong old man, older than his beauty wife. He was doing the right thing by trying to kill us, because he had long ceased to 'know' us. He was protecting his property, as he saw it, from strangers.

It was my first half-term out from my English boarding school. I had a major scholarship, but it was effectively my grandfather's money that was paying the rest of the fees. The wheel of separation of child from antecedents by self-made money had begun. I could see that my grandparents were more conventional and right-wing than my father and mother had been. My Henderson grandparents didn't like my father; my father's family looked down on the Hendersons. Their separate, profound, kinds of musicality were incompatible. Professional musicians on both sides, on one the Church, the other the stage. I was the oil and water shake-up. My mother had been dead for four years when Grandpapa tried to kill his wife and his granddaughter, thinking us intruders, in his folly.

Grandpapa went for Nana with the hardwood truncheon he had used in the Army in Jaffa in the war; she yelled to me in her deep grand stagey voice, that never slipped, even as he thumped her (she was Scots-Irish cockney with the loveliest and most gold-rolled speaking voice of my whole background, including those backgrounds that were yet to arrive), 'Candia, call the police.'

I did, but I couldn't tell them how to find us, and my grandmother, holding down her spouse, himself strong with fear and insanity, gave me calm, self-possessed instructions to relay down the telephone to the police.

She had spine. It must have been worse, I think now, because I'm sure that she loved him, and she had a long widowhood to endure alone after who knows how long of concealing his decreasing stability. She did it all with poise. Her happiness in her widowhood lay in producing opera and operetta. I cannot think that I contributed to any happiness at all. I was a nuisance and a let-down, plain, brainy, a lefty and a snob.

Her engagement diaries are lists of small sums and presents she has given. She was generous and well-regulated. She was more hospitable than greedy and had no appetites but cigarettes and music and like-minded company, which I was not to become for her. She watched, it is clear from my inheritance from her, those little frightening diaries, my marriages and my giving birth and my small success as an author as perceptible through the press and 'kind' neighbours (she took the *Daily Express*), with increasing disgust. She would ask herself in her diary whom I had paid to get all this attention. Even reviews that I wrote she noted carefully in her diaries, not from familial pride but because she felt that they were bids for attention, that I had somehow paid to appear in the paper. She regarded my defection to the toff-class as a betrayal of decency. I didn't know my place. Yet she was the grandest woman in her manner, as she smoked, or took out the wrapped sandwiches from her refrigerator before an after-rehearsal impromptu around her piano, or as she hailed the bus from Caversham into Reading, and stepped out to take coffee at a department store with a kind of film-star duchessly hyper-demeanour.

How odd England showed itself to me, a Scots child through and through, and how late I have been to grasp how I must have hurt my grandmother and let her down, by making what some few souls thought was a marriage advantageous in worldly terms. My mother failed her parents by marrying a man far more educated than she was, a man educated, toxically, as her parents saw it – socialistically – to place value on things other than money and respectability. And when I married a man who was many things superb beside his station, my educated father briefly – for he came to love my first husband with a deep affection – felt, momentarily only, a stab of something surely analogous to my grandparents' sense of class betrayal when he had married Mummy. My father blamed me; he mistrusted my appearance, I think, and thought of it as a spangled meretricious lasso. I suspect my father pitied anyone who was going to marry me; I do not know this. I didn't know I had the lasso to throw; we scarcely ever had a personal conversation, though all our exchanges were elliptically personal in their encryption; we shared matters of the eye.

Nana vowed upon my first marriage never to speak to me again. She was hurt. I married a toff and then a Pakistani. I did not have a respectable job. I was horribly visible. My grandmother never knew the odd congruence – starting from so different a place – of her own emotions and those of my Parsi in-laws, who so disliked all the publicity I received, reflecting, entirely reasonably, that one pair of ridiculous fashion tights, credited as costing some shocking sum, might water a village in India, and that no proper wife, no proper person, no proper writer, appears in evening clothes not her own in order to help publicise a book that is in literary terms respectable.

My grandmother thought that the education she had effectively paid for had separated me from her and made me pretentious; she was fed in this apprehension by friends who passed her all the disobliging cuttings they could. An equivalent drip-feeding went on to my poor parents-in-law. Neither of these things – the separation, the pretension – was precisely the case, but it helps worsen the hurt to coarsen the terms, naturally, and my grandmother and my mother-in-law were each attached to private suffering, a plot laid out for one by starting to earn her living aged five on the stage and caring for a blind sister, and for the other, perhaps, by the Partition of India and Pakistan in the year of her marriage, for she was from Bombay and her husband, her first cousin, from Karachi.

That my grandmother and I did speak again is due to telephone calls, made by each of my husbands, and each call concerning the arrival of a child, her three great-grandchildren, separated from her, as she understood it, on account of the bitter prejudices that rack this country still, by class in three cases and colour and creed in one, and yet – when at last she met them in her final year of life – she felt them entirely hers, her great-grandchildren, the older of whom have her posture and her gamut of social smiles and the youngest of whom has her appetite for libretti.

I have at last started to let go of the dear stone, that cherished discomfiting notion that my grandmother did not love me or my mother.

She loved us too possessively, too angrily, too silently, in the way of the day. It was her stone, a stone axe, beautiful and held behind her lovely face like obsidian, never letting her yield. I won't feed my own stone by rereading her hard, withheld diaries, but must instead recall that at the end she let me hold her hand day after day, whichever one she thought I was, my mother or me, and that she left me in her will an envelope of mica windowpanes for a solid-fuel stove, each the size of half a playing card, little slips of crackly pearl for feeling heat through and for looking through, into the fire in our pasts.

My mother very occasionally brought home from her trips to the grocer Young and Saunders, or from Rankin's the fruiterers at the West End, a pomegranate, in tissue paper. She would give me a pin and two plates. (Is this the sort of thing to which people refer when they say, 'We made our own fun'?)

Mummy would cut the pomegranate into four, put on my apron, which was modelled on a French child's smock and sewn by her, in her constant search for rational and appealing clothes for children, and let me take the chambered, compressed, treasure apart, with one plate for the leathery but blushful skin and the membrane that you could look through, and the other for the pressed red jewels, which I was allowed to eat with the pin. So long did this task take – a whole afternoon – and so magical a treat was the process that I was not surprised, when I read in my anthology of myths, *The Tanglewood Tales*, about Persephone – to learn that she had tumbled to a pomegranate's charms in Hades, and that the seeds were measures of time spent with or without a mother.

LENS I: Chapter 7

Painstaking effortlessness, *curiosa felicitas*, was my father's, apparently idling, actually supercharged, gear. There may have been something irresistible to him about my mother's lavish appearance and her extremer way. But it was also, time showed, at some level repulsive. The quick term for this is, I suppose, a fatal attraction. They were stuck under the net of convention and another net of passion that had charred to distaste on his side I think. All this is speculation.

In marriage, and this is less speculative, since I have twice failed to understand, to implement and to reverse the disintegration of this, we are, or I was, trying to answer the loss and absence that the other has felt. One hopes the other's gaps will be filled by something that one carries within. But somehow instead we may create what we most have feared because it is familiar. Perhaps everyone but me knows this.

I saw my mother be craven to my father. Cravenness has no place between any two people. Craven is the claw of the mode most repulsive to me of any, that of ingratiation. I hate full frontal flattery and its oils the more, the longer I live. My father lived perhaps a little too sternly by the exigencies of understatement; my mother's overstatement I know, because I am like it too, *was* authentic, *was* intensity of feeling, terribly banked down. I'm like them both, dry and pyrotechnic; but you need to keep powder dry. I don't like slobber. It is the slaver kills and not the bite.

———◆•◆◆———

Marilyn Monroe killed herself in the August of 1962. I was already much taken by suicide, but only as a means of transformation, the death of one way of being in order to catalyse the birth of another,

47

as in the Beast becoming Jean Marais in the film by Cocteau of *Beauty and the Beast*, to which my parents were attached and which they took me to see whenever it was showing. Cocteau himself had designed the programme and poster for the first Edinburgh Festival. That was one of my parents' worlds, the Edinburgh arts world. When the Traverse Theatre was born, Mummy cooked for the actors. The Incredible String Band lived in one of my friend Janey's father's barns. Our street had the poet George Bruce and even Chopin had stayed in the Crescent some time before, no doubt on his way to visit Miss Stirling at Keir, where there was said to be a piano he had played. There were recitals in the Chopin house, which belonged to a musical family. I remember my mother making zabaglione for the mime artist Lindsay Kemp. I felt at once a bond with him, to do with discipline, extremity, outsiderness. I was drawn very young indeed to the company of gay men. A matter of talk and of establishing hidden ways to utter; puns, jokes, playing around. This line in transmission ran deep. My father totted from a skip quite late in his life an old ironmongery sign made of cast-iron letters. He reordered them up the stone stairs of the house: IRONYMONGER.

I read all I could about Marilyn's death. I remember reading *Life* magazine, lying on my stomach, of course, on the floor of another family, and getting the first intimation of why she really did it that made complete sense to me. *Life* had silky pages that smelt of my lino-cutting set.

The words that made sense were, 'Breasts, belly, bottom, soon all must sag.' The alliteration, the coarse mimetic bounce of the words and the downward fall of the sentence added to its crude potency; the misogyny agreed with some knot within me of self-dislike, and I saw that that was one reason to die (or transform yourself, as I saw suicide at that time, before it had come closer), that Marilyn had *shifted shape* by choosing to stay the same, by dying. I collected information about female suicides long before there was one at home, whose case I have refused to study until recently. I was interested as a quite small child by women who kill themselves and that they will often choose to wear make-up to do so. This may have changed by now. Many suicides are drunk or otherwise chemically changed, and grooming, as I have cause to know, is not a part of the throes of advanced addiction. Women used to get into their prettiest under-wear, their nicest negligee, in order to be negligent of themselves in the highest degree. I don't know what happens now that there is so great a passion for pictures of women falling short of the impossible standards they have set themselves in life. And if we think at all, we know, even without seeing photographs of really dead beauties, that the prettification will in time be all undone: the mouth falls open, the stomach rebels, the bowels let go, the worm or the fire do their work.

I was keen on the self-betterment side of suicide, so convinced of angelic afterlife was I, on account of knowing for sure that I had a guardian angel, partly because on my nursery wall was a reproduc-tion of Ghirlandaio's painting of Tobias, slung with the fish, gall from whose liver was to cure his father's blindness, and his Angel, and partly on account of my guardian angel having told me firmly not to turn on my bedroom light switch which went on to give my mother a great shock later that day. My mother was undoubtedly attractive to shocks.

Also, someone had written on my nursery window with a diamond, which showed that a child or young woman (the writing made that clear) had lived in that small tall shuttered room before. The words were 'October 1893'. What was important was that all the letters had serifs, so once someone with a lot of time had looked out over the garden and over the wall to the river and up and over the narrow walkway to the railway bank, maybe, and certainly within knowledge of the cemetery over that bank, where The Red Lady, it was known, walked by night and had done since thirty years before my guardian angel had written her tidy date on my windowpane.

The idea that suicide is a way of refining oneself is not new, to humans, to children, to girl-children, to girl-children of religious bent, nor to anyone who seeks a solution. Often the solution sought is temporary, and this temporariness cannot be ensured. Anorexia is its slower mode, taking appalling hostages. The joke of it in my life was that the long suicide I took on was the perfect undoing offered by alcohol, and I really didn't know that I was doing it until very nearly too late, by when I had indeed transformed myself by taking the clear liquid solution.

Marilyn died and as a child I loved the most the pictures of her with her intelligent husband, always so evidently and photogenically intelligent, Arthur Miller. His dark looks established, together with almost all medical doctors whom we knew and the cold Edinburgh weather, which necessitated that men wear long tailored overcoats, what could be called my 'type', as in Proust's 'she was never my type'. Later this received a top dressing of Sydney Carton from *A Tale of Two Cities* and of the hopeless clever drunk Charles Stringham from *A Dance to the Music of Time*, Prince Andrei too. About the only thing I can say in my defence in this area of daydream is that I have never fancied Vronsky.

Hopeless, clever, drunk; that trio of adjectives reminds me of something that happened on the same day as I read that sexy and offensive sentence about Marilyn, and it reveals what conversation was like in the long afternoon winter drawing rooms of Edinburgh among my parents and their friends. We were some doors down from the house where Compton Mackenzie would hold court in his great downstairs bed. 'We' were, I suppose, another family, of two parents and four children, a grandfather and a very thin aunt who I realise now was dying, and my parents. The oldest daughter of the house, about sixteen, was reading *The Flight from the Enchanter* or some other novel by Iris Murdoch that I had seen my mother read.

'Why do the adjectives in Iris Murdoch's books come so often in threes?' she asked.

So the game was to use only triplet adjectives for the afternoon and all of us played it. The taste of that house was black treacle with yellow cream, in bowls of uncooked oats. Over the dining table there was an oil painting of the mother, Marjory, in a hat covered with flowers. The father was a landscape architect. All the children save the boy, Simon, had dark eyes. Simon told me not to let people know how much I knew if I wanted more friends. We were six and took turns on the rowing machine that was there for the frail ones in the family. Simon and Polly were twins and I was a severe bore for them because I tried to copy them in order to be normal; copying twins who are not identical is a tangle.

But who to be?

When my mother died I had someone to be, perhaps. But it was in the days before people spoke about such events after they had happened, and we were in Scotland, where speaking was less the done thing, even, than in England, or speaking of dramatic personal matters, or personal matters at all.

I suppose there was some mongering of scandal.

But Scotland it was that saved me. I am sure of that, for all that I was sent away quite soon. The being sent away very possibly fixed Scotland for me, deep-laid as it was in a way that I had not under stood was happening, as my father drove me and my mother all over the roads, never as the crow flew, but round and deep about and through the sea lochs and mountains and glens of the North to look at the houses, castles, villages, mills and towns he worked to preserve.

In the back as he drove, I sang my sagas and sucked on a fresh lemon against carsickness. The lemon had come, my mother had always said, as she pulled it from her travelling-basket the moment I started to whine, from sunny Italy. Sometimes it had the leaf to show for it.

LENS I: Chapter 8

I do not need to invent her because I can see her in the children. She had a terrible temper, slanting eyes, outrageously long gesticulating hands, cheekbones like a Russian, a faint overbite, too much height, a silly voice, a gift for making rooms and occasions with nothing more than, say, sweet peas, a matchbox and herself. She put nasturtiums in salads, she was unnecessarily kind, her heart was tender, she got things a bit wrong and said sorry, she held her hair up with paintbrushes, she shouted, she gardened passionately and hopelessly, she loved peculiar expressions – 'touch not the cat' – and was irresistible to old men; she was a bit of a snob, she had beautiful shoulders and threw bits of cloth round her home and herself; she gave too much away, she tried to save the lives of shrews, birds, mice and tramps by bringing them home, she had an extra-ness that some fell for and some resisted, she cooked on her budget as though for a family of eight, she turned heads and ended up talking not to the prince but to the scarecrow; she was untidy with spasms of obsessive reordering, she collected small heterogeneous things as though her life depended upon it; she remembered names. She wrote rather good doggerel. The nearest thing I have to a suicide note is one such poem. I cannot hand on the misery by sharing it.

In aesthetic terms, then, she hadn't my father's unerring line, but she did have colour. She loved magazines, as I loved comics. She longed to subscribe to the (then) French magazine *Elle*; her first copy of it arrived the week after her death. I would have tea with other families because they took comics. Fat use I was as a playmate when all I did was lie on my tum and read comic strips about large families in the midst of a large family, like the Mitchisons who had an au pair and Patum Peperium for tea, or the Michies, who were Communists and had a nanny and had married one another twice and were to die together in a car crash in 2007. Then there were the Ordes who lived at Queensferry and sang madrigals and whose mother herself was so beautiful that she made cakes rise like her golden bun, and the Waterstones who taught me the Lord's Prayer with 'debts' and 'debtors' in the Scots way and whose mother made me baked beans and of whom I said to my own mother, 'Why can't you be like Mrs Waterstone?' in the last weeks of her life. I meant, 'Why won't you let me use the grill?' or something, I suppose. God knows how Mummy heard those words.

Mrs Waterstone's condolence letter arrived very soon. People were good to my father.

I don't know exactly what my mother did. A pupil, some thirty years my senior, at a course I taught once told me that my mother had changed her will and my father had changed it back. What kind of person tells one these things? Another told me that she had broken up the flat of someone outside our family the day before she 'did it'. I can't see it. Is that the thing I'm refusing to see? That my mother was incontinent with grief during her last days? How could she not have been? Why else choose to die?

It would be frivolous to die without reason, wouldn't it? Death is better perhaps than such consuming rage or misery.

All I want, for her, is to soothe her.

I do not swallow the 'cry for help' theory in her case, just as I don't swallow the idea that she had a rotten go of flu, which she did, too.

She did not want to wake up on the following day. That day was to include events that she could not countenance.

I don't even know if suicide was legal when she did it, or where her ashes are. I think she died in October. I know that I wore school uniform to the funeral and that I was horrified by the tidy curtains as she went away through them in her coffin. My friend Janey Allison, Janey who had never joined the anti-Candy gang, who grew up to be champion downhill ski-racer of all Scotland, and who could like Paul Klee hold a line boldly, in crayon as she could in snow, Janey's mother cried at the funeral. She was a terse Scots blonde, Mary, née Ingalls, who was given to ticking us off in Latin at table in the farm kitchen out at Turnhouse, but she showed an affection I cannot forget. Janey I never see nowadays but can, right now, in her button shoes, aged four, or in her ballet gear, with the petersham belt. Our mothers were such friends as I hope we are still.

———◆◆◆———

Mummy put me to bed in her and Daddy's bed, and she told me that she loved Daddy. I have no idea whether she got down the pills, which were transparent and turquoise, with alcohol. Their name was Oblivon.

The next day took one of two forms.

Either I was taken to the home of the Professor of the History of Art, Giles Robertson, and his wife Eleanor in Saxe-Coburg Place, or I was taken by my mother's cleaning lady, Mrs Stewart, whom I loved and called Sooty, to her house on an estate in Pilton. I can remember moments selected from each very disparate residence. Perhaps there were two days inside that one day. Oddly, I don't know the year, though I think it was the year after President Kennedy was shot. I know that I wrote a long encomium to the President after the assassination, and that my teacher didn't like the way I mentioned Mrs Kennedy's pink Chanel suit; to mention garments was not 'suitable', a very Edinburgh concept at the time. If she'd known he was going to be assassinated, though, maybe she would have chosen something a wee bitty more practical? (Is this an especially Edinburgh consideration? In Muriel Spark's *The Driver's Seat*, the protagonist selects a specially non-stain-resistant dress to be murdered in.) I knew that it was peculiar, even distasteful, to think like this.

I can remember when President Kennedy was shot, and not when my own mother died?

I know. But it was so.

I knew that something was wrong when I saw my mother on her tummy in my bed. I think that she had on not a nightgown but a green wool dress. She had sewn me a pink pillow with grey kittens and pussy willow branches on it to help combat my nightmares about the Cauliflowers, who came out of the walls and stole your breath. I do not recall whether her head rested on this pillow at her end. That is all I saw, except that her head was to one side. It will never cease to appal me that my children have seen me from this angle on account of drink. How can I? How could I? How did I?

There's nothing so dreadful-tasting that, if it is your poison of choice, will not make you take it. That is what addiction is. The worse it is, the more 'unsuitable', the more it seems to be what is made for you, your final course of just desserts, not someone else's cup of tea at all.

That day, whichever day it was, that Mummy died, I waited for my father. At first it seemed to be with Sooty.

When Sooty's husband Sandy came in from the Ferranti factory, Sooty took him into their kitchenette where their son David would sometimes melt lead to make soldiers. Sandy had braces and the family had a television. Sooty called Mummy 'Maggie'. She said to Sandy, 'It's very bad with Maggie. I think she's gone.'

Sandy had a blue shirt and the lino was like coloured pebbles. In the garden was an aviary for budgies. The kitchen furniture was yellow plastic with dots and lines in black and white. I loved Sooty's curtains. They were printed with pictures of onions and carrots and Italian things like peppers, and implements, whisks, which we called beaters then.

Sooty let me beat up some evaporated milk till it got frothy and eat it off the spoon. Did Daddy come and get me? How much worse it must have been for him, exposed to his wife's grief and pain for good.

How terrified he must have been. What could he do but what he did?

He told me the truth in the bedroom of the two youngest Robertson boys, Charles and Robert. We played together all our childhood, the three of us. The Robertsons were Quakers. The house, home of clever articulate children and a scholarly pair of parents whom I loved, was always filled with wonderfully tempered vocative tones of 'thee' and 'thou'. Their father, Giles, was a Bellini scholar. He read to us, very fast, in the drawing room, under the Venetian chandelier. He read, for example, *A Flat Iron for a Farthing* by Mrs Juliana Horatia Ewing. If we grew restive, we played. Our favourite game was 'Siesta Time on Mount Olympus'. We put on our counterpanes and played at being gods and a goddess. If we grew more restive, their mother, Eleanor, or one of the older children would say, 'Thee must not *romp* in the drawing room!'

Maybe a year later I was to embarrass Charles by pretending that he was my 'boyfriend' so as to stop being nagged about the existence of such a person by other girls at school. I said that he looked like Napoleon Solo from the *Man from U.N.C.L.E.* television programme and the bubblegum cards that were a modish collector's item among schoolgirls at that time. Charles had heard of neither. The Robertson children and I were all avidly reading *Pale Fire* at that point. More secret languages were being learned but I had grown too drawn by the double tongue of trying to fit in. We were preoccupied by the work and pacifism of Bertrand Russell; also by his home life.

In Charles and Robert's bedroom, my father told me nothing but the truth, upon which he never again enlarged; very likely, for him, the only way.

'Candia', he said. 'You will never see your mother again.'

People ask, 'Are you angry with your mother?' I am angry with neither of them though I feel vivid disgust at myself still.

I went down the inside stone stairs and out into Saxe-Coburg Place, a green square; after that, I walked around the quadrilateral autumn pavement, feeling important, shut out, and singular.

I started to tell myself the story on that day whose end is my writing this down. I shall try to tell it as exactly as I can. I thought on that day, whenever it was, that this new swerve in my story made me interesting, but I see that in fact it is a story that makes us connected, not myself singular. It is the story of loss.

That exchange, of desolation for empathy, disclosed itself to me quite close upon my mother's death, the click of a new consciousness that I would be better advised to listen than to assert when it came to suffering, that it is not a game of trumps, and that the suffering of those one loves cannot but be worse than one's own.

My poor father read to me all night in the basement at the Robertsons' house, *The Sword in the Stone*. Can you imagine his peril and his tiredness? The sheets were linen, an act of sure hospitality on the part of our hostess. Linen sheets are chaste luxury and comfort.

Later, I became a sort of succubus upon the whole Robertson family. I was to do it with other families, too.

That night I had – or so my memory, which is as reliable as my eyelids, tells me – a dream after I fell asleep in the early morning, that foretold the future. I would go away, far away.

If this were a novel, you would learn at what chapter of *The Sword in the Stone* my father and I eventually fell asleep. Let's pretend it's when the Wart becomes a bird of prey and there come the Latin words of the Scots poet Dunbar, from his 'Lament for the Makars', 'Timor Mortis Conturbat Me'.

I don't know really. I did become rigid with fear that my skinny father would slip away too, and I took, in the coming weeks, to waking him, shaking him awake, like a first-time mother with a baby. What sort of caricature of his dead wife must I have represented at those times, reborn, younger, desperate, alive?

LENS I: Chapter 9

My mother and I were jealous of buildings, first.

My father worked for the National Monuments Record of Scotland and then for the National Trust for Scotland. He was away a good deal, and at first he went on his own. They didn't have a car in the early years and I imagine that a baby might have been a worry, even if allowed on field trips.

If people mention the conservation of buildings now, they think at once of something almost aspirational, associated with a style of life, a type of person, a version of the past. All this could not be further from how my father thought and worked and lived. He was working to save buildings that were being blown up, set alight, anything to get rid of them and to realise the cost of the land they sat upon and to be rid of the fearful costs they and their upkeep demanded. Roofs were pulled off Scottish houses in order for the rates to be avoided. There was a cull of castles, palaces were dynamited, streets fell to the wrecking ball, squares came down in the name of progress, tenements fell in stone and dust. The war had left the sides of buildings gouged, their innards shockingly exposed, wallpaper making its sad prettiness plain, a chained mirror blitzed to wood and a shard of looking-glass.

I played on weekdays in a playground called the Wreck, down by a bomb crater near Drummond Place. Years later I realised that it was called the 'Rec', short for recreation. The swings at the Wreck and at Inverleith Park, where you might catch minnows in a hairnet tied to a pea-stick, were tied up on a Saturday night by the park keeper, so as not to be usable on the Sabbath. Park keepers were renowned among the children who played all day at the playgrounds, and who were worldly-wise, for being great wielders of the belt or the strap. Certainly they fiercely guarded the pavilion in the park at the end of our crescent, where I never really did dare to play, except in the rough grass. Even a fat child could get through the railings that smelt of iron, rust, coally rain and lead paint. After I got thinner I played walking along the railings on the park side. On the side of the houses, most of the railings were topped with *flèches*, acorns or fleurs-de-lys, except where they had been uprooted to contribute to the war effort. I felt pity in my own body for the hurt buildings, encouraged by my parents, who took me with them everywhere when they were together. Later the National Trust gave Daddy a car for work, a fat Hillman we called the Tank.

I loved to sit in the back, my head against the rattly window, watching the rain make shapes, especially in the dark and under a rug, and most especially of all, when we were going north. The humming window gave me a pitch against which I could sing, like a drone behind a bagpipe; I think the noise I made was worse than any pipe (I love the pipes violently. Until recently, I would have said that they make me hold my head up, but now my failing sight is making me do that too, so let me say that they make my blood race). My father couldn't abide my mother's singing, which was flat, nor mine which was flatter, and booming, and often built around long stories whose heroine was me, assisting medically at some point during Bannockburn or helping at a crisis with the Argonauts. I was very keen on Jason.

I was in love always. Odysseus seems to have been its first really intense human object. My mother heard me calling out his name in my sleep when I was six. I'd started reading the *Odyssey*, in the E.V. Rieu translation, under false pretences. My father said that my mother was reading it because she thought that Homer was some kind of an animal called an Odyssey. He was teasing, but patronising also. In both senses, she wanted his education. That was for sure what I think that I thought, but I don't remember. I identified with none of Odysseus's womenfolk, not Athene of the grey eyes, not patient Penelope, not beastly Circe, not tall Nausicaa, head and shoulders above her handmaidens in height, but preferred to confect an extra part for a brave agile young female doctor. I was very taken, when it came to the *Iliad*, with Achilles for his sulkiness and with Hector for his fearful sufferings; but he was never going to pull through no matter how thoroughly I bandaged him.

———◆———

Comics were early stirred into the reading mix. With some tact, my father pretended to like comics too and would pay me half the price of my *WHAM!* in order to 'read' it. *WHAM!*, which had an excellent strip called Georgie's Germs that had those satisfying battles between microscopic life forms that are always so rich a culture for silliness, cost threepence-halfpenny a week, pronounced, I should perhaps tell you, 'thruppence haypenny'. Where can one begin to translate?

The source of most comics, especially in Scotland at that time, was the ultra-conservative publisher D.C. Thomson of Dundee, to whose products I was early addicted, and still am. They did not come to our house but I knew where to get them. The *Dandy* and the *Beano* I could manage without, but still must have my *Broons Annual*, my *Oor Wullie*, reassuring and harrowing in equal part. They have moved with the times. While they were stuck in the forties or so in the sixties, with a few references to Mop-Top laddies or jukeboxes, they are now shockingly less sexist and no one is picked on for being fat and or ugly.

No one was ugly in the world of the comic that addled for good my drawing style, *Jackie*. ('Be bolder! Be bolder!', my father would say, and once I heard my parents saying to Janey Allison's parents at kindergarten, 'She can't yet *get* Klee.') *Jackie* was thrilling pap, tame girl-friendly romance. Other girls brought it to school. I can to this day draw any Jackie type you will, daffy blonde, speccy brunette with latent romantic promise, spirited redhead, polo-necked love-bruiser, handsome toad, reliable mother's boy. Golly, that sugar, that romantic sugar, it rotted my line. I can draw nothing like as well as either parent did, having trained myself to be more decorative than truthful in the shapes I make on the page when I draw.

But look! The blinding may be helping that, too. I'm starting to learn to draw again, teaching myself from a book given to me by my second husband. The book is called *The Tao of Sketching*, and it is by a Chinese artist called Qu Lei Lei, who has made an enormous portrait of our son, with a kind of predella feature, about the size of a bath, of his beautiful, strange, extra-bendy hands, folded, which is to be framed separately from the vast head.

So, there will be two ways of looking anew, with these modified eye sockets and with the help of *The Tao of Sketching*. I have had a good deal to unlearn, my cramped pretty curlicues, my symmetries, my velleity that tends to tidy, stretch, elide, as in fashion magazine drawing. My mother was trained in fashion drawing, and it was her work I copied at the kitchen table as we made all that fun on our own.

My father *could* draw, where 'to be able to draw' means to be able to transcribe that which you see, and pleasingly, in a way that does not betray but rather finds out, and is true to, the object seen. He could also draw decoratively from his imagination, with that trick that takes knowledge, so that he could make a line look as though it were taken from a certain architectural period, or even a period of design-influence. It is not surprising that he loved the architectural jokes of Osbert Lancaster. He had a friend, Peter Fleetwood-Hesketh, who had a similar talent. You are never quite alone with that percipience of eye, that witty strand. You can always make something of what you see. I have a few letters written by my father when he was still very young; he cannot restrain the pen. Finials grow, acroteria sprout, domes swell, columns are tactfully broken to accommodate the script; it is like wandering in a neoclassical garden, a spritzed Piranesi. He could cut paper into Corinthian capitals, into palm trees, into knights on horse-back, into fretwork minarets, into a vista of a city. In one letter to a cousin he makes of a telephone receiver an Ionic capital.

My mother could make patterns, strings of cut-out dancing dolls, and she did *such* things with colour. It was her habit to buy second-hand clothes and to dye them in the big jam pan. Often when I got home from school, she would call out 'I'm dyeing' from the basement. Her colours were always changing but her favourites were silver and pink, smoky grey and mauve with no red in it. We mixed colours a lot, at the kitchen table. Guessing what the outcome would be if we mixed powder paint or watercolour or oil paint or Smarties or icing or ribbons, this was a good game. She let me paint potato crisps and offer them around when her friends came to drink coffee or – at Christmas, I think – Cinzano Bianco. She scribbled with wax crayons on cartridge paper – very expensive – and let me colour in all the little moons between the waxen boundaries of scribble, and to try never to have a colour adjacent to itself; was that possible? We used her paints from her student days, a Rowney set with little replaceable pans of watercolour, and a Cotman set whose replacements came wrapped in paper like sweets from Aitken Dott the art supplies shop on Hanover Street.

I had some triangular wooden mosaics with which I made patterns, and some wooden sticks named *Cuisenaire* that my poor parents hoped would make me better at mathematics, and architectural wooden blocks from Germany in a duffel bag. I would ask my mother all the time, 'Which do you like best?', 'Which is your favourite?' She would make a case for each. I do it with my children. The youngest gets cross. He thinks that I am being politically correct, that I am in thrall to the tediously New Labourite phenomenon he calls 'the Equal Elves'. I'm afraid I am just copying my mother.

———◆◆◆◆———

I cannot remember much about my mother, but I shall try, now, to do it. I am looking for her and with her for my ability to look.

I have looked away from it for a long time while pretending to look at it. God knows how it is for people who contemplate the disintegration or physical fission of someone they love. At least she was in one piece in my bed where she, at thirty-six, lay dead.

I regard (a word of seeing, I see) that last sentence as too aggressive to the reader, too showy, to remain. It is bad form. I cannot, I observe, look at it. So I'm going to make an experiment, and leave it.

I will now try to remake my mother's last day during which she took me to the Nubian goat farm at Cammo to choose a pointer puppy, a dog that must have been a sop to me, or perhaps to herself, like the drugged meat burglars are said to throw for guard dogs. I remember the lop-eared goats and the brindle pups.

When with either of my parents, I had the sense that each was fragile. I asked them that disturbing incessant question, 'Are you all right?' a lot. His breathing sounded wrong, they fought too much, she cried on the edge of her bed. I avoided them on account of this, and hung about after school with the boarders, or walked home with other girls, bribing them with the bus fare I would save by walking. I had friends by now, other children of bookish homes, or daughters of my parents' friends. I wasn't popular, but I was on the verge of being a cult. Something was happening at home and other girls' parents talked about it.

By no means all fathers liked finding me at the after-school tea table when they got in from work. There was something provisional and not respectable about me. It wasn't just that my mother was tall and sexy and wore sometimes a silver and sometimes a pink wig, that she smoked or had that Englishy voice, the Siamese on a lead, the black poodle-cross (named Agip after Italian petrol – '*supercorte maggiore, la potenta benzina Italiana*') or the yellow Labrador Katie. It wasn't really anything as simple as that I was not named Fiona or Elspeth. I was a Mc, after all, if not a Mac. It wasn't as though she didn't hand out jars of home-made, misspelt 'blackcurrent' jam, that delicious staining preserve with something of its leaves' cat's-pee tang to the black fruit.

It wasn't Mummy's awful driving. She learned only late in her life and had a half-timbered Mini van that got into scrapes. She might put the card discs from tubes of Horlicks tablets in the parking meters in Charlotte Square instead of sixpence.

That's the worst thing, morally, I saw her do.

She was pursued by more than one man who was not within her marriage. One of these, later, after I was the mother of three, came round for lunch with me in my marital home.

'What happened to your mother?' he asked.

'She died,' I said.

'Oh,' he said. 'What are you doing this afternoon?'

———◆◆◆◆———

As I've said, a number of people have wanted to tell me what my mother did in her last days, or on her last day. I have no desire to know. I may be wrong in this. Other people are involved, and I don't want them hurt. I don't want anecdotes or gossip. I want the emotional truth, so I can make her better. And that I cannot have. I want the printout of her human heart.

I do not think that we can at this distance know the truth.

I do not think that we could even then have known the truth or seen it.

I have very often wanted to take from her thoughts whatever it was that so hurt her that she felt she had to die, and to replace it with the complete certainty that she is loved, and that by people, my children, their fathers, who never even knew her. I do not know how I know this save that she has grown less fragile, less contingent and less fantastic in my mind, the longer she has been dead. In life she felt frail to me, like a story, unless stories are not frail.

Bridge

My house in Oxford lay, and still lies, last in a Regency cul-de-sac of artisans' houses behind an almost Georgian street that is at right angles to the comely parade of Beaumont Street that itself holds both the Ashmolean Museum and the Randolph Hotel.

I finished writing the last chapter you read on Ash Wednesday 2007. I am now speaking to you.

Deeper into the year on a hot May day, I very nearly burned my house to ash. Being an old terraced house made of wood and lath, it might as well have been a blue touchpaper.

As had become usual, I couldn't see that day. I had become used to groping my way up and down the narrow staircase of the house, much as you do on a boat. For reasons to be seen, I have spent a good deal of my life in boats. Nonetheless, I am no good in on at or with them. I had acclimatised myself to the layout of the house but still banged into things and fell over frequently, especially over the piles of books. The things I loved had, though I didn't know it, become a danger to me, and twice I slid gratingly face first down a flight of stairs over a slither of hardbacks, old *TLS*s and magazines. I was used to having bloody knees like a schoolboy and bruised hips like a mother with a granite baby. That hot day I was as usual pretending to myself and to the nobody at all who was looking that everything was all right.

I had run dry on doctors. My condition's intractability either exasperated or baffled them and such significant words as 'referral' and 'Queen Square' had been muttered. One psychiatrist who vividly reminded me of the Scottish wizard Michael Scott who is mentioned in the *Purgatorio*, said that I had chosen to close my eyes against the unbearable sight of Fram's happiness with his new love Claudia; I came back with the old argument – that since I love him I wish him to be happy. There was an air of psychological manipulation in that expensive room that might be better kept for playwrights than appointed healers.

There was the episode of the wonderfully named Alexina Fantato, who turned out to be not a strapping Italian glamourpuss with sexy but stern spectacles but a dear lady from Scotland married to an Italian. There's a tradition in Scotland for these feminine-ending masculine names, Donalda, Kennethina. It seems that all note of disappointment is unintentional, unlike those long declensions of heir-hungry hermaphroditic names to be found in *Burke*. Alexina shrewdly saw that I had 'issues', as she kindly expressed it, with self-esteem. I made my usual noises about preferring to live by suppression than by spillage. She made a sensibly pawky face of disbelief at how someone this old could so mismanage her life.

When Proust comes to his account of the death of Marcel's grandmother, the old lady and her grandson pay a visit to a distinguished doctor whom the narrator will not even dignify with an invented name. Simply referring to the smug physician with his failure in humane understanding, the prerequisite of good doctoring, as Professor E——, Proust has the man manifest his heartlessness and hypocrisy under cover of a decorous but fishy anonymity. My own Professor E—— washed his hands of me in sight of a witness, Claudia, whose sharp large blue gaze saw and recorded it all. She is more direct than I could ever even try to be. Professor E——, intelligent, disinfected, effective, spoke:

'I have done all I can for you. Some people may suggest that there is a non-physiological aspect to this unhappy condition of yours, which is always a distressing one. They are wasting their time and they would be wasting yours. You will not find it profitable to go down that route.'

I am still cleaving my way down that route, although the route itself has sometimes seemed to be narrowing, the stream drying up to reveal only little pebbles, hard stones hardly wet at all even by the grace of artificial tears, and this book is part of the walk following that diminishing way to some kind of resolution, if not the open lens of sight itself. Of course it is physiological; *of course* the cause of my blindness is neurological. But who says the life lived is separate from the body that has lived it?

———◆◆◆◆◆———

Back to that stuffy day in May, my cats and I shut in the small wooden house. I was in my workroom and felt my eyes' heat and discomfort become sharper. I pulled them open, unsticking my eyelashes. Even peeled, my eyes saw nothing. But this nothing was not black or stippled or veiled or any shade of the blindings I had grown used to; it was thick white.

That is how slow I was to realise that my small house was full of smoke. I did not think at all, which must have saved my life. Usually I am a great one for telling myself not to make a fuss and certainly not to bother other people, especially not the already overloaded public sector. I banged my way to the telephone, rang 999 and got a woman in Glasgow.

For the first occasion in my life, and not the last, I used my newly acquired unfair advantage, and I expressed it in words that felt like rhubarb in my teeth. 'My house is on fire. I'm partially sighted.' The woman with the reassuring Scots voice asked where I was and I replied to her as if we were sharing a sofa and a biscuit, 'I'm in Beaumont Buildings. It's a street in Oxford. It's not a building.'

On I prattled in my burning house.

'We'll be with you right away, dear. Hold on and get out of the house right away, closing all doors you can behind you.'

'But I've two cats.'

'You'll have to leave them.'

Now I see how patient she was with me, with all the flaming nation clamouring for her attention.

I didn't obey and I did try hopelessly in the, I was now aware, reeking house to find my cats. I chased them, for some reason I can't understand, into the basement and shut them in, or so I thought, but my thinking was as fogged as a choking drunk's, and I was left to reflex alone and to action, perhaps my two weakest behavioural suits.

All that in a whisker. I was soon in the street with three fire engines and a score of strong young competent people. Yes, a firewoman too, and all of them concentrated on reducing harm and bringing later calm.

A neighbour took me in. A fireperson like the young Hector stayed with me and asked my neighbour to make tea. He actually asked me whether or not I took sugar. We conversed. Again it was the sofa and biscuit feeling. I learned that he was a keen hunt-follower, and that he and his wife couldn't afford to buy a house in the Oxford area so that he had a long commute to his extraordinary work.

'In fact,' he said, 'we're really grateful to you because we had a city councillor visiting the station with a view to cutting down the service. Then you came through. You won't mind my saying that it's extra good you're blind.' How could I not love him?

Two hours later, everything but my oven was spick and span. Having seen smoke damage and water damage and having lost one house to arson, I was astonished. It was just like magic. The 'emergency services' had been heroic, the staled newsreader's words had immediate Homeric meaning. These stern-faced young people had entered the house, located the source of the smoke, hacked the oven out of the wall, taken it outside, extinguished what turned out to be spontaneous chemical smouldering, sucked all the smoke out of the house, swept the kitchen, wiped the surfaces, and all but put a nosegay on the draining board. They had also attended to any overspilling olfactory offensiveness that might have been caused to my next-door neighbour who had of course been regrettably interrupted by the bells and smells of the fire engines.

I asked them all when they stood round me, helmets off, after it, what I could do for them.

'Write a letter to head office, that would be great. If you think we did our job properly.'

I wrote several such letters in my best writing that looks like my old worst writing. These were love letters.

And the cats? Of course, an officer had been deputed to find and liaise with them, so much so that his uniform may never recover from the cuddling.

That night, without my knowing it, my translation was organised. My second husband telephoned to my first husband and got my older son. It turned out that the fire, which could have been so much worse, came like a catastrophe in a play, a kind of relief, so that at last my family could talk about my blindness and where to put it and me and my two cats.

The novels of Iris Murdoch are, for the time being, out of fashion. She has become someone in a film, someone pitiable even, someone who has been impersonated by souls who haven't read her work. It is not my place nor intention here to play reputations but in her time she was an enchantress and her philosophical work contains much that is luminous; as a girl, she presciently noted Simone Weil's words suggesting that deracinated people can be among those who cause the most damage.

I mention Iris, whom it's only fair to say I did slightly know (in case someone wants to niggle about Oxford's closed hive), because what happened to the cats could only have been invented or written, in its full richness, by her. My cats, for the duration of my move from Oxford to London and the first precarious London weeks, were cared for by a couple named Leander and Rachel.

Leander and Rachel, at the insistence of each of their mothers, had moved from their flat in Stockwell with their own at the time five cats to Oxford where Leander lectures at Brookes University. The couple first met in the Lemon Tree cafeteria on Platform 8 at Reading Station.

There was a theory to this, the Ancient Greek theory of buying off expectation, like calling the Fates the 'Kindly Ones'.

If you meet, the theory of Leander and Rachel ran, in a truly awful place, your relationship will prosper and your love be lifelong. When they first met, my younger son was seven. He started angling to be pageboy at their wedding when he was about seven and a quarter.

He was finally the ring-bearer at their ceremony of civil partnership on a summer afternoon in 2007. Leander, a stunning redhead, as the old social magazines might have said, wore a frock modelled on that of Mrs John F. Kennedy, designed by Oleg Cassini, at the Presidential Inauguration Ball. Rachel, a beautiful petite brunette, wore an ivory silk sheath.

Leander, which is her real name, arrived in our lives with as much competence and fabulousness as Mary Poppins. She came with an emerald dolphin nose-stud and streaming red hair, to be my daily lady. She has stayed at the core of our lives as good genius, role model, Christian example (of course she's an ex-Goth), Green activist, mentor, cat counsellor, nearest thing to a nanny in every good way and none of the bad, sci-fi nut, baker of weekly cakes and friend of the heart, together with her lovely wife, archaeologist, academic, beauty and the driest wit this side of Campari. Lists like this can be lazy, but there is a crammed goodness to the pair that has almost literally sustained me during the locust years.

At the reception there were fifteen wedding cakes including one topped with a bride and bride, and, for the duration of that hot green garden afternoon with children playing in several languages around us, I sat under a tree with my son and Leander's mum and dad and allowed a new thought to cross my mind: that all *could* be well.

◆·◆◆·◆

It was late June of that same year. My older son Oliver and I met in, as the nonsensical phrase has it, a 'residential' part of London where, even with my photophobia and flinching face, I perceived that I would feel like a thistle in a plushy meadow if I pretended to live hereabouts. My son had taken time off work. He is half a foot taller than I am. I love to be in his shadow. He was in a suit. The day was unbreathably hot. I could see he was missing important phone calls.

We were nearing the end of our list of flats for rent. We had squeezed our frames into several highly accoutred provisional and meretricious spaces with nice keen girls. We had viewed eight leather sofas and three very thin tellies. How did I see this? By doing as I'm doing now, to read this through, by pulling up my eyelids' raw skin, and by making mad faces.

I feel like Mrs Tiggy-winkle with the spikes growing inwards especially over my eyes. I move like Mrs Tiggy-winkle too, tentatively shuffling as though in slippers and very old. I climb upstairs like a child of two.

We had one flat left. We had heard about it only that morning. Over breakfast, Olly's godfather had told Fram, who is his great friend, that he had just inherited somewhere off the King's Road, its owner an American artist who had lived for many years in Italy before moving to London in the nineteen-seventies. He painted right up till almost the very end and the last two squiggles of pigment he chose are still sitting on his palette under an inverted toffee tin. Mauve and ochre, the colours of shadow in Rome.

We sat in Olly's car. I could feel his thin skin not liking the heat of the day. He has hair the colour of the flame on a firelighter packet and slanting green eyes. I was melting like an old cake. We were only just not tearful, like hot children on a birthday.

We shook ourselves down, he clicked shut his car and we ambled to a house that I had not entered since having dinner there thirty years before in the company of my father's old schoolfriend Simon Raven.

The street was a chasm of heatwave. We pressed one of four bells. Two heavy doors were opened and we stepped into what might as well, that afternoon, have been in its shaded refreshing dinginess, a segment of a palace in Venice.

Oliver, who is formal in his manner and composed of jokes and understatement, said, 'It's like your old life, Mummy. Look at all the books.'

I could smell home. Books, linoleum, dust, polish, oil paint, soot, laurel and the very faint note of drains. Edinburgh, Cortona, Karachi, the Hebrides. And now Tite Street.

LENS II: Chapter 1

I f I'd stayed at home, would it all have happened? Or is this every runaway's question when chased down by shame?

It's certainly a question you might have wanted to ask of my uncle Clement, who, if he'd been able to stay at home at 'Dunkeld', my paternal grandparents' home in Sydenham, or at his and my grandmother's grace-and-favour house at Windsor Castle, where he was organist and choirmaster at St George's Chapel, might not have married or become a father. Would his musicality, sheltered, have made him a more sung English composer of the twentieth century? Or would he have chosen, as he did, his own merry means of death as one of the seven Noble Gentlemen of Poverty at St Cross in Winchester? Fewer than a dozen of us went to his funeral at Basingstoke Crem.

Clement's son, David, one of my only two first cousins, who looks lugubrious and is funny, very handsome in the darker Italian fashion, stepped forward and stuck on Clement's coffin as it slipped through the curtains the label he had steamed off his daddy's last bottle of Gordon's Gin. 'Mrs Gordon', Clement called it. For him, not mother's ruin at all, but quite possibly a mother's boy's compensation for that mother's absence.

Winchester Cathedral rang with voice at his memorial. He paid for his gin by giving maths tuition to the children of takeaway proprietors and late-night shopkeepers, ambitious for their children's rise up the slippery pole Clement had negotiated by ignoring or perhaps remaining innocent of it. He saw the sad and funny, not the worldly, in the world.

McWilliams do this thing of fading out. They die young and they stay in touch with the aid of telepathy, of not writing letters and certainly not making telephone calls. They tend to eat unhealthily, to be musical and scholarly to the point of dust in their habits, with strong genes for self-effacement, religious faith (C of E in the rest of the world and Episcopalian in Scotland, or converts to Roman Catholicism), medicine and spying. They have been explorers and teachers but mostly they have been naval surgeons, musicians and secret poets. Their habits are gentle and they have a sweet tooth. Almost sickly thin in youth, they may get tubby later. It could in only some few cases be something to do with drink. It is not hard to see why they were only briefly kings of Scotland. My daughter Clementine compares them favourably with that reproductively inefficient animal, the panda. 'McWilliams are rubbish at dating,' she says, 'but pandas are *really* rubbish at it.'

Clement himself loved the detective stories of Edmund Crispin, King Penguins, of which he had collected almost the entire run, the music of Buxtehude, Wilkie Collins. He knew his Bradshaw intimately, which of course gave him heartbreak as the railways were privatised. He slept from time to time on park benches. He wrote operas for children, preferred tinned fruit, and hummed as though continually about to hatch.

My father was not a drinker. He was a Capstan Full Strength Navy Cut untipped man. He gave up after his stroke, simply smoked seventeen in a row in the hospital and never again. Not that there was long to go. His stroke had hit him while he was walking along reading a Posy Simmonds book in Charlotte Square. Perhaps it was an excess of pleasure that felled him.

Up ahead of Clement and me is my robust Cousin Audrey. A dead ringer for Christine Keeler, Cousin Audrey is a Champagne girl, and I hope she won't mind if I say that she is now to the north of seventy, in her cloud of fragrance purchased at Jenners, the Queen of Edinburgh department stores, and surrounded by the ghosts of terriers and horses. Cousin Audrey is my mother's first cousin and is a Young of Young's Malt Loaf, delicious, healthful and profitable. Young's Malt Loaf will be remembered by some for its acronym: YOUMA, long since, to Cousin Audrey's righteous and splendid ire, munched up by United Biscuits, now a mere crumb in Nabisco, which may be just a corner of Nestlé. Cousin Audrey keeps tabs on us all; she is *not* a McWilliam. McWilliams are mainly socialists and Cousin Audrey, to whom I can't not, as you will have seen, give her full title, *does*, energetically, use the telephone. She has graced stages from Pitlochry to London. One of her dearest friends, a Miss Balfour-Melville, she addresses as Miss Balfour-Melville. Miss Rosalind Balfour-Melville will this week be one hundred years old; we are in May 2008. For her birthday present she has requested a new white frock with a lot of wear in it. That's Old Edinburgh for you.

When Cousin Audrey is puffed out, she declares, 'Whew! I'm peched.' When she's feeling dotty, she says, 'I know you think I'm up the lum.' Cousin Audrey is an alumna of a now-defunct Edinburgh school called St Trinnean's, which is, you understand, not remotely the same as being a girl from St Margaret's, which is quite distinct from Lansdowne House, George Watson's Ladies' College, Heriot's or St George's, which as it happens is where I went. St George's is to the naked eye intensely Scots but to the understanding of mockers of a tubby wearer of its uniform in the nineteen-sixties, almost up-itself English.

My plaits often got filled with chewing gum on the bus or tied to the seat handles. The girls did the gum, the boys the tethering. Maybe it was the scarlet cockade on my beret embroidered with St George piercing his curly dragon and those four nouns from 'The Knight's Tale', TRUTH, HONOUR, FREEDOM and COURTESY. In summer, we wore white gloves with our lightweight, fine puppystooth check, A-line coats; in winter the older girls sported a suit, known as a 'costume' and a cardigan in a shade named Ancient Red. I was only a 'big girl' for a year, but during that year was privileged to enter the mysteries of the Senior-style undergarments: white knickers, navy knickers, white cotton suspender belt and stockings, in the shade Aristoc 'Allure', the colour of strong tea with evaporated milk. There was a racier option, American Tan, that was a shiny auburn, the tea without the milk. The uniform came from Aitken & Niven or Forsyth's;

it goes without saying that there were distinctions between the two shops. Forsyth's had a slightly swingier clientele and had perhaps less Old Edinburgh tone; it sold sportswear (tennis, croquet, skiing, cricket) and you sat on a polar bear to get your shoes fitted.

One of the things people ask, if they notice that you are female and gather that you might have been schooled in Edinburgh, is 'Were you at one of those Jean Brodie style schools?' There is of course no such thing; how Miss Brodie would have abhorred this sloppy generalising. But there's no denying the precision of the echoes for St George's. We were superbly taught by fine Scotswomen, mostly unwed, who had been unmanned by war. We started Latin and Greek before these languages could alarm us, while we were yet in our baby-pinafores.

My parents could not afford the fees. I got some kind of scholarship. My mother's parents paid the rest, and I think minded. My parents fought about it. My father was vehemently agin private education. (I believe he married two women who may at least once in their lives have voted Conservative.) My maternal grandfather was self-made and highly suspicious of education beyond the respectable zones of business, boxing and golf. He read the *FT* and the *Reading Gazette*. He was quite right about the power of learning for its own sake, its huge and blessed leverage for freedom, the vital key it hands you should you require to escape.

Cousin Audrey's hot on business too and to this very day often berates me, quite correctly and very loudly, for my pointlessness and the pointlessness of what I laughably do for a living. Nonetheless, she has in her time loyally attended readings given by me and at least one gentleman known in the wider world to be 'that way'. She's a bonny heckler and one of the bravest souls you will ever meet, a glamorous spinster of the old school, shrewd, courageous, greatly loved and on her own. She reads the right-wing press with close attention. It broke my heart when I suggested the *Guardian* or the *Independent* and she took up both. I feared for her imbalance. Her favourite paper is now officially the *Independent,* her favourite man in the world Boris Johnson, with two little pouches for my sons Oliver and Minoo. She is a man's woman and has the hairdo to prove it, confected weekly by her dear friend Muriel Brattisani, of the famous Brattisani family, whose lobster and chips and cairry-oot Champagne are the talk of the entire globe.

My German publisher wrote to me once describing Oxford as 'the Omphalos of the known world'. He went on to become Minister of the Arts for Germany and then, with some relief, the editor of *Die Zeit.*

Anyhow, Edinburgh knows that it is the centre of the known world and *wheesht* to your omphaloi. Has a doughnut an omphalos? We're talking baked goods here. Omphalos? Can you export it? Well, of course you can, and we are an emigrated race, the Scots, bringing our notion of civilisation wherever we go, bridges, sugary snacks, books and stories, fighting and drinking.

What I'm trying to get round to is my birthday, the 1st of July 1955, the birthday of Julius Caesar, for whom my third name is Juliet. In October I was christened at Rosslyn Chapel, burial place of the Earls of Orkney, scene of *The Lay of the Last Minstrel* by Sir Walter Scott, reputed resting place of, among other things, the Holy Grail and the True Cross and scored with a number of unexplained Masonic symbols. I wrote in a novel twenty years ago about this numinous jewel in stone. Of course, its anonymity has since been rather blown by Dan Brown. It contains among countless other solid beauties, the 'Apprentice Pillar', a piece of carving so virtuosic that the chief mason is said to have murdered its maker, a mere apprentice, for his presumption, and then hanged himself in remorse. There is a small carving of the grieving master mason, his mouth an appalled hole. This pillar is depicted on the front of one of my father's volumes in 'The Buildings of Scotland' series. Daddy died in the middle of writing *Dumfries and Galloway.* On the front of that volume is one of the Duke of Buccleuch's palaces, Drumlanrig House, out of which, not very long ago, someone walked unnoticed carrying a small painting by Leonardo.

That's carry-out for you on a scale beyond even lobster. The painting has since been returned. The late Duke was once our Member of Parliament and I remember him canvassing in Thistle Street, a tall curly-headed long man, before he broke his back out hunting. His father, the old Duke, had a silver wine cooler the size of a cow trough into which I remember being put for fun as a small child. Like being in a huge deep ladle of precious reflective metal, it fitted me fine. All made to hold drink.

My lips had never touched liquor then.

I was an only child, but even then somehow stood aside from properly inhabiting a self, even though at the beginning it was a fairly chunky self to inhabit. I played with dolls, glass animals, and small unmatching china tea services that my mother collected in junk shops. Wherever she went, I was. I followed her stuck like a limpet to its home-scar. I loved the scent of her forearms and the smell of her hands that combined acetone, coffee, Atrixo hand cream and cooked garlic.

In our crescent lived many mothers of families to whom Mummy became close. Constance Kuenssberg was a doctor and the wife of Ekke, our doctor, who came out day and night for us.

Ekke's father had written to him when Ekke was a boy at Salem in Germany, the school set up by Kurt Hahn who later founded Gordonstoun. It was 1935 and the Nuremberg Laws had just been passed. In Ekke's father's letter were the instructions to walk out of Germany into neutral Switzerland, down into France, and thence to Great Britain. Ekke did this. He was interned as an enemy alien on the Isle of Man, which some have described as being a kind of university then, a virtuous Babel. On his arrival in Edinburgh, Ekke trained to become a general practitioner and married Constance, who was part of the Edinburgh establishment, being daughter of the Rector of Edinburgh Academy. This extraordinary couple did much to set up the National Health Service in Scotland. Ekke's son is now still my stepmother's doctor.

For a more expansively raised generation I should say that you had, at that time (if you had shoes at all), indoor shoes and outdoor shoes, the line between each being the front door of any dwelling place. The purpose of these designations was cleanliness. It did not do to bring the outdoors in. You might spoil someone's good housekeeping. It was a matter of everything in its proper place.

The cold: each day was a fight to keep the cold outside where it belonged and not let it into the house, though houses were freezing inside too; there was an unsleeping vigilance against cold as it came in from the sea and down from the hills and off from the mountains and into our bones. If the air was not misty with human breath and surreptitious attempts at thaw, it was misty with the haar, the mist off the sea, of which some Edinburgh residents were in my childhood very proud as it was yet another way of keeping yourself *to* yourself.

It was not unusual to see people ski the winter streets. Mothers would pull children on toboggans to fetch the messages, which is Edinburgh for 'do the shopping'. Old ladies walked as I do now that I'm blind in the snowless streets of London, side-shuffling along the pavement while nervous hands feel for the next railing. I cracked today into a column of sixties brick, the corner of what used to be a rather ritzy rehabilitation clinic. The bruise is coming up nicely. Today's blepharospasm doctor wryly remarked, 'The clinic got out six months ago, or you might have been able to sue. It belongs to a property developer now and they're a bit more hard-headed.'

My mother's and my favourite junk shop was Mrs Virtue's, in a basement on a corner with her name up in subtly shaded sign-writing emphasised in gold. The steps down to Mrs V's had iron handrails curled to right and left. She herself wore a hairnet, a navy angora hat, a musquash coat, a pink-flowered pinny, many cardigans topped by a maroon one, a Clydella vest, fingerless gloves, varicose veins, stockings and socks, and what were called indoor shoes.

Mrs Virtue's shop was a tunnel of mattresses twenty deep on either side, damp with cats' piss. It was hard to imagine Mrs Virtue outside her musty nest. It is likely that she and her cats had a shared diet, though she smoked more than they did. I can't think why I never stole anything from Mrs Virtue's shop. Can it have been original virtue in me? The place was so chaotic and I so young that I understood the set-up as how things were meant to be and would not have dared spoil the careful arrangements Mrs Virtue appeared to have made. She had a face like chiffon for wrinkling and intermittent sets of teeth. Her eyes were dark and missed little.

Mummy spent hours talking to Mrs Virtue. They had far more than cats in common. I didn't know then that these long conversations with people outside her marriage were a symptom of her loneliness as well as of her curiosity and friendliness. I am certain she was not signalling this loneliness to anyone intentionally, leave alone to me. She wanted to be the best of mothers.

It is not easy to say this out loud and before I went blind I would not have had to, but this greedy obsessive recall of trivial (and, it's not lost on me, mainly visual) detail has clamped to me even closer as a habit since I lost my capacity to see. I was made of what I saw. I saw in panorama and in focus. I saw things at and even over the edge. I wasn't half so good at hearing.

I'm scared I've become like an inventory for the sale of an old dead person's house, what Scots call a displenishing; here I am, picking up lost bits and pieces of my scattered life to try to make something whole by putting it all together, my own flotsam and jetsam.

I plugged up my ears against the parental fighting. I think I knew that my parents, as a pair, were growing terribly demarcated from within, she the indoor and he the outdoor shoes. There was some scuffing. She threw and he hit. She slapped. He didn't throw.

Both were sociable and attractive to the opposite sex. They took me with them to dinner parties and I either sat up with them or was put to bed in a guest room or the hosts' bed. I remember falling asleep in a nightie from Mrs Virtue's that my mother had laundered and starched. I had a tube of Smarties, too precious to open, in one hand. And I had done my teeth. The couple my parents were dining with encouraged me glamorously to call them by their Christian names, Gerald and Denise. He was what is called in Scotland a sheriff and she was French. From the age of three I had attended the Institut Français. It wasn't a particularly fancy thing to do at that time in Edinburgh; it may have its roots in the Auld Alliance, that tie between Scotland and France against the old enemy, England.

When my parents woke me up, after dinner with the Sheriff had run its course, the bed was stippled all over the clean sheets by the gay fugue of Smarties.

It seems a pity to interpose 'real time' yet again, but it occurs to me that my use for Smarties as a child was only chromatic. I sorted them into colours, hoarded, hid and lost them or gave them away, mainly to my father who, being skin and bone, loved chocolate. From the first I knew that different characteristics inhered in each colour and that colours related to numbers and to letters of the alphabet.

I don't like chocolate but I love to look at its outer casing. I am attached to those maps that come in chocolate boxes, with fanciful names for each mouthful. I still can't face chocolate, unless, and this is awful, it is white and therefore not chocolate at all.

In fact, it's probably my version of mother's ruin nowadays and certainly this breast-fed baby's only approximate mother substitute.

There was a sweet named Treets. Treets were like fatter, and merely brown, Smarties, and they had a slogan: 'Melts in the mouth, not in the hand'.

I was first approached by a flasher when I was four. Actual manual work and melting in the hand not the mouth followed soon thereafter. There was one try to broach my milk-toothy mouth. I recall the feeling, as of a large eyeball with a thick lid forcing itself past my uvula. I didn't seem to think this was unusual at the time. Families living many to a room in freezing poverty cuddled together for warmth;

there was often a 'simple' son, who might wander the town. Having found the means of making a productive sensation, why might he not have taken it into his head to share the feeling? I simply stood aside from myself. I still have some of my milk teeth.

This intervention was exactly the opposite of reading. Reading was safe and something you went into. This invasive unshared business was something you stood aside from. It didn't go on for long either in fact as an act or as a sequence in my life. Nor was the practitioner even someone whose name I knew, poor boy, trying to find a vessel for his pleasure.

Where was my mother at these times? She was being preyed upon too, by someone certainly less innocent than my poor urban simpleton.

Someone was circling her and smoothing her vanity, seeping into the crevices left by her dearly loved husband's absence, away with his unsleeping work.

———◆———

All my life I've had words that got stuck in my head as tunes do. When I was three it was San Francisco and Benozzo Gozzoli. I had no idea of the meaning. It was the sound that stuck. During other parts of my childhood, the needle stuck on various phrases or sometimes single words; 'Pretty ballerina' bounced in my brain for the obvious reason that I wasn't. 'Pink' chaffinched away in my head for months. Ever since the fire in my Oxford house, the word that has been rolling around behind my eyes is 'epilimnion'. I even wake up saying it. This may be a bad case of 'Candia McWilliam's swallowed the dictionary', because I've only the slightest idea of what it means, which is, I think, the top surface of a large body of water, for example a lake. What I don't know is how many meniscuses make up an epilimnion. Then other words attached themselves to it and now I'm bothered by the assonant but dead-end statement, 'we swim the epilimnion'.

It has become impossible to write of my far past without being somewhat open about the present and its tense surface.

A carer brings breakfast to my cousin Audrey in Edinburgh; if it has not arrived by noon she's fair mad with frustration, diabetes, hunger and very possibly loneliness. It is with grave difficulty that she gets about. Today, when I got up at six and started blindly doing my chores, I realised that I was like this, in inverse, about the arrival of Liv at 9 a.m. Just as Cousin Audrey is hungry for her breakfast, I'm hungry to pour out words and get them down. I have already after only six days become dependent upon the process and the presence of Liv. I no longer pace when dictating but sit slightly behind her to her right and hope that does not make her feel haunted; I'm less shy than I was, and can feel the sentences consequently relaxing. It's less like doing a reading, and more like having a conversation, where the other person is not gagged but doesn't talk quite as much as I do. I'm not naturally one for monologue, and was never, even at my most drunk, the life or soul of the party; one of the fears consequent upon my blindness has been that of becoming a big fat bore. The note I most resist in a female voice of any age is the note of complaint. Only French women do it at all attractively, and even then it seems to me too close to cleaving to the privileges of servility and aggression.

Say the present is the epilimnion, then, of this book; as we swim it so we shall feel the changing temperatures of the past rise up, the weed brush our legs; we may or may not sense schools of trout or a biding long-jawed pike. All over this house are pairs of spectacles, many of them purchased for one pound each at a Pound Shop in a subway under Basingstoke. None of these spectacles came with a prescription. I just like to have a pair of specs to hold and fiddle with and put on and wave around as though I were a person who could see. In my old life, before blindness, I had only just started to wear reading glasses, as was normal for my age. Before that, I was always seeing, watching, gorging my eyes.

What is enough to see?

What is enough to look for?

For the last two days, I have been conducting an experiment, and attempting to use my ears to catch secrets and the almost unheard, as, I realise, I used to use my eyes. Of course I've always eavesdropped; it's a form of collecting irresistible to the spy side of being a writer. But I'm trying now to hear and listen supernaturally, around corners, within trees, into birds' nests, right into the egg within the nest. So far it hasn't come up to the level my seeing skills were at when they departed. That sounds ungrateful; I'm aware that it will take another fifty-three years to tune my hearing skills up; I'm just a hatching tuning fork, like the one emerging from the lyrebird's egg drawn by my father larger than life size with his Flo-Master pen on the basement wall in Warriston Crescent after another row with my mother.

So far, my only auditory revelation occurred in a doctor's waiting room. Unless I'm with Liv or asleep or actually with a doctor, these waiting rooms are where I spend my days. I was in a department of Guy's Hospital that is a house built upon the place where Keats did his medical training, opposite the Old Operating Theatre whose motto is COMPASSIONE NON MERCEDE, near London Bridge. I heard three pieces of scaffolding being conjoined and the dead sound was exactly that of a wooden xylophone; distance had turned metal to wood.

Occasionally, fashion demands that very pretty people wear spectacles for what is called in the world of magazines a 'story'. This is the run of editorial pages with some ostensible narrative connection using the same model or group of models. Sometimes film stars wear specs not on account of their trouble with seeing but on account of how they wish to *be* seen. They may for all we know be short-sighted, but these are specs for being seen in. Today, the left-hand lens has fallen out of my favourite pair of such specs. That's what my specs are. They are all a put-on.

I trod upon what I thought must be a very thick and large toenail with my bare foot. I felt around and realigned my mind. The only sort of animal whose toenail it could be simply could not have fitted into this flat. I thought directly of our Latvian lodger, who often babysat me. That's how my mother was able sometimes to leave me, I remembered all at once. I was left with the lodgers. One lodger was a sculptor in clay, his favourite subject crouching beasts, tigers in the main. His glaze of choice was an intense Middle Eastern turquoise. His hands and feet were interesting to me. He was a sweet man. I remember him clearly saying that at least the clay didn't get under his nails. The nails of his feet and his hands had been pulled out under torture.

Unlike our lodger, my mother's courtier was a fabulist. I would think this, wouldn't I, but I feel it was less to my father that she was unfaithful than to the strictures of a certain Edinburgh that just couldn't take her. If I look at this more closely, I'm aware that there was, together with the kenspeckle, right-and-proper city, a bohemian life stirring that she sensed but perhaps never quite managed to reach and that has since her death flowered orchidaceously.

It was not that my father did not love her. They were so unalike by extraction and temperament that it is evident, even to me, their child, that theirs was a real passion. It was just that he loved buildings too and the buildings of Scotland at that time were being blown up, knocked down, blasted, wrecked and swiped down by permission of the state in a way that called directly to my father's dedicated curatorial heart. It was a love, and it was a love for life.

Several times, Mummy's admirer turned up at our house dressed in costume. This wasn't to fool me but to amuse her. I don't think I crossed his mind. I seem to remember him turning up as Mr Toad once, but maybe that was a mufti-day. He certainly had a veteran open-topped vehicle of some sort, that necessitated the putting away inside our overcoats of my mother's and my waist-length hair. Mummy had a circular thing like a fur hoop; it was called a 'rat'. You pulled your hair through it and arranged a bun or a beehive or a twist or a chignon or a cottage loaf. You fixed the arrangement with long hair-pins of the sort that come in handy in old black-and-white films, for lock-picking, car-starting, etc.

Just as she was an early user of the contraceptive pill, my mother was a pioneer hairdryer user. Like all her machines, it had a name and broke almost at once, to be half mended by her. One morning as we sat in my nursery, I on her knee, Morphy Richards sucked instead of blew and we spent a morning disentangling, you could almost say lock-picking, our long hair, hers pale blonde and mine more brown, from this space-age machine, with its cunning design suggestive of weaponry and air travel.

My mother followed with complete involvement the lives of many of the animals who lived at Edinburgh Zoo. We wept together when the elephant seal perished after choking on an ice lolly stick someone had given him. Why had they not given him a cornet? We observed the high-held pregnancy of Susu the giraffe. My mother tried to correct me for mourning the zoo's elephant, Sally, more than my great-aunt Beatrice, known as Beadle. The defining triumph of my mother's animally attached life was when, unanswerably, the zoo's golden eagle, William, laid an egg. We both of us feared the sala-mander and the electric eel, looking at their flaccid yet potent inertia in absorbed disgust. My mother was warned off by zookeepers for hanging around the penguins and the ring-tailed lemurs. The keepers were right. She wanted to bring the creatures home with us. After she died, I was turfed out of the zoo for trying to catch a chipmunk. Actually, I wanted a pygmy hippo.

When you fly up to Edinburgh, if you look under the left oxter of the plane as it commences its descent into the airport, you will see what remains of my parents' idyll. Its name was Craigiehall Temple and we went there on summer weekends towards the end of my mother's life. It stands above the banks of the River Almond, a folly three storeys high growing among the wild white raspberries and enclosing beeches. Its stairs wound through its three octagonal rooms, the top one with a golden ceiling around whose cornice ran plaster ribbons held by plaster doves. It had a doll's house portico and no amenities at all. My parents furnished it from street sales and Mrs V's. The piano in the top room cost half a crown, of which there were eight in the pound. There was a large cane chair that extended and had a pocket for magazines and a place where you could put your sundowner. My father called this chair 'the British Fascist'. The middle room was where we all slept on camp beds that rolled away in the day. I lay on mine in my sleeping bag pretending hour upon hour to be a caterpillar, then a chrysalis. I was usually asleep by the time I was due to break open as something more glamorous and winged. There was a chemical lavatory and at night, with much care, as though handling moths, my parents lit the gas mantles of hurricane and Tilley lamps. The smell of paraffin makes me feel sick, as do all petrol compounds including Cow Gum, which we used to stick down layouts at *Vogue*; but to the paraffin-nausea there is also a dizzy homesickness for me since it was the source of much of our heat and light when I was a child.

I don't know how long we leased the Temple; I'm sure I want to think it was for longer than is true. In the end, my parents gave up mending after the vandals who would come and play football in the top room and turn my mother's pearl-poppit jewellery out on to the floor looking for real stuff. We did spend one Christmas there and nothing mattered at all because the world was white and we were in a stone tower with no one near us and our dogs and our cats, log fires and drawing things. I had, too, one birthday there and remember thinking that the silky-shivering fields of barley all around were not green but blue and sometimes, under the wind, silver. My father made a rope swing for me and, insofar as my first childhood goes, this was the most physical my life ever got. I had a pet snail named Horatio and a stickleback named Lindsay. We lived very considerably on hot milk with crusts in. My mother and I liked salt with it, my father sugar. We went, as Scots say, enormous walks and I could tell my mother was pretending she was on a horse. The woods were full of smoking bluebells and white windflowers that, like the spirit they're named for, lose breath when cut. It astonishes me, now that I am a mother, to observe in retrospect with how few elements both my parents could conjure magic. She was more confident at the Temple; she knew what to do in the country. She could name flowers and she knew how to kill a rabbit with a stone when it was wet and blind with myxomatosis. He was less romantic about the country-living side of things, probably because it was he who got to deal with the chemical lavatory, the log-sawing and the drive out to reach his wife's dream-place. There was some other occlusion that I can only guess at; to do with my mother's admirer?

To return to the epilimnion; this morning it came clearly to me that my father's apparent absence of human demonstrativeness was just that, apparent. So intense were his emotions about buildings that he has left to me, and I believe to my half-siblings, a characteristic that sounds chilling – the capacity to be completely changed by a building, to be inhabited by it imaginatively and emotionally. Three times in my life I have been rescued by architecture. The flat where I'm staying now exemplifies this. At my blindest, I can still be consoled by the feel of the door handles in the studio where Liv and I work, their satisfying relationship to the human hand.

I used to be sorry for myself as a very small child because my father was so often away or, when present, actually utterly preoccupied by a building. It was only in my twenties that I even began to read this as not over-aestheticism but as deep humane connectedness. It is easy to misread so silent, so cultivated and so cool a character.

The history of architecture, the study of human habitations great and small, was not then fashionable. The National Trust was on a rescue mission, no mistake. The heritage business did not exist. Progress was the watchword; new was good. This leads me to a complicated personal muddle. It never crossed my father's mind that what might be called a 'social' interest might be taken in great houses, but it may cross that of my reader, so much have the times changed. Great houses were being pulled down at the rate of one a week in Scotland, more in England, during my childhood; my father was, as it were, their protector, champion and physician. My father had no interest in who was who and indeed rather regretted anybody being anybody on account of his shyness about the personal. Naturally this made him an ideal friend of anybody who was used to being sucked up to; such people found themselves refreshed by his disinterestedness, his consuming interest. He engaged with houses, less so with home.

Where this is muddling in any account of my own life became clear to me in a horrible but revelatory way after the first ever interview I did when my novel *A Case of Knives* came out 1988. My trajectory, which has felt to me, naturally enough, just like my own life, is legible in various disobliging ways and it's not lost on me that one of these involves what that genius Kingsley Amis calls hypergamy. He meant that a clever man who can make people laugh can marry any woman he wishes, even the most beautiful. It's not the same for women. I mean that I started off what I think I still am, an Edinburgh girl, but somehow time and events have made me seem to be an Englishwoman; an Englishwoman, at that, of some privilege.

Then we did just stay in, visit, talk and think about houses. Some of these were small and some were not. What they had in common was that they were at that time imperilled.

Where were you when you first read *Struwwelpeter*? I don't know if you can buy it now; it may be available from antiquarian or 'special-interest' booksellers. The first copy of it I found was certainly from the century before last. Its terrifying vigorous bossy pornography has set some of my rules for life. The red-legged scissor-man visited me only last night, oddly enough with the face of Richard Dawkins, with whom, how can one's dreams be this trite, I was playing chess. Augustus the chubby lad – 'fat ruddy cheeks Augustus had' – is still, on bad days, my picture of myself, and, even when I got down to the pin man Augustus in my thirties, I still felt like the fat boy before he started rejecting his nutritious soup. I found *Struwwelpeter* under a bed I was sleeping in at Culzean Castle in Ayrshire, built by Robert Adam on a cliff over the sea. Daddy was restoring it, quite considerably with his own hands; the castle has a high oval rotunda with a sweeping exaltation of staircase, arising with composure like written music up inside its shell. Daddy would be up a trembly ladder with his cigarette, re-limning cartouches or re-plastering crumbled bits of Vitruvian scrollwork. I was never, while he breathed, not worried about my father. When he died, there was at least that; he couldn't fall off a battlement or dive through a skylight. Or, indeed, he couldn't ever again get arrested for trespass or burglary.

The grateful nation of Scotland had just given a wing of Culzean in perpetuity to the American people for the use of their President should he find himself on the Ayrshire coast. I was left to potter about while Daddy worked. I had at the time a broken right arm and dislocated shoulder so I had learned to draw and write with my left hand. I was four but was very proud that I had a duffel coat made for a fourteen-year-old to accommodate my plaster. I was sleeping in President Eisenhower's bed, or at any rate having a rest in it, when I found *Struwwelpeter*. Who the Dickens can have left it there?

Culzean sits on the Ayrshire coast in replete beauty among its gardens. We would always be there for daffodil time, later in Scotland than in England, and the creak of daffodils as I walked among them and smelled the sea from within the castle ramparts was safety itself. The spring of the broken arm I spent secretly memorising *Struwwelpeter*, being spoilt by the tea-room ladies who gave me glacé cherries, and sitting atop one of the stocky little cannons that defend this gracefully parodic masterpiece. I tried daily, failed daily, to lift a cannonball. The balls were arranged in neat pyramids beside each gun. In the evening after a sunny day they held warmth until the light had gone and if you licked them the rusty salt taste was delicious. It's the taste of oysters. Blood, iron, iodine.

Around 1960, the National Trust for Scotland hired a cruise ship from a Norwegian shipping line and invited archaeologists and other enthusiasts to take a tour of the Hebrides on the SS *Meteor*. Particular attention was to be paid to brochs, early structures sometimes so early as to be hardly perceptible to the uninitiated. My father was overseeing some aspects of the tour and giving informative evening talks.

For a greedy only child who *was* the only child on the ship, it was a taste of the high life. One evening there really was a swan made of ice at the Captain's table and, during the day, a childless American couple made much of me. We passed the great organ pipes of Staffa and Fingal's Cave, we stopped at Iona where I heard the turf praying. No one had yet spoken directly to me of God, so I had built him for myself.

I had not become a liar yet and I am not a liar now, but I do believe that we made harbour at the island of Colonsay, disembarked and toured its surprising tropical gardens that surround the pretty open-armed big house. It only takes one more squeeze of my memory to have it believe that we met the handsome wife of the island's laird. She was nice to me, my false memory tells me, because I was the only child aboard and she knew that plurality can nourish a being.

One of seven children herself, and mother of six, she seems in my mind's eye to be wearing a flowered dress and gloves. Knowing what I know now, I realise I must have made it all up.

◆•••◆

Perhaps on account of my father's absent-mindedness about my mother's birthday, I felt some unease around 3 September each year.

On her thirtieth birthday, her cat Nancy Mitford fell two stone storeys from her bedroom. My superstitious mother *really* did take this as an ill omen, to which she often referred, to do with cats having nine lives but herself just the one and her birthday being the day the Second World War began. On my own thirtieth birthday, I was making supper when a large white rabbit fell from the sky. It screamed horribly, for its back was broken. Our neighbour from the flat next door kindly despatched it. Or should that be our neighbour from the flat next door despatched it, kindly?

A large and floppy-eared rabbit, the poor thing had been bought by the tenant of the top flat in our building as part of his pet python's supper. The RSPCA visited in due course and found quite a selection of reptiles, including, tear-jerkingly predictably, a crocodile, diappointingly not resident in the lavatory.

Even at six, though, I had come to see that birthdays were the teeth of time and that things were not improving between my parents. My own high-summer birthday was celebrated with strawberries and cream. I was allowed a friend over. I chose a girl at random because I didn't have a best friend yet. She was called Gillian. I thought her very dainty and pretty. When the time came for cake and strawberries and cream she cried and cried because she did not like what she called 'real cream'. She was scared of my parents' English accents and had met cream only once before, when it had been nice, between two pieces of meringue. It was 'shop cream'. Real cream, she said, was dirty because it came from cow-juice and gave you an illness that made you cough up blood.

In embarrassment made worse by the need for festivity, my parents said goodbye to our poor little guest with her white socks and angora bolero. Later, the childish part of the day was over and the dinner table was full of adults, the blue and white plates, hot food. In the sky were both the sun and the moon. There was one more, and most beautiful present, a dress made of the best velvety cotton, cut exactly to my dimensions and embroidered inside its neck with lavender silk thread spelling out my full name Candia Frances Juliet in beautiful clear handwriting made with a needle. This gift was to go deeper with my mother than any tattoo on skin and I was one year closer to becoming a fat little liar.

A vacancy had been filled in our family, no larger than a needle's eye.

LENS II: Chapter 2

In the life of the present I am reading, that is listening to, *Paradise Lost*. It is read by Anton Lesser, whose intelligent doubt-filled voice somehow emphasises the clouded giants and rivers of pearl he speaks of through the mind of Milton. So far in my blindness only my accountant has been sufficiently innocent and jolly to mention Milton to me, over the receipts.

How consoling and terrifying it was to hear the words: 'the mind is its own place; and in itself / can make a heaven of hell, a hell of heaven'. When first I became blind, Fram, who lives sixty miles away, suggested that I would never be quite alone because I have 'my art'. I felt at once consigned to live off something that I was not talented or morally courageous enough to address. It was like telling a deer to build its future around raw meat. I'm doing my best and I'm quite aware that whatever my 'art' was, it will have been changed by my blindness. It remains to be seen, if I may use that word, how. I was never alone when I could read.

My parents and I visited England only for very specific familial reasons. I was always carsick and usually moving between anxiety and terror, relieved by daydreams, at this period all about being a doctor of great bravery during a selection of historical scenarios; I suspect I was usually disguised as a boy in these roles. My father had never passed a driving test, braked on corners and both parents smoked in the fuggy leather cupboard that was our car within. It wasn't our car, really, but the National Trust for Scotland's. This non-ownership was significant to my sense of our hardly holding on to our ledge in life.

Our reasons for visiting England included my parents' bookseller friend Ben Weinreb and his family. Ben gave me the dummy of a book called *London 2000* to draw in. Both date and city seemed lifetimes distant from me and my life; now we are years beyond it and Ben is dead. We visited other friends, a couple called Myrtle and Bear; he was known as Bear, since, as a diabetic, he couldn't have sweet things. He too was a book dealer. Myrtle was a potter. There were some rather glamorous friends in Hampstead, he perhaps a sculptor, she certainly a sexpot. She struck me as the best sort of sexpot because her warmth went out in all directions, not merely to men.

The main reason that we ever went as a family to England was to visit grandparents. This was never comfortable. My widowed paternal grandmother lived at Windsor Castle in a tiny house in the cloister that nonetheless had a speaking tube to call long-departed servants. She had been a nurse at Great Ormond Street Hospital and bore the loss of her husband with a daily exercised Christian faith and ingrained modest fortitude. My grandfather, Ormiston Galloway Edgar McWilliam, a man whose temperament was made for peace and the arts of peace, fought as a teenager in the trenches in the Great War and was killed at the end of the Second World War while laying a smokescreen in the tail end of an aeroplane that was shot down, I believe, by our own side. Among his close friends was the painter Henry Lamb, and the letters between them show a relish for family life and a sensitivity to preposterousness both at war and in the smaller frays of family life. Lamb's letters are often illustrated with quick sketches of his children being dried after a bath, paddling and so on. In one of his letters my grandfather describes tucking my six-year-old father back into bed after the child had been awoken by the flare and crackings of the Crystal Palace burning down, of which my grandfather gives an eyewitness account. My grandfather wrote and illustrated a published book before he was twenty. It is about the battle at Suvla. He must have known he was going to die then.

But he didn't, or not in that war. I have the photographs of him as the captain of both rugby and cricket teams at Charterhouse. On the back of each photograph he has written in almost every case the date and place where each smiling young man in the fading picture had fallen in war.

His widow, my grandmother's was not a false piety; she was a deeply believing Anglican whose daily notebooks used to shock me with their probity when I was ten and thought I knew a lot. Clearly I knew nothing. What decent child goes through the notebooks of her grandmother? Each day she recorded the church services she had attended, to whom she had written, and from whom she had received, letters, and how much money she had spent. The amounts were very small. She had an expressed quality of humility that enraged my mother and there is no doubt at all that my humble grandmother looked very far down upon her tall, ostensibly worldly daughter-in-law. The word, though it was never used, would have been 'vulgar'. Certainly my paternal grandmother regarded my maternal grand-parents as being 'not quite . . .' or, that damning deprecation, 'too grand for us'.

My mother teased my father unkindly about his attachment to his mother and referred to her mother-in-law, also unkindly, as 'Navy Blue Throughout'. These had been the words that my grandmother had replied with when my mother's mother asked her what she would be wearing to the wedding that would conjoin their ill-matched families.

I called my paternal grandmother 'Grand'mère'. I suspect this was to get over some difficulty about my own mother refusing to address her as 'Mother', as convention might then have asked. In due time, my stepmother would address her thus.

My mother's own mother wasn't that fond of Mummy either. My grandmother Clara was from theatre people; her own mother and grand-mother, with their long beautiful legs, had been male impersonators on the stage. My maternal great-grandmother was a friend of Vesta Tilley. There are lost photographs of my transvestite ancestresses looking wonderful in tails and tights. How I wish I had them now. I packed them away in a trunk before I moved into my first marital home. The trunk was stored by a friend. The friend died sadly, surprisingly, dreadfully, young. How could I even mention my trunk of keepsakes to a family that had lost its head? As it is, the trunk of travesties sounds like the framing device for one of those dull novels that are meant to show us some flat tale of parallel lives separated only by time, whose moral is that we are all sisters under the skin. I worry, too, that my long-lost trunk may contain things of which I might be ashamed, satin trousers, proposals of marriage, lists of things to do that will resemble in every way those lists I write thirty-five years on.

Neither Mummy nor I inherited the great legs. My grandmother Clara's first speaking role on the stage was as Little Lord Fauntleroy, aged five. She was so symmetrically and astoundingly elongated and so facially beautiful that she was continually stopped on the street. I have one photo of her, singing the part of Mad Margaret in *Ruddigore*. Considering the town's later importance in my life, it is odd that I should, for the earliest part of it, have thought that 'Basingstoke' was an invented word that you employed to calm female lunatics. In the Mad Margaret photograph, my glorious grandmother's glorious hair reaches to her calves. Later when she cut it off her father, who owned a string of theatres in the East End and on the South Coast, didn't speak to her for months. He could eat twelve dozen oysters at a sitting. My grandmother Clara was known as Clare; she had two sisters, Ruth and Edna. Edna married and lived in Guernsey, impossibly exotic. I remember meeting Great-Aunt Edna only once, during a half-term out from my English school. We sat in some silence. Nobody's accent sounded real except my grandmother's self-invented grande dame tones. Poor, blind Ruth became a counter in my parents' stony game that no one could win.

My father was a dab hand at playing ducks and drakes, making flat stones bounce off the, I suppose, epilimnion. As their marriage worsened, my mother would say, 'Throwing stones can blind people. My Aunt Ruth was blinded, aged seven, *for life* by a boy throwing stones.'

You could see my father was getting bored with my mother. This boredom made her anxious. I was anxious for them both, with their separate damaged hearts. I can't remember a time when I didn't know that my father's heart was literally fragile since he had had rheumatic fever during his National Service. He was meant to avoid physical risk and exertion; of course he didn't. And since I lived with my face as far up my mother's sleeve as I could get it, so as to smell her, I knew all about the heart that was worn there too.

Our visits to my maternal grandparents were approached with sublimated satire and some dread by my father. God knows how my mother felt. I think the person with whom she was easiest was Ernest, who had been her father's soldier-servant and stayed on. She was adored by Ernest in a way that she was not by her parents to whom her gender, height, appearance and marriage were all a disappointment. Her father called her 'Scruff', not kindly meant.

The Folly, West Drive, Sonning-on-Thames, Berkshire, was England to me, and how it scared and stifled me. I could not then have placed what it was about this single-storey brick residence made, as I could never forget, with my grandfather's blood, toil, tears and sweat, that took the air out of me but I never entered it without knowing I was going into another country where they did things differently. I recognised the claustrophobia when encountering it again in Elizabeth Bowen's great wartime novel about escape from a certain England, *The Heat of the Day*. There is in it a house called Holme Deane, that is not The Folly, naturally, but has some of its effect.

I don't eat ham or pork, sausages or bacon. I have a number of Jewish friends who really like sausages or will eat a bacon sandwich. My refusal to eat pig-meat started off as a gesture of wholly pointless identification, and maybe its motives aren't as grand as I thought they were, when I was seven. Maybe they are a pettifogging, grandiose and utterly pointless boycotting of a certain England. I was scared of the flatness, the enclosure, the sense of being tinned. One could not, as in a home in the North, stretch and shout and breathe in and out.

One was in a tin and on a shelf and set in place, the place to be, to sit and stay sat, set.

Ham and salad was what we had for lunch at The Folly, the ham like big wet hangnails, the salad made of units, one lettuce leaf, a quarter of tomato, a slice of egg, a pinch of cress, and that incontinent flitch of beetroot. My father loved Heinz Salad Cream and got his lunch down with the help of this; for pudding it was ice cream and tinned fruit salad. This was for the times a perfectly festive family meal. My mother had spoiled me by her Italianising of our life, her olive oil, aubergines, herbs. At The Folly, meals were taken because what you did at one o'clock was have lunch. It was almost an act of patriotism, a contribution to the resettlement of the world post-war, the healing deployment of routine against chaos or otherness.

My father, never a fan in other circumstance of healthy food, would 'forget' not to say, 'Do you know, Clare, that Wall's make pork pies too and that this ice cream is probably – delicious of course – pork fat with a bit of air whipped in?' This was mean of him as he consumed quantities of Wall's all his life, regarding it as a special delicacy not perhaps related to real ice cream, certainly not to ice cream in Italy or as made by the Italian immigrants to Scotland, Mr Lucca at Musselburgh, Mr Coia at the end of the Crescent, Mr Nardini at Largs, but certainly a treat in itself. This was the man, after all, who, when Lyons Maid brought out the new line in lollies they called a Fab, with hundreds and thousands on the chocolate tip, spent a weekend afternoon chasing one down.

I think my Christian name was a bother to my Henderson grandparents. It was ostentatious, foreign and pretentious; they had not heard it before. Grandpapa did not like what he did not know. Of course they were defensive; there had just been a world war; they had but the one child, who seemed to have decided to marry a man who was not only uninterested in making money but deprecated the process and the idea of a society arranged around it.

My grandmothers addressed one another as 'Mrs Henderson' and 'Mrs McWilliam'.

It is all unspeakable and it was all about class, tone and education. My maternal grandmother, despite her beauty, a dowry that can reassure a man who purchases it that there has been a straight swap with no small print, was cleverer than she dared show her husband. He was older and controlled the purse-strings. She cleaned the house, starting at five in the morning every day, wearing what she called a 'house dress' before she changed into her proper – on show – clothes for that day's part, and brushing her regrown waist-length hair one hundred times before dividing it into six, making plaits and coiling it up like Dorothea Brooke's crown of hair in *Middlemarch*. She did the housework daily like this although there was Ernest's wife Florrie to 'do' for her. Yet it was at The Folly that I found one of the books that changed my life. It had been my mother's. It was a big coral-coloured cloth-bound book containing black-and-white reproductions of old master paintings and modern works with captions encouraging you to look harder into the picture. It had been published during the war and has something of the perspicacity of Kenneth Clark's *One Hundred Details*. It was written by someone called Ana M. Berry and now belongs to my children. It must have taken faith in civilisation to produce such a book at such a time. Its name is *Art for Children*.

All her frustration my grandmother poured into systems of control that eventually grew inwards and harmed her. She was so proud; she would like it to be said of her that she never took a penny from the state, that her home was spotless, that she was a good wife, that she had kept her figure, that she wasted nothing. I think now that inside her stone self was a good deal more sweetness. I think that she was lonely and used pride and dignity to kill pain, in so doing closing over her heart an awful fist of calcification till it resembled flint and was not. All the creative dash she had been born with in the Mile End Road, where she'd kept her ponies as a little girl, she turned to producing light opera and operetta for the Sainsbury Singers of Reading, who became as family to her.

McWilliams think Verdi vulgar (I don't. *Don Carlos* is my favourite). I learned about my father not caring for Verdi at the very start of the existence of the Sony Walkman. Daddy was in a ward of old men after his stroke. I flew north to see him with this exciting new invention and a stack of Verdi on tape, all in cellophane. Daddy, who had an immoderate passion for the NHS, was even quite chatty to me, and introduced me to a new friend he had made in the next-door bed.

'Bob, this is my daughter, Candy', said Daddy. 'She is not a very keen swimmer as far as I know.'

He explained to me later, as he ate with real gusto his eleven o'clock lunch of Finnan haddock with extra bones and mashed tatties, 'Bob likes girls. His daughter was a local swimming champion. He had an unfortunate experience with her and was sent to prison. He's a charming fellow. Do you like Verdi, Candybox? I don't think I could bear him at all up close.' Long before it was fashionable to be keen on Handel as a composer of opera, Daddy was. I took my Verdi tapes back to England. We never had the time together to find that we both adored Britten and that I am nearing his feeling that Richard Strauss is the sexiest of composers, though I first met him in the Four Last Songs when I was sternly above sex, being fifteen and torridly in love, at that point, with one who was as remote and cool as the North Star.

I do not know why music should cause more curdling in matters of taste than literature, but so it sometimes seems. My parents' parents each mistrusted the other's form of musicality, taking it, unfairly and unsubtly, on either side, as a metaphor for much more.

I loved each of my grandmothers for physical reasons: my McWilliam grandmother had a nice little bob held in place with a kirby grip and read nineteenth-century novels to me; she had catch-phrases such as 'Would patrons care for a cup of hot chocolate?', and 'Would you v.s.k. close the door?' where v.s.k. stood for 'very sweetly kindly'. My Henderson grandmother I loved for her waistline, her ankles, her deep voice, her extraordinarily stagey diction; but I knew to be afraid of her. She believed in posture, in scouring, and in never complaining. I never sensed that she had faith in anything but the joy music gave her and in discipline, while my other grandmother was suffused by her religious faith and knew and played ecclesiastical music.

We took a trip to the Highlands with my maternal grandparents. Grandpapa kept his Homburg hat on his left knee all the time he was in the car and on his head all the time he was out of it. He held on to the leather strap that cars had at the time in the back as we drove up to Blair Atholl and other photogenic castles. The idea may have been to convince my grandparents of the respectability of my father's source of employment. My grandpapa Douglas Henderson was a pure Scot, his wife an Irish-Scot. It was impossible to detect any reaction to the operatic landscapes we were toiling among, no reaction save to changes of temperature in that claustrophobic vehicle. Although my grandmother on my mother's side was a woman of habitual kindness, she was perhaps not kind to her own daughter. My grandfather simply was unkind to her. At over six foot, my mother was nonetheless a woman who expected to be knocked about.

We made forays to England, obedient to the proprieties of family life. Things at home were tightening up. My father crashed his car on the edge of Duddingston Loch, upon whose frozen epilimnion the Reverend Walker serenely skates in the famous painting. The car was of course not his but that of the National Trust for Scotland. Daddy had been driving on ice, and fast. There was but one tree on the edge of Duddingston Loch and that tree it was that saved my father's life; the car's registration number was LSD 414, in those days when LSD stood for money: pounds, shillings and pence.

I was beginning to start trying to stay the night with friends in order to avoid either the silence when he was not there or the shouting when he was. My mother cannot have been easy. She longed to work, she was lonely and dislocated; and yet she continued to pour into me the sort of imaginative care that may so easily be put out by what we nowadays have learned to recognise as depression. For there is no doubt that my mother was a woman in despair at a time when divorce except among the uninhibited rich or the very free-thinking was an extinguishing scandal and when a woman's portion was her husband's.

There is the awful irony that when a marriage is most in danger the couple behaves in exactly the way guaranteed to rile, madden and repel one another. If only they might be nudged to recover their actual as opposed to monster selves, the marriage might yet survive.

In this case, such a thing was not possible and did not happen. Matters were moving too fast, in ways that I could sense but could not know. It was a little ship, someone else was coming aboard and my mother took what I am convinced she thought was the most logical, kind and unselfish step that she might take for the sake of her husband and her child. She jumped ship. She couldn't see another way.

I had always been a pamphleteer, boring my father with various documents that I had carefully written out in extravagant proclamatory hands. I remember writing a lot about the tensions between Greeks and Turks in Cyprus, and I devoted screeds to the long dying and eventual death of Pope John XXIII. I never wrote a word about this disaster nearer to home.

My mother loved clothes that sparkled. She made a mauve silk ballerina-length skirt and bought to match it a mauve polo neck shot with silver. It was her best party outfit and before putting the polo neck over her face she would wrap her whole head in a chiffon veil so as not to mark the polo neck with make-up. She spent days deciding whether or not to wash these garments by hand with Lux Flakes or to take them to the, costly, dry cleaner.

Without conscious intention I wore on the occasion of my engagement to my first husband, a mauve silk ballerina-length skirt with a mauve sparkly T-shirt. Someone, of course, spilt red wine all over me and I remembered then that I must not send these symbolic clothes to the dry cleaner or they would come back only after I had died. I hand-washed them and they are my daughter's now.

I suppose my mother's sparkly mauve party outfit went, all nicely dry-cleaned, to the shop known as the 'Dead Women's', where she did a lot of clothes shopping herself during her short spell as a living woman.

———◆◆◆◆———

To be asked to be stepmother to any child must be an alarming prospect. To be asked to be the stepmother of a grief-stricken solitary with nearly a yard of hair must be devastating. Nonetheless, at the age of twenty-seven, in the April after the October of my mother's death, my Dutch stepmother Christine Jannink took me on.

Christine's parents, Dutch though they were, lived in another England, very far from The Folly in Sonning, on a farm that reached down to the banks of the River Wye and ran to other routines entirely. The routines at Llangetts, near Ross-on-Wye, ran on a mixture of ultra-English and ultra-Dutch lines that were to me both exhausting and really quite exciting.

At the wedding reception I sat under the festive table on which lay a long pink fish taken from the river, and I eavesdropped. The flowers my stepmother had chosen for her bouquet were white and yellow freesias and also, more unusually, the velvet black *Iris tuberosa*, more usually known as the widow iris.

The men wore buttonholes of this same velvety flower. It remains, peculiarly, one of the flowers that I most love and I first saw it on that day. It is associated with the best in my life; I thank its gardener for that, and my stepmother too.

My stepmother's clever needle had run me up a coffee-coloured raw-silk frock. Unlike almost all brides, but just like an ugly sister, I got fatter and fatter as the wedding approached. My stepmother let in a cunning broderie anglaise panel across my stout front.

Although I was never able, without complicated feelings of disloyalty towards my mother, to address my stepmother as 'Mum', as she wished, I was able to call the grower of those irises 'Mama'. I loved my bossy Dutch step-grandmother at once and with passionate feeling. Here was someone, I felt, as I sulked under the long pink and silver fish and the concealing damask cloth that covered the festive wedding-breakfast table, someone with kindness and style who had got through something very dreadful, the war, occupation, flight, and survived with love to spare.

Oddly for an only child, I had never had an imaginary friend. But now I was to have a real, pretty, new friend, about whom I'd heard such a lovely lot.

We had first been brought together, my new friend and stepaunt, two years my junior, the Christmas before. It cannot have been easy for any of the adults but they acquitted themselves nobly. Nicola, my stepmother's adored baby sister, was the fourth and late child of her handsome parents. So special was she that she had been given the first name 'Engelbertha', literally brought by the angels.

She was being asked to love a gigantic ruffian in a kilt, two years older and ten sizes bigger than herself, with an inner life populated very considerably by the ancient world, North Britain and death.

Nicola no sooner looked than she loathed. I no sooner looked than, I guess, I envied. We were to learn over the next few years how veritably to torment one another.

❖

Rushing up to the surface of today, no doubt in shame, I should tell you that while Liv has kept her chair at the computer, I have vacated mine at her side. This has been taken over by one of the two other personalities as well as my own that poor Liv has to deal with daily as we write this book together. Rita, the Russian Blue cat, who has the sagging undercarriage common to spayed queen cats, has turfed me out of my chair and I'm on a piano stool. Yesterday her resting place of choice was the so-comfortable computer keyboard, so we had to exile her. Today she is taking her revenge. The other cat, Ormiston, whom Rita disdains, and who resembles a minky koala bear with an owl's face and leaves tennis-ball-sized clots of fluff everywhere, is outdoors pretending to be a dog. His loyalty, kindness and obedience are among the many reasons that Rita despises him. She takes much more seriously her feline duties, being spiteful, sneaky, narcissistic, and almost purely selfish. Her triangular face, large turquoise-emerald eyes, long legs and ever-questioning silver tail mark her out as what she is, a beauty from Archangel, a double-coated ship's cat, used to men and to small territory. She very clearly prefers men to women and cannot abide the smell of any products made by Elizabeth Arden. I run all my scents past her for approval. If only she did the same for me.

Smell becomes very important as sight is lost and one scent that at once wakens me in the night is that of Rita when she has decided to take a territorial stand against the feral cat who lives in the Royal Hospital Gardens that are over the wall from the garden of where I am living. Cat's pee wakes me up as quick as a flash. At the last count, there were at least thirty-nine foxes in the Royal Hospital Gardens. Today, as I write (Liv is ill so I'm tapping blindly myself), it is the first day of the RHS Flower Show, so the foxes will have much new excitement to look at and chew on and tonight a fox may look at a Queen.

⟵◆◆◆▶

My poor stepmother had to deal with a stepchild itself almost feral. There was so much that, aged nine, I simply did not know was essential to the sustaining of normal everyday life. Brought up in a large prosperous house with siblings and staff and a mother with a talent for domestic organisation, my stepmother was faced with a sullen lump who knew nothing of the arts of husbandry or of the activities of any proper, let us say accompanied, child. As she understood it, I did not even know how to play properly. Her own father had won a gold medal for hockey at the Olympics, she had played at junior Wimbledon, her brother had been athletic at Winchester, as a family they went to Switzerland each year for what they called the 'wintersporting'. Her nursery life had involved games not of the imagination alone but with equipment and rules and competition. I was physically inert and evinced not even much mental movement. My stepmother called me once the least curious child she had ever known. We were walking along the Crescent at the time. I was of course thinking about myself and how I was perceived (I was by then in double figures). Did people think I was the au pair? I was wondering at that precise moment, the moment of my condemnation for incuriosity. But that was to come.

The first thing that had to go was my fat. Christine instituted the healthy habit of a run before breakfast. She monitored my diet with maternal care. My father and she made an attractive pair of newly-weds. My father always looked younger than his age and they were patently content in and respectful of one another's company.

But there was me. Even as I diminished in size, I did not diminish in number and this cannot have been easy for either of them.

Thorough regime change commenced. My mother's cats were destroyed, her yellow Labrador Katie sent to go and live therapeutically with the inmates of a lunatic asylum. I was given a blue budgerigar, whose death by careless starvation remains on my conscience. Nicola had at the same time been given a green budgerigar that lived a long and, one can only presume, happy life. Budgies don't confide much. I named mine Sebastian. I do not like the proximity of birds; they are like escaped hearts in full panic, beating, beating, unable to help you to help them, unsusceptible to rational appeal, flickering, filamented, electric, random.

I was learning systematically to lie. Frequently these lies were pointless, for example that I had to stay late at school on account of a play I was in, when of course there was no play and I just didn't want to go home.

I was hopeless with money so my stepmother initiated an account book; we did the accounts after Saturday breakfast, after my run and before I cleaned the brass. Our front door had the numerals 2 and 7 in brass, a letterbox, a large handle, a keyhole-plate, and to the right, set in stone, a square bell-pull of chaste Georgian elegance. There was the brass threshold cover and all the internal door handles and elegant acorn-tipped window raisers to do as well. I preferred using Duraglit wadding to Brasso and a cloth, because I was wasteful with Brasso and tended to splash it on surrounding painted areas.

The large square bell-pull was most rewarding. Was this because the neighbours could see that I was a good girl really, as I polished, those Saturday mornings?

Together, with their pared-back taste, my father and his new wife overhauled the house that had been so reassuringly stuffed and quite possibly unhygienic in my mother's time. New spaces were made; a modern airiness not unfaithful to the Georgian whole prevailed. The tatty affectations of my mother's gardening were levelled and a new aptness of intelligent planning for a growing family introduced.

Routine appeared where it had very probably culpably never been before. A goat's bell was rung at mealtimes. Grace was said. Appropriate napery attended every meal. I laid the table for breakfast before I went to bed. A wedding gift of good china, navy blue vine leaves on ridged white porcelain, was the everyday service. There was other, Dutch, ancestral china for dinner parties. My stepmother's magical needle confected dressings for every tall window and my father stencilled or carpentered witty architectural effects throughout the now, it seemed, much larger house.

In time for this largeness, the couple's first baby was born, at home, my half-brother Nicholas Charles, named for Nikolaus Pevsner. We had become a churchgoing family, attending the highest of high churches in Edinburgh, Old St Paul's. Some Sundays Father Chancellor, with or without his curate Father Holloway, would come for Sunday lunch. I loved Father Chancellor with his beard, big voice and golden robes. He was later said to have taken to drink. Father Holloway became Bishop of Edinburgh, then the chief Episcopalian bishop in Scotland, then lost his faith and is now a prolific writer and opinion-former. He gave the address at my father's funeral though, quite possibly by arrangement with God, I never got to hear it, as will become clear.

The density of the frankincense, dispersed during the very long Sunday services by the swinging ball of the thurifer, was difficult for my poor stepmother during her two pregnancies and she sometimes felt faint. I developed a taste I have never lost for the ritual and intoning and chanting and bobbing and bowing of the High Church and indeed it is very confused with my faith, which is, as I write, giving me some trouble.

My first conscious taste of alcohol was after a church service. I am unconfirmed and have therefore never tasted Communion wine, and, even should I become confirmed, I shan't taste it (confirmed alcoholics avoid the wine and take only the Host). This liquor was in an eggy Dutch drink named advocaat, to be eaten off a spoon, so guileless was the substance that was to reduce me as low as you can get this side of whoring and the grave. As many drinkers boringly say, I didn't like the taste of the drink. I loved the Roka cheese biscuits that looked like the wattle fences on my toy farm in the blue and yellow tin that had in Dutch the slogan *'De andere half van uw borrel'* (the other half of your cocktail).

My half-sister Anna-Sophia came next. Both my half-siblings are a charming combination of their parents and I can never believe or understand why they are so nice to me. I like them a lot and we stay in touch in the usual way; by not getting in touch. Nicholas, who has cycled across the Ukraine, made maps in Afghanistan and is on speaking terms with the North and the South Pole, is perhaps the most outstandingly silent of us though he will suddenly send a book of Tanzanian recipes or a picture postcard from Thule. Anna and I have been known to share a meal. We share the same jokes but we don't need to talk about it. I think we loved our father from something of a similar angle.

After my father's death, I was stopped in the street in Oxford by a handsome young man who asked me the way to somewhere. I started to describe it in the usual manner, giving helpful details but not very long on such things as north and south.

'Do you mind my asking this,' said the young man, 'but are you related to the McWilliams?'

It turned out that he was the doctor who had had to break the news of my father's sudden death at work to my stepmother. It was the precision and uselessness of my directions that gave him the instinct that told him who I was.

I often try to imagine how it must have been for my stepmother faced with me. All I wanted to do was read, and reading doesn't shake off the fat. To her credit, she got me out on to the street. I skipped and skipped and skipped and skipped and skipped. There were plenty of rhymes that went with the skipping:

> 'Edinburgh, Leith,
> Portobello, Musselburgh –
> AND Dalkeith,'

And:

> 'Andy-Spandy
> Sugardy-Candy,
> French Almond Rock
> *Bread and butter for your supper's all your mother's got!'*

I skipped a minimum of one thousand whirls of the rope a day. My record at backward skipping was 305, and, fortunately enough, I forget the record for forward skipping. People did play more in the streets in those days, it's true, and not just something said to make today's young feel bad. We played hopscotch, we stilt-walked, and my stepmother even taught me to ride a bicycle. It is unimaginable to a person of Dutch extraction that any human being cannot ride a bicycle.

Dreadfully, because I felt and expressed no gratitude, only fear, I became the owner of an expensive new bicycle and soon I was cycling to school and guiltily getting off and pushing the bicycle and walking whenever I could. This bicycle, a generous gift from my stepmother, remained in my life all through Cambridge, when I used it once, and right up till the time when I worked at *Vogue*. Its last ever ride was between Warwick Avenue and Vogue House. Even in the nineteen-seventies, Hyde Park Corner was challenging to a wholly uncoordinated cyclist, attired as a matter of course as a flower fairy in buttoned boots and skeletal on a diet of vanity and fear.

I started to dread going home after school because I knew that I would in my absence have fallen short. Something quite evidently needed to be done with me, aged nine, and my stepmother rose honourably to the challenge. I could not have gone on as I had under my mother's sway, just reading and drawing and emoting and inventing worlds, completely certain of at least one person's love, dawdling in affection's shade.

My stepmother did a good job. I did get thinner and I am quite a good housewife, though I do not have her gift for making of any space a dustless geometric zone of purity. I am like my mother and like my daughter, a collector of clutter, but I have a nice healthy case of obsessive-compulsive disorder and replicate many of the routines that I learned at my stepmother's hand.

The really bad thing was the lying, and that was of course, of my own invention; QED. It hurts to lie, damages the understanding of the self and bruises any love that might be about. I seldom lied to give myself importance. I'm not interested in boasting. I'm afraid I lied in order to find some peace, which of course I did not, and in order to find love, which I then found on terms that were not healthy, or, rather, it was not love that I found, whenever I thought I had.

I just wanted to be left alone to read. I did not seem to be able to become the kind of child that was familiar to Christine, that she and her siblings had been, that Nicola, so close to me in age, evidently was.

My father and his new family were relieved of me during the holidays by the inspired intervention of my step-grandmother Mama, who would have me to stay either in Herefordshire or, in the summer months, at the progress of Jannink family houses across Holland.

It is said that Scottish writing cannot be separated from the idea of doubleness, and I feel it to be so as I speak private things aloud to Liv. I hear the echoes as I confess in my unbelonging-anywhere voice in this tall cold English room.

The first time I tasted milk fresh from the cow was at Christine's parents' farm. They had Jersey cows. Mama brought me a mug of milk in bed. She took it for granted that she would listen to my prayers. No one had asked this of me, or given this chance to me, before. I was enchanted. When she told me off I could at once see her point of view. It must have been upsetting for her to see her own daughter struggling with the ugly child whom she herself could handle with ease.

I took a sip of the milk after I'd said my prayers to Mama. It was absolutely disgusting, so rich, so sappy. Like little Gillian at my unsuccessful birthday tea, hating the real cream, I longed for town milk, milk, at any rate, that did not proclaim so gutsily its provenance from a cow.

Mama and her husband, whom I called Papa with a long last 'a', were from different parts of Holland, she from Amsterdam and he from a large estate near Enschede, close to the German border. She had been an actress and had the poignant features all her long life of a sort of bespectacled Ava Gardner. He was tall, blond, handsome, beautifully dressed, very quiet and subdued, by the time I knew him at all well, by Parkinson's disease. This meant that Mama had to undertake not only the feminine side of English country life but, increasingly, the running of the farm and the decision-taking, all of it. Her care of her husband disguised itself as nagging. In fact she was keeping him alive by making him stay as fit as he could by not giving in and letting her do everything. She forced him to feed himself, to do his buttons, to walk tall. Yet again she was evidencing imaginative, maternal, love, in this case to her unmanned and, possibly, previously dominant husband.

Every summer until I ran away Mama drove Papa, Nicola and me to one of the seaports for the Hook of Holland or for Rotterdam. She managed everything, from teaching me how to pack a suitcase, to the passports, the seasickness and carsickness, my heavy resistance to Nicola, Nicola's distaste for me, the maps, the driving, the shopping, the cooking. She even got me to play cards.

I had long been afraid of card games. At some point in my life before Christine, I had met playing cards; I put about the untruth that my religion forbade me to play with them. I was simply bored by them and very likely too innumerate and idle to take an interest.

The first part of our Dutch summers was always spent at the Jannink seaside holiday house, Duinroosje, which means Little Dune-rose. The dune rose is what we know as *Rosa rugosa*, whose tomatoey hips make excellent jelly and whose pips make good itching powder. Papa was one of seven children and there were many pretty little blonde cousins. Naturally Nicola spoke Dutch to her cousins. Naturally, too, my Dutch took a while to get off the ground. There was the additional problem of my height. Nowadays Dutch people are often tall but it did not seem to be the case then and once or twice there was real trouble when I was queuing, after our early morning swim in the sea, for our daily buns or *kadetjes*, because people thought I was German. On our *kadetjes* we had little seeds of anise in sugar, called *muisjes*, that is, little mice. They were pink and white and blue. When an heir to the House of Orange was born, Mama said, all the *muisjes* in Holland were orange. There was chocolate hail for breakfast too, *chocolade hagelslaag*. The softness of the Dutch language is delightful and my step-grandparents' English was winningly softened by their Dutch accents, so they said 'of' for 'or' and 'v' for 'w'. It is a language I have long ceased to resent, though for some summers I felt it shut me out, till I got the ear for it. Italy had come more easily to me, but Holland is quite deep in me by now.

Mama managed the business of feeding me while controlling my fatness with the kind of commonsensical grace she brought to every aspect of managing me. Dutch food is delicious and highly calorific, featuring much bread and butter, plenty of red meat, pancakes the size of sunhats, snacks between meals, these snacks baffled under drifts of icing sugar or slathered with mayonnaise and washed down with bottles of stuff the milkman delivered called Chocomel, which is just chocolate milk. Mama wilily discovered that what I like best in the way of food is herrings and fresh fruit and that I loved to swim in the sea; and so she too helped reduce in dimension this seal-like child that had been washed up on her family's shore.

It was at Duinroosje, where we lay having a rest, as we had to every afternoon, in the yellow-painted metal-tubing bunks, that Nicola told me that she came from a different, more elevated, social class than I did. She explained this in terms of the size of her parents' garden and the amount of land lying thereabouts. I looked at the metal rungs of the yellow ladder that led down from my top bunk to hers below. I'd never really seen class in terms of stiff rungs or layers, but of continual change and adaptation, as something rather diverting, like picking up shells on a beach, knowing that each one was different, identifying how so, but not saying which was more or bigger or better, or, indeed, less, smaller or worse.

Soon enough, love distracted from class. We were at the next house on the summer progress through Holland, Springendaal. Set in a pine forest close to the German border, this was a gingerbread playhouse for plutocrats built in delicious brown wood and curtained nattily in red and white. This was the house where I learned to put off going to the lavatory for as long as two weeks. It is a trick that is unprofitable; you might say it backfires. But I was scared to go into the woods and crouch and dig and bury. Who was watching? Only God, but still I imposed this mannerly constipation upon myself, afraid of nothing more than my own body. It was merely a physiological version of what I was up to within more perilous recesses in my mind.

Other matters of hygiene were also mortifying. Nicola and I bathed, each with her own enamel basin of cold water, her flannel and soap, out of doors in the heather every morning in the slanty light among the cobweb-silvered heather. She was a perfect little cherub and I was shape-shifting in ways I would rather not notice myself, never mind have anyone else notice.

The air at Springendaal made up for everything. It was as I imagine the air must be in *The Magic Mountain*, bracing and curative. Although the land was flat the air was drinkable it was so refreshing; something to do with cleanliness and those inhospitable but sweetly breathing pines above.

The family's large house outside Enschede was named Stokhorst, and it was here that the matriarch, Oma Jannink, lived, to whom, each summer, we paid our respects. It was a high cube of a house with yellow shutters and deep rooms, the kitchen painted that furious strong Dutch blue to keep off flies. The toy cupboard at Stokhorst was marvellous, stuffed with Edwardian dolls, complex tin merry-go-rounds and wonderfully articulated puppets. When we stayed there, the maid, uniformed, brought dry biscuits called *beschuiten* with strawberries squashed into them and fresh milk when she came to wake us up. Nicola and I generally shared a room.

It was with her cousin Alexander that I fell in love, in no very serious way, but it gave me a repository for my longing to be unaccompanied and to daydream and make up stories. Maybe this longing to be alone is just an attribute of only children, though I'm dead certain Nicola longed to be without me too. No one named Alexander can ever be quite unheroic. I chose Alexander to love because I was really in love with Alexander the Great. The very thought of him at his lessons with Aristotle or astride Bucephalus gave me a thrill.

Nearly all the worst fights that Nicola and I had in our childhood were semantic. She was practical, able, efficient and literal-minded. I was in a place where I could not express myself in language and took refuge in being dreamier and more in-turned than ever.

Nicola knew how to get a rise. She would talk Dutch to herself when we were alone in a room together, or (and she scored every time with this one) she would start to talk about the complete pointlessness of learning Latin and Greek. I still rise to this today. I feel my glands swell, my lecturer's voice settle in my throat, the old arguments conjugate themselves within my enraged brain. Was it for this the Spartans fell? Tell them, passing stranger.

You can see Nicola's point.

So we riled one another through these summers and became, probably, quite fond, each of each. I remember that I told her when I had the frightening experience of an elderly maid at Stokhorst getting me to put my tongue into first her parrot's and then her own mouth. The parrot was an African Grey and its tongue the colour of an unopened black tulip. It was quite dry. The maid's mouth was wet.

The happiest house, which I remember with love and where the atmosphere of devotion was so strong that one almost dared not spoil it by lazily falling into our bad sniping patterns, was named De Eekhof. This was the home of Christine's Tante Lida and Oom Nico. They had no children, yet the house was arranged as though for children and the disciplines and routines led to mental ease and stimulation in a way that any family might envy. The maid Helli wore a white kerchief and everything about the kitchen and the dining room and where we played seemed clean but not sterile, and, which is irresistible to a child, even to a very tall one, all our equipment was one size smaller. We played, after our morning swim in the pool that was simply a sandy crater at the end of the garden, with a toy grocer's shop, its name het Winkeltje (the little shop), that had come from the store of toys at Stokhorst. There were enamel weighing scales, little iron weights, jars of dry goods, small wax paper bags, churns, dippers, ladles, and carved wooden vegetables of every kind. Even when we were too old to play with this toy it was irresistible to us and peace would break out between Nicola and me. There were gravelled walks and flopping buddleia covered with tortoiseshell butter-flies. At rest-time, we really did rest, like happy children tired out by play in some ideal of family life. Tante Lida and Oom Nico were cultivated, curious and sophisticated. They left their considerable collection of paintings to the Dutch people. I remember walking drip-ping after a swim past a picture that I know now was by Monet. There was no fuss. No one ticked me off for my wet footprints. Halfway up the stairs on the way to our bedroom was an automaton we were allowed to play with once a day each. You wound it up and then the real, stuffed, fez-wearing monkey under the glass cloche would begin to do magic tricks, lifting a bowl to reveal a different surprise every time.

The last time I went to De Eekhof I was reluctantly adolescing. Oom Nico took me for a walk. He had read my diary, in which I had written that I was so unhappy I wanted to die.

'It is a waste of time,' he said, 'to be unhappy. And at your age it should be impossible. Believe me, I know. One feels important if one is unhappy. But it could all be so much worse, you know.' He had the great gentleness to mention no other diary, no other unhappy teenage girl, to be found in Holland no time at all ago.

Oom Nico had hairs growing out of the end of his nose, and large, sad eyes. He wore bifocal spectacles that magnified these eyes. He was bald and was driven to the factory by a chauffeur. The factory made fragrant bales of cotton and printed it gaily. Nicola and I were allowed to choose a bolt each for Christine to sew summer frocks for us. We chose, that last summer, after lunch. Helli had made *biftek* and afterwards she had drained yoghurt in a cheesecloth and served it with strawberries that had got hot in the sun so that they were between fruit and jam. Nicola chose a white cloth punched with lacy flowers. I chose something pink, feminine and rosaceous, as though for curtains or some large expanse. I chose it for the girl I would have been had I been a better girl. My lukewarm but useful, merely theoretical, crush on Nicola's cousin Alexander transferred its points completely to devotion and gratitude when Oom Nico said, 'You will be pretty, you know.'

He had found me out. I had always known that it was lucky I was good at schoolwork because I was so ugly. The odd thing is, why did I not think that this relation, this *non*-relation, of mine was telling the truth? After all, I couldn't imagine him telling a lie. During those summers in Holland, I too took a holiday from telling lies.

LENS II: Chapter 3

The first large family in whose cousinhood I tried to affix myself was the great clan of Mitchisons. It was a joke in scientific circles at the time that more than half a ton of human flesh answered to the name Professor Mitchison. Naomi Mitchison, the sister of J.B.S. Haldane, was the matriarch and pivot of the family. She lived to be one hundred and three, the oldest Old Dragon that doughty prep school has yet produced, and one of the first baby Dragons. Doris Lessing has described in her autobiography the atmosphere of intellection at Carradale, the Mitchison house in Argyll. I doubt if I can match her for I recall the passage as absolutely spot on and now of course can't find it, though maybe I should learn to delegate now I am blind. That *would* make a drastic and rather late character change.

Naomi was known by her children, her grandchildren and her friends as 'Nou'. One son, Geoffrey, had died in childhood from meningitis. The death is described by Nou's friend Aldous Huxley in his novel *Point Counter Point*. There were five remaining children, Denny, Murdoch, Lois, Avrion, Valentine. Murdoch was Professor of Zoology at Edinburgh, his wife Rosalind Professor of History. Rosalind was known as 'Rowy'. Rowy had been a close friend of my mother and her daughter Harriet was my friend; each pair of friends was as dissimilar in the same way as the other. That is, where Rowy was effective, certain, dark and convinced, my mother was indecisive, unsure, blonde and ductile; the same was so of Harriet and myself. Harriet's younger sister Amanda went on to become a journalist who came from the *Independent* Magazine to interview me. When she was a refinedly pretty little girl, I had, with Harriet, tormented Amanda by telling her long, plotless, essentially theologically based stories about a monster we called the King Devil. I can't think where we got him from, since the Mitchisons were sternly rationalist and unbelieving. Harriet's reading tastes ran to *The Lord of the Rings*, which I could never hack, though I was a sucker for Narnia, so it looks as though I should bear the brunt of the responsibility for the King Devil. When Amanda came to interview me, I felt it only right to give her, in every regard, the upper hand. I was ashamed of my beastly stories in the dark at the commodious Edinburgh house of her childhood. The interview was perfectly nice, though it implied, which may be possible, that my mother's suicide was the result of incompetence rather than volition. I've always comforted myself with the thought that what my mother did was what my mother wanted, but maybe it is good, if sore, to keep an open mind.

Harriet and I both wanted to be doctors. Harriet became one and I still think about it. That's a difference between us.

The village of Carradale lies in a bay on the eastern edge of the Mull of Kintyre. In recent years, it has been tragically newsworthy because almost every member of its small fishing fleet was drowned. That guts a community for generations.

The big house was harled and painted white, pepperpotted and roofed in slate the colour of lavender when dry, of thunder when wet. There were never, it seemed to me, fewer than twenty adults in the house at a time, always a few babies and then there were middlies and, what we were becoming, teenagers. That I did not fall completely into internal delinquency is almost certainly due to the Mitchisons, Rowy at the core of it, but all those others each of whose names I can remember, with their faces, for ever, at the age they were when I was turning twelve, though most of them now are professors themselves and members of the intelligentsia, whatever it is now called. Certainly not the 'chattering classes'. They were nothing as trivial as chatterers, rather forceful, indeed irresistible, asserters.

During our teenage years, we were sent to sleep at The Mains, the Scots word for the home farm. This was a sensible decision. Dressing for dinner took me about four hours, though I've never met a vain Mitchison, including those who possessed beauty: Clare and Kate, Mary, Valentine and Josh. It was in the bathroom at The Mains that I first saw underwear made for the delectation of men rather than at the behest of spinsters. It had been hand-washed, evidently, and was dependent from the taps of a washbasin in the freezing bathroom. It was at once very small and very emphatic, lacy, red, and belonging to the girlfriend of Francis Huxley.

The drawing room in the big house was full of the sort of silence that is made by eight or nine good-quality brains working hard and separately, absolutely not a library silence, more like being in a vast digestive system. Small, fierce Naomi sat typing at her desk that looked out over the unsmooth Highland lawn, a hedge of Rugosa roses, the path to the sea, Carradale Point itself and the sea beyond. She wrote well over ninety books. The light in the room was low and seemed to be green. There was a sizeable mobile made of metal fish that very probably interpreted Darwinian theory.

In the plain, loaded shelves was a tan first edition inscribed to Nou by its author of *The Seven Pillars of Wisdom*, on top of which I had one Easter found a chocolate egg hidden. This was a rare success for me since the annual egg-hunt clues had as a rule a scientific and mathematical bias, with a strong seam of Scottish history. After Nou's death, this volume went up to auction and I saw it again in a newspaper; what it was and what it meant to me so separate.

Nou was, in addition to being an Argyllshire councillor, though devoid of any whiff of landlordism or lairdliness, Mother of the Bakgatla tribe in Botswana, and frequently one or more of her honorary Bakgatla children would be staying at the big house.

Nobody said, but Nou, as well as coming from the intellectual purple, was also, though it infuriated her to be addressed thus, Lady Mitchison. Her late husband had been made a Labour life peer. I mention this at all only to introduce the ticklish subject of what to call the people who worked for her, since she was at once so clearly the product of at least two kinds of aristocracy and a good old-fashioned Red.

One evening we older children were asked by Percy, who did the gardening, although one did not call him the gardener, to gather caterpillars from the kitchen garden. The cabbage white has a caterpillar that is fat and striped like a wedding cravat; when you pick it up it looks interested at both ends. We took our catch, if you can call anything as docile as a few bowls of caterpillars a catch, in to Nellie, who certainly was not the cook.

The caterpillars, dipped in flour and nicely fried, appeared as the first course that night in deference to the palates of Nou's guests from Botswana.

The dining table was enormous, thick, not polished but raw wood, aged, stained, practical; it was a rectangle with curved ends; there must be a geometrical term for this figure but I lack it. I do not mean an ellipse. There seemed in that atmosphere of intellectual certainty so little that was elliptical in the way my father was in person and in the way his mind worked. I am ashamed to say that I escaped from his intelligent failures of certainty to the Mitchisons' apparent categoricalness with the cowardice that goes with a callow mind aspin. My father's way offered no shelter, while that of the Mitchisons offered much of it and, or so it seemed, to spare. I was, as I am not now, sick for certainties. I now find them infertile and too often rooted in prejudice.

I wonder now whether I was ever actually invited at all to Carradale or whether I just hid within one family or another's capacious kindness: Rowy was kind all through my youth in a sort of improvement on her late friend, my mother's, way. An improvement, I mean, in that Rowy was alive. Nou's daughter-in-law Lorna, married to Av (Nicholas Avrion in full, meaning the Victory of the People), came from Skye and always seemed to be carrying a baby in her arms. She never raised her voice and had the balanced selflessness that comes to only very few mothers. She was impossible to lie to. It was

Ruth, Naomi's oldest daughter-in-law, whom I loved and to whom I clung like stickyweed for years, though she never complained about it, even when I started sticking to her in the South as well. She was not a physically large person, nor did she shout. She seemed to see a great deal and to interpret it correctly but in silence. She was a doctor, musical, wore slim brown or grey shirts and sat at a tangent to the table. She was tangential in manner yet direct in thought; a mode I find increasingly appealing the longer I live. I wish she were alive now; hers was a singular note amid so much information and embodied, biological almost, confidence.

At the far end of the dining room was a sizeable brown painting, thickly impastoed. It was known as 'The Goat in the Custard', and worked surprisingly well as a splashback for the kippers that were left for each individual to fry for him or herself at breakfast, in a then remarkable item of culinary equipment, an electric frying pan. It is a miracle that the house smelt not of frying red herrings but of heather, wood, pipe smoke and wool. Heather smells like dust and honey both. Intellectuals smoked pipes then.

Sometimes, a piper would come up from Lochgilphead, and, perhaps, a squeezebox player, and we would dance in the library, which was called the ping-pong room. Nou, short, dense, wore garments of fantastic tribal splendour and simultaneous rationality, sandals, bright yet serious skirts and perhaps a serape or sash in acknowledgement of one or another of her encyclopaedic interests and convictions. She was unbending, solid, frowning; she looked like strength itself, like an animal, an armadillo or a Galapagos tortoise; absolutely not a pangolin. The pangolin looks as though his armour has only recently been donned. Nou was born in hers. She danced in a stately manner that attested to her sublime physical confidence. She was an advocate of the benefits of free love. I feared to be addressed by her, yet longed to get a smile from her. I felt easier in her house when she was not in the room and that this is not a particularly healthy state of mind. I do not think that she cared much for my mother or me; even as lame ducks, a class for which Nou had time, we were not interestingly lamed. I can imagine my mother getting Carradale all wrong, talking in the drawing room during the daytime or gossiping or noticing clothes or foods or smells. Certainly she would be overdressed. We were there together only one time, when I was two, so I cannot speak for her outfit during that summer of 1957.

Mealtime conversation was on the whole abstract or theoretical, whatever age you were. There was little people-talk unless it be of use, attached to a paper written, a law made, a proof offered. Avrion had made butter with Lorna's breast milk, I seem to remember, and there was talk of self-made blood-pudding.

Two years ago, wandering around the Scottish National Portrait Gallery, I came face to face with Nou. There she was, miraculously at about my height, as never in life, dressed in blue, frowning, chin on hand, looking me straight in the eye. It was her portrait by Wyndham Lewis, which had been on the ping-pong room wall and under whose gaze, dancing this time to records of Scottish dance tunes, I fell in love for the first time with a grown human not resident in the ancient world. It is a love that came to nothing in the conventional sense so that it remains, for me at least, complete. Nor is it untried. The one who generated it absolutely without intent remains today a beloved friend and provided for years as it were an internal moral thermostat that I fell short of, but knew when I was doing so. It is not coincidental to my life as a novelist that he was a child in India and is a musical scientist. Nor is it coincidental to my private life.

Wyndham Lewis was a good choice to paint the young Nou. He got that density, that energy, that intellectual force. In the corner of the painting to the sitter's right is a curious pair of antagonistic marks, written in paint, like scallops inverted, or fists opposed, conjunct yet fierce. If they encrypt Nou's character, they do it well. The other attribute caught is her uncompromising seriousness, combined with an irresistibility, like that of some metal.

In the long-playing-record trunk in that library, there were also to be found the speeches of V. I. Lenin and a Russian phrase book from which I copied into my diary at that time 'A rose is a flower. A man loves a woman. Death is inevitable.' I also found a book on medieval Latin lyric by Helen Waddell and remember the words:

'Vel confossus pariter
Morerer feliciter,'

that she translates as:

'Low in the grave with thee
Happy to lie.'

I've used these words as soothers for years. They work as phrases whose meaning either dissolves, leaving you in a state of meditation, or tightens up, giving you plenty to think about.

I had discovered a great pleasure of the painful side of life: its relief, or exacerbation, by literature. Of course I'd been doing it all along but hadn't realised.

It was typically bifocal of me to have lit upon the object of my distant love since his delightful brother was my first proper boyfriend. Between them, they constitute immortal disproof of the proposition that all Mitchisons are brilliant but not always super-subtle. Terence Mitchison was an undergraduate medieval historian at St Catherine's College, Oxford, a place that was to recur and grow in my life. We met during the famous summer that Anthony Appiah, the grandson of Sir Stafford Cripps and nephew of the Queen of the Ashanti, said, and we were *just* thirteen, 'It depends whether you have an eschatological *Weltanschauung.*' The thing about Anthony was that he had some paisley flares and a blue rollneck and he could play the piano. The other thing was that we became best friends and that he's never shown off in his life. He just was that far in front – like Prospero, but kinder.

Terence courted me with letters that would, if anyone knew where they were, constitute the most colourful archive you could wish for, literally. He breathed jokes, mainly of the verbal kind, and sent them to me colour-coded, brown for medieval jokes, green for rural jokes, pink for jokes to do with the history of Empire and so on. And, of course, puns resulted in multicoloured words. It was not that Terence was, as I am, a synaesthete whose synaesthesia is redundant or at any rate useless; he was an etymologist with a grip on detail. So considerable was this grip that when we took a holiday, later in our friendship, on a barge on the Brecon Beacon canal with schoolfriends, Terence had embroidered his Admiral's cap with the barge's name, *Samuel Whiskers*. Everything about Terence was thorough and good. He had embroidered another cap: *HMS Leaky*.

Which makes that swivel of disloyalty, or whatever it was, in me towards my idol, his older brother, extra mortifying, and I only hope Terence was well shot of his schoolgirl correspondent. At the start, I suspect that I fell, as through a trapdoor, for the blameless older brother for the simple, no doubt tediously biological, reason that he was, and remains, the single individual who has, since my mother and father, been able to carry me. His areas of specialism included blue-green algae and dreams. I used to read books about finite-dimensional vector space and Riemann surfaces to try to make myself appealing to this distinguished ludic individual. When he remarked, glancingly, that he thought blue more becoming than pink, I did as my mother would have and made a stew of woad, or rather Dylon dye, in Strong Navy and bunged all my clothes in. Nothing could have prepared this poor man for cause and its effect upon his silly child-friend.

I drooped around after him for pretty much a decade, during which his circle of friends, to some degree, took me up and conducted the kindest of intellectual experiments upon this peculiar child. So it was that I found myself building sandcastles (one, for example, of the Gesù in Rome) with the right-wing philosopher John Casey, being introduced to green Chartreuse by the composer Robin Holloway who later wrote me properly critical letters about my work, which he did not like; and becoming a friend for life of my idol's lodger, with whom he would play piano duets, Roger Scruton, who was then a boy of twenty-seven with hair that flamed over a face that also burned white with seriousness. The architectural historian David Watkin taught me to dance the *galope* and asked me to marry him, which he must have forgotten, or at any rate I notice that we don't seem to be married. They gave me books to read and were, I suppose, waiting to see what the result would be when I had ground my way through whatever it was: *The Anatomy of Melancholy*, *Hadrian VII*, *The Quest for Corvo*, all of Firbank, *Memoirs of a Mathematician*. Unknowing, I was a kind of Maisie. Their patience with me and tolerance of my mooncalf presence among them was admirable. I was a bit of a liver-enriched goose, I'm afraid. What kind of egg they expected me to lay I cannot imagine, but not this life that I am laying out now, I'm sure. I still possess the label of the 1955 Veuve Clicquot bottle that we shared, perhaps eight or ten of us, on my fifteenth birthday, over lunch. It is, with all my possessions, not to hand but in store, awaiting a return to a life unpacked.

Before these loves, though, came rupture and detachment from my father's house in my early teens. He and I never exchanged words about it, but I left his home and did not come properly back to it again, and certainly not to live.

I had become compact of lies, a child of flies, a beelzebubbler, as my stepmother apprehended it, and she did not, quite understandably, want me near her children. I suspect too that I was growing to resemble my mother and that my father could not face another unhappy marriage; since the only thing that was wrong with his marriage to my step-mother was me, might there not be benefit for all concerned were I to be removed from the sum?

I had always fancied boarding school and now its allure was unequivocal. Several prospectuses were sent for. I liked the look of Cranborne

Chase and Bedales. It turned out that my mother had left enough money for me to be sent away. I sat scholarships.

It was to Sherborne School for Girls in Dorset that I won a major scholarship. The adjustment from a school whose houses were called Argyll, Buccleuch, Douglas, Moray and Strathmore to an establishment for young ladies of England and the Commonwealth was actually not all that painful. The only sad thing was that I lost all trace of a Scottish accent, though my children tell me my voice changes as we cross the border north.

In the scholarship examination I had scored fewer than ten points out of a hundred for mathematics and these points given merely for the sake of face. A special division below all the others was created for me and for a girl who had been terribly damaged in a car accident. We were patiently taught by a Miss Hayward, who challenged us with such problems as: 'You have a curtain rail that is four feet long. You have four curtain hooks. At what intervals do you place the curtain hooks?'

My housemistress was a Scot, Jean Stewart, and a place had been found for me under her care because a glamorous-sounding girl named Augusta had of a sudden decided to leave. I was no substitute for this Augusta. Huge, foreign, by now crop-haired, queerly named and in my old school uniform, I was an odd fish.

I learned to love my housemistress, who combined suffering with beauty and reticence. She was a devout Scots Presbyterian, later retiring to the Western Isles and becoming a minister, but I simply could not abide the diamantine, pearly, glorious heroine of a headmistress, the radiant Miss Reader-Harris, later Dame Diana Reader-Harris, who is revered beyond her death to this day. I have no doubt that she was good and that she had star quality of the regal, cinematic sort. She would have made a wonderful-looking wife for a dictator. I am almost certain that she, who wore a large, three-stoned diamond ring, had, poor woman, like so many of our other teachers, lost her fiancé in the war.

Etiquette demanded that we say goodnight to our housemistress with a curtsey and a handshake each night, also that we curtsey each time we encountered the headmistress in whatever circumstance we found ourselves. I was in the sanatorium with flu when the head-mistress made a visit, and hopped out of bed to curtsey to her. She smouldered bluely. Her crown of white hair, her aura of lavender, her good tailoring, her well-manicured hands, her lovely face, all flinched. She knew satire when she saw it and she didn't like it. She'd taken me on halfway through a term and I was absolutely not going to prove to be a disappointment after all the Christian kindness she had shown me.

So it was that I discovered institutionalised duplicity. That's a harsh term for it, but how I got happily by at Sherborne was by succeeding academically and, within that cloak, doing whatever I wanted, so that when there was a putsch against smokers, I could say that I'd been smoking which was an expellable offence, but they didn't want to get rid of me because, in their terms, I might be a success and go up to university, Somerville or Girton. It was understood that one would not apply to King's College Cambridge, the only 'mixed' college at the time.

At first I didn't have to work very hard at all because my Scottish school had been so far in advance of its English counterpart. This was bad for me and I hung about idly reading novels. We were permitted five items on our dressing table, including a picture of our parents. I haven't owned one of those ever. There were dormitories divided into cubicles and a few rooms for sharing. Nothing at all about boarding school struck me as more disciplined, demanding or impinging than had been my recent experience of life at home. I'd have been happy to spend the holidays at school, and in some cases did spend half-holidays and other times with some poor teacher, mainly Mr Hartley who taught Scripture and referred to the Minor Prophets as 'this Johnny Haggai', and 'that fellow Habakkuk'. We all longed for him to say 'this Johnny Jesus'.

It didn't strike me at the time that my departure to Sherborne might be the cause of any grief to my father and I have no idea whether or not it was. He sent the occasional elegant postcard with an architectural feature depicted on it, for example the star-pierced dome of the Royal Bank of Scotland in St Andrew Square. He was not a rich man and travel was expensive. He had a new family and I was very little fun for them to be around. On Sundays, we had to write to our parents. Very soon I started writing to other people's parents instead of my own.

I had big feet with my full name written on the soles of my shoes. We were often at prayer, so when we knelt I could not avoid giggles from behind.

(Liv, who was once a chorister, has just told me, to my outrage on behalf of the bride, that she sang once at a wedding where the groom had taken the precaution before the service of writing on the bottom of his shoes: 'HELP ME'.)

I'd only the sketchiest idea of how to make friends, as must by now be clear. Throughout my years at Sherborne, I was often ill and spent a disproportionate amount of time in the sanatorium being nursed by Sister Parrott and Nurse Greene, who in winter put goose fat on one's nose against chapping.

On one such visit, I was in a sickroom with the eldest sister of a family from Scotland. She turned out to be the oldest of six. She was Jane Howard. Then came Katie who was apparently in my year, then Caroline, then Alexander, then Andrew and Emma, the twins. They lived on an island in the Hebrides. Its name was Colonsay.

Jane was a brave talker; during my cosy illness I listened spellbound to her stories of home and family. It was another kind of falling in love, and a kind I was used to. I was falling in love with a family. The parents, whose real names were Jinny and Euan, were known as Mummy and Papa (pronounced Puppa). The parents were young, busy, and alive. The mother wrote weekly letters to her daughters and sons. These letters were spicy with adventure and displayed a dashing tone that made of any material whatsoever an excellent story.

After some sniffing, because we were both used to sitting at the top of the class, Katie and I became the sort of inseparable that maddens adults. We remain so today, though were we to meet now at the age we are we might not care one bit for what we saw. She is practical, carries no fat and mistrusts display of or reference to emotion; she loves *Hornblower*, Patrick O'Brian, Nevil Shute, Alastair MacLean, *The Lord of the Rings* and Melville. I've read *Moby-Dick* only since I've been blind, and loved it. I am fond of *HMS Ulysses* and *A Town Like Alice* for love of Katie. We both dote on James Bond. She is a Bond girl type, too, and can quote pages of the sacred texts. I'm just asked to write forewords to them, that no thriller reader in his right mind would read.

Unlike Katie, I am not in practical terms resourceful, and am trying continually to put a name to emotion since I have discovered that apparently to suppress it makes you go blind. Katie is beautiful. Her father, whom soon I too was calling Papa, is partly Native American. His great-grandfather married a Cree. All the children, even blonde Emma, carry the stamp. Caro, who has married a Neapolitan and 'become' Italian, looks entirely Mediterranean till you look for what it is that makes her so. It's the flashing teeth, the gesticulations, the mobility yet grandeur of feature, as though a pagan goddess spoke. She is taller than most Italians. So you see that several generations down, the consequences of this union with the Cree are apparent; perfect white teeth in wider mouths than human, almost lupine, intolerant eyebrows, flashing eyes, long bones, narrow pelvises, weirdly semaphoric flat-handed hand gestures, and a capacity to start bonfires with no materials but moss and flint.

For reasons that I don't understand, fraternising between the school's houses was not greatly encouraged; Jane, Katie and Caro were in a different house from me. I was in a house with a name I still only cautiously comprehend, Aldhelmsted East (it's something to do with the ontological argument), which was over a bridge from the rest of the school. Katie and I were both passionate fans of a substance called junket, made with milk and rennet, an enzyme extracted from the stomach of calves. We made it in jam jars that we carried across the bridge in the pockets of our green tweed cloaks as gifts for one another. This is how our life has gone on to this day, carrying incomprehensible but to us amusing messages over whatever obstacle life has put in our way.

The dark star of the school was our friend Rosa Beddington, who was on her mother's side a Wingfield-Digby. This family, who live at Sherborne Castle, had founded the school, so Rosa, in spite of her chain-smoking and early and dramatic effect upon men, became Head of School until she was demoted for being seen 'drinking shorts in male company'. Rosa had grey hair when she was twelve and I was sitting behind her in Latin, which was one of the very few things she could not do, though she would have been able to had she decided that she approved of the subject. Like almost every femme fatale I have known, Rosa made no effort with men. She had a vocation and she fulfilled it. She became one of the very few female fellows of the Royal Society, shortly before she died aged forty-five, of cancer that had eaten every bit of her except her daily-fumigated lungs.

It is hard to know where to start with Rosa since it is a story of extreme compensation for absences. Her beautiful mother had been an Olympic equestrian and killed herself when Rosa was very young. Rosa lived with and was raised by devoted cousins who became mother and father to her. Her father, with whom she felt furious, came of a distinguished Anglo-Jewish family. Ada Leverson, Oscar Wilde's Sphinx, was a distant relation. Her father was a competent painter and so was Rosa, who was also an observant draughtsman, which was one of the things that made her a unique microbiologist, since she could draw what she saw through the electron microscope and she saw more than had been seen before about the processes of cell development in embryos. Rosa's father published several books, including a tribute to his Labrador, *Pindar: a Dog to Remember*.

I was with Rosa when she was told that the cancer that had been in her breast was now in her brain. We were in the old Radcliffe

Infirmary in Oxford. Her husband Robin, who had already lost one wife to cancer, had rung me up and told me to go to Rosa right then. I got to her in time to hear a smartly dressed Australian lady doctor saying to Rosa, a young-looking woman with long silver hair, terrific curves and a moonstone on her hand,

'You're bright, so you must know it's curtains.'

Rosa sent me out for two bottles of red and two packs of Dunhill. She lifted her booted legs on to the narrow hospital bed, crossed them at the elegant ankle, and lit up.

For the rest of her life, Rosa railed against the fact that because she had 'Doctor' before her name, other doctors presumed that she had no feelings. Not that she was railing on her own behalf, but on that of patients who weren't even doctors; how did the doctors treat *them*?

In her dying months Rosa made a freehand and exact botanical tapestry that would cover a good-sized double bed. Every stitch was an act of will. Its ground is black, the most difficult of all colours in which to sew large areas. Yet not the tapestry but Rosa was being nightly unmade. She did tell me she was well in her dream-life but at the end she fought angrily with some apparition that made itself felt at her deathbed, perhaps her father, turning up at the last.

Rosa made a surprising schoolgirl because of her poise, deep voice, and innate aversion to wasting time. It's pointless to speculate whether she knew she had to cram more into less time. She was a superb drinker. Hard spirits had no perceptible effect upon her; they certainly reinforced her already devastating effect on any man in her vicinity. She was drawn to much older men of powerful intellect. She is the only woman I know to whom a man has sent an entire antique ruby *parure* after only one meeting. Years later he shot himself, on Valentine's Day. Rosa was fundamentally, and realistically, sad, which lent her a gunpowdery vivacity. Rosa also became attached to the Howards; large families have this fuzzy magnetic edge that pulls in others. The Howards deeply loved her. Her gap is shaped like that of a sibling in many lives. To and in her profession her gap is incalculable.

Rosa's personality was in torsion, her character silver threaded with steel. Its quality was recognisable in her person, in her writing, in her work, and in the calibre of the men who loved her. Her widower, Robin Denniston, is more than twenty-five years her senior; it is cruel. Still he writes and still he reads and still he lacks her company.

At her end, it was not Katie or me whom Rosa and her body's dying animal needed, but our other close schoolfriend, Emma, who has inherited from her own mother the gift of healing hands. She helped Rosa to peace and comfort by her presence and her touch as Rosa neared her death.

Emma's mother wears a lipstick called Unshy Violet and is named Kiloran after a bay on the island of Colonsay. Emma is called Emma Kiloran. The name of the Laird who gets the girl in the Powell and Pressburger film *I Know Where I'm Going* is also Kiloran. In the film he is considerably less glamorous than Papa, who is first cousin to Emma's mother. Emma's mother remembers children's parties given by Nancy Astor at Cliveden, where the children had a little parade of shops and went 'shopping' with their own paper bags. Over eighty, she can still touch her toes, is a corking dancer, and mother of six. My first term at Girton, Emma's mother took me out to lunch with her own godmother, who was Kipling's daughter, Elsie Bainbridge. She was wandering in her mind and I was no help, very likely wandering in my own. Kiloran held things together. It is what she does.

She has never married again since the children's father shot himself late one summer. Lucy, the youngest child, was still tiny.

That day, we were all, Rosa, Katie and I, going to Emma's home on the farm in Dorset for lunch, a swim, a glimpse at the newspapers and to visit the local steam fair, which had become an annual treat. Emma's mother was the first person I knew who peeled cooked broad beans so that the little vegetable was bright green and digestible. She served them with thick home-made mayonnaise. On that day, we did still go to the farm for lunch.

Emma's mother fed us, sat with us, looked after her still young children. A widow for under a day, she gave time to all these things.

Where does pain go?

Emma's father was a joy to get a laugh out of. His was a languid slim English beauty. He loved jazz and secret jokes. I only once *really* got a laugh from him and it was when he came down to the disintegrating tennis court on Colonsay and saw something he thought he would never see in his life, which was me playing tennis. His daughter, my friend Emma, who is half my size and vitally bossy, had the same reaction when she saw me driving. We were going along a perfectly ordinary road and over a perfectly ordinary bridge.

'Claude, darling, can you get out now and let me take over?' she said, and completed the movement, exactly in the manner of her elegant father relieving me of the implausible tennis racquet when I was thirteen on the tennis court by the lupin field, where the tall pink and lilac flowers grew like a crop. Made into patties with water and cooked on hot stones, the flour made from ground lupin-seeds may have composed part of the diet of ancient man. Just think of the labour in collecting the stripped piplings, like lentils, their silky podlets discarded into frilly heaps.

As the slaps of my own familial tide broke repeatedly upon me, it seemed that the choice was to stay and be damaging or to slip away.

I did not run away from home. I took a boat.

I don't know whether it was natural buoyant pessimism, self-paining good manners, a slight aversion to his oldest child, or simple exhaustion that led my father to take my disaffection with such quietness. He was a man not without anger, but the complications that came with keeping me at the heart of the home were painful and distasteful. Since his consciousness was of a piece with his tentative but utterly confident draughtsmanship, it is perfectly possible that he decided without even consulting himself to leave the area in his life that was concerned with me with rather more outline than shading. Unlike me, my father was absolutely not a monster of self-control. His life made intolerable demands upon him and he bore them apparently easily as though born to the task. I wish we had spoken more together. At the time, if we chatted, so attuned was our language that it seemed somehow discourteous to my stepmother whose English is perfect, but not highly nuanced. The responsibility for the jagged edge left by my departure was all mine and I only hope it healed as swiftly as it seemed to. Both my father and I had been so trained to be retiring that I have no idea whether he was as I felt myself to be, when I dared to think about it, haemorrhaging in my own nature internally, having somehow betrayed both parents, a stepmother and her children, by the time I was fifteen.

The internal valve used to decompress such feelings is commonly some means of escape or oblivion; I took one and was to take the other.

———◆◆◆———

Today, in blind-time, it is the Wednesday of the Chelsea Flower Show. Staying in the flat last night was my landlord's mother, a gardener by profession. Since she was coming to her own son's house she need have brought no gift, but she had chosen for me Ted Hughes's translation of Ovid's *Metamorphoses*. I hadn't read it since 1997, and was at once excited to see the russet cover. But that was all I could see. Somehow it seemed a perfect present and I remembered how struck I had been by Hughes's translation of the story of Daphne; in my recall, the bloody words sprang leaved with green.

As if by telepathy, my landlord, who had accompanied his mother, asked, 'Have you read Christopher Logue's Homer?'

'I love it. *All Day Permanent Red*,' I replied. The luxury, for even two sentences, of an exchange about reading, after these dry months, was delicious.

It became plain to me only two days ago that we are in the season of sweet peas and peonies. One of my doctors lives within creeping distance and I feel a sense of achievement if I can get there and back without falling over or crashing into someone. Chelsea Week, I thought to myself, with plenty of nice country people up in town, would be a good time to make this stab at normality. It began as a treat. The King's Road was the usual troubling sequence of negotiations and feints. Then there's the big island to be gained in Sloane Square. Once in Sloane Street, I was sure I'd start to smell floral displays set out by the shops to attract the pollen-gatherers up for the Flower Show. I passed two neoclassical tubs of sweet flowery spikes, missed a lady who I could tell was very smart from her heels and her smell and from her polite, 'I'm so sorry', wobbled on for a bit more and bashed into someone around my height, gender female, coat weatherproof, accent cut-glass, shock utter, who shouted, 'You fucking bitch.'

Perhaps she had just come from the doctor where she had heard bad news, or maybe the parking had been impossible or the train up from the country running late. Who is to say that none of us might not have said it?

There are some doctors who are in themselves curative. They lower your anxiety and your pulse as they speak; you sense their truth. This doctor is one such and I left his surgery capable even of seeing my way down the front steps. I walked home remade to a degree by this insightful man. It was only in my own street that I noticed my skirt had fallen down and that I was shuffling along inside a puddle of grey jersey that it had made around my shoes. The white stick was handy at pulling it up and re-establishing it. Another benefit of not seeing is that I didn't see if anyone saw.

I am for the moment perching in this flat like a gull on a cliff. The metaphor isn't overstretched. I am a bit of a gull, being blind, and gullible at the best of times. The flat might certainly in one way be likened to a cliff, for it is enormously tall. My friend and land-lord has tucked me in under his wing in what was once one of the

Tite Street studios of John Singer Sargent. Liv and I work in his studio, whose windows face north and south, twenty feet of sheer light, with muslin soothing or baffling the light over the street-side window.

It is not possible to be in this room and not feel better. It is exhilarating and it feels full of the ghosts of work. At present, it is not decorated, save accidentally and provisionally. Dressed or undressed, done-up or bare-boned, it is a room that in itself provides breath. I don't believe in inspiration of the kind you wait around for, but this room has breathed some life back into me.

Sometimes in the night, between about 4 and 5 a.m., I can see a bit to read. I took down a book by Michael Levey called *The Soul of the Eye*. It's an anthology about painters and painting; mostly it consists of painters themselves talking about painting and drawing.

I fell on two things, and now it is the day it is very painful, literally, to read them, but here they are, first Sargent himself in a letter of 1901: 'The conventionalities of portrait painting are only tolerable in one who is a good *painter* – if he is only a good *portrait painter* he is nobody. Try to become a painter first and then apply your knowledge to a special branch – but do not begin by learning what is required for a special branch or you will become a mannerist.'

In the pale gap of reading time that I was granted I came too upon this, from *On Modern Art* by Paul Klee (1924): 'Had I wished to present the man "as he is", then I should have had to use such bewildering confusion of line that pure elementary representation would have been out of the question. The result would have been vagueness beyond recognition.'

This last refusal of distraction is entirely true to the line my father in his life took and the lines he made and the lines he drew.

Looking, now, at the high window and the plain grey of the walls, though I see very little clearly, I do see a composition that is timeless: a young woman of lovely form at work at a table on which rest some vessels and a jar of flowers. If I scowl and make horrible faces,

I can see what I already know, that the young woman is Liv, that the vessels are mugs, glasses and bottles of scent and that the flowers are what must be gathered in their season and cut and cut again, sweet peas.

All that is required is a frame, and it is that which I'm attempting to construct with these words. By opening my mouth very wide, as though I'm screaming, but without sound, I can open my eyes in sympathy and read from *The Soul of the Eye* what it is that Poussin has to say about framing his picture *The Israelites Gathering Manna*:

> I beg of you, if you like it, to provide it with a small frame; it needs one so that, in considering it in all its parts, the eyesight may remain concentrated, and not distracted beyond the limits of the picture by receiving impressions of objects which, seen pell-mell with the painted objects, confuse the light.
>
> It would be very suitable if the said frame were gilded quite simply with dull gold, as it blends very softly with the colours without disturbing them.

It is very difficult indeed to prevent the memory from confusing the light; as for the frame, I am attempting to gild it not at all save where it is of its nature golden.

———◆·◆·◆———

Fram says that he never reads the childhood part of any biography, since childhoods bore him. He also used to say to me that one of my benefits as a wife was that I had no family, which is, strictly, very nearly true.

But I did have and do have the long, and for the most part by definition insular, since it took place and takes place on an island, family romance with the six Howard children and their parents, their stepmother, their beastly dogs, their fantastically frightful paternal grandmother, who on first sighting me enquired, 'Who is the common

140

girl in the corner?' and who ended up by making revolting but much-loved bargello cushions for my first wedding present, embroidered with the coat of arms of my husband, and to whose wheelchair we tied fifty pink and fifty white balloons on the christening of my first son, so that the tiny fierce termagant was lifted up in her chair to the summer sky. She once again became, as she must have been in a hundred ballrooms when she was Di Loder, one of the identical Loder twins Diana and Victoria, who were on nonspeakers for half a century, a red-haired beauty afloat in white and pink, the cynosure of all eyes.

In order to make the crossing to the island of Colonsay it is necessary to end this chapter here.

LENS II: Chapter 4

Liv, who is twenty-two, has just asked me, at the start of our working day together, whether it would be better to be stone-blind than to be in this flickering and changeable state. As it happens, I have been up working for several hours and am therefore very close to stone-blind, but still it is inflected and there are colours within my eyelids. I seem to remember from accounts written by 'properly' blind authors like Ved Mehta and Stephen Kuusisto, that 'real' blindness can also be continually modifying within its veils and infinite shadings of black, or, more often, white. Of course, it depends on the kind of blind you are.

Liv's question is an intelligent one. Perhaps it is *the* question; I'm certainly honoured she asked it, since it demonstrates a levelness of attitude to her employer and the peculiar situation she finds herself in with that employer, who is me. She made the point that her mother is averse to change, but that she, Liv, were she to be visited, heaven forbid, by such an affliction, would attempt to extract from it all the good that could be.

I recognise myself when Liv speaks of someone averse to change, but my life has been so zigzagged in its shape and so full of abrupt change, much of it caused by me, that I am unsure what not-changing – one might call it security – feels like. Perhaps this blindness is just another, negative, attempt by my mind to deal itself some security, by reduplicating the loneliness in which I found myself with that loneliness's thickening through blindness. This remains to be seen.

I made a short, parodically adult, not totally convincing speech to Liv about acceptance of whatever comes one's way, and the necessity to make an honest attempt at turning it to the good. I also told her the plain truth, which my friend Julian Barnes regards as tosh, that I feel as though, if I'm hurt, others whom I love will not be. The scapegoat theory, he calls it, and I thought of the dreadful Holman Hunt painting.

Still, *dum spiro, spero*, otherwise why would I be visiting so many doctors, at least three of whom seem resistant to the concept of my registering as blind, even with the promise of a guide dog, parking concessions, and other benefits that come with such officially recognised status?

My grey cat Rita has occupied the chair I sit in to Liv's right. Fram has just rung to say that he is going with Minoo and Claudia to stay with mutual friends in Yorkshire over the bank holiday weekend and that he had a happy birthday yesterday. Sometimes I cannot be sure when I'm going to wake up and realise that it's all been a dreadful dream and that I am well again and not alone and can sit in my own chair and read a book.

I say to myself, 'Worse things happen at sea.' After all, none of what is sad is happening to anyone but me. I must take Fram's advice and detach, detach, take sannyasa insofar as a middle-aged Episcopalian can. I'm not made of the material that makes a modish new age Hindu or Buddhist. Fram is a Zoroastrian, a faith that accepts no converts, although it is so very practical a religion and way of life. But all that is for later.

If Liv hadn't asked me her plain courageous question, we would have begun this chapter with a meditation on the place of magazines, especially fashion magazines, in contemporary life. Let's get it over with and then we can set about the serious business of addressing the ferry that takes you over to the island of Colonsay.

We were not allowed to read magazines at boarding school. This heightened their value dramatically. We had in our house at school at least one accredited beauty and I think it was she who smuggled in a copy of *Vogue*. Her name is so apposite for a beauty that let me put it in; she is the granddaughter of Daphne du Maurier and her name is Marie-Thérèse de Zulueta. Although we were not allowed to watch on television the funeral of the late King Edward VIII, then

Duke of Windsor, because he had been an adulterer, Marie-Thérèse was allowed to watch the film of *The Birds*, because her grandmother wrote it. She was allowed to sit up with our matron, Mrs Fraser, and watch all that avian horror on the little brown box.

Marie-Thérèse had hair thick as a squaw's and the colour of corn that reached her waist. She had an olive green velvet hair ribbon, bendy eyelashes, a glamorous stepfather and a glamorous father and was like me addicted to Nestlé condensed milk sucked from the tube; that bears some looking into. Boys fell on sight of her like ninepins. This in the days when we had to cross the road if we saw a group of boys from the Boys' School approaching. Men fell too for her mother. They both had faces of the ideal proportion, clear brow, low large eyes, perfect mouth, the features disposing themselves in baby-like proportion in the lower two-thirds of the face.

Edward Heath was in power. Electricity was rationed and for several evenings a week we were without it. This copy of *Vogue* fell into my hands. On page seventy-five, an announcement was made about *Vogue*'s annual Talent Contest. I've always entered competitions, the motive mostly publication or cash. In this case, it is fortunate that my habit was so undiscriminating, or I am sure that I would have been expelled for having entered this one, let alone running away from school for the day without telling anyone to have lunch sitting between Lord Snowdon and Marina Warner (who had on yellow satin hot-pants with a heart-shaped bib).

The competition rules stipulated that all entries be typed, double spaced; I had no typewriter. I wrote and drew my entry after the long school day by candlelight (absolutely forbidden for obvious safety reasons) with fountain pen and (contraband) make-up for colouring in my drawings. There were several parts to the competition, the only compulsory part being to write one's autobiography. I had no very long life to write about, being fifteen, and caused great offence to my family on all sides by describing my poor stepmother, fatuously, as resembling a 'beautiful milkmaid'. I also designed a Summer

Collection around a moth motif and selected whom, alive or dead, I would ask to dinner. I can remember only Elizabeth I and Evelyn Waugh. I'd never made dinner or held a party.

There were in those days telegrams and I returned to Aldhelmsted East, after that disorientating day at Vogue House in London, to find that I had won by unanimous vote the *Vogue* Talent Contest for 1970. Thank God, and I mean thank God, the headmistress had also received the news on that very day that I had won a national essay prize sponsored by the Sykes Bequest, the topic to be selected by the entrant, anything at all as long as it was to do with Missionary Work. I had written a long, very boring, wholly invented, essay about smuggling Bibles. It was fictitious but full of detail; never did I feel so grateful for it as when Dame Diana Reader-Harris announced the double news concerning me at prayers the next day; that I had won five pounds in a national essay competition dedicated to Missionary Work and that I had also won a prize given by a magazine called *Vogue*.

The *Vogue* prize was a huge sum of money, fifty pounds, but the real prize of that contest remains to this day an astonishing one; every winner of the *Vogue* Talent Contest is awarded the chance of working on the magazine. What in my case this achieved will be seen; for most people it is an incomparable entry into an impenetrable world and a golden opportunity. I fear that for me it was a reason not to become an academic or a teacher and then it led to many of the things that are worst about, and worst for, me. But that comes later. All I will say for the moment is that magazines are, without a shadow of a doubt, addictive.

'The Earth is the Lord's, and all that it contains
Excepting the Western Isles, for they are David MacBrayne's.'

Anyone who has been to the islands of Scotland will recognise the truth of this. MacBrayne's run the ferries that are quite literally a lifeline to the islands. Every sheep, every jar of Marmite, every tank of petrol, every cornflake that you consume on an island in the Inner or Outer Hebrides will have been brought there by MacBrayne's and will consequently have a surcharge that is referred to as 'the fright'; that is, the freight. There are perhaps only two travellers over the last century of whom I've heard, who have travelled between the islands – save of course for those on private transport, yachts or planes and such – under their own steam and these two valiant travellers are a bull who swam from Barra to Vatersay and Hercules the grizzly bear, star of the Sugar Puffs advertisement, who set out on his own after a tiring afternoon's filming, and made landfall a day or two later with a fine appetite for his next bowl of cereal. It's probably fortunate they didn't meet midstream or the food chain might have reasserted its sway.

The first trip I took to Colonsay was on the MV *Columba*. She was a much smaller vessel than the big drive-on ferries that are now used; vehicles were swung aboard her on davits in a great heavy net and positioned with much swearing and vehemence in the Gaelic by the MacBrayne's men. The *Columba* had a writing desk with its own headed writing paper and tea was served, including cake stands, unless the sea got what is called lumpy. That first trip, I was sensibly attired for arrival at a small Scottish island in a voile maxi dress, bare feet and some sunglasses that had snap-in snap-out lenses in a choice of shades: turquoise, peat or rose. For my arrival I selected the rose-tinted spectacles. That crossing was a fair one and I wasn't sick at all, though I had to visit the Ladies with its astonishingly heavy doors, fit to cope with a bad swell, to reapply my Biba eyeshadow which was also pink and frosted. I have in my life made this journey only twice, I realise, on my own. At the start of this book I thought it was but the once, when I left the island to do my bit for Man Booker, but of course I arrived alone the first time.

Arrival at the pier at Colonsay, or at any other island, is a mixture of a gathering intensely social and ferociously practical. Families reunite, sick people leave for hospital, children depart for school on the mainland, tractors roll off, the dustbin lorry arrives, a wedding cake must be unpacked with utmost care, a new baby may meet its father for the first time, a bull must be unloaded, a funerary wreath disembarked with due dignity, a body, even, must be consigned. So it's fortunate that I have no recall of my own arrival at Colonsay. Perhaps, if anyone noticed at all, they thought I was a cabaret entertainer who had got on the wrong boat. Oban was not then the sophisticated burgh we now know.

Scalasaig, the port at Colonsay, is, however, inordinately sophisticated. Let no one think that because a community is small, it contains less nuance than a larger one; the reverse is so. There is no end to it; the place never stops. Like all life lived up close, the feeling intensifies with the proximity. The lens is tightened in upon you and your behaviour, your coloration, your profile in flight, your integrity.

There is a big book about the geology, archaeology, botany, ornithology, zoology and highly variegated civilisations of Colonsay and its tidal neighbour Oransay. Its name is Loder on *The Islands of Colonsay and Oransay in the County of Argyll.* I mention it because once you have a sniff of the place you will want to know more and here I can but represent it with a puff of cloud, a pinch of air, the smell of crushed bog-myrtle, or the call of the corncrake that lives protected within the island's shores.

Another addiction warning must in fairness be issued at this point: one of the lowest blows about my blindness is that I can no longer really see to read the island's online newspaper *The Corncrake*, that once read takes up its place in one's reading pattern with a good deal more monthly tenacity than many glossy magazines. It is certainly more European-minded than many broadsheets.

As for the island itself, it grows through your circulation like a tree whose pip you have swallowed without knowing it. It is quite possible to make the world of Colonsay. It is an Eden. St Columba drove all snakes from it.

Oransay, which is attached at low tide to Colonsay, is a holy place. If I were told that I might never return alive, I would ask to be placed with the least fuss in a wicker basket and taken to Colonsay for the residence of my soul. Just as long as, mind, it was no bother. The freight on my cadaver might be crippling. Oransay is for other souls, to whom we shall come.

The island of Colonsay is the ancient home of clan McPhee. There is in Canada a town in Saskatchewan called Colonsay, witness to the Clearances. The *New Yorker* writer John McPhee has written a book of lasting value about Colonsay called *The Crofter and the Laird*. In my life I have had the luck to have known that crofter a little; the laird is Papa about whom it is impossible for me to be objective. Even John McPhee has trouble, writing in the early nineteen-sixties, resisting him; the same goes for Ian Mitchell in his far angrier book, *The Isles of the West*. In addition to looking just right for the part, Papa is an astoundingly sweet fella, as he will say of others.

It is 2008 and Papa, thank God, is still alive. Nonetheless, he is known on the island as 'the old Laird' because he no longer lives in the big house, so it falls to his older son Alexander to be the young Laird and responsible, not unlike God in an unblasphemous way, for everything that goes wrong.

But that is now. When first I met Alexander, he was portable. I took to having little children around me with passion. The twins were six, I think. Among ourselves we use the terms brother and sister, and I fell into a habit of ambiguity. It is perhaps among our children that the position is best and most tactfully made clear. My children refer to their 'not-cousins' and love making jokes about how they have genetically 'inherited' aspects of the Howards simply through closeness and osmosis. They cannot imagine how touching this is to me or how grateful I am to them for it.

It pulls together strands that I myself cannot pull without feeling them heavy as sodden hawsers leading to sunken hulks.

Not only is there no drop of blood in common, save in the most primordial sense, but temperamentally and in every other way I am as unlike a Howard as could be, save perhaps for my height. However, I like to think that this otherness makes me of some use to them as a sort of conduit or adaptor, a useless person when many useful ones are around. The autobiography of a person even temporarily blind must skirt sentiment with care and the subject of a childhood that was at once delayed, invented and almost impossibly beautiful spells danger for the glowing, softened, recreating memory.

There were of course rocks under the dream, but they have proven negotiable, which is a benefit, insofar as I can see it, of family love. From a distance of over forty years, it is not possible for those long holidays from school not to blur into one another, though actually I can tell the years each from each in a fashion with which I won't trouble my reader now. It was a late childhood and with very particular conditions.

When I arrived in the lives of the Howards, there was no electricity save from little coal generators that stopped at midnight and sulked if you had a Hoover on at the same time as, for example, four light bulbs. This in a house with twenty-five bedrooms, albeit eight of these simply comprising a bachelor floor, as though for visiting swains, ready for eight dancing partners. We had candles by our bedsides, stone hot water bottles, coal fires in our bedrooms and, when I first arrived, ate with the grown-ups in the dining room only on special occasions; otherwise it was the nursery. I suppose I regressed appallingly. Certainly I fell with indelicate speed into calling the parents Mum and Papa instead of Jinny and Euan. Mum read to us after tea, which arrived on a trolley: gingerbread, Guinness-and-walnut bread, drop scones, soda scones and blackcurrant jam. We played dressing-up games and every day involved a physical adventure of some sort during which I would come to some safe small harm, be chaffed a bit about it, and be nursed out of it with affection from one or other parent or child. The parents had that dash and carelessness that goes with having a large number of children. It wasn't actual carelessness. It was confidence of the physical sort.

When I arrived, the house's harling was weather-washed with pale pink; it is now pale yellow. At the front it holds out accommodating wings around a sweep of pebbles and an oval lawn, each wing terminating with an elegantly arched Regency window. All around the edge of its front façade at the foot are pale green glass fishermen's floats like heavy bubbles. From the back, the house looks surprisingly French, an impression not dispelled by the palm trees and tender plants that embrace it. The lawn bends twice deeply down to a cedar tree of great size, a stream and a bridge that leads to the many scented acres of subtropical garden that rise beyond and up and over to the pond and the gulches planted by nineteenth-century enthusiasts collecting from China and the Himalayas. In May and June the deep womanly perfumes of rhododendrons and wet earth almost make the air sag. The Polar Bear Rhododendron smells of lemons and tea with cream. You could make a tea tray from one of its leaves. All rhododendrons of the family *loderi* have leaves whose backs are soft as a newborn baby's head, with a downy covering called indumentum. Many of the hedges are wild fuchsia or escallonia. The fairy-like white fuchsia is the loveliest and leads to a part of the walled garden where Papa put (with much indentured child labour) the great glass ridged tower of a disused lighthouse lens from Islay. Sit within it and the world splinters into its seven constituent colours. On a bright day, screw up your eyes for a blinding white inside your head. The lens itself is big enough to hold two or three people. I have been into it once since I've been going blind. Its gift on that day was to dress the closest tree of pink blossom in long light-ribbons of green and blue.

The oddity of a closely remembered late childhood is that I might not perhaps remember it in such detail had it genuinely been my own. Nonetheless, it did its binding work. Above the house is a loch called Loch Scoltaire. Each child kept his or her wooden boat slung in the boathouse there. In the centre of the loch is a small island, surrounded by other islets on which terns nest and dive-bomb your head as you row or swim to the central island. There is a Victorian pleasure-house, suitable for picnics and sketching, from which, in the nineteen-twenties, Papa's glamorous mother might have gone swimming naked before setting up her easel. One summer when Andrew was about six, it was mooted that he was brave and old enough to have me in his charge overnight for a camping expedition in the little house on the island. He was an enchanting child, with a head like a broad bean and an enormous mouth. We set out up the hill through the heather and gorse and over two rusty stiles with our equipment. Andrew was in his striped pjs, maroon dressing gown and those old-fashioned slippers that little boys used to have resembling those worn by elderly gentlemen. I can't remember what I was wearing, but it wouldn't have been anything like as practical as Andrew's attire. It had been made very plain that Andrew was the expedition leader, as indeed he was, since I can't row. We pulled out the littlest dinghy, *Duckling*, climbed into her, trimmed our weights as far as we could and Andrew rowed lustily to the small island where we made fast the painter.

We settled down in our sleeping bags. We had brought two eggs for the morning and firelighters and matches. I was to be on wood collection duty. The island is maybe the size of four king-sized beds, the wee house the size of one. We told one another a few scary stories and soon Andrew, dear bean, was fast asleep. The next thing I knew was that we were participants in a really creaky Enid Blyton or *Swallows and Amazons* plot. I heard the muffled sound of oars and saw the fairy fire. I heard the deadly tread. All the other siblings except Jane, who was too grown up, had accoutred themselves as ghouls and skeletons and beasties. Anyone else in the house who could be persuaded to come along had done so. One house guest had had the idea of laying paraffin on the water and lighting it. But Andrew and I slept through that part of the invasion. It was such a comfortable haunting, safely to be teased by people who had gone to the trouble of frightening one just enough and then arriving to reassure, so that there we all were on the tiny island inside the already small island of Colonsay, sitting in the brick house with six little wooden boats pulled up stern to and painters tied with a round turn and two half hitches. In the morning Andrew and I went home to the big house for breakfast even though our disgusting boiled eggs had been so filling and nourishing.

With great patience, Jinny and Euan allowed me to tag along on all adventures and duties, or to absent myself from them. Katie has also been a lifelong task giver. One summer we were in the fruit cage, collecting gooseberries for jam and bottling for the winter. It was a boiling day and we were in swimsuits and shorts. Little Emma was with us and it was on that day that she told me that the feel of damp grass on her bare feet gave her an occasional sense of nausea. I knew she was a pea-princess then. We had several heavy baskets of red, furry goosegogs and a couple of trugs of harder green ones. Suddenly I made a noise. Katie had trained me to sneeze soundlessly and never to cough, even if I felt like it. But this was a loud noise and Katie didn't approve of it. We went on picking among the prickly bushes under the net in the walled garden. About ten minutes later I tried to talk and found that I'd lost the capability. I made some more noises. Katie was bent over her picking. She is an efficient and excellent gardener, cook and household manager. She very much dislikes being touched suddenly, but I had to get her attention somehow. I tapped her hand with mine and poor Katie turned round to find me not quite doubled in size and gagging. I can't remember what happened after that. Someone found some old Wasp-Eze in a cupboard and squirted it on to where the sting was still sticking out of my cheek. I love gooseberries and love picking them, like most gardening chores and especially doing them with Katie, but that time was nearly fatal and now I carry the syringe and pills that the terminally allergic wasp-stung need.

The best of the wasp incident was that every day Papa would say, 'Claude darling, are you sure you're all right, you seem to have got bigger.' So, yet again, he made a comforting repetitiveness that when I started to deflate meant that the other children could tease me painlessly by pretending to be Papa. Later, we discovered that I was also allergic to Wasp-Eze, allergic both to the attack and to its prescribed redress.

The length of the summer days in the North, and the delicious light that lingers, retreats and is reborn, fills my memory with summer evenings when we smoked the mackerel we caught or made moules marinière in a bucket. The sea in summer can be purple or it can be aquamarine and so it is with the sky. Coming back from long days on a beach with one's young children in a flotilla of boats, watching the kittiwakes and chugging into harbour with the remains of a picnic and piles of sandy tired children has become part of my deep life. One day, we were at sea in a small chunky boat, about eighty years old, like all Papa's boats an orphan. We were just off a bay named Balnahard where the mackerel crowd. We had our darrows down and were waiting for fish. As a child I loved the gutting and it used to be my job to gut at sea, but since having children I can't do it. Suddenly everyone's darrows were leaping and on each hook were not one but three or sometimes five mackerel and then we found ourselves witness to what might have been an illustration of the food chain. From the sea leapt a sparkling cloud of colourless, minute fishlets, followed by a jacquard silver-and-blue arrow of mackerel followed by three perfect, classical dolphins as though posed upon a vase and then, enormously, slowly, holding back time with its size, the huge bridge of an emerging basking shark, three times the size of our boat.

Sometimes Papa might be persuaded, if the evening was flat calm, to take us, as children, and later with our own children, through the strand between Colonsay and Oransay, but at low tide so there was a danger of going aground. The benefit, however, was that when he turned the engine right down and steered as he can by feel, we were among seal families, for it is just off Oransay on Seal Island that the seals go to pup and we could watch them suckle and kiss and roar and chat and sing, the mothers so confident (so long as we kept quiet or did nothing but sing rather than talk) that they did not flop into the water leaving their babies but stayed with them on the kelpy rocks. We have been no more than six inches from those white baby seals with their awful cat-food breath and their black marble eyes. The sea on nights like that was like milk and, going home, there might be phosphorescence in our wake. We would tie up the boat in the harbour and unpack the box full of gutted fish, the exhausted picnic, Papa's bottle of pink wine and our beach bags, a different colour for each child, with our names embroidered on. I was proud when Jinny said I could sew mine.

I cannot calibrate what the value of this family, and of its home, is to me; perhaps that is what having real siblings is like, but I think not, because I am conscious that it surprises me and delights me constantly, therefore I cannot be expecting it, therefore I surely don't take it for granted, as one perhaps does the love of a sibling. I also feel that I am more use to them semi-detached than attached and homogenised.

Katie and her second husband William, who have been married for almost thirty years, grew tired of London. Katie is a country girl and needs to hack and dig to make a day feel lived through. William is extremely adaptable. They and their three children moved to a house on the Firle Estate near Charleston. They rented Bushey Lodge, a house that Cyril Connolly and his wife Deirdre had lived in. With driven application they commenced to become organic market gardeners just before the idea had caught on. Katie and William's market gardening produced aesthetically pleasing vegetables in magnificent abundance. Katie loved the names; she was especially fond of a floppy lettuce called Grande Blonde Paresseuse. They grew purple potatoes and Japanese artichokes and cardoons, tigerella tomatoes, yellow beetroots, rainbow chard and a host of products that the supermarkets have now made familiar. Their project foundered on an unready market and perhaps too much generosity when it came to the accounting. There had also been an element of using hard physical labour as an anaesthetic, for at this point there was a shadow of unhappiness over each of their lives.

Enduring town life but not attached to it, Katie was delighted to be asked by her brother Alexander to come and live on Colonsay and work with him. I told her she must keep a diary. Colonsay isn't like anywhere else at all. There's an adventure every day. You could write a poem every morning and every night. I would like to live there for a good stretch of my life. I began to worry that Katie would get sad when the days got shorter and darkness came down at three, but she has the great gift of Arachne, and every minute is filled. William has now followed his wife to the island. He works as woodman, binman, soothant, impresario, baker.

The topography of the island offers all terrains in little, as though it were an ideal or invented place. It has its great peak, just under 500 feet, its isolated lochs, its whistling, golden, silver, black and pink sands, its cowrie beach and its fulmars' crags; it has its deserted blackhouses and its wild flags, its own orchid, *Spiranthes romanzoffiana*, its fairy rings, its Viking burial ship, its standing stones, its overdressed choughs that look ready for town; it is the only place where herons nest on the ground and it has a pair of nesting golden eagles. Its turf is dense and full of wild flowers, including the smallest rose, the pimpinellifolia.

The islanders peopled my childhood, my growing-up, my middle age; some have left, many more have died, several tragically, needlessly. Some, over the years, have been brave enough to dance with me, or even come south to toast my wedded bliss. From the residents of Colonsay I have received steadiness, grace, jokes, music, irony, continuity in the sort of quantity that I would hope to offer a child, or, for that matter, a dumb animal. I have been privileged in this.

———◆◆◆◆———

There is no avoiding boats on an island. The miracle of the ferry, for as long as I was at boarding school and then at university, was that there might be periods for as long as three weeks when the island was stormbound and the *Columba* could not get through. This must have been both worrying and tedious for all the adults concerned, but I was having a honeymoon with infancy and felt it bliss to be stuck safe at home, with its routines and rules and habits.

We did run out of food. We tell people we ate curried dog food. I can't remember if it's true. It might as well have been. We did eat any quantity of a magnificently Scots viand, buyable in bulk, named SwelFood. It had a connection with the vegetable kingdom. It lived up to its name should you add water. A little heat improved things. I ate and ate on Colonsay and, though not lean, like the others, I didn't get fat, because I was living a life beyond books, though not without them.

I have never quite got over a bad tic I taught myself, very likely unnecessarily, under my stepmother Christine's regime – to leap up as soon as one heard footsteps approach, to hide one's book, and 'look busy'. I didn't do that much on Colonsay, at Colonsay, in Colonsay. The nature of my anxiety changed. I wished to fit in. In this I lost bits of myself. This was all my own fault. I think the Howards wanted me *as* me, if they thought about it at all.

<hr />

When people look knowing and talk about the popular music of their childhood, I can honestly refer to both my childhoods, in Edinburgh, and on Colonsay, and look blank. When the electricity worked on Colonsay, the gramophone played classical music. Quite by chance I had lit on another musical household. To reach the drawing room from the front hall, you had to go through a curved room called the corridor-room; there was a smiley bison with a centre parting in his horns over the pianola that had sheets taken from Paderewski's own playing of Chopin, and a piano that we sang around. Mum or Caroline played. It was from the corridor-room gramophone that I first learned to listen for the style of a conductor, though frequently the tempi must have been affected by the wind or the rain outside. We listened a lot, together, to music. I remember the

Brahms Violin Concerto and his Hungarian dances, the Mozart Coronation Mass and Litanie Lauretanae, *The Marriage of Figaro* and *The Magic Flute*, and Haydn and Boccherini. Just sometimes, Edith Piaf, whom Mum and Papa had seen in Paris. No Messiaen, no Mahler, no Russians, no Wagner, all of whom I love, but came to later. Papa, as on every 'cultivated' topic, knows more than he affects to know. He is a natural teacher, the only man I would allow near my younger son with a fretsaw, or near me with an explanation (all done in salt cellars and napkin rings) of how the universe works or what diatonics are. He is intriguing for many reasons. He has not grown old where old means bitter or incurious. Of course he repeats himself. That is because we force him to. We say, 'Pop, Pop, do the one about . . .'

We are in our fifties and forties, he halfway through his eighties. I'm lucky to have been caught in his slipstream (he will correct the term, no doubt).

His brother Barnaby, who is perhaps eighty-two, was dying last year. He had had three wives, three children, seven stepchildren. Papa went over to St Louis, where Barnaby has made his own version of Colonsay, to say farewell for good to his younger brother. Papa officially hates death. Barnaby's nurse fell in love with him. Instead of a funeral, there was a wedding. Barnaby shares his brother's good looks, though without the beard. Height, black hair, now white but still thick, and cruel blue eyes belied by that smile wide as a wolf's and as perturbingly white. Papa smiles while he is working, biting down on a small piece of his tongue. His children and grandchildren do it too.

They all carry multifunctional knives around their waists on lanyards, though have had to rethink this since airports grew difficult. Each one's knife is of great sentimental value, having been given as a reward when, one by one, the children learned to sail their respective wooden boats around the tiny island in the loch.

I've never been in danger of possessing such a knife.

The Howard children were sent away to school considerably later than many children of their background, as it might convention-ally be imagined. All the children owe their general knowledge and handwriting, their sense of lore and their manner of keeping things shipshape to their governess, Val, who had also been governess to their mother and her six siblings. The big house is full of things Val made with the children: tables with glass tops covering labelled shells gathered during afternoon lessons and laid on old green velvet; lists of birds seen and illustrated; children's books carefully inscribed in the same fluent rounded hand as each child came to learn it. Val never taught me but the others had that kind of skater's grace to elide this so that I might sink my roots deeper into the family myth.

Yet I was unconsciously deceiving myself on far too many levels. The fact remains that there are six Howard children, whom I love, and that they are not my siblings. Nor are their parents mine, though it is my belief that I love their father very much as people do love their fathers, as far as I can see it. It is far too late to untangle anything that goes so deep, but it is not too late to be clear about who is whose. I speak in this apparently chilly dissecting sort of voice on account only of knowing that it is with the precise naming of things that my sight will, *if it will*, return; and that the truth matters.

It is with reference to boats that I am able, perhaps, to express the intensity of my affection for this family. I trust my life to each member of it and have been hauled from the possibility of a watery grave, as has my younger son, by their strong arms more often than I can admit. (Minoo and I have spindly, useless arms.) Life on Colonsay is lived, very considerably, on boats. Given the chance I would rather step out of a boat than into one, be this into a harbour, which has happened countless times in Colonsay (and once in Tonga), or at sea, or into a loch (or into the South Pacific, where I hadn't a Howard with me and which comes later). Perhaps at root there is little higher one may say of another individual with whom one has spent a mort of time than that one feels safe with them. The Howards make me feel physically safe, which is a state I achieve in few other circumstances. What these circumstances are will make itself plain to readers.

───◆◆◆───

It was from Colonsay that Katie was first married at the age of seventeen and a half, in her wedding dress ironed by Val. Rosa and I made bowls of philadelphus and daisies. There was a marquee and the honeymoon was taken on the Isle of Barra.

In the photographs we all, including the grown-ups, look like children.

Marriage was still at the time the suitable terminus of the story of a childhood. Girls were married 'from the nursery', like trees taken for grafting.

During the time we were at Cambridge together, Katie and I were, I think, unsure of what narrative to follow. The times were changing, but nothing like as swiftly as retrospect might have you think. Girton was quite as sequestered and well-behaved as Sherborne School for Girls had been. Many of my contemporaries in college arrived engaged and left after their degree to enter into marriage.

The first night in the dining hall at Girton, which is a red Victorian Gothic structure, designed by Waterhouse, three miles outside Cambridge on the Cherry Hinton Road, a sturdy pink blancmange was served; I said I wouldn't have any, thanks, and a shiver went down the table.

Later I sustained two approaches, one from a quietly spoken American girl who turned out to live just off Washington Square with her grandmother and two giant poodles and who became a friend for life, Miss Sarah Montague, gymkhana star and radio performer; the other from a girl I regret having lost touch with, who said, 'You went to fucking public school, didn't you?'

I think the truth is that I only went to fucking public school because my mother was dead, and that is the answer to the question

I asked some chapters ago, would it all have happened if I had stayed at home? I wouldn't have fucking talked like this. I might have talked like fucking that, and that in itself might have been a great big fucking relief. Not that, actually, all Scots do swear all the time, nor *pace* some English critics, does that brilliant writer James Kelman use such language, save where to do so holds to the truth.

If I had stayed at home, I wouldn't have talked like this and I might have married a nice Scots boy who really could dance (though in the East Coast fashion) and we might have settled down to the couthie Edinburgh life for which, I think, I hanker so, now that I definitively have not lived it.

Scotland itself is zigzagged with strifes and loyalties, with roads that wind north in listlessness, desolation and ancient war; there are many sects and septs of Presbyterianism and many families who raise a glass to the king over the water. I won't here go into Rangers and Celtic, for I'm ignorant, but so little is the country, so small its population, so deep its habit of talk and of remembrance, that the past lies over and within everything. While it is a hard fact that Papa's great-grandfather received the Island of Colonsay in lieu of payment of a lapsed debt by Sir John McNeil, it is also true that if to own a boat, as the vulgarism goes, is to stand in a shower tearing up fifty-pound notes, to inherit an island is to stand in a maelstrom doing much the same, with added responsibilities for its human residents. Papa was born in South Audley Street to parents of improbable wealth, deriving in the main from the Canadian Pacific Railway and the Hudson's Bay Company. His great-grandfather endowed McGill University and Papa said once that he seemed to remember a lintel over a door in the 'Old Man's' house in Montreal that was made of solid gold. His great-grandfather, Donald Smith, became first High Commisioner of Canada and later Lord Strathcona (Gaelic for Glencoe which he also owned) and Mount Royal (which is just Montreal). Goodness knows if this lintel was a metaphor or what he literally saw, but Papa's own life has been entirely unembittered, as he saw most things except for Colonsay go. He is a born master craftsman.

The words 'private island' come nowhere near Colonsay; it is not a plaything but a society, and most of the boats, houses, cars that pertain to the family that accidentally presides amid it with patience, beneficence and nothing short of love, are held together, bodged in some way. Papa is a genius at bodging. So are his children. It's my sense that they don't really like things that do not need fixing.

When we were younger, Katie, Caro and I shared clothes. Jane was careful and neat and very sensibly kept us off. Caro had a red jumper knitted for her by Val, Katie a becoming cream jumper knitted by her grandmother with a repeat motif of the Strathcona crest, a beaver chewing its way through a log. I had two jerseys, one of which I'd received for Christmas from Mum and Papa so it was sacred and came out only for evening wear. My other jumper was grey, knitted on needles the size of rolling pins, edged in grey velvet ribbon, large enough for a shire horse and had been thrown out by Daniel Day-Lewis, the weedy younger brother of our friend Tamasin. No. I don't know where it is now. It disappeared with my dried-out and reassembled lobster, some old love letters, and the Clarendon Press George Herbert, all of which were by my bed, when I 'grew up' and Alex and his wife Jane took over the house.

There is a strong bohemian streak in the Howards. Papa's mother, confusingly known as Oma, really could paint and her many swift oil sketches of the island catch it just so. Papa was brought up with Peter Ustinov, whose mother, Nadia Benois, used to paint with Oma. There are two 'reciprocal' paintings made by the two women on a summer day on the island in the nineteen-thirties that hang in the corridor-room on Colonsay. Tulips in a vase, dropped-waist dresses, a departed Hebridean afternoon seen through differing eyes. Many of the Howards' close relations are artists; one, Linda Kitson, who briefly married her cousin, Papa's brother Barnaby, was a Falklands

War artist. Papa's sister Didon was a creator in her every gesture and she leaves girl twins who have the very same trait; one of them, lying in Barcelona, felled in her forties by a stroke, is literally drawing herself out of it with pencil and paper. The Howards are not spoilt. Their affection for things is greatly enhanced when that thing is to some degree damaged or, even better, hopelessly broken.

It is my private belief that Papa rather resents things that work perfectly first time. I don't mean he sabotages them, but he perceives less of a challenge in the spanking new than in the clapped-out old. He is without doubt an artist in wood and metal. It was a sad day when he moved out of the big house and his entire run of *Wooden Boat* magazine was on the line. He had first subscribed to it aged thirteen. In the end it went, though he has kept the squared notebooks in which he draws inventions and improvements upon machines that have caught his attention. One of the most happy days of my second childhood was spent not actually on Colonsay but off the old A40 in a disused church with Papa, Katie and Caro; we were there to meet one of Papa's innumerable correspondents. His family used to say of Papa that he kept a steamboat hidden on most canals as other men keep mistresses, but that day we were privileged to enter the largest steam-driven Wurlitzer in the known world. We climbed inside its entrails, saw the real coconut husks that made clip-clop sounds for the movies, and Caro was allowed to play it while Katie and I stood inside and watched the bellows do their elephantine work. Papa, although he is, as I have said, a man resistant to the soapier sides of faith, is a soul whom it is a pleasure to see transported, whether by a Wurlitzer, the Queen of the Night, the way the bark grows on eucalyptus trees, or when a rope goes clean around a cleat.

❧

It is this feeling of docking cleanly that grows more elusive with blindness. I will, if I may, give an account of my mornings at this time of my life. I get up at six, run a bath by ear, turn it off, feel for my electric toothbrush, load it with toothpaste, making sure by smell the toothpaste is not foot cream, do my teeth, get into the cardigan that I know hangs from the bathroom door, go into the room where the cats' litter trays are kept, find a roll of dustbin bags, somehow discover the mouth of each one and put one inside the other, in case of horrible leaks, fill these with the used litter and any old cat food and the newspaper the cat dishes sit on, give the cats clean litter, wash their dishes and dry them, put clean food into each dish, making sure not to spill any cat food on my hands or I shall smell it all day. I then take the bin bag downstairs, holding the grabs and banisters, to the catacombs of this Victorian house, undo by feel three deadlocks and put the full bin bag in the appropriate dustbin. I re-shut the deadlocks and move slowly towards the kitchen where I know how everything is stowed, though I still fall. I half fill the kettle (I can do this by weight), take the coffee from the upper shelf in the freezer door, shake about as much coffee as a squirrel's tail would weigh into the cafetière, wait for the water to boil, pour it on to the coffee grounds and commence my daily quarrel with the plunger. By now it will be 7.20 and my bath will be of any temperature at all, so that's a surprise to look forward to. When first I became blind I was determined to be well groomed, something I have never in my life been before. I'm not sure it's worked, although I know that I am clean. On my shelves however, await the jumpers of a well-groomed blind woman, each arranged in its own bag with lavender or cinnamon or clove (sovereign historic but useless remedy against moth). My jumpers are arranged from white to black through all the misty colours of grey and pink and blue and lavender and olive that I wear, the naturally occurring dyes of Scotland, where my jumpers were born. In its way my cupboard of jumpers is like Des Esseintes's organ of perfumes in Huysmans's *Against Nature*. In another way it's just me trying hard to kill two birds with one stone; that is magically to become tidy and, even more magically, to unbecome blind. I did the colour-coding holding open my eyes with my left hand from the top of my forehead, like holding a cracked watermelon together.

◆◆◆◆◆

About the time of Katie's first wedding I made a friend who is everything I am not. I met her through my Czech friend Cyril Kinsky. He has twenty-six Christian names, wanted to be a theatre director, and was for many years. Then he fell in love, started a family, and trained for the bar. He is a QC and a virtuoso of marquetry, indeed all forms of DIY. He is also cool, unusual in a DIY-er. Kafka lived to the side of his family's palace in Prague. His father Alphy smoked more eloquently than any man I've seen in my life.

Cyril brought to Cambridge his cousin, Sophie-Caroline Tarnowska. We've got an elective affinity. She knows what I think. Her husband Gilles is my son Minoo's elective affinity. He is a red-headed Protestant left-wing banker of vertiginous musicality. He is so nice you want to take him home. I have loved Sophie-Caroline over thirty years. Recently they took a second honeymoon in Scotland. Gilles reported that the rain was 'so delicious, so varied, so interesting'.

When Minoo went on his French exchange to the Paris home of this family (all of whom speak better English than I do, so it was pretty silly), he telephoned to say that everything was perfectly all right, actually very homely, for example there was a red-headed *grand-mère* who lived upstairs with her dog Gavotte and who wore jeans and the oven had fallen out of the wall, 'just like at home'.

Twice in my life Sophie-Caroline has given me the courage to act as I could not have without her. She has never had to be explicit because she reads my mind.

When I went blind she rang me and I was transfused with a reason to go on. I know that she is devout and she gave me some of it, like a lozenge, or a bit of mint cake on a steep climb, a viaticum, without actually mentioning the name of the Manufacturer, the Almighty, but she was too clever and too kind to be so coarse as to say outright, 'Do not harm yourself.'

For some of the time, they live in the Gers, in a sublime semi-ruin called Mazères, the ancient archiepiscopal palace of the archbishops of Auch. This house is the great romance of Gilles's parents, their last shared project, all still very much in the doing. The Angelus tolls daily in the tower. The fields around and the earth and the cows and the farm dogs are the colour of pale bread. In the roof of the palace is a library as long as a church. Minoo lives in this room when he visits. Next to it through a glazed rose window is the music room. It is quite possible to go from the music room into the library and miss Minoo, for all that he is tall, petrified with deep contentment into the room. Down four flights of stone stairs red griffins, faded after centuries, are stencilled in rhythm on the pale curve of the chalky walls. The history of the Cathars and of the Albigensians is legible in one layer after another in this fortress. A corner of a fallen room is blocked up with stone of another shade, from a time long before the already far time that seems to be the closest, yet is already centuries away.

There is an enfilade, falling, snowing, with whitewash, of mirrors laughing thinly into one another, the panelling tactfully bracketing itself around each tall looking-glass. The ceiling asks for chandeliers but incompletion is the keynote. How to describe it? Perhaps if Ely Cathedral grew like an opening stone rose and softly half fell down . . . ?

In this house, at the age of fifty, one night in 2005 I listened out for hornets in my bedroom. I knew I had to change my life before I lost it. A wasp will kill me, but hornets carry more poison, so I'd die sooner. I know, because I was stung by an orange hornet the size of a conker at sea just off Tahiti and that was nearly it for me, before even marrying for the first time. My then fiancé whizzed me by rubber boat into hospital and by the time we arrived my arm was a washing-up glove full of jelly.

Decades on, I waited for hornets, standing with a shoe in my right hand in the hortensia-wallpapered room in the hot Gascon night. The small double bed was occupied by the semicircular body of my then companion. Marcel contemplates the sleeping body of Albertine in like pose, reflecting on the infinitude of traits one human soul may possess.

Such was nowhere near my reflection that night. I knew that to be anything like truthful or kind, I had to get away while there was still time for him to locate another comforter, before I turned on him for nothing worse than his own fulsome nature.

It was nothing anybody said save he himself. It would take Proust's cumulative genius to show how, feeling himself closest to truth, he most lied. To be with him through time was to see through him like a hoop. So, a profession can take the soul. It was politics that he professed.

<hr/>

In fewer than three months' time, I shall leave this flat for, as its delicate state attests, it is in need of structural and architectural attention. Its ceilings sag a bit, its draughts are tempestuous, and aspects of its layout, although I have come to love them, are certainly dated. Liv and I get our fizzy drinks from a suavely concealed mirrored wall that you press and it magically opens to reveal a cocktail niche. There is a flip-over serving counter for when the studio was in use for private views in the seventies. There is a door into the studio that obviates the necessity of entering the artist's private apartment, a system put in place for Sargent. The colours, that will of necessity have to go, are kind to pictures, ranging from every kind of dove grey through to lichenous greens and, in my bedroom, a colour that combines pink, blue, brown, grey, white and black and yet is very light; the colour of the gill of the smallest, freshest, field mushroom. The sitting room, that we call Henry James, might be any colour. It is the colour of memory, a tactful background, a recessive, becoming, dark but festive, shade, making everything hung upon it look better.

Five or so years before his death, the owner of this flat sustained a stroke that made movement difficult, although it did not stop him painting. In order to help him remain independent, banisters and grabs were installed exactly as though it had been a ship. They save me from sinking.

I could have done with more of those grabs, on a metaphysical level, when I was at Cambridge. I did not know that there lay within me a thirst nothing could quench that would nearly kill me. There were signs, but they were illegible to me and my friends at the time.

My room at Girton was called F6; it took some ascending to. I was next to a popular girl whose parents visited most weekends bringing lox and bagels. I was very grateful one Sunday when the mother of this family gave me a bagel, stuffed full. Some kind of fear set in. I did not understand how to get out of one's room except to go to the college library or for meals in hall. I knew that when women were first up at university they joined one another for intense conversation over mugs of hot chocolate. I had two mugs, so that was a start. Further research revealed a row of three baths, each in its cubicle and each the size of a lifeboat, so I spent a good deal of my first year at Girton just sitting in the bath reading and getting wrinkly. I was an unreliable and irresponsible student, having come straight from school where, during the last term that Katie and Rosa were there, I had worked as a housemaid and kitchen maid, because I had got into Cambridge before my A levels, didn't want to be separated from them and needed to earn money. It was interesting to see the modification of girls' behaviour towards me as I changed from senior to skivvy. Mrs Rock, the house cook, was kind to this unhelpful pair of hands and gave me jobs she knew I could do like emptying the commercial dishwasher, grating fifteen pounds of cheese, or slicing ox liver and onions for fifty-six people with a knife whose steel was whippy, sharp and thin as a line.

The school train started at Waterloo and ended at Sherborne. For some happy reason, one summer day when we were in our A-level year, it dawdled at Basingstoke. We were told that we might go and purchase refreshments at the station buffet. We were not yet changed into our school uniform, and no one in their right mind would want to challenge Katie's raised eyebrow. We purchased two pork pies and two miniatures of brandy. Brandy is rage and turmoil to me, gin the taste of isolation.

Otherwise strong drink hardly made its appearance at Sherborne, though there was a rebarbative cocktail offered by the headmistress to those girls considered made of the right stuff to meet visiting preachers such as Sir Robert Birley, formerly headmaster of Charterhouse and Eton. Katie and I were chosen for this privilege and liked him a lot. Neither of us felt the same about Dame Diana's refreshing sherry, tomato and orange juice cocktail that was the speciality at White Lodge, the headmistress's house.

In the first weeks at Girton, should someone have asked me what was wrong, I would have replied that I was simultaneously anxious and bored. I seemed frozen to the spot. I couldn't leave my room. In my room was a bottle of sherry. Everyone knew that undergraduates offered one another small glasses of sherry. I drank the bottle on my own and went to sleep. I imagine that this sleep will have been the first blackout of my life, and that having glimpsed this option, my brain's biochemistry was on the very tentative lookout for more.

There was a bus that took Girtonians into town for lectures and seminars. I ended up sleeping on the floors of my patient friends, Anthony Appiah the most patient of all, playing me his records of Marlene and Mahler and Noël Coward and allowing me to cramp his love life.

Of course there were some friends from school. Edward Stigant, descendant of the Archbishop Stigand on the Bayeux Tapestry, was reading History at Christ's under Professor Jack Plumb. Edward looked like a very naughty Russian girl. He had the profile and eyelashes of a Borzoi and was short, lissom and bendy. His gift with languages was prodigious. When we did our examinations for Oxford and/or Cambridge, which were in those days separate from A levels, there was a translation paper from which you had to choose two longish passages from among a dozen or so languages to translate into English. Edward had done them all, with time to spare, and waltzed off with a scholarship. This took courage. His older brother had earlier achieved distinction at the same college and taken his own life while still at university.

Edward did not live very much longer than that brother, but oh the delightful nuisance he caused in his life. He was completely kind and, of course, when we first met at the school classics club, 'The Interpretes', which was a decorous means of meeting boys, I lapped him up. He was having an affair with a Turkish air stewardess at the time. This strange reversion to what might be thought of as deviancy in the context of someone quite so camp, also struck him during the week of our Finals, when he fell head over heels in love with a magnificent girl, and sent her a dozen red roses every single day. They both emerged with congratulatory firsts.

I'm astonished that I have any friends from Cambridge. I was a dilatory worker, a shocking shirker of essays and supervisions, and I did not understand that it was perfectly possible to say no at any stage of the transaction should you be invited out by a member of the opposite sex. I had a powerfully developed sense of my own repulsiveness that cannot have been helped by the fashion for platform shoes that coincided with these years. Thus, when I did leave F6, I was six and a half feet high and, in some senses, quite unstable. There were three dons at Girton whom I feared and respected, though they might not have guessed it: Jill Mann for Chaucer, who spotted me at once for a coaster; Gillian Beer, who has, despite it all, become a friend; and Lady Radzinowicz, who, with her dachsund Pretzel, taught me Milton and Spenser. I was so nervous about leaving F6 and actually getting on to the missile-launcher bus for central Cambridge, that I attended relatively few lectures, though I developed a fondness for Professor J.A.W. Bennett who must have been about twelve hundred years old by then. It was also compulsory, for reasons of cool as well as literary curiosity, to attend the lectures of the poet J.H. Prynne. I adored watching him take words to bits.

One day a vision entered the lecture theatre. Of course I had seen beauties before and there were even two at Girton, but this was different. She was attired in a coat of a red fox and it was clear that her electrical and crackling head of hair weighed more than her etiolated and fashionably attired body, from her Manolo Blahnik boots to her Joseph jeans and her Sonia Rykiel jersey (I was a *Vogue* reader and could do the semiotics). We had a catwalk model among us and she was one big cat: Tamasin Day-Lewis.

Tamasin was at King's, a college full of interesting people who were not Girtonians. They included descendants of old Bloomsbury, precociously brilliant philosophers, a girl who lived with a man who had already sired children, and my beloved friend Rupert Christiansen, who allowed himself four minutes off work between breakfast and lunch and five in the afternoon for the ingestion of a cheese scone. Every vacation Rupert worked in the Arts Council bookshop in Sackville Street. He had one, orange needlecord, suit. Rupert is colour blind. He saved up every penny to go and stand in the gods at Covent Garden.

It says much for Rupert that he took me out to see the ballet *La Bayadère*. After three days' thought I dressed for this occasion in eight-inch cork platforms, white tights, a wraparound white cheesecloth skirt, a scarf tied across my by now ultra-skinny chest and an enticing new bubble perm inspired by the film of *The Great Gatsby* with Mia Farrow and Robert Redford. Rupert is a good six foot two and he weathered this fearful first date to become my daily correspondent, my test of decency, my measure of honour.

It was during Prelims that I realised that I could speak in tongues, or rather that I could do so if drunk enough and if the drink were whisky. Today I do not drink at all or I would be dead, and when people ask, 'Do you miss anything about drinking?' I can with perfect truth say no. But I do miss the smell of those island malts, that are nothing more or less than the smells of the islands themselves, of sea, of kelp, of heather, of peat, of wrack, of mist, of slow, slow burning.

I gave a party at the end of Cambridge, for my twenty-first birthday, for the friends I had somehow made. I sent out invitations on which I had drawn a bough with golden apples. The words written below invited each recipient to help me take my golden bow. The house in which the party took place belonged to none other than my present landlord, to whom, that first time, I was a lousy lodger, borrowing his tank tops, sending telegrams via his phone bill and continually introducing cats into the ménage. I remember Peggotty and Portnoy, who was a Siamese and therefore always complaining. In this may be glimpsed something of the golden character of Niall Hobhouse, who was Anthony Appiah's cousin. To my twenty-first birthday party, the golden bow, I wore a jumpsuit made of paper that I had sprayed gold, and gold cowboy boots. I had not neglected to spray my hair gold.

For some reason, just as the party got going, Katie told me to cook some crumpets. She talks so quickly that I frequently mishear. I have before now jumped out of a boat when she was just telling me to 'go about'. I set to with the crumpets and continued being my entertaining self, welcoming my friends and no doubt swigging along. For the record, Katie tells me that she was in Singapore on this occasion; so memory casts its dramas.

The grill began to send out little flames. I bent to attend to it. There was a thick smell of burning hair. The paint with which I had sprayed my hair and dungarees was gold car paint, highly flammable. I rushed upstairs dressed in flames, a zip, underwear and cowboy boots, drenched myself in the bath and returned later to my own party re-attired in some no doubt fearful ensemble, maybe even the £2.99 pink rubber dress from Sex on the King's Road.

At the party was my very quiet friend Amschel Rothschild. He wore a navy blue velvet suit, an expression of amusement on his face, one that might have been painted by El Greco, and a cymbidium from his hothouse in his buttonhole. He had neatly sprayed the orchid gold.

But for him, who took me out of Cambridge for the last weeks before Finals and set me to my books as you might set an animal to exercise, I should have had no kind of a degree, let alone the pleasure of discovering what it means really to work at a subject and how that pleasure has no end. While it may be solitary, it is, at its best, love and sight, or, rather, vision. A love in which there is no doubt that you wish to do the best you can, not for your own but for its sake. Amschel died far too young and I shall miss him till I die. So I owe him my 'good' degree and many more degrees of gratitude.

LENS II: Chapter 5

In the summer of 1976, there was a heat that dried the green out of England. It was possible to faint away when you stood up. Water was rationed. There was even, I believe, a Minister for Water, or perhaps he was a Minister for Drought. During that summer, I fainted on a train that was crossing Suffolk and woke up with words branded on my arm in sunburn: Second-Class. I had seldom travelled far; after all, England was quite far away from my first home in Edinburgh and Colonsay was in itself both domestic and utterly exotic. There had been Holland, Italy, Switzerland; nowhere outwith Europe.

Amschel had at the time the use of his parents' house in St James's on Barbados. The house was reminiscent of Caribbean life as it's not often advertised, a life of conversation, books and ideas. Amschel invited Tamasin and me to stay at the house and then to travel with him to Cape Cod to join his sister Emma.

Two days before travelling on this, to me, unimaginably complicated journey, I was on the tube on my way to work at *Vogue*. A nice young man called Simon Crow greeted me. I was standing; it was a crowded carriage. Simon was sitting down. He asked me what I was up to and I said that I was going on an aeroplane to Barbados and America. Simon was in the Foreign Office and knew his stuff, clearly.

'Have you got a passport and a visa?' he asked, still half asleep.

I had neither, but I did have a pair of pink stripy lounging trousers I'd sewn that I considered very suitable for Caribbean nights.

Simon Crow, who I think was at Oxford while I was at Cambridge, got me a passport in one day and stood in line to get me a visa. The sort of man you need in diplomacy.

The reader may not believe the following story. Or rather, it could not happen now, as old people say. Two days before my first wedding, my husband-to-be asked if I had a passport in my married name, since our honeymoon destination might require one. I really don't know whether I quailed within while looking noncommittal or if I confessed. What I did do was telephone the Passport Office in Petty France. The telephone was answered in those times by a person. I blurted out my story in all its idiotic detail:

'Getting married in two days; new surname going to be Wallop, yes that's right W-A-L-L-O-P; don't know where I'm going because it's my honeymoon; yes very happy indeed; I have got into a mess like this before and the person that helped me out was called Mr Potts.'

'This is Potts speaking.'

❖

But I'm travelling ahead of myself. In Barbados I learned how delicious are limes, that mace is the web that wraps itself around the nutmeg, that really good manners go all through a person, that Tamasin would be pre-eminent in whatever world she decided to take on, that you must never sunbathe under a manchineel tree or its tannic fruit will drip poison on you. I read all the books save for the esoterica concerning the world of spermatology (Amschel's father Victor Rothschild was a world expert on sperm as well as many other things including Jonathan Swift and the safe defusing of bombs). I sat on the white sand reading books and going blotchy in my Celtic fashion. Only one beach boy tried to pick me up during the whole ten days and he gave up on about day four when I said I was happy reading. 'You not a woman, you a machine.'

It's the quiet of the luxury of the place that I shall not forget, the white coral walls, the polished white coral floor, the stuffed white sofas and chairs, the delectable shade, the pale, light-lipped sea. In the library, the books were plump with sea salt, hygroscopically swollen. Books literally holding water is an theme for me since so much of my life has been spent at sea or enislanded.

The rain came promptly at siesta time, when Amschel would retire with verbally sophisticated modern authors whose drift he might sometimes explain to me later. Tamasin and I occasionally set out upon adventures, certainly the least bearable of which was a trip on a pirate vessel named the *Jolly Roger*. This vessel pumped out reggae for an hour in the middle of each afternoon, anchored offshore, offered limitless orange petrol to drink, and was operated by a captain with a strong line in innuendo; the voyage's highlight was a mock marriage involving a good deal of crazy foam and rice. I do not mind if I never have that kind of fun again. Tamasin, in her unapproachable beauty, fared rather better than a poiseless Scot absolutely lost without her book. The drink was at this stage of my life too nasty even for me to drink.

We flew to Boston and drove down boulevards of thrilling tackiness; here the Leaning Tower of Pizza, there 'Dan's Clams: the more you eat the more you get'. The house Emma and her friend Alexander Cockburn had taken for the summer was a silvery clapboard house with verandas, perfect for a reader of Updike. You could walk out along the quay and swim from it through soft yet salt water edged with rushes. Intelligence was again the air of the house, this time fashionably radical and very fast moving. Alexander made us Manhattans to drink. For some reason, although I had in Barbados been soaking up four or five daiquiris a day, that Manhattan did me in. I spoke in tongues, I howled, I went on and on about the things about which drunks go on and on, the things they drink to forget. I remember being excruciatingly boring about Colonsay, and going on too about mothers. I was out of my depth in all senses after two measures of bourbon, a sugar lump and some bitters.

Emma did what she does, which was remain white and cool. Alexander, having much and distinguished Irish blood, must have seen a drunk Celt before but I was terrified to meet anyone's eyes at breakfast, so I stayed upstairs for as long as I could reading *Paradise Lost*. I also found, read and was scared by *Hollywood Babylon* by

Kenneth Anger. Its photographs of dead people in undignified settings, head in the oven, perfect hairdo hanging out of a ruined car, stays with me. It set one register of my bad dreams. Somehow the shamefulness of the book attached itself to my shame about having got so drunk.

I reassembled myself and occurred brightly into the others' normal day at about eleven with the gelatinous acted normality that will be familiar to all who are or know alcoholics.

We progressed to New York, where Emma lived on Central Park West. Again the note in the house was of the Left, of books and the want of show. I discovered that New York was a walkable city, like Edinburgh, and loved it. I was unprepared for its expressive beauty, the variety of shapes, the quality of reciprocated light thrown between the buildings. Amschel fell for a Moholy-Nagy in the Guggenheim and drank gimlets at the Plaza Bar. We visited a bookshop at midnight and called in meals; what could be better?

Years later, when I was just over thirty, my Girtonian friend Miss Montague of Greenwich Village got married. She asked me to be one of her matrons of honour. There were, I believe, eight of us. I was much the tallest and the smallest was a groovy society photographer called Roxanne Lowitt who could look good in a brown bag. Sarah herself was a vision as a bride, lacy, light, frothing. I may have to go into the background of the garments worn by those of us in her train. Her mother was a balletomane and was to be found, as a rule, wherever in the world Nureyev was dancing. Sarah had one precious piece of material designed by Bakst for the *Ballets Russes*. It was a shimmering jungle silk, but there was hardly enough of it to go round eight people, so a plan had been devised. Each of our dresses, cut exactly to fit our disparate measurements, would bear at its neck a lozenge of the precious cloth.

So it was, on the afternoon after Sarah's graceful and affecting wedding ceremony, that I was accosted by Christopher Hitchens, somewhere near Union Square. I did notice that we were surrounded by people who were not conventionally dressed but, hey, this was the time of club culture and I must hang with it.

Christopher has one of the most compelling voices alive. I confess I bought on CD his book *god Is Not Great* simply in order to hear those tones, so smoothed by cigs, so enriched by the booze, so clever and hardly vain at all, so lubriciously dated and grand.

'Hi, Claude,' said Christopher. 'Happy Halloween. And what are you dressed as? A parsnip?'

As we returned to England in the aeroplane in 1976, Amschel asked if I'd like to be his lodger in Warwick Avenue. When I said yes thank you, I had no idea to what I was acceding. I did not know London in any sense at all. I had visited Madame Tussauds, a few antiquarian book-shops, Vogue House which is at number one Hanover Square, and perhaps a handful of fashion boutiques, Biba, Bus Stop and Laurence Corner Military Apparel, whose khaki siren suits were, with gold stiletto-heeled boots, my relaxation wear throughout the nineteen-seventies. I had no idea about the wires that hold a life together. All I knew was that I had that job on *Vogue*.

Warwick Avenue is a boulevard running down from Blomfield Road and the Regent's Canal. Ava Gardner had lived around here. The green cabmen's hut is famous among cabbies for the quality of its fry-ups. Amschel's flat had been lived in before by his sister Emma and Alexander Cockburn and had clearly lain at a nerve centre of sixties radicalism. The journal *Three Weeks* was published from there. The chastity of the décor was something that I have come to think of as a particular form of *le goût Rothschild*. The first flight of stone stairs was bare. At some point a large quantity of serviceable elephant-grey carpet had become available and there it was on the floors of the drawing room, the serious library, all the way up the next flight of stairs and into each bedroom beyond and so right to the very top attic room, which was to be the epicentre of some heartbreaks. Amschel himself was fastidious and exquisitely dressed. His trousers came from Beale & Inman, his suits from Anderson & Sheppard. He was twenty-one, his jeans were ironed, his shoes from Wildsmith. But he looked like a saint, not a dandy. He was attending the City University. He would return from the country with his clothes for the week beautifully ironed and ready for his week's study. Later he became the circulation manager of Ian Hamilton's *New Review*. No situation could have been more elegantly suited to him in all its minimalism. At weekends he raced classic cars. His room contained his bed and, leaning against the wall, one ormolu-framed mirror that may have come from Mentmore.

The drawing room at Warwick Avenue was furnished with a desk made of a single curve of wood, a sculpture by the Greek artist Takis that when switched on at the wall flashed its alternating yellow, green, purple and blue lights, and an elephantine set of sofa and chairs, comfortably expiring. We did have a telly. I think it sat on a pile of telephone directories. There was a pencil drawing by Léger over the desk. Occasionally, Amschel might visit the kitchen, halve an avocado with a surgeon's care, ease away its stone, and spoon a little Hellman's Mayonnaise into the depression. Once or twice I saw him cut a slice of bread and turn it by various processes into toast and Marmite.

His generosity in having, as lodger, one so improvident and domestically gifted only at cleaning rather than cooking, was typical of the sweetness within the formality of this complicated yet simple-hearted man. I paid no rent. We had no romance. I suppose it was poor Amschel upon whom I learned to cook. I spared him the dish that got me through much of Cambridge, rice cooked with Bovril or tomato ketchup or, when the occasion demanded protein, whelks. I am not sure I could look a whelk in the face now. I am not talking about winkles, but whelks, that have a keratinous front door the size of a thumbnail, a flesh-coloured body that looks like a plastic model of the inner ear, and, tremendously evident khaki digestive arrangements.

Amschel's father, who had mesmerising and often alarming charm, asked me one day whether I could cook Sole Colbert. I liked saying yes to Victor and sometimes his early morning calls demanding, for example, a crested ear trumpet, were challenges that it was amusing to rise to. I cannot imagine how his tenderly beautiful wife Tess and he got down the astounding brew I had made over three days' reduction of beef bones. I had reinvented Bovril itself. I suppose Tess, as she always did, made it all right.

Meanwhile, I was learning the magazine trade from the bottom up. I am uncoordinated and not good with knives. Layout in those days involved the cutting out of individual letters with a scalpel and their placing at the actual point upon the page demanded by the art director. *Vogue*'s art director at the time was the innovative Terry Jones. The really fascinating people in the art room were the retouchers, who did by hand what computers do now, that is, make perfection real, with eyes as minutely observant as those of a jeweller, using brushes as fine as the tip of an ermine's tail. With almost buddhistic patience and only the most cryptic of chat, these quiet, gifted people would lift a face on film from pleasantness into beauty by the application of tiny dots. At least one was a refugee from Austria. I could imagine her retouching for Horst, for Baron de Meyer. I imagine the retouchers spoiled their eyesight, though they did have lenses much like those a watchmaker might use. The rhythm of our weeks was ruled by 'The Book', which was the magazine itself. Copy dates were long and dictated by the seasons of the couture, so we lived always in an unreal, future time. There was nothing more precious than the dummy of the next issue, which would be full of 'stories' that had been thought out by the fashion room well in advance and dictated by some shift in collective mood as mysterious as the great annual migrations.

My first summer at *Vogue* was a summer of cream. All the girls in the fashion room had the look. If you didn't understand how to have the look, you couldn't be in the fashion room. The girls in the fashion room were riveting to observe. They had a susceptibility to trend and nuance that is germane to what keeps capitalism rolling round. In some this amounted to pure artistry; I think of Sheila Wetton, who had been Molyneux's house model and who wore gloves to work every day; of flame-like Grace Coddington who cannot but breathe out new trends as she exhales, yet moves in classicism like the night; of Liz Tilberis, who epitomised for me fresh-faced, freckly, friendly, calico-wearing chic even though she ended a perfect size four for couture, thanks to cancer. The girls in the fashion room hardly spoke to the girls in Copy, or even in Features, where I ended up.

Our editor, Miss Beatrix Miller, was to me like a far less specious version of the headmistress of Sherborne. It may seem crass to compare a fashion magazine with that excellent girls' school and the Church Missionary Society to which Dame Diana dedicated her life, but Beatrix Miller was an individual who was utterly committed to seeing and getting the best in and from everyone she worked with and who worked under her. Her leadership was generous; she was not an icon but an inspiration No liberties were to be taken yet her thoughtful-ness was boundless, her private kindness silently conducted. Her office door was guarded by the magnificent Ingrid Bleischroder who was delivered to work in her father's Rolls. Miss Miller, which was what we called her, seemed to live on fizzy Redoxon tablets. She had good hands and pencilled the underside of each nail in white crayon. Everything was in the detail.

Having acquitted myself hopelessly in the area of layout, since I vomited every time the Cow Gum was used, I was shuffled magnani-mously into Features via Copy. At the time, *Vogue* had such writers working for it as James Fenton, Charles Maclean and Lesley Blanch. Polly Devlin, Antonia Williams and Georgina Howell were staff writers. The standard was high. I was allowed to start with writing captions. This isn't an easy matter. You have to consider the ego of the photog-rapher, the needs of the manufacturer of any garments depicted, who may be an advertiser, the size of the page, the demands of the font, and of course the story. I spent days thinking up the words 'Double cream layers'. The photographer was Eric Boman, the model Beska and the lingerie was made by Janet Reger and Courtenay of Bond Street. The story was 'Girl alone in bathroom in Grand Hotel with many diamonds and very few clothes. What, this side of decency, does she get up to?'

My particular incapacity was to remember to ask what the price of the garment was, so that sometimes a page might go to press with a pound sign followed by a hopeful row of zeros waiting for the real price to come through. The practicalities of working co-operatively on a magazine are similar to those of working on a film and require many of the same adaptive qualities. You need to be practical, quick-witted, resourceful, outgoing, good at working with other people, unflappable, not remotely touchy, able to cope in extreme tempera-ture conditions and capable of soothing persons spoilt to the point of psychopathy. Miss Miller and her team did all this, and more, and evidently loved every minute. I was as bad at working on a magazine as I was later to prove duff at writing a film, though that film work did bring me two invaluable things; an attachment to Stanley Kubrick, who had asked me to write a film for him, and the startlingly prophetic words for my affliction, blepharospasm, which is indeed Eyes Wide Shut, the name of that film about my failure to write which Stanley was wryly graceful.

I came into work on my bike and left it in the *Vogue* car park under-ground. I worked out a uniform that would keep me unnoticed at first which was a pair of Amschel's jeans, my school beige V-neck and a fox-fur scarf I had got for ten pounds (a lot of money) in a junk shop. I gave up eating, following a regime larcenously entitled 'the doctor's diet'. I ate a boiled egg and four prawns per day, but I did feel I was starting to fit in a bit more. I was moved from Copy, where my boss had been a pretty grey-haired lady who was fond of bird-watching and possessed unaccountably right-wing views, on to Features, where my boss was Joan Juliet Buck, Hollywood name to conjure with, playmate of the stars and later to be editor of French *Vogue*. At this point in her life she wore only the colour purple. It was to do with something Karl Lagerfeld, a close friend, had told her. Her eyes were purple, deep purple all around the iris's edge. Her skin was white.

Joan was precisely the sort of person who is unique in style and therefore frustrates those legions who emulate her; that is part of being truly chic. I thought I might take up this monochrome business and I chose as my colour, probably because I am so chromatically indecisive, pure white. Between Joan and me was the admirably sane Lucy Hughes-Hallett. One day it was Lucy's twenty-seventh birthday. 'Oh my God you are so young,' drawled perfectly *maquillé* Joan between taking calls and reading the celebrity bulletin to see who was in town that day. Her furs were good, and embroidered, as proper furs should be, with their owner's name on the silk lining. Joan was interesting, kind and clever and I wanted to do something to please her. She was off out to lunch. Would I take her messages? Of course I would. Joan was engaged at the time. In a density of tailored yet clinging mauve, her black hair cut so perfectly that it had a ring of light around the top, Joan set forth for lunch, I just happened to know, with Donald Sutherland.

Joan knew all the stars, so I wasn't surprised and I sat close to her phone to be really helpful and take messages in case it rang.

In due course Joan's telephone did ring.

I picked it up.

'May I speak to Joan?'

'No, I'm sorry.'

'Who is this?'

Although I had won the *Vogue* Talent Contest in my natal name, Candia McWilliam, I was very confused about names and many people knew me by my nickname Claude and the surname Howard, so, more often than not, I got into great knots of explanation. I can't remember the name that I gave to my interlocutor but he did turn it on me. Let us say that he said, 'Well, Claude Howard, where is Joan?'

'Oh that's easy,' I chirruped, 'she's out at lunch.'

Forms of breathing that I should have had the instinct to recognise were audible. This was a powerful individual, changing into another conversational gear entirely.

With horrible adult lightness this man asked me with whom Joan was having lunch. The part of my brain that knew that Joan was engaged to someone ceased to function. The thought that this man might be that someone did not proffer itself. I just remembered the interesting bit and walked into the dragon's mouth as I smiled daffily into that cupping receiver, 'Oh, she's having lunch with Donald Sutherland.' There was a tremendous roar and a slam.

Joan, who arrived back at the office after coffee and petits fours, was sweet about it. I was so lucky in her and the other features writers that I did what I can do when things seem to be going rather well. I sabotaged them.

In the interests of this fascinatingly changing, daily thinner everyday me, I had forsworn alcohol. But it is perfectly possible for an alcoholic to be drunk on mood, tension or state of mind.

I was being courted by a number of countervalent men, at least three of them alarming on account of age, force, tastes or marital status. They took me at what was increasingly my face value, or rather decreasingly my face value, a skinny babe (that word was not yet coined with reference to people older than two) who worked at *Vogue*. I had no idea how to transmit to them that I was a trapped bookish fatty who was no good at working at *Vogue*.

I don't know when I stopped going into the office, but I do remember, and I thank her for it, that Miss Miller sent me telegram after telegram asking me if I was all right when I imagine she could have sued or sacked me. I wrote her letters that I never sent and some, years later, that I did send, and do not even know where she is or if she is alive today, but I must be one of the most disappointing outright winners of the *Vogue* Talent Contest ever. I was just too scared to go back into that office. Having turned myself into a caricature of what I saw, I behaved like someone with an empty head. I froze like a thin white woman with a head full of snow.

It's not a secret that *Vogue* in those days ran on the labour of gently reared girls with private income, so that, for example, it was possible to find Lady Jane Spencer in the Beauty Room, and a descendant of Pushkin and the Wernher mining family, who later became a virtuosic mime artist, in the administration department. It would be unfair on Condé Nast though to ascribe my defection simply to my not being able to afford to work there.

Addicted to magazines as I am, I could not bear seeing behind their pages. I was like the opposite of a conjuror who likes to make magic from his practical skills. I could not bear the bright light shed upon my dreams. I had grown ill within the very breeding ground of consumption.

There was a bad period of hiding and pretending to be going to work, but the 50ps ran out and even when I had pawned my mother's jewellery box for eight pounds (it was ebony, silver, mother-of-pearl, had crystal phials and a box of mercury powder for wigs, was made in the eighteenth century and contained its bill of sale, handwritten; she had given it to me for my fifth Easter), even when I'd saved up cider bottles and taken them back to the off-licence to redeem the 10p on each one, even then I knew that the only sort of work I could do, with any honesty, was writing. I had dropped a stitch somewhere by not applying for a doctorate, by lazily, unthinkingly, slipping into my prize job at *Vogue*.

Happy outcomes from my time at *Vogue* were friendships. Two friends I had made just before *Vogue*, one the little sister of Alexandra Shulman, who went on to edit *Vogue*. Alex and I were friends but I was, I felt, too impractical for her; I remain devoted to her and impressed and rather intimidated by her. Her little sister Nicola became a friend of the heart. Beauty is an impossible characteristic. Women want to have affairs with men who have had affairs with beauties, as if it will up the octane of their own looks. Nicky is shrewd and innocent, a real writer, scholarly and kind. It just so happens that the capsule her soul is contained in is a beautiful one.

At school at St Paul's with Alexandra were the famously terrifying

Fraser girls. The Frasers lived in Camden Hill Square. Notoriously, a neighbour of theirs had been killed by an IRA bomb intended for their father Hugh Fraser. Hugh Fraser was an example to me of everything a man might be. He looked like an eagle, he took mustard on his smoked salmon, he sang to his dog, he was upright, noble and all the Alan Breck virtues.

Flora Fraser possesses that smile to be found on some ancient sculptures, referred to as the archaic smile. It is the sad smile, the smile of an all-knowing Clio, muse of history. When first we met, Flora was reading Greats at Wadham and I was at Girton – no, it goes further back. I remember a sixteenth birthday party at Camden Hill Square and precisely what I wore, footless tights in strong pink and a knitted transparent pink lamé nightgown together with my, at the time, candy pink and hot pink striped hair all twisted up in a bun. Flora married very young her peer in intellect and in love. She was still at university. Her husband Robert Powell-Jones had read Russian and Chinese. His intelligent beauty shook with the tension and pitch of his mind. He danced on a high wire in that head.

They learned Turkish and Italian together, living on love and carrot sticks. Their daughter Stella was born to them one glorious May the 15th. But Robert carried in him what I carry too and he did not escape it. They tried everything but in the end he died before Christmas 1997. He had just completed his translation of Pushkin's *The Bronze Horseman*. It might almost be as though Robert's own subtlety, that was compromised by the harm drink did him, has after death joined itself in posthumous conjunction with Flora's own subtlety. I could not have managed my life without this strong friendship that she has thrown to me when I thought there was no one in the sea but sharks and minnows.

So somehow I ended up after *Vogue* working first in a joke shop and then for a decorous old-style pornographer on Old Street, which was not the fashionable area it is now. In addition to packing tired copies of *Fanny Hill* and trying to get off the ground a rather interesting-sounding book about the Blunt family and equine blood-lines, I ended up, thinner yet this time, and attired in white, but in rather the same situation I had found myself in at the very beginning of *Vogue*, ineptly laying out a magazine with scalpel, cardboard and Cow Gum, though now in a small room in Old Street with one man instead of Vogue House with all its varied and often congenial wildlife.

This time it was the AA membership magazine that I was laying out badly, the AA being a large organisation that comes to the rescue of motorists in distress and whose headquarters are in Basingstoke. My new boss, the Old Street one, who regularly paid me in cash on a Friday morning and borrowed much of it back on Friday after-noons, took me on a trip to Basingstoke. We underwent a lunch with the bigwigs from the Automobile Association in their local hostelry. Mention was made of my having worked on *Vogue*. This to demon-strate experience with layout. I deprecated loudly but no one was reading my body language. The AA headquarters was, at that time, one of the tallest buildings in Basingstoke and from its boardroom might be viewed the Wiggins Teape building, known locally as the Hanging Gardens of Basingstoke. I laughed, then saw that my reac-tion was not the right one and sucked in the laugh.

I knew that I was acting and that I shouldn't have been given the part, should never have auditioned for it. Anyone in their right mind would have sent me away as had the kind lady at Konrad Furs in South Molton Street, who simply said, when I went in there and asked for a job, 'Do you really think you're suitable, dear? Aren't you a bit over-qualified? How much do you know about selecting pelts?'

Out beyond the edges of Basingstoke, a town that grew almost as one watched it, were roundabouts, aspin with vehicles, their owners very likely members themselves of the AA. Our presentation having been accepted, we were appointed designers to the Automobile Association of their monthly magazine. Going down in the lift, my boss said, 'Seems a pity all that land being built on around Basingstoke. Still, you've got to put people somewhere and it's as good a place as any.' And so I got the layout job for the AA. The prefiguring of my being practically laid out before I got to the other kind of AA is not too neat to be true.

I stayed with this job for about a year, my ineptitude in most areas outstripped by that of my boss, over whom there was a Mr Big of whose visits I lived in fear. In another part of the building, doing I do not know what, worked a tired-looking man named Mr Bunce, whose assistant Nanette came in one day with what looked very like a broken jaw. The one solid benefit of the job was that opposite the office there was that beautiful repository for the dead, Bunhill Fields, where I walked when I could, reading the stones.

But by now I was learning to take a certain amount of care of myself. Our lugubrious next-door neighbour in Warwick Avenue, Tobias Rodgers, a dealer in Spanish incunabula, threw a tablecloth over his ping-pong table and had a party. At this party I enjoyed a conversation about Hogarth, about building wooden ships, about the deliciousness of non-fizzy Champagne, about how weird it was to be the only Jewish family in your small town in New England. I had met the man who was to stop me going out dressed inappropriately, make me eat more sensibly, and show me, in the Cosy Fish and Supper Bar in Whitecross Street, opposite my workplace in Old Street, how to eat a gherkin properly. For a start it was called a pickle. His band was called The Forbidden and their number 'Ain't Doin' Nothin'' was number forty-three in the New Wave charts. His *nom de guerre* was Jet Bronx. He is now more ordinarily known as Loyd Grossman.

<hr />

As we worked on this chapter together and I gradually lost sight, Liv and I speculated as to what lies at the root of the changes that dictate fashion. I said to her that I'd always thought of it in two ways; that, as it were, there might be a cobalt mountain somewhere and therefore, to keep to cobalt prices high, blue must be the colour for the coming season. So I'd thought of it visually, the colours laid out as you see great heaps of pigment in soft triangles set in low brass bowls at the roadside in India.

The other way I'd thought of it is as an enormous sneeze of influence, so that everyone under the age of forty suddenly thinks that she has invented the notion of edging a cardigan with velvet or pinning an outsized rose on to her lapel. The great trick is the usual one with capitalism: how to make everyone feel that they are expressing their individual self by purchasing the very same thing as many millions of others. Who are the great sneezers of influence? People imagine that it is the fashion editors, but I think the truth is more mysterious and lies deep at the root of the levels of discontent with themselves that are imposed upon women and that we embrace with such delight and appetite.

———◆◆◆———

I had, in London, broadly, two milieux when I first arrived there in 1976: homosexual men and grown-ups. Of course they often overlapped. The first world set me at my ease when I talked, as the purely heterosexual world did not quite. Drawn as I was to art historians, architectural historians and painters, I found myself often the only girl in a room. I was fond of dancing and with my close friend James Fergusson, an individual of impeccably sober mien, antiquarian bookseller and revolutionary of the newspaper obituary, I used to jump about a lot in gay clubs. Jamie is entirely of the marrying kind and I have the privilege of being godmother to his daughter Flora, who would be horrified to see how her father and I, whose common ground is fundamentally bookish and topographical since we are both Scots with a close interest in stone carving and every matter of calligraphy, font or letterpress, cut capers in the Embassy Club, Country

Cousin and other dives. The other thing we did by night was drive in James's Mini-Clubman van, looking at churches and the streets of the City. On these drives I would come closer to understanding my father's detailed love of London.

What was I living on during these days? I sold a lot of my clothes, I didn't eat unless I was taken out, I had a little overdraft, and I got mortifying jobs. I ghosted two books and modelled for Levi's Jeans. It is a nice point that my first husband's second wife was auditioned for the Levi's job, but her bottom wasn't big enough. I was conscious that I was wasting time and that I should be spending my days accumulating and building words or else teaching in some context or another. I wrote tiny pieces for the *TLS*, the *Spectator*, anyone that would have me. Essentially, these publications were doing me favours. I had no sense of building a career. I was flashy-looking but recessive.

The moment any form of recognition or success looked as though it might be looming, I scarpered. I longed for routine, for a project, for a means of making something with what I was fairly sure I had, some kind of baker's gift to leaven things.

Instead I woke up every morning with my heart battering in fear of I did not know what as the cavalry horses trotted down Warwick Avenue in the dawn. If I had enough money I would buy a newspaper, occasionally applying for jobs. On the way to get the paper, I would say good morning to Stanley, the tramp who sat on the bench outside the house in Warwick Avenue. Of course he knew my name. I always gave him the money I didn't have.

One day Stanley was reading a rather thick-looking book.

'Good morning, Stanley,' I said. 'Is it any good?'

'Don't look, Candia,' said Stanley. 'I'm masturbating.'

I was reading all the time, munching through the shelves at Warwick Avenue and rereading *Under the Volcano* suspiciously many times, though I still didn't know what was wrong. I remember overhearing Christopher Hitchens recommending *The Blood of the Lamb* by Peter de Vries to Martin Amis. I read it. I wanted that kind of steer on what to read next.

One or two properly adult friends had the energy and gumption to tell me to sit still and write a book, but I still hung back. My friend the publisher John Calman was angry at how I was, as he saw it, wasting my life by failing to write. He shouted accurate and therefore even sorer accusations of time-wasting and expense of spirit at me in an echoing restaurant. I took umbrage, mainly I guess because I knew he was right. We fell into a stand-off. John was murdered in France at the age of thirty-seven by a hitch-hiker who used as his weapon cooking knives that John's mother had given him. Nothing seemed susceptible of redress. This talented wilful passionate man had cared enough to say what should have been said. He paid me the honour of interfering as too few adults had in my wilful self-sabotage. If I had been attentive to John then, some disasters of my own if not of his life might perhaps have been averted. It is dreadful like a red spider shot into the head to think of his end. I dream of it never less than once a month, hoping to have reversed it by the time I waken. His mother outlived her son.

A new lodger came to Warwick Avenue. She had superabundant talent but also required system. When first she came to live with us the contained, feline Angela Gorgas was executing a series of quasi-tantric Indian miniatures for the *Playboy* millionaire Victor Lownes. Angela was angel-like, too, from every angle, actually embodying the entirety of her implausibly suitable name. She had hyacinthine locks, sooty eyes, a tremendous laugh, seemed to talk without moving her mouth, was half my size and was at the epicentre of more love polyhedra than one telephone line and front door could easily accommodate. If your arm was worth having then Angela was on it. She also made a sweet friend.

I became distracted from my own life's path in the plots of the lives of others. I had no very strong sense, except when I was dressed up, of who to be. When dressed, I often overheard things that I disapproved of or feared. At one dinner party, evidently culled from the tips of various social icebergs, I overheard the unforgettably wrong-headed sentence, 'That man is a traitor to his adopted class.' I want one day to write the novel that fits around those self-revealing words.

I was learning the Lily Bart lesson but not taking it in.

Some of my friends were starting to get little dry coughs that wouldn't go away. One friend I nagged at for a whole evening to go to the doctor. How he must have wished to back me away and how politely he concurred and said he would. They started to die in threes, the more outrageous ones, the ones who had given themselves girls' names or only wore leather. Surprising people got thinner and thinner and then were dead. It was like a race that you did not want to win whose starting pistol had a silencer.

I received a long letter about the importance of d'Annunzio and about the health of his two Afghan hounds from my schoolfriend Edward Stigant weeks after he died in hospital in Milan. So his mother lost two of her three sons too soon.

Then, at last, I found a proper job rather than a hand-to-mouther. When people asked me the name of where I worked, they said, 'You've made it up!'

Well I hadn't, and it was a wonderful job, though I was a rotten employee. I was hired to write copy for an advertising agency whose name really was Slade, Bluff and Bigg. It was of small size and, which was startling for an advertising agency in the approach to the nineteen-eighties, radiant with principle. For every flashy account we had, there was a charity, for every glittery client, a quietly decent one. I was happy in my work, though I cannot believe how patient were my employers. Mr Slade, who was very musical, was a dedicated Liberal, the only Liberal indeed on the Greater London Council. His brother Julian wrote *Salad Days*. Mr Bigg had had a distinguished career in a much larger agency and lent calm authority to every meeting. Mr Bluff was a real sweetie and could handle such tricky clients as Gucci and Kutchinsky with his velvet paws. The agency was in bosky South Kensington. I had a room to myself.

I shall never forget the art director because he told me two things: one was to write a book right *then* and the other that drink was no good for me because my character changed when I drank. And this was someone who had never seen me drunk. He himself never drank. I took neither piece of advice.

Loyd was in America pursuing his career in the world of punk. Actually, now I come to think of it, I suppose the answer to the question posed in passing above, about who creates the world's fashions and trends, is probably none other than Loyd Grossman, sauce-supremo and anagrammatical arts tsar, and other such poly-national panurges.

To a considerable degree, the meta-Loyd whom the public sees was a creation of the nineteen-eighties. When first I met him he was writing a doctorate at the LSE about the effect of distilled spirits on the eighteenth-century working class in London and the author of a crisp book about the history of rock music. How less direct might his trajectory have been had he settled down with me and written treatises on the lesser-known pupils of Verrocchio.

Many of my Cambridge friends had departed to become profes-sors in America. Perhaps it was a Hogmanay on Colonsay that drove Simon Schama off these shores for good? He certainly hated it so much that he mentioned it on *Desert Island Discs*. I felt so sorry, but I understood exactly. It was a mixture of heartbreak, weather, and what he apprehended as a glimpse of unreconstructed Philistia at play. He took refuge in the library at Colonsay House that he pronounced to be a decent though unadventurous Whig library. The record he chose to epitomise his short sojourn on the island was the Sex Pistols' 'God Save the Queen'. I'm sad he got that glimpse, and I have seen things through those eyes too, but the truth is, as always, more compli-cated. My Oxford friends had settled into their vocations, Rosa into cell biology, Jamie Fergusson into the world of antiquarian book-selling, my friend Fram Dinshaw into becoming himself a don at Oxford. Niall Hobhouse had left Cambridge early and set up as an art dealer specialising in art and artefacts relating to India. He is now profoundly involved with the philosophy and practice of architecture and of public housing. His public service genes came to get him.

◆◆◆◆◆

In the story of a life, according to the best-conducted experts on etiquette, there are but three times when one should appear in a newspaper: when one is born, when one dies and, in the middle, when one marries.

On our first date, Quentin Wallop told me that he would never ask anyone to marry him.

We became engaged not very long thereafter. We married on 10 February 1981 in the church of St Martin-in-the-Fields in Trafalgar Square. We chose the church with its sublime spire and then un-restored and umbrageous interior because Quentin was a dedicated circumnavigator of the globe under sail and it is the church of seafarers, and for its architecture, and on account of the charitable work it does among the addicts and the homeless of London.

My father, that is, my blood parent, had suggested that we marry in St Magnus the Martyr, for T.S. Eliot: 'Inexplicable splendour of Ionian white and gold'. But there was some problem with parking.

Eyes were very important in our swift courtship. Quentin saw me across a room in Marsham Court where he was living. My impression was of hand-painted wallpaper, celadon in tone, and a young man with gold hair not apparently enjoying his own party. We did not speak. No one introduced us. I had just returned from India, where I had gone to convince a friend that it was home that he was pining for and not me, so I was rather thin and must have seemed interesting on account of not having slept for some days. Quentin made enquiries as to who I was and moves were made towards an introduction. We were both motherless, both tall, both longing for affection, both serious about children and animals and we each believed that we could make the other happy. With so much breakage in our pasts, too many house-moves, too much unsettledness, we married, we felt, with our eyes and hearts open.

Another romance was shaking confetti over the nation at the time. I was surprised when pretty Lady Diana Spencer chose my dress-maker to make her wedding dress, but who could be annoyed for very long, when *my* handsome prince was there? Our (I cannot say 'my'; it was 'our' wedding after all) wedding dress was entirely covered with glass sequins, each one colourless, each one exactly like a tiny pierced contact lens.

My dress had a million eyes and it was to the future that they were turned as I went down the aisle on Papa's arm towards my groom in the soft gloom of that great church, thirty feet of Argos-eyed glass and white taffeta train pouring itself down the aisle behind me. Daddy was in a front pew, having professed himself delighted not to have to take a central role; I wonder now.

From the tiara that held up my hair, released for the day from the Bank of Montreal, fell a long veil over my face. It too was scattered with brilliant lenses that made me feel as though I was seeing the day and the man to whom it gave me through shining tears of unquestionable joy.

Were marriages so tidy as to be best composed of opposites, how well we might have done; but in some ways I think we were too profoundly alike and are able better to love one another when not under the same roof but equal in our love for our children. Quentin is incontrovertibly the hero type. He camps under the stars with the Tuareg, he walks the Karakoram Highway, he loves the Hindu Kush, he is involved in the rehabilitation of boy soldiers in Sierra Leone. He works for the Red Cross. He does hidden good. When we met I thought he was ridiculously handsome with golden hair and a terrific beak like the old Duke of Wellington and he knew how to do things. I thought that it was pretty much as exotic as being able to stay on a bucking bronco to be able to drive, so it was inevitable that I became infatuated with this person who could do so much that I could not and to whom I felt I had so much to give. I did feel he was a kind of merman and it is the cruellest of fates to which, to this day, he will not allude, that his beautiful boat, *Ocean Mermaid*, launched by his mother, was burned in an accidental shipyard fire long after we parted.

However, it is restorative to see him on one of his hunters, Gus, Monty or Graf, and realise that he is once again connecting himself with the life for which he was made and that is in his blood.

In the dining room at his house at Farleigh are two tall portraits by Sir Francis Grant, depicting Isaac Newton Wallop, the 5th Earl, and his wife, Lady Eveline Herbert. The 5th Earl refused a marquessate and the Garter from Gladstone, thinking them 'beyond his merits'. This Earl and Countess had twelve children and she embroidered a chair cover during each pregnancy, still managing somehow, in between all of it, to gather up into her social life, albeit briefly, Henry James, who wrote to his father from Eggesford, the Portsmouth house in Devon:

I am paying a short visit at what I suppose is called here a 'great house', vis. at Lord Portsmouth's. Lady P, whom I met last summer at Wenlock Abbey and who is an extremely nice woman, asked me a great while since to come here at this point, for a week. I accepted for three days, two of which have happily expired – for when the moment came I was very indisposed to leave London. That is the worst of invitations, given you so long in advance, when the time comes you are apt to be not at all in the same humour as when they were accepted . . .

The place and country are, of course, very beautiful and Lady P, 'most kind'; but though there are several people in the house (local gentlefolk, of no distinctive qualities) the whole thing is dull. This is a large family, chiefly of infantine sons and daughters (there are twelve!) who live in some mysterious part of the house and are never seen. The one chiefly about is Lord Lymington, the eldest one, an amiable youth of twenty-one attended by a pleasant young Oxford man, with whom he is 'reading'. Lord P. is simply a great hunting and racing magnate, who keeps the hounds in this part of the country, and is absent all day with them. There is nothing in the house but pictures of horses – and awfully bad ones at that.

The life is very simple and tranquil. Yesterday, before lunch, I walked in the garden with Lady Rosamund, who is not 'out', and doesn't dine at table, though she is a very pretty little pink and white creature of 17; & in the p.m. Lady P. showed me her boudoir which she is 'doing up', with old china &c.; and then took me to drive in her phaeton, through some lovely Devonshire lanes. In the evening we had a 'ballet'; i.e. the little girls, out of the schoolroom, came down into the gallery with their governess and danced cachuckas, minuets &c. with the utmost docility and modesty, while we sat about and applauded.

Today is bad weather, and I am sitting alone in a big cold library, of totally unread books, waiting for Lord Portsmouth, who has offered to take me out & show me his stable & kennels (famous ones), to turn up. I shall try & get away tomorrow, which is a Saturday as I don't think I could stick out a Sunday here . . . it may interest you [to] know, as a piece of local color that, though there are six or seven resident flunkies here, I have been trying in vain, for the last half hour, to get the expiring fire refreshed. Two or three of them have been in to look at it – but it appears to be no one's business to bring in coals . . .

I have come to my room to dress for dinner in obedience to the bell, which is just being tolled. A footman in blue and silver has just come in to 'put out' my things – he almost poured out the quantum of water I am to wash by. The visit to the stables was deferred till after lunch, when I went the rounds with Lord P. and a couple of men who were staying here – forty in numbers, horses, mostly hunters & a wonderful pack of foxhounds – lodged like superior mechanics.

Although I have a soft spot for the 5th Earl, who is good-looking and sounds decent, one can feel that Henry James wasn't perhaps putting his back into those so beautifully maintained dumb animals. During these blind years, I've been playing all sorts of silly games along the lines of who would you rather among the great writers be stuck in a boat with, and at first I thought the answer was a toss-up between George Eliot and Proust. But now I think, if we're ruthless and it had to be one, let's have Henry James. We can hide his correspondents Robert Louis Stevenson and Turgenev in his greatcoat pockets.

LENS II: Chapter 6

If my own is a story of uprooting and its effects, so is that of my first husband, about whom I shall take the course of writing as little as he would wish. We married in love and in good faith and are the parents of two beloved children. We come high in one another's lives and have only kind thoughts for one another. We are both of a romantic temperament, both shy and both with an instinct to place trust in a metaphysical belief system that includes God. Quentin is a confirmed Christian. When I stand next to him in church, which I do quite frequently, I feel my own shaky faith strengthened by the directness of his.

I did not become confirmed when the opportunity to be so arrived at boarding school, taking the pi line that most of the other girls were doing it to please their parents and to get a nice string of pearls or a pretty diamond cross. I should have become confirmed then, because it would have so pleased my McWilliam grandmother. Quentin's story of deracination and its redress is geographically (and in other ways) more dramatic than my own and I shall tell it sparely. Born in Spain, he was a young child in Australia. He loves the sea and ships. At a very tender age, he was sent to prep school at Farleigh House School. His grandfather, sensing after the war that big houses might be doomed, had leased his own to this institution, a primarily Roman Catholic prep school, and moved to Kenya. Thus Quentin was at school among boys of a different religious denomination; he had an Australian accent and was being schooled in a house that was, actually, his own. While he keeps many friends from those days, it was greatly to his satisfaction when the lease expired in 1983 to be able to restore and to re-enter his ancestors' home. The school relocated to Red Rice in Andover. There is now no sense to the house that it ever was anything but a happy family home. People who were at the school are astonished by the difference.

One way of being evasive in a memoir or whatever it is that my mouth is making in an attempt to get my eyes to open, is to take refuge, as Anthony Powell so gruesomely enjoyably and teasingly does in his own memoirs, in genealogy. I shan't do that. Histories of the Wallop family may be found elsewhere.

Perhaps the most humanly relevant fact about the Wallop family is that they are known as the Red Earls on account of the heir more often than not having ruby-red hair. Our son Oliver, who was named for Cromwell – one of the Wallops was a regicide – was born on 22 December 1981. His names are also Henry Rufus. I got to choose this third quite unrejectable name. As soon as a little bit of the baby's head was visible, Quentin was convinced that he would be a boy, and a boy indeed he was, with a fiery head, at birth and ever since, of scarlet hair. It was a hard snowy winter and we spent Christmas at Basingstoke District Hospital, dizzy with joy and completely ignorant of how to feed our huge son. The NHS gave us a knitted Santa which is still in the day nursery at Farleigh. It was the middle of the shooting season, so Quentin would be busy in the day and then slide in his Land Rover back to me in the hospital with big dishes of salami that he had bought at I Camisa in Soho and sliced paper thin. Other mothers who gave birth in December 1981 may remember this handsome man handing around plates of cured Italian meats in his delight at being a father, and it was indeed to be a father that Quentin himself was born. His story of deracination makes for an absolute fix on steadiness as a parent.

Our honeymoon took place in Mexico. I had forgotten to get an American visa and even Mr Potts couldn't swing it. This time, the crazy luck came from the fact that Papa was very briefly a Minister of State for Defence under Mrs Thatcher, who sacked him I think for being too left-wing; 'wet' was the word of the day. Phone calls were made and on our stopover in Los Angeles I was guarded, including on 'comfort visits', by armed police. Quentin is an experienced, hardy, courageous, adventurous and curious traveller. He was completely thrown to discover that he had married someone who turned to jelly at the thought of arranging a train trip from Basingstoke to London. He says that I offered to do the washing-up on our first long-haul flight together. In those days there was a sort of drawing room in the forehead of very fat aeroplanes, which I used to like. It felt solid. It was like being a citizen of Celesteville, Babar's immaculately rational and so French city, all curves and absence of threat, while sitting up in the top of those fat jumbos.

We arrived in Mexico City in the middle of the night. I sent my sparkly pink and grey going-away outfit to the dry cleaner and, true to form, it returned doll-sized the next day. It made for a good grounding that I had read *Under the Volcano* so many times

But I was completely unprepared to conceive of the minds that could build the pyramids of unmortared stone that we climbed in the Yucatan. The solidity of such abstraction, the mathematical judgement and forethought required to cut each constituent stone just so and to cut it but with another stone, that obsidian axe, all this not only overwhelmed but terrified me. I found myself thinking about their thought and failing to conceive of how even to begin to think about it. It argued mental processes of such developed abstraction, whose result was transformed into something solid, and that felt deathly itself. There were no merciful flaws, was no tolerance of looseness.

It is common knowledge that the Mexicans go and picnic on the graves of their ancestors, taking food for the dear dead. Perhaps that was what I couldn't supply imaginatively as I stood in the court where allegedly a game had been played with human heads, or when I looked into the stone face of the rain god Chac Mool at the summit of one of the pyramids. It was a relief to see that his uncomfortable pose and lugubrious features looked exactly like James Fergusson, who would have made an improbable Mayan.

In between visits in the dawn before the great heat rolled over these ancient sites, we drove with our guide Mr Cervantes, prodigiously belted around his generous tum, and visited churches whose inner gold was like being swallowed by the burning sun itself, though they were lit low and only brushed by little candles.

In Oaxaca, I was briefly kidnapped. Quentin found me in the police station. There had been a misunderstanding and a perfectly genial crowd of kidnappers had thought I was Jimmy Connors's new wife, who was apparently a Playmate of the Year in *Playboy* magazine.

In the way of new couples in a new place, we found 'our' restaurant and 'our' waiter. We fell for an elderly waiter whose deep melancholic physiognomy was so paintable, so Spanish, that he seemed to have walked straight from the frame of a painting by Velázquez. Having been born in Spain, on the feast of Santiago, Quentin has an affinity with Spaniards, though a Mexican Spaniard is another kind of Spaniard. I feel a strong attraction to that Spanish Greek, El Greco, born in Candia.

It was at the metal table tended by this beautiful waiter, wrapped in his pure white apron, that I learned that of all spirituous liquors, tequila is to me the most dangerous and powerful. I saw black visions. The iguanas didn't help, purposeful and with empty eyes. They look repulsively knowledgeable, hardenedly social.

Quentin had planned in detail a long honeymoon involving deeper penetration of the jungle to see Mayan ruins – than we eventually made. We spent some time self-catering in Cancún, an outpost of one kind of American civilisation. When I say self-catering, I mean that we got shy of the communal dining room of the resort we found ourselves in. Somehow it was common knowledge that we were newly-weds and the combination of being serenaded and of not giggling at the menu ('Pork Chops Deutsch' got us every time) drove us to spend time in our little cabin on the beach. Since he had been to Mexico before, Quentin had developed a taste for Huevos Rancheros; since I was in love, I ate them too. The other thing we lived on was avocados. I never became quite used to the flat-footed arrival into our bedroom of a grumpy seven-foot-long iguana, who seemed to want to play. He did that thing that creatures in thumpingly hot countries do of staying very still indeed and then making a sudden movement that chills the blood. I think he was in love with Quentin too and wanted to drive us apart. He certainly saw it as his business to guard Quentin from any overtures from me. He was very dusty and I wondered whether he was polished at all underneath. His sides ticked. He stood, it seemed to me, for disappointment, aridity and a general sense of having missed the party. There was no reasoning with him.

In the end, for a Malcolm Lowry fan, it was the perfect way for a Mexican honeymoon to come to a halt. We ran out of money. Quentin, who is good at that sort of thing, made several phone calls. The iguana watched us. Perhaps he was even jealous of the telephone.

At last, after, it seemed, more than a dozen abortive telephone calls conducted in Spanish, Quentin got through to someone who said that they were the secretary to the British Consul. Naturally grave and courteous, Quentin enquired whether he might speak to the Consul.

It was the middle of the afternoon.

The reply came from the secretary, that no, Quentin might not speak to the Consul, since the Consul was taking his rest.

It was irresistible not to hope that the Consul was sleeping it off.

In the event, we flew home, happy in the almost certain knowledge that Oliver would be joining us at some point fairly soon. Over the next nine months I doubled in size. This is not a figure of speech. Quentin was gallant about having married someone of ten stone who very shortly became someone of eighteen.

After Oliver's first Christmas in the hands of his doting but un-practised parents, help arrived in the octogenarian form of Nanny Ramsay. She was the real thing. Her best friend was also a nanny and had, like our nanny, been nanny to three generations of the same family. When they telephoned each other for a chat, they addressed one another as Nanny, as though it was their given name. I do not know Nanny Ramsay's Christian name. She smoked one cigarette each evening, out of the window, one foot crossed over the other at the ankle and one hand on her narrow hip. The very old-fashioned sort of nannies used to come in two shapes, fat or thin. She was a thin nanny. She wore a white overall, a belt, a hairnet. Michael Foot was leader of the Labour Party at the time and Nanny said of him, 'Poor Michael Foot, I can't imagine who his nanny might have been. Look at his hair.'

Nanny was a Scot from Crieff and had retired aged seventy-five. She came out of retirement to do some babies, as favours. She liked to weigh the baby before and after each feed, in proper scales such as a grocer might use, with weights going right down to an eighth of an ounce. Nanny made me keep a notebook to see how Oliver was getting on. It was quite clear that he was thriving. In the scales, he looked much like a person who is always going to hang over the end of things.

There had been but one tricky moment in the haze of delight that surrounded the arrival of Oliver, which was when Quentin's aunt Camilla visited just before the birth. I had stencilled the cornice of the baby's room with mermaids and Aunt Mickey, as the family called her, was perfectly content with that. My instinct told me, though we never actually knew from a scan, that the baby would be a boy, and I had purchased what I thought of as a very sensible selection of blue clothes for his arrival, jumpers, jeans, a blanket.

Aunt Mickey instinctively took over the matter of babywear for an impending heir. She took me to the White House, now long gone, where she ordered quires of monogrammed poplin handkerchiefs for the small face to rest upon. Dozens of long white nightgowns with no more than the faintest touch of forget-me-not on the smocking, drifts of shawl made in the Shetland Isles, Egyptian cotton sheets with the discreetest of 'W's in the corner, were all were amassed for this most weighty of arrivals. Any other equipment we acquired at the also long-gone Simple Garments of Sloane Street, where it was simply impossible to buy anything synthetic or with animals on it, or anything at all that looked as though it had been confected after 1953. Quentin's Aunt Philippa Chelsea sent silk bibs. She was the family beauty, lushly voiced, clever, small. She had worked on Jocelyn Stevens's *Queen* magazine.

Thank goodness for Aunt Mickey. She had set me on the path of rectitude. And so it was that Oliver and then Clementine were dressed as the kind of children who wore tweed coats with velvet collars and strapped sandals and short pure cotton socks. It is only fair at this stage to say that Clementine complained about this from the age of twelve to the age of twenty-three. She would say, 'Mummy made me wear smock-dresses and strappy sandals till I was *twenty*.' For a long time another line of Clem's has been that she doesn't want daughters though this has, by a recent miracle, been lifted during my blindness. The last time we touched on the matter of how she would dress her female children, she said, 'I'm keeping them in smock-dresses and Mary Janes until they're *thirty*!'

Aunt Mickey had worked at Bletchley Park, was widowed young, and lost both her older son and only grandson. For the weeks before my marriage to her nephew, she mothered me at St James's Palace where the family lived when they were in London. It was at lunch on one of these pre-nuptial days that I learned that one must not cut the nose off a piece of Brie; to do so is called 'nosing', as in, 'My dear, you've nosed the Brie'. It was at Aunt Mickey's table during this astounding week that I looked into the bluest eyes I have ever seen up close, those of Clementine Beit.

Of course she was a Mitford. I fear blue eyes. I like them and I fear them. They freeze the mongrel in me that expects to be whipped.

I must here say something of Aunt Mickey's brother, Quentin's father Nol (Oliver) Lymington, my father-in-law. Nol had badly wanted to be a doctor but it was not felt that this was suitable to his station. He was a sweet man, with beautiful legs that he has passed to his son and grandsons. He was frail after a bout of TB and a long

stay in Midhurst TB hospital. I am not sure that he received many
visitors there, though I know that Mickey was a champion sister to
him. He had a wide selection of talents. Towards the end of his shockingly short life, he apprenticed himself to Bill Poon, of Poon's Chinese
restaurant in Soho. Bill Poon was said to be descended from the man
who invented the stock cube. Nol came away with a magnificent
certificate from Bill Poon, certifying in cursive black ink that 'Viscount
Lee-Min-Tong' had completed, with distinction, his cookery course.
And so he had.

At this point Nol was living with us and I was pregnant: so were
many of my friends who lived near us in Hampshire. Nol cut no
corners and found every last elephant's-ear fungus in the stores he
haunted in Soho and gave us girls weekly lessons of such detail and
panache.

After Chinese food, there was a lull; maybe it was in this lull that
he produced my yellow retriever pup Guisachan, dropping her on to
my bed as I slept after giving birth to Clementine. The next phase
was altogether more esoteric and demanding; Nol became an apprentice chocolatier. He joined the University of the South Bank and
learned a tremendous amount about the temperatures at which chocolate is shiny, less shiny, not shiny at all, completely screwed up and
so on. He purchased a white overall and he worked in beautiful white
gloves. There was nothing he could not do and boxes of chocolates
so complex and so pretty that it was impossible to imagine eating
them started to appear at family occasions. Nol was the most patient
enrober, glosser, crystalliser, ganache-maker and praline-crackist. At
this stage in his life he had not yet separated from his third wife.
They lived in a house of airy elegance with a parrot named Albert,
who had plucked off all the feathers save those on his head, so that
Quentin would say he looked oven-ready, and three wire-haired dachs-
hunds named Charlotte, Anne and Emily. The minute precision
required by chocolate technology was a challenge to domestic and
marital life and it was perhaps a manifestation of their internal schisms

when forty-five gallons of enzyme for making soft centres turned up in a drum on the doorstep. Each chocolate requires but one drop.

Nol would have made a good teacher and, in happier times, he could have been an intimate and loving parent and grandparent, had his heart spared him.

The night before our wedding day, I lay in Aunt Mickey's elder daughter Angela's maiden bed in St James's Palace and prayed. I do not remember sleeping though I must have. I remember quantities of indecisive, pleasant February rain falling and the wide view from my window over the sentry box and up St James's Street. In a box in the cupboard were my white suede shoes, size six, in which I was to walk into my future.

Quentin and I moved to London, renting a house in the Portobello Road, because his bachelor house in London had been set fire to by an arsonist – an episode terrifyingly and more extensively described in Janet Hobhouse's novel *The Furies*.

I am incapable of thinking about this with any precision. It occurred around the time of Oliver's birth. I hardly know about it save through fiction. Quentin had lent his house off Westbourne Grove to Janet when she casually mentioned that she had nowhere to live on a visit to us that snowy winter of Olly's birth. Janet was living there and lost the manuscript of a book that she was writing on Braque in that fire. Thank God she did not lose her life, though that too was early extinguished by the cancer that drives *The Furies* into being the stupendous novel it is.

The arsonist had seen Quentin's car and formed an idea of us for which he evidently did not care. He made a pyre of everything moveable in the house, which was not a great deal, poured petrol over and lit it. Both Quentin and I have, with increasing reason, a deep horror of fire.

During our time in the Portobello Road, Oliver learned to turn somersaults and his sister was conceived. I would not mention this did she not like the idea; it has remained 'her' part of London.

While I was expecting Oliver, Quentin himself had been at sea for a good deal of the time, completing his own private circumnavigation on his ketch *Ocean Mermaid*. Quentin is one of the few people in the world who is entitled to wear the tie of the Association Internationale Amicale des Captains de Longs Cours Cap-Horniers. That is, he has been around Cape Horn, more than once, under sail. To attend the meetings of this society even as an appendage is a privilege. On one occasion, I was lucky enough to see a film made on a full-rigged tea clipper when one of the nonagenarians present had been just a boy holding on for dear life to a spar as the great ship rounded the Horn. No soundtrack, but you read the sails.

Quentin can name the stars and navigate by them. He can find land using dead reckoning. He stopped hunting after his mother's death and took it up again the day it was made illegal. He has a passion for justice, a tenderness for the underdog, and a mind that works patiently and logically through to the bone of the problem. There is something of Plantagenet Palliser to him. He is quiet, but when he speaks, he has a beautiful voice.

When Clementine was born, Aunt Mickey presided once more like a more worldly angel of maternal lore, and Nanny Ramsay came too. We had a new house to move into, an estate house just beyond the gates of Farleigh House where the school still festered. Clementine had expressively conversational hands and was a very slow eater. She decided not to breastfeed and very early conquered her larger brother, who referred to her as 'Birdy' until her birth and was her subject in love as soon as he saw her. He would stand with his feet tucked into the bars of her cot and loom over her, shedding a shadow that was bright orange at the top where the sun fell upon it. They were, and are, each other's stalwart best defender.

After the birth of Clem, the health visitor suggested that I might like to get out of the house a bit and do some A levels with a view to gaining some qualifications – and perhaps some other 'interest'. I was reading avidly, though that is not invariably deleterious to the raising of happy and balanced children, and both children seemed to be flourishing. I was one of the first people to read *Midnight's Children*. As well as the seethe of the book, I liked the look of the thin, modest, exhausted author. Shrewd of me, if not precisely prophetic.

Things between Quentin and me had shifted and held us apart at an undeclared pitch of difficulty. We could not find the words with which to row our way to safety, then found the wrong ones. Not for the first time I lit upon escape as a solution. My father wrote me a, for him, unusually direct letter of concern. It suggested that although powerfully drawn by temperament to Italy, he had come to place a higher value on the aesthetics of the Dutch School. He loved Quentin.

I left Farleigh. I went to stay with my friend Rosa Beddington in her tiny house in Oxford. The telephone rang. It was Lucinda Wallop, Quentin's sister. She said, 'Daddy's dead.' I said, 'No, he can't be.' He was only sixty-one and Quentin had just found a home for him close to us on an island on the River Test. He was a loveable, un-realised man.

I visited estate agents. I am not at all sure how lucid I was. One estate agent assured me that very few rental houses accepted children, most particularly not one house I liked the sound of that lay deep in rural Buckinghamshire. 'No Children', I read. There were no pictures of the property.

Very uncharacteristically, I found myself driving down a half-hidden road signed to Wotton Underwood. I could park my little car because there was a large gravelly yard to the side of what seemed to be an architectural hallucination, a golden pink central house flanked by lantern-shaped pavilions, behind delicate wrought-iron, golden-berried gates. It was a sleeping beauty. I looked to my right and saw that there was a gate leading to a wishing well on a wide lawn that ended in a ha-ha and beyond that at least one lake. I rang a doorbell at the side of the house. A funny bracket, as though for a pub sign the size of an equestrian portrait, stuck out of the side that faced where the cars were parked. It was high summer. I realised that this bracket must be for swinging in enormous paintings, pianos, furniture through the great windows of the house. The door was answered by a woman with my maternal grandmother's very voice. She took one look at me. I was not a pretty sight, fat, wretched, scared, uprooted, unaware that alcohol would never make anything better. The witch who opened the door, for a white witch she was, said, 'My child, you will live here. And you will bring your children.'

This phenomenon was Mrs Elaine Brunner, who, going one day to a garden clearance sale in the 1950s had seen the house to which that garden was attached. The house was due for demolition, having in its last usage been a school for delinquent boys. She had on that day a powerful instinct that underneath the Edwardian modernisations by Sir Reginald Blomfield there still lurked a Soane house. It had been built for the dukes of Buckingham and Chandos as a companion house to Stowe.

She saved it, buying it for a sum, I think, close to £5,000. She was, right up till her death, one of the most compelling, sexy yet maternal and grand-maternal women I've ever known. She was one of the beloved monsters of my life and she worked untiringly for that extraordinary palace she saved.

My first night at Wotton, I slept in a slightly-adapted-for-lodgers ducal apartment. The telephone went and it was Quentin. It seemed to be ridiculous to be separated from someone whom one so wished to console. I asked him whether he wanted me to attend his father's funeral and he said, 'It depends on whether you cared for him or not.' Of course I went.

And so we parted, as though our lives were happening to other people. We held hands in court and there seemed no question but that the children, on account of their situation, must stay at Farleigh. It was more unusual then, and my sense that this was the right decision was not one that I could ever make clear to any but the most intimate of my friends.

People have tackled me about this, thinking it unnatural or weak, but it laid between the children's father and myself a small island of trust amid the perilous currents of divorce. It was the children who mattered. Whether or not it was right for the children can only be gauged by them. I wanted Quentin to trust me and knew that the next thing we had to build was a safe place for our children.

Mrs Brunner it was who insisted that we all, including Quentin, have Christmas together at Wotton. On the years when the children were with me at Christmas after that, Quentin went and worked for the homeless at Crisis at Christmas. I received a letter from Aunt Mickey that told me among many other things I had lost 'a place in the world'.

LENS II: Chapter 7

Wotton became my place in the world, by which I mean my place quite far away from the world. Perhaps it was here, in its tall rooms and in its perfect self-contained hiddenness, that I relapsed into my inborn habit of reclusion. Wotton never did feel lonely, because I discovered that Mrs Brunner shared my affection for in-house mail, so that we left one another letters almost daily if we had not met in the rose garden or taking a walk under the chestnuts by the first lake. The park had been laid out by Capability Brown and there was, to the small landscape in which the house lies, an adaptation to mortal scale and vision that made walking along those lakes past their half-resurrected bridges and temples a humanising experience. Before the first lake there were two Doric-pillared Grecian temples. Oliver and Clementine and I would take bread to the swans who lived here. On the farther lake lived Canada geese with their two faithful watchmen-geese standing apart from the flock. Returning from walks to the house with the children was each time almost impossible to believe. We would pass a herbaceous border, leave the rose garden to our left, go and sit in the long grass on a bench by the wishing well and be paid visits by Solomon and Sheba, Mrs Brunner's peacocks, who, she said, had probably flown over from Waddesdon, which looked down at Wotton from the east. If it was a sunny day, Mrs Brunner would call us up on to the back steps of the house that led in to her own quite breathtakingly sparkly apartments. She always had a treat for the children, though her appearance was in itself the greatest treat, for she was brightly manicured and preferred to wear the colours of the rainbow. She smelt good too. Inside the house the tall windows had shutters that were barred at night across the dizzy original glass. Each shutter had its hole, an oval about eight inches tall, through which to look out for the moon in its transit.

There were secret rooms and rooms filled only with ebony knick-knacks. One room contained only objects made of mother-of-pearl. Clementine's and my favourite had a high curved ceiling edged with shining pearls, each the size of a tennis ball, in freehand plasterwork; below this lay disposed Mrs Brunner's own extraordinary wedding dress and that of her daughter, so that the whole room had a silvery-fragile bridal air, as though from the story of Beauty and the Beast. It was like the dream of a princely wedding that the poor Beast might have prepared.

If Mrs Brunner was attached to fairytale stage sets, she was also a brilliant chiseller at all possible architectural or state-related organisations that might help her to protect, conserve and reveal her exigent treasure trove. Even when I lived at Wotton House, she discovered an eighteenth-century ha-ha behind the nineteenth-century one, an indoor fish pond laid with tiles and braced with elegant bronze pillars, and several further follies in the woods beyond the second lake. I do not know how old Mrs Brunner was, though I imagine it would be easy enough to find out. Her role in our lives was so supernatural that I prefer my ignorance. I never called her by her first name.

The house within has a trembling stone staircase with wrought-iron work by Tijou that quivers as one mounts the stairs. The vistas within the front hall suggest the receding background of a Renaissance painting, exemplifying and playing with perspective. The hall is full of light, very high, and paved with black-and-white marble in squares on the grand scale. In winter, an open fire was set in the fireplace in that front hall, where the children and I left carrots and biscuits and, at Mrs Brunner's insistence, a tot of brandy for Father Christmas.

It was at that first Christmas after the sadness of our parting that I saw how a pure flirt like Mrs Brunner made things easier between me and Quentin. The great lack in our lives, probably thanks to the premature death of his parents and my mother, was grown-ups to teach us how to pull the splinters out instead of driving them further in.

We developed a pattern, familiar to many families, whereby the children spent half the holidays with me and half with their father, and alternated, insofar as it was possible, at weekends. Thank God there were the two of them to sustain one another and grumble about this together, since it was to go on for a long time. I remember standing on the nursery floor at Wotton having tidied all their toys away and looking at the departing car, thinking, 'What is in their heads?' At around this time I wrote a children's book and illustrated it. It was really about Oliver and Clementine, of course, and it was always going to be destined for Quentin, who has the paintings now, which are portraits of his children.

❖

There was no sense of unsafety at Wotton although we were an old lady and a younger woman and two small children alone. The whole place was barred up so snugly that its only burglar, during my time, was a ferocious wind that punched holes in three fragile windows, whose panes simply couldn't take the brunt in spite of their delicate ductility, like that of sails.

I had the notion that I would write some short stories to make a bit of money. I sent five to Auberon Waugh at the *Literary Review*. He sent them back with a kind note saying that he and his wife had enjoyed reading them in bed. I imagine this was a tease. I then tried applying to *The Archers* to see if they would like a new scriptwriter, but they wouldn't.

There's nothing for it, I thought, but writing a novel. I had bought my father an electric typewriter that he had seen the *Observer* newspaper was offering at a reasonable price. He passed me his old typewriter, whose keys you really had to think about pinging down like those of an old till.

I wrote my first novel, *A Case of Knives*, in my bedroom at Wotton House, a room whose mirrored cupboards chopped up the images thrown by the circular mirror the size of the shield of Achilles on the opposite wall.

In the South Pavilion lived Sir John Gielgud. In the morning, you could see his partner Martin taking their shih-tzu for a walk. Opposite Sir John lived an elegant German lawyer who worked between Washington and London and kept this celestial pavilion as his country hideout. He often entertained my children and me to Sunday lunch. His line in girlfriends was terrifying to one who has never seriously in her life thought of wearing leather. On the whole they turned out to be very nice and, moreover, to do things like run Lufthansa's legal department or own a chain of supermarkets in the old Austro-Hungarian countries.

Behind this exquisite pavilion was a courtyard containing a long house that had at one point been where beer had been brewed for all the servants employed in the main house. In this house lived Graham C. Greene and his family, including at one point his mother Helga, with whom Raymond Chandler had been in love. Quite briefly, Clarissa Dickson-Wright was his housekeeper, and once she babysat for me. At this point she and I were both what is called 'practising alcoholics'. I had no idea.

Every day when I woke up at Wotton, I was glad to do so. I suppose that means that one has found a place in the world. Once I saw fox cubs playing leapfrog on the back lawn. I so loved being there and when the children were with me it felt as though beauty in itself might feed them the things that disunity was taking from them. It was a hopelessly over-aestheticised view, I can see. But to this day, I like it when I know that they are in the places where there is beauty.

Mrs Brunner met and charmed my father; they were exactly each other's sort of thing. Daddy, possessed by architecture, crazy about Soane and handsome; and Mrs Brunner, obsessed by her great charge, her house, and very fond of flirting. Mrs Brunner welcomed other friends as well, though she was a great one for taking what the Scots call scunners. She was absolutely beastly to the boyfriend of one of my best friends whom she regarded, quite correctly, as treating my friend unkindly. If not a witch, she was an advanced telepath.

She could also dismiss people simply on the unfair grounds of their want of physical attractiveness, and she was extremely fussy about fairness between the children so that if someone bought a present for just one of them, there would be a note requesting the presence of the giftless child in Mrs Brunner's drawing room where would be laid out a fairy feast and some compensatory present.

It is quite a feat for a mother of an only child to think in this way. She had at some level remained not childish but fierce as children are, and we were all her cubs and felt it. I hope that it is no shadow to Mrs Brunner's own daughter to say that Mrs Brunner made me feel, if not mothered, protected.

<hr />

My friend Rosa was a fellow of Brasenose. My friend Fram Dinshaw, whom I'd known since I was less than twenty, was a fellow at St Catherine's College. My friend James Fergusson was working at an antiquarian bookshop in Oxford. Jamie and the children and I would meet in Oxford for greedy Chinese lunches at a restaurant where in the fish tank were those carp whose eyes stick out and who seem to be dancing with their floating veils of fin.

Long before my first marriage, Fram had, outside Rosa's house in Oxford, given me a kiss. Shortly afterwards he wrote to me. I read the letter standing up on the Bakerloo Line between Warwick Avenue and Oxford Circus, on my way to *Vogue*. In it, he adumbrated that if I did not smell so horribly of smoke he might conceivably take an interest in me and that there was something about me that reminded him of blackberries and that we might, if I calmed down, end up together.

But by now, many years later, I was a vessel with cargo, my children. All the smelling of blackberries in the world doesn't mean that you can be careless with human souls.

Our first date, or rather what reveals itself to have been,

retrospectively, a date, was to Rycote Chapel. In the car Fram put on 'Soave sia il vento'. Later he made me a tape recording of some Larkin poems. I found myself playing them when he was not there. I listened again and again to 'The Trees':

> Yet still the unresting castles thresh
> In fullgrown thickness every May.
> Last year is dead, they seem to say,
> Begin afresh, afresh, afresh.

Once, when the children were with Quentin, I agreed to go and stay with Fram at his family's house outside Cortona. It was to be reached by a dirt road cut into the hillside. Opposite lived a couple called Gina and Nino Franchina. She was the daughter of the artist Gino Severini and granddaughter of the poet Paul Fort. Nino made tree-sized helical metal sculptures. Further along lived a family who would prove to contain the novelist Amanda Craig, though I've not met her.

Early one morning, taking a walk up the lane and between the strawberry trees, I looked in the damper gullies at the edge of the dry thin path. I couldn't believe what I saw. There they were, growing wild, those black velvet irises that I love. They were everywhere at that spot, and beyond them red tulips, with reflexed petals and thin stems like veins, which preferred to be on flatter tilth, as though they knew that they were a motif on a million Turkish carpets.

The house at Cortona was simple, two storeyed, whitewashed within and then decorated by Fram's mother, who had a gift for drawing that had won her a place, that she did not take up, at the Slade. The house smelt of woodsmoke, lemons and basil and was set amid olive groves. It had a particularly non-Italian garden because the whole family had that passion for flowers that may have come from living beside a desert in Karachi. Outside the house was a large *Magnolia grandiflora*, crinum lilies grew along the front and a catalpa shaded the terrace where, in good weather, we ate outside. Troughs of basil were everywhere and 'Heavenly Blue' morning glory twined around the kitchen door. The rose that changes in colour, *Rosa chinensis mutabilis*, grew around the front door. At Easter peonies we never identified, which had come from the villa below, would flower with pink heads considerably bigger than my own children's. The bottom of the garden was hedged with a vine of that most fragrant and intoxicating grape the *uva di fragola*, the grape whose taste and scent is that of a strawberry and makes a wine that for some reason the European authorities disapprove of, so it is drunk in secret among friends. Rosemary and sage and all the herbs that flourish in dryness lent their oil to the air. By the well stood a fig tree and another deeper down the garden. At the side of the house was the kitchen garden, or *orto*.

The family who originally lived just below and later moved into the local town still came up to work for *gli indiani* on the hill. Franca, the wife, worked in the *orto* and as cook, and her husband Guido came and fixed emergencies such as wild boar in the garden or a plumbing disaster.

Negotiations between a Tuscan peasant and a fastidious Zoroastrian, as Fram's mother Mehroo temperamentally as well as religiously was, were nothing like as difficult as they might have been had the two women not decided that they liked one another. Franca therefore simply fitted in with what she was told, that only napkins with a person's initial on might be given to that person, that never must bedspreads be put on a bed with the foot part at the top, that all sudsing had to be done before all rinsing when washing up, and that the rinsing must be under flowing water, that dirty utensils must never be laid down on the side but on a dish and so on. Much of it was common sense and the rest she took as part of the charm of this little family who had decided for part of their year to move into the house that had proven such hard work for her own family.

Out in the *orto*, copper sulphate was sprayed and dried to a high abstract blue on the tomatoes, grapes, aubergines, peppers and zucchini, whose flowers Franca would fry and scatter with salt.

To watch Fram's mother cook was to watch an artist at work. Her fine, beautiful hands had nails like almonds with that natural line of white seen in some Madonnas. To take the bitterness from a cucumber, she would cut off the narrower end and – often gently telling one a story and meeting one's eyes with her own – turn and turn and turn the cut piece of cucumber until it had drawn out all the bitter white milk. Then, and then only, would the cucumber be ready for peeling and for slicing into lenses as cool as ice for hot eyes, cut not with a mandolin but with a little knife. She did everything domestic beautifully so that it must have been, for her family, like living with a ballerina or an antelope, something incapable of ungrace or disgrace. She was lovely to behold. It was a quality that resided in tempo as much as in address and gave each act its own dignity. She made, rather than took, time.

When I read Edward Said's autobiography, I was pierced by the similarity of his own relationship with his mother to that of Fram and Mehroo, though, unlike Fram, Said seemed to have established some wafer of air betwixt she who bore him and what he could bear.

———◆◆◆◆———

Today, 5 June 2007, is a flawless high blue June day in Chelsea. Some days ago, we were puzzled as to why the air was full of low, close, mechanical noise. It transpired that the Metropolitan Police had chosen to shoot a young man, unhappy in his marriage, desperate for the return of his wife, far gone in drink, and wielding a gun with which he could have killed no one. The police marksman shot him in the head; that is, he shot to kill. What of talking to him? What of tranquillisers? That young man might, a hundred times, have been me.

It is when such things happen that people around my age thank God their parents are dead.

Last night I had a visit from the film-maker Amy Hardie. We have a friend in common and she was keen to tell me about her experience of a shaman in Edinburgh, who she believes has saved her life. She feels that my eyes might open if the doctors could be more humble and eclectic when it comes to the hidden paths of the human brain. I had wondered if I blinded myself when I left Fram, whom I married on 27 September 1986. I left him in November 1996.

The onset of the physical condition, ten years later, seemed like the reification of a metaphor I had inhabited for a long time. This way of thinking enraged the more mechanical of my doctors.

Amy's film threw me back on the dear dead. When I was drinking, I summoned them and held long conversations with them; I could actually see them. It was a solid experience. Among my dearest dead is Fram's mother. You might say that it is easy for me to love her now that she is dead, but we do not love the dead on account of the relief they offer us but on account of the personality that has gone for ever. My mother-in-law was one of those who can turn a room to flowers and air or fill it with frost and razor blades. It gave my mother-in-law pleasure herself to give pleasure and yet sometimes something dreadful took and squeezed her. The persons who most understood, loved, overlooked and steadied this were her doting, hugely intelligent, husband Eduljee (Eddie) and her daughter Avi.

When, as a family (which is what I then believed we were), we visited Karachi, it was a time without flaw. Of course the city itself was growing more dangerous and I did not leave the house alone since in myself I constituted a western cliché, with my yellow hair and pink face, maybe even an affront. Fram's childhood house had been eaten by white ants, so the Karachi house was built, oddly enough, by a Scots architect the Dinshaws came across who was working for UNESCO. The house dated from the nineteen-sixties. It was set around a cool quadrangle where we took tea and *batasas*, a kind of dry, cheesy, Parsi shortbread. The years fell away from my mother-in-law. Her husband's sister was in Karachi at the same time with her family and there was much toing and froing, not quite the same as living in the extended family system in the Indo-Italianate villa of Fram's grandparents that had been sold just that year and which we visited one day for tea.

We drove up past lawns edged with bright red bedding-plants to the façade of this house near the Victorian Gothic Frere Hall in the middle of old Karachi. We mounted the stairs, and in contrast to the other houses we visited during that happy fortnight, encountered the electric interference of modernity. Every room was dominated by a telly and video. There were at least two sons of the house, under ten and chubby. We took tea and talked. There was a year's worth of Karachi gossip to catch up on, although it was not the inner gossip of the Parsi world. There was talk of conditions worsening in the city, of men with guns at night, of the chowkidars having dreadful fights. On a table to the side of the room reposed a selection of small-eats, or rather enormous and challenging cakes, clearly as much for show as for ingestion. I noticed that the chubsters had disappeared. The table that bore the showy cakes had a nice hand-blocked tablecloth that fell to the floor. It was a homely touch in a house otherwise fitted out by Sony, Sanyo, Bang & Olufsen. The chocolate cake was the most splendid of all, turreted, godrooned and melting. The attack it was receiving from the warm day, despite the chattering air conditioning, was being assisted by four hands that were hollowing out the cake from under the tablecloth with quite as much assiduity as if they had been white ants.

Fram remembers the mango tree in the garden of the house of his babyhood where he was born at Breach Candy in Bombay, within sound of the sea. He used to say that he was the monkey who played and ate and swung and made himself safe in the branches of me, who was that fertile, glowing, mango tree. How can I have taken an axe to its roots?

Back in Karachi, where my parents-in-law had made their first marital home, I had the sense that my mother-in-law was so secure that she could trust me. Her lifelong servant, Munsuf, served us at meals with a different cockade in his turban depending on the formality of the meal. I learned a, very, little Urdu because Munsuf was Muslim and I wanted to make it plain to him how happy I was to see him and the family at home. He began to work for my mother-in-law when he was still a boy and she not that much older, so their closeness was telepathic. One afternoon, my mother-in-law relaxed with me enough to show me her saris. She shook out each one and told me when and where she had worn it. In a woman so averse to show yet so sensible to beauty, this was the showing of a miles-long florilegium. The saris were stored with balls of cedar wood and muslin bags of lavender that she had grown in Cortona. Each sari was a woven story and there was what she didn't say too, which was that she loved and quite clearly looked beautiful in that pink which is almost blue and that I particularly love; it is among the last colours to fade from flowers at twilight.

My father-in-law read the *Dawn*, Karachi's newspaper, daily, and looked, as he always did, at the stock-market prices. In the evening he was reading Flaubert's letters on a small upright sofa in the drawing room. The routines of daily life were congenial, airy and natural between each of us, I believed, at the time.

One night, because we were young, Fram, his sister Avi and I and their cousins were invited to a beach party. Many aspects of it were curious. The young women whom I had met as Parsi wives and daughters, ravishing in the modesty of their garments and the flat shine of their Indian-set jewels and pearls, had changed, since it was nighttime and no one but their husbands would see them, into western beachwear or into some designer's idea of western beachwear. Many of these couples, after all, had houses in New York too. We were driven along the spit out into the Arabian Sea where I doubt that anyone much keeps a beach house any longer, but in those days it was like a more expansive Southwold. The servants settled to making the barbecue and the wives to comparing their outfits. How much lovelier, actually, they had looked before. Nonetheless their husbands seemed pleased to see their wives turned out so with their crazy sunglasses – although it was pitch black outside – and marvellous sarongs covered with logos. Even the jewellery had changed and become the faceted hard jewellery of the West.

Yet perhaps they were right to be so strangely attired and that only for the cover of night, for it was to prove to be a night of nights, the night when the turtles know to emerge from the edge of the sea and un-dig from the sand the clutches of leathery eggs they have left there.

So there we were, all of us quite young, and everyone apart from Avi, Fram, their cousins and myself, dressed for a blazing day in Portofino, when out of the sea came lumbering animals large enough to ride on yet made almost completely of horn and leather, tanks on the sand, ballerinas in the water. Then it began. Hundreds and thousands of perfect models of their mother, but the size of a Jaffa Cake, came scrobbling out of their nests and hurled themselves into the sea, which indifferent, hauled them in its wave further up the beach to leave them high and dry. It proved to be a whole other way in which you can't beat the sea. We picked up handfuls of the perfect, scratchy little things and went quite deep into the sea with them, but back the waves came with their freight of bad pennies. Exhaustion killed many; it's not surprising to learn that so few survive.

⬥•◆•⬥

While working in our high cliff of a studio, Liv and I are receiving more visitors than we used to, because this handsome, crumbly house is about to be taken to pieces and put together again. Contractors, builders, civil engineers, architects, curtain-makers, come and go with their laser tape measures and their pickaxes. We are polite but so far haven't offered tea. We are working too.

So if I felt that I was contingent and perching on a small ledge before, I now feel the ledge is thinning and the sea beneath me is crawling, and I must get on with this story.

———◆◆◆◆———

When we were nineteen or so, I knew from his appearance, which is elegant and slender, and from his colour, which is a light caramel brown, that Fram was not English. I assumed that he was Indian. He is in fact Parsi. He is a Persian, descended from that group of Zoroastrians who, at the time of the Arab invasions, fled from Iran in boats and landed in Gujarat. The Parsis made a deal with the indigenous ruler, fortunately for them a Hindu, that they would neither break any of their host's taboos nor proselytise. In return he allowed them to settle and trade, originally in a kind of palm toddy. During the time of the Raj, Parsis found a thirstier market, purveying whisky, brandy, soda water and so on to the sahibs.

Zoroastrianism seems to me, who have less than no business to opine, but a Zoroastrian son, a commendably rational way of leading a life. That son, for example, really does implement the instruction left to him by his Parsi grandmother on her deathbed, 'Good thoughts, good words, good deeds.' It is a religion that institutionalises charitable giving and that reminds each member of the faith that he has brought nothing into the world and will take nothing out. Each Parsi wears a thread around his or her waist called the *kasti*, as a warning against excess; below the normal daily shirt of even a westernised Parsi you may find a *sadra*, which is an almost gauze-like vest of simple white muslin to remind the wearer that, no matter his prosperity, he is the same as any other man.

It is an ancient faith and I feel shy writing anything about it. However, its importance in my life cannot be overemphasised, both for good and for, entirely unintended, harm. Perhaps the thing that most outsiders know about Parsis is that they bury their dead on Towers of Silence, leaving them there to be eaten by vultures and

223

returned, therefore, to the cycle of life. The other thing that people know about Parsis is that they are worshippers of fire.

There is in the world a dwindling number of pure Parsis. This is not helped by people like me, who have married pure Parsis. There has come a ruling from the Parsi Panchayat, the ruling body, that the children of male Parsis born to *farangi* women may still be Parsi, but this is not entirely popular with ultra-orthodox believers. One may read frightening things on websites. It all returns to the cruel question of purity, an inhuman phenomenon that is presently igniting all flammable faiths, creeds, tribes and dictators as it has immemorially done. Purity posits the notion that we are not one another; whereas clearly, to live, we must imagine how it is to be one another. This is where fiction, though it is not a utilitarian art, or anything so simple, cannot but come in. We need urgently to know how other people feel.

The closeness and decency of the Parsi community, insofar as I have ever encountered it, comes as refreshment to the soul. There are fewer than 100,000 Parsis in the world. Zoroastrians have been actively persecuted in Iran, and in India a really unexpected modern glitch has compromised their ancient burial customs. Indian vets have begun to treat ailing cattle with Voltarol, a painkiller that – if they eat one of the treated cows – attacks the liver of Indian vultures. The vulture population of, for example, Bombay, has dropped by ninety per cent, which presents a public health hazard and portends disaster – or change – to the Parsi community as it holds up the liberation of the soul and the rejoining of the body to the creation.

In fact for the last two generations, Fram's immediate family have been buried in the Protestant Cemetery in Rome. I am glad of this in some cowardly ways. The thought of my shrouded husband or my son in his cerements being loaded on to an aeroplane to be taken to the Towers of Silence, where women may not enter, is a lonely one. Lonely for them, I mean.

So how does this relate to Rycote Chapel, with its stars cut out of contraband playing cards on the ceiling? I had always known that Fram was clever and could be exceedingly cutting. What I had not expected was a complete unevasive answering of every question I had asked or even thought to ask. I think that I knew I loved him when he referred with exotic normality to Marks and Spencer as 'Marks'.

I thought, here is someone with a perfect ear for seventeenth-century poetry, here is someone who never misses a trick, here is someone of whom I was afraid because I know his tongue has blades, and yet he is still, despite all his schooling and conditioning, that tiny bit unassimilated. All children brought up between cultures become felinely bilingual, trilingual, whatever it takes. Fram had in his time acquired illiterate smatterings of Urdu and Gujarati; more Latin, less Greek; French and Italian. His English modifies according to with whom he is speaking, so that when on the telephone to his parents, whose English was the hyper-English of let us say, the Third Programme in the 1960s, you would hear that note leaking into his own tone. When he is with his sister, they speak English at one another like birds. When he is teaching or giving a lecture he speaks naturally in a pure Latinate English and in paragraphs. I love his clarity. When we talk, I wave the butterfly net; he does the pinning.

Very slowly, and it was slow because the children were my main trust, I introduced them to Fram, mostly with Mrs Brunner or someone else there too. He was, at that stage of his life, as he expressed it, 'agnostic about children'.

The curious thing is that while Fram was not disinclined in principle to undergo an arranged marriage should his parents wish it, and despite there being one candidate who sounded suitable and lived in Paris, his parents never did arrange such a match. For as long as possible, his mother ignored the fact that her son might be having relationships with non-Parsi girls, for so he was. His taste ran to beauties; quality not quantity was the characteristic of those who might be found in his sway. But somehow he managed, throughout his twenties, to remain the apple of his mother's eye, unpunished as yet for having grown into manhood.

Meanwhile, happier news was coming from Farleigh. I had been nervous lest some hard-faced blonde direct herself at Quentin and the children, but I should have had more faith in him. My old friend Jamie Fergusson had introduced Quentin to his cousin Annabel, I believe on the Isle of Wight, maybe even over a bucket and spade. I do not know where to begin about Annabel. She is the A to his Q. But how was it then? Was I jealous to hear that Quentin had a friend whom he had introduced to the children? I was not. I had known Annabel since I was about seventeen and much liked her parents. Her father was a general physician in Richmond, one of the old school, who wore striped trousers and a black coat. He was very funny, but you had to wait for the jokes, because, like his brother Pat, the father of Jamie, he spoke incredibly slowly. I once missed an aeroplane because Pat Fergusson enquired over breakfast one day when I was due to fly to Glasgow, 'Whether..........or.........not...............you............are............... ...an...admirer...........of..............the.................novels.......of... ....Ivy Compton-Burnett?'

One of the treats available to a Fergusson-fancier, when the two brothers were still alive, was to get them together and overhear their conversation. It was like waiting for the Mona Lisa to wink.

Annabel's mother is something quite else. Spirited, *croyante*, a Catholic convert, she is one of those people very much one's senior who combine wisdom with knowing exactly what's hot at Top Shop. I loved her from our first meeting, which was long before anyone in our generation had married anyone.

Annabel herself I first met at a party where what was striking was the blueness of her eyes, the grooviness of her physique and the old-fashionedness of her garb. I think maybe at her christening there was a fairy who arranged for Annabel to dress in an especially old-fashioned way, otherwise her effect as she walked down the street would, like that of Zuleika Dobson, have left men even more stupefied than they already were. The other thing I knew about Annabel was that she was clever in the practical, realistic way that I am not. People would say of her, 'She looks like a Botticelli angel but do you know she can do the *Times* crossword?'

No one could possibly accuse me of either of these attributes and I was happy that Quentin himself might be growing happier. I also knew, most importantly of all, that Annabel was kind and good. Later it was my pleasure to find that she is really, properly, funny. It's like medicine.

For reasons to do with the house at Wotton's beauty and Mrs Brunner's scarcely perceived but very present hand on the tiller of the life that my children and I led, we never felt transient or uncared-for. She combined bossiness with affection and the sort of over-partiality you do, on the whole, only offer to your kin, so that we did feel we were living with, if not a fairy godmother, a fairy grandmother.

I hate competitive games, maybe for the base reason that I'm no good at them. At New Year, Mrs Brunner, who had an entire room called the Oak Room dedicated to stage costumes, held a charades party. How I dreaded it. I can't act to order and I can't act if I know I'm acting, but I loved her and would have to attend. I couldn't pretend I had to stay with the children because they were with Quentin, and Fram was with his parents because New Year's Day was his father's birthday. (Parsis have two birthdays, one dependent on their mama and one dependent on the moon.) Mrs Brunner had arrayed herself that night as a mixture of Catherine the Great, Elizabeth I, the Empress of Bohemia and all nine muses. Her golden hair was up, her face painted. It was possible to see the captivating young woman she had been. But in this incarnation she was authoritative.

The script was complicated, a good dinner had been had, much

Champagne drunk, a charming set-designer named Carl Toms, who had worked with Visconti at Covent Garden, was on hand, while to direct us there was none other than Nicholas Hytner. I'm glad to say that he recognised my acting potential at once and that I played my part as a poisonous mushroom with the sort of grace and sporing-ness you might expect. New Year was also the birthday of Annabel and I believe that it was then that Quentin proposed marriage to her. I hope that I am right. Perhaps I am giving them a few more years of marriage than they have had, in which case, lucky them.

In the case of Fram and myself, things could not but have been more complicated. When I consider myself from my mother-in-law's point of view, I can see that what her beautiful only son was bringing home was a gigantic, *Angrez*, previously married, too old, and completely untrained animal. My mother-in-law could not help feeling these things. In complex ways, the West that she had been raised to admire, whose literature had arrived by steamer-trunk throughout her children's childhood, had become grotesque, appetitive, grasping, vulgar. The particularly bad part of it all was that I entirely saw her point of view and agreed with her, so replete was I with self-disgust, self-distaste and the willingness to believe that I smelt and took filth with me wherever I went. It was an unhappy concatenation.

My father-in-law Eddie, who I always thought liked me a bit more than did his wife, actually liked me a good deal less.

Nonetheless, all these feelings were, for some years, hidden by my parents-in-law. It might have been better to have released them by some means other than the slashes of the razor that my mother-in-law chose as her means of attack. It was mainly her son she punished. Yet they themselves had been to school in England, had sent him to prep and public school in England, so to punish him for being what she called a 'brown Englishman' was cruel. She never stopped loving her son, so the hurt she felt compelled by her anxieties to cause him harmed her much more.

My mother-in-law was a woman who could make a room a paradise or a slicing unit on account of her mood. Her family were used to it. My sister-in-law Avi, who stands at under five foot and has known severe long-term medical pain in her life, simply and beautifully neutralised all malice ever afloat in the room by her own blessedly even nature. She has a keel. I don't know if it's a faith or her natural acceptingness, or both.

I fear that I was all too keen to condemn myself. At the very beginning, when Fram first courted me, I think my mother-in-law and I wanted to love one another; I certainly wanted to love her. I think she genuinely tried to love me, but my own sense of my unloveability rushed to greet her instinctive condemnation and they wrought, over the years, a terrible mischief together. In order to be married in Italy, we had to fulfil residency requirements and stay in the house in Cortona for something like two months. Quentin was happy that we were being married out of England – it seemed more natural that way.

We did have one happy day, the day of our Parsi betrothal in Cortona. My mother-in-law had threaded jasmine and marigold ropes and set in shaken chalk auspicious designs all around the perimeter of the house. Fram's aunt and uncle came from Rome, a coconut was broken and rice placed on our foreheads and sugar on our tongues to make sure that we would only speak sweet words to one another.

The wedding itself took place under the aegis of the Communist Party of Italy. The Mayor of Cortona made us freemen of that beautiful town. We were garlanded with long strings of carnations that my mother-in-law had sewn. We were young, thin, blazingly in love and tremendously close at every possible level. There was a feast at Vasari's house outside Arezzo, with Italian and Indian food alternating. Fram's kind and smiling Aunt Khorshed had provided Niazi, her old cook from the Pakistani Embassy in Rome. Yet in the photographs my mother-in-law is holding her sari over her face so that she cannot see what is being enacted before her. If only I could have taken that pain from her and told her that I would look after and love her son for ever, that I could love her, that I was I, not a foreign culture. But it didn't happen.

Months later, after our honeymoon, the photographs of our wedding came back and Fram noted on a visit home the distaste with which they were regarded. The poison had started to run and could only get worse, most especially when I began to make some small name for myself in that thing, the world.

Mrs Brunner had been simply furious when we got engaged, though it was in a direct and catty way and once she'd said her dreadful piece, we did make friends again. What she said to me was, 'Go and live with an Indian beside a bus stop in Oxford.' But in the end she was tremendously chuffed by the next lodger I was able to conjure, up to whom I could not come in any regard, for he was a boy and a handsome one and Mrs Brunner saw at once that here was something greatly more glamorous than I, Edward St Aubyn.

We settled into our flat by the bus stop in the Banbury Road, and I remember Brigid Brophy sending me a postcard saying that to live on the Banbury Road must be much like living in Persepolis. In several regards she can't have been wrong at all, for I did indeed try hard, and mostly failed miserably, to keep a Parsi house. Even though my mother-in-law chose the sinks and all the sanitary ware and I never cooked onions because Fram hated the smell, I did not keep a Parsi house. My hair moults and Parsis have a horror of dead hair, wrapping it up before throwing it away, as 'we' might and 'they' certainly do with nail clippings. It was, of course, idiotic to attempt to ape a culture I had not been born into, no matter how open to it I was – and I was. The cracks in a performance, no matter how rounded it be, will declare themselves, through nerves, self-consciousness, or even that sense of falsity that goes with the attempt to imitate, be it never so innocent and good-hearted. How could I, brought up in Edinburgh, gather what had been handed down through thousands of years from the high plains of Yazd and Bam?

The following awful truth is so. My father was expected at our wedding, but mysteriously cancelled. On our wedding night, over dinner in Orvieto, Jamie Fergusson casually let it fall that Daddy was that day having open-heart surgery. Later that night, before retiring, we went for a walk in the town. When Fram saw someone whom he thought attractive, he said so, as he always did. I thought, 'That's fine. It'll all feed back into me.' Now I think I know that I should have said, 'It's our wedding night. Please look at me. I am here.'

I learned these things too late and from Fram's new companion Claudia, who has only just not got my name. She enacts these things and is in this respect my beneficiary, as well as being someone who knows instinctively how a properly adjusted person should behave.

Having been raised in habits of unassertion, I have learned inadequate systems of self-defence that may seem suspect to outsiders especially when manifested by a person of such size.

There is on the face of Orvieto Cathedral one particular dancing angel, her mood choric, her hair loose, her mouth laughing. I did feel that happy on that first day of our marriage and often thereafter too.

Our honeymoon was short and busy. We drove the elderly white Lancia on which Fram had learned to drive in The Hague fifteen years earlier, when his uncle had been Pakistani Ambassador. You could see the autostrada through the floor. We drove south to Ravello and Amalfi. Lorna Sage had given us Gore Vidal's telephone number and told us he'd love to hear from us.

Not much he didn't. At Fram's amused insistence (maybe he was bored) every day, after caffe latte and for Fram toast and croissants (I was constantly, in those days, starving myself) I would ring the Vidal house and get a very dusty answer indeed. We drove to Pompeii, Herculaneum and very early one morning Paestum where the air smelt of sage and rosemary and our only companions were two ghosts.

The ghosts were tidy and well turned out, clearly having died around the mid nineteen-twenties. Her bob, her filet, his hat, his pince-nez, their faded Baedeker, his ancient plate camera, her button shoes, her clocked silk stockings, his punched co-ordinate brogues, everything chimed. It was years later in England that we realised that they must have been Stephen and Oriel Calloway, doing a spot of rubble-romping.

It was Fram's first sweet act as a stepfather that our honeymoon lasted only four days because we had to surge up to Rome again and fly home so that we might take the children to be page and brides-maid at the wedding of our friends Cyril and Natasha Kinsky in Dorset. There was no grumbling at all and I recall, as the dancing began, having a sensation that should not arrive as a form of self-consciousness, since it is an absence of self-consciousness, that I was where I should be, with whom I should be. It was wonderful to be with the children again.

There was from the start something not good for our marriage in the routines that I collaborated with. Because I had never forbidden anyone anything, I encouraged Fram to spend as much time with his mother as he had when he was a bachelor, rationalising that this was an adjustment that I had to make as the junior partner (junior to my mother-in-law) and in deference to her increasing sense of alienation. I was atoning for the Raj, perhaps. I don't know how. It is interesting that she had a Scottish governess. When she visited Edinburgh, long after we had parted, she said that it could have been somewhere she might have lived and that she wished she had seen it and understood before. This is very sad to address for me.

Her home, or any full concept of that home, had been ruptured by the Partition of India in 1947, the year of her marriage. She and Eddie were first cousins, but his father came from Karachi; hers from Bombay. They had married entirely for love, but the romance had been furthered by their common (Bombay) grandfather. It was an unusually tribal hybrid: a love match that might as well have been arranged. My parents-in-law were everything to each other and regarded their children as extensions of themselves. They began to pity Fram for not, apparently, conforming to their model.

My in-laws' distaste was certainly not helped when it came to my first entering the world of being published. The Common Reader had all but died out. Publicity was in the ascendant, about to gain a grip even on the then fusty world of publishing.

Such was Mehroo's charm, and so profound my longing to have a mother figure to love, that I often felt it could have come right, but she was undoubtedly massaged in her nascent, perhaps at the time only half-formed hostility towards me, not remotely by the family in Rome who were steadily loving, but perhaps by others unseen by us. Someone certainly ensured that my poor mother-in-law received every single press cutting referring to me. The sophisticated reader (and my mother-in-law *was* sophisticated until blinded by emotion) will realise that one has little control over how one is depicted in the press. When my first novel came out, there were a number of photographs of me, none indecent, but very few in my own clothes. I stayed with my in-laws while being photographed by the late (and notably serious-minded and intelligent) Terence Donovan. They were appalled at the stylist's contrivances when I returned after the shoot. Fram was later given to understand that my painted presence would discomfit his father in his immaculate dressing gown over the breakfast table.

When it became clear that I was having a baby, we went to tell my parents-in-law the happy news. Something was very wrong in the atmosphere of the flat. My mother-in-law made what was meant to be an overture of friendship, but said something on the self-deluding lines of 'Can't we agree that these misunderstandings have all been Fram's fault?' I stiffened and could not agree. The atmosphere rapidly soured. Doors opened and closed; hurried consultations seemed to be taking place in other rooms. But whatever the thing was that I was missing or catalysing, I could not identify, nor would for many months later. My father-in-law had just been diagnosed with leukaemia and my mother-in-law in some measure associated this with a piece that had appeared in the *Daily Mail* about a German literary prize that I had won that made some ribald play over *lederhosen*. A kind friend had sent her a cutting.

Our son was born at 4.03 p.m. on 22nd February 1989. Fram was at a meeting in College. The baby lost oxygen at the last minute and arrived blue. A very smooth gynaecologist whispered the word 'Resuscitator' into a kind of grid in the wall and then the room was full of focused people doing the thing they had practised to do: to bring back life. Minoo changed from navy blue to mauve to almond brown. We met, liked one another on sight (I can speak for him too) and were at once separated to our respective units of intensive care. I had lost so much blood that they wanted to give me a transfusion. Luckily my blood slowly made more of itself. I was already making those deals you make when it is life or death. We were gently told by the well-meaning wife of a colleague that Minoo might never be mentally or physically quite right. My parents-in-law visited Minoo in intensive care, peered through the glass wall and noted with some relief that he looked very much like his father. I was not surprised that they didn't come and see me. They would have characterised it as not wanting to disturb me. Now, almost twenty years later, I think that there should have been less of that sort of stuff in my life and that my son's grandparents should have come to see his mother who was also, perhaps, in some danger.

Fram went home and prayed hard all night for our small son. In Italy while I was pregnant we had toyed with naming him Bruno or Gabriel, but, and I think this is quite right, the moment he was born it became clear that he should have the customary Parsi names: his great-grandfather's, his grandfather's and his father's. So I have two sons whose names were foreordained. I have never minded this in the least; their names fit them like gloves. The birth of Minocher Framroze Eduljee Dinshaw was announced in the *Telegraph*, I suppose, and maybe *The Times*. It was also, thanks to the ignorance (let's be gentle and not say racism) of *Private Eye*, announced in Pseuds Corner, as bearing witness to the fact that my pretentiousness knew no bounds, since I'd even given my infant son invented and show-off names.

For some months after his birth, we took Minoo for check-ups, and he learned very late to sit up. It's certainly true that now I have Minoo, I believe that dyspraxia is real, not just a newfangled term for clumsiness. But those prayers Fram sent up seem to have achieved something. Minoo will never make a waiter or a footballer, but his brain functions, may the saints preserve it. He is presently exercising it swotting for his Mods at Balliol, having long outstripped, in literary terms, his exhausted mother. His brother and sister met him with the gentleness and curiosity towards babies that are characteristic of their own father.

LENS II: Chapter 8

J ust in time to start this section of writing, two things happened. My eyes closed down and the doorbell went. Liv helped me to pack away the typical over-reaction that I enact whenever I have tidings that a child may be looming, in this case Oliver. I will not show him all that he is expected to eat or I will receive a well-made and entirely merited lecture against stockpiling perishables in an under-performing economy. I just want him to have the right level of bake to his water biscuits, the right absence of bubble to his mineral water, the correct ratio of cocoa solids to his dark chocolate, and of course the all-important mint tea bags, since he regards fresh mint tea as less satisfactory than the enbagged product. So, you might reasonably suppose, isn't a woman who is this pedantic about her son's grocery welfare set fair to be a hellish mother-in-law? I do hope not, and most of it, my intensive pampering and consideration of my children, is as it were love in microdot form.

So why did the lids over my eyes glue themselves together just like that when it's an Olly day and Liv and I are, I think, quite relaxed together? The only reason I can adduce is that at the age of thirty-six, my mother decided to stop right there, just like that. Had she lived, she would be eighty-one, an auspicious number for Orientals as it happens, since it is divisible by three and compounds of three. I cannot imagine the sort of old woman she would have been, though I am fast imagining the sort of old woman that I shall become.

In fact, anatomically, I feel that I have become that old thing. I creep, I peer, I fall. I have very nearly forgotten how it felt simply to stride along a street with one's head back and one's hair falling down one's shoulders. Yet this feeling was mine not two and a half years ago. I have become timid, from a very low base, since I was already really laughably, in many areas, psychologically timid.

I remember at my friend Alexandra Shulman's twenty-first birthday party a wild Irish boy called Connor said to me, 'You're no use for anything but tossing your hair and making big lips at people.' It looks as though he was right, in a way. Certainly I bear him no malice because he was one of those characters who bring event and warmth into a room, a plot-turner.

My father's death was sudden too, like my own *coup de vieux*. My stepmother telephoned. I picked up the phone. The children were all three one room away. My stepmother's clear tones said what she had to be ringing to say:

'Oh Candy, it's Colin, he's died.'

I said at once what the celestial scriptwriter told me to say and replied, 'You were a very good wife to him.'

My stepmother explained that essentially Daddy, exactly like Quentin's father, had burst, his pacemakered but weakened heart haemorrhaging in that slim chest, and gore pouring from that witty mouth. Fram was in Jersey with his parents. I insisted that he should not cut short his weekend. They thought this odd and were uneasy. I told myself that this was selfless, that there was nothing he could do for me to bring my father back, and there was plenty he could do with his parents on Jersey to make them happy.

There was of course a baser motive, the motive that had been pulling me into quicksands ever since my twenties. If Fram were not with me in my misery, I could drink, and drink I did.

We were already at the time seeing a psychiatrist about my drinking. He was expensive but good. From an orthodox Jewish background, married to a black woman, he had experienced much that was helpful to us when it came to the atavistic flinch. Yet every time we visited, I wasted at least three minutes by making the 'I know we're lucky' speech, the speech of guilty shrink-attenders everywhere.

By the time Fram returned from Jersey, I was the sort of drunk that he must, each time he approached our house, have learned to dread. I was a talking doll with a small vocabulary and stiff limbs. My brain, my spirit, my soul and my spirit-sodden body were unavailable to him at this most dreadful time, when he would have known in every wise how to calm and console me.

Five days later we left the children for the day with a babysitter and of course a list of telephone numbers. We drove to Heathrow and entered the aeroplane in our dark funeral clothes. At the then friendly and rather cosy part of Heathrow where one used to embark for Scotland were further mourners including my cousin Frances and Jamie Fergusson. Frances had been evacuated as a child to the house where we now lived in Oxford. She had known it as the house of one family. We knew it divided up by a developer; our kitchen was the old butler's pantry. Frances had particularly disliked my first novel and wrote me a long letter explaining why, resting her case on the reasonable enough complaint that there are sufficiently many nasty people in the world without writing about more. She also very much disliked the business of my drawing attention to myself by being published. Nonetheless, she made a gay-hearted and kind companion during the long cold exhausting farce that was to be the day of my father's funeral. In the morning I had rung a florist and asked for a big bunch of mixed anemones to be placed on his grave, with a note saying, 'To Daddy, with all my love from Candy'. Once in the air, we felt all set for this impossible event, Daddy's last ever slipping out of the room. Considering that he was only just sixty-one, what a lot he did with his life. He'd meant to die. He hated falling to bits.

We sat with our thoughts. Jamie is perfect at these occasions and knows to tease me but not to make me cry. He had written a personal obituary of my father for the *Independent* in addition to the official art-historical one.

Over the border, something started not to go quite right. Our captain came on to the public address system. Lovely, reassuring doctor's voice. We were in the middle of a blizzard that had suddenly burst over Scotland and we would have to divert to Glasgow.

The funeral was in Edinburgh.

It was a bumpy flight with much flashing in the air and sudden darkness at the windows. I wondered if Daddy had anything to do with it. When at last we got out at Glasgow, we were faced with really only one practical possibility, to hire a cab and screech along the M8 motorway. We got out of Glasgow's tentacular ring-road system, with its tall noticeboards reminding you in twinkly lights not to take a drink or smoke dope at the wheel. The motorway was completely blocked and the visibility was, exactly as my father would have liked it, minimal. There was a good smoky fog. Obviously he was going to slip away while the going was good. We had already overshot the time for the commencement of the funeral service, which was to be led by the Bishop of Edinburgh, the Father Holloway of my childhood. We drove cautiously – no screeching possible – over what was nothing less than thick black ice. No one was crying and I knew that if I started to, everyone might.

On the radio, Radio Scotland reiterated news of the sudden descent of a blizzard across the central belt. I was trying to think when exactly Daddy would be put into the earth. Frances was in the front seat, Jamie, Fram and I in the back. Blizzard lights over the road kept us aware that we were in ferocious rather than merely dim conditions.

As I had so often done as a child, I leaned my head against the window and listened to its hum. I cleaned the window with my cold fingers. There, to the left, reversed out as though in a print or a linocut, was a black horse galloping across a white field, with above it, on a hill, the thorny crown of Falkland Palace. Somehow, we had got lost. I felt that the horse was white, the field was black; the message was that my father was free. His contrary soul, his dear soul was free.

We arrived in time for polite drinks at Edinburgh College of Art and I was cornered by a girl who told me, at length, how dreadful it was for her that my father was dead. I agreed but couldn't do much more to comfort her. She had clearly enjoyed a unique relationship with my father. That's the charm problem. The last mourners left. Edinburgh College of Art's staff annexe seemed, once empty, a cheerless place to have travelled so far not to see the last of one's remaining parent. Jamie and Fram suggested that despite the thick snow, we go and find the grave at the Highland Kirk of the Greyfriars where Daddy is buried close by Robert Adam. He is memorialised in the Flodden Wall of Scottish Heroes. We set off almost skiing downhill in our thin wet shoes.

Lightly clad for a southern funeral as we were, we slithered and slopped and froze. But at last we did find the fresh earth, snow-blanketed now. And we found my cheerful anemones with their card, 'To Dad, from Mandi'. The 'i' had a special dot on it like a Polo mint.

Most things about this vexing day would have been to Daddy's taste.

In Edinburgh, which, to me, has always been an hospitable city, we could not find even a cup of tea. We returned to the airport, flew back to Heathrow, said our goodbyes and Fram and I returned home to Oxford where my older children had for the first and last time comprehensively destroyed their bedroom, very possibly egged on by their grandfather who was making such a spree of it.

When I undressed the baby he had a horrible welt, open and sore, on his left-hand side, the size and shape of an adult man's thumb. I enquired of the babysitter what it might be. 'It's impetigo,' she said. 'I have it all the time.'

───◆◆◆◆───

Apart from – and it is a very considerable 'apart from' – those weekends when Fram was with his parents and I therefore corroborating to myself the unlikeability my mother-in-law sensed in me, we were often very happy. I have been close in the mind to no one unrelated to me by blood as I have been to Fram and in all other parts of our lives that remains true also. Every day when he dropped me at the market to choose our dinner while he drove off to work, I thought, 'This is how it is and this is how I wish it to be.' I worked hard and loved it.

Our joy was later increased by the presence of Clementine, who had come to the Dragon School in Oxford as she had outgrown her school in Hampshire. This thrilled me for all the obvious reasons, and also because it had been Fram's idea and indicated trust between our two households, Quentin and Annabel's and ours. Clementine proved to be a fire-breathing dragon. Soon she was in the scholarship class and schoolmates with exotic names were sending her Valentine messages. Her literary tastes grew. She loved *A House for Mr Biswas*, finding the episode where no brown stockings are available very poignant, and reading *A Suitable Boy* round and round.

Fram was working too hard and on too many fronts and I knew that he was often exhausted beyond endurance. I also knew – how could I not? – that there was something abnormal about my relationship with alcohol. When we entertained, I did not drink, but often disgraced myself when making the coffee. When we went out, I hardly ever drank. If I did do so, there would be a terrible script waiting just inside my larynx to tell itself. Fram would write down the awful things I said and read them to me the next day. It was like listening to another person. I had a bad person within me whom I mistakenly identified with my dead mother. What neither of us realised was the toll this was taking on Fram, not by nature immune to his mother's melancholy.

The years rolled round and I produced my books. I lived by reviewing, which was congenial and constructive. I loved the chewiness of the process, miss it greatly in blindness. The children were flourishing. Fram had discovered a passion for being a patron of interesting architecture. Clementine disliked the boarding school she had moved on to, but, when offered the opportunity to leave it, decided entirely characteristically to stick with the devil she knew. Oliver was growing taller and taller. He played athletics and rugby for his school, in spite of his slenderness. We did not yet have a word for the clumsiness that ailed Minoo, but Minoo had a word for almost everything else.

When the three were small enough and allowed me to do it, I dressed them alike. Oliver is to this day very brave about this, though he will touch lightly on his determination never to wear quite as much pink as his mother introduced into his early sartorial exposure.

Frequently and especially at birthdays, we went to Farleigh or Quentin and Annabel came to us with their new baby Rose, an individual of early drollery and beauty. The four, apart from one short fracas when Minoo annoyed Rose at Farleigh by telling her that her bunk bed was a frigate in full sail, were as close as close.

'It's not,' she said, 'it's a bunk.'

<hr />

Something has gone wrong with my listening patterns. When first I started reading talking books, I gobbled first all my favourites and then those I'd been shy of. In that way I had, although my physical world was becoming distressingly straitened, my fictional world, or rather the worlds I was reaching through fiction; they were rich, orderly, coherent and bottomless, so that, for example, I remember a weekend of real physical discomfort and fear, but within it, telling human truths and diverting me from myself, lay *The Mill on the Floss*. Even through that patchy weekend, I knew that I was still I, because I could feel where George Eliot's writing was strained, woundingly self-referential, and where it simply spilled out in its beautiful, thoughtful, human reams, as for example when the showy aunt whose name I forget shows off her hats to poor Maggie and Tom's about-to-be-dispossessed mother.

I seem just now to have run out of reading matter, or at any rate to have lost the road I was following into the great heart of fiction. My new unities are shaken. Over this last weekend I have listened without discipline to a life of the young Stalin, to *To the Lighthouse*, to *The Guermantes Way*. I began to attempt to listen to either *Hamlet* or the *Sonnets* but the chaotic base I had stirred up for myself made this impossible and instead I seem to have made not a space for unclouded thought but a prescription for damaged sleep and violent dreams. Perhaps it is because I am so often alone that the book within which I am living at any time sets the mental weather and I can do real damage by simple accident or by running out of the steady material of genius that has the capability to crowd out my repetitively cycling thoughts.

The thing is that the steady material of genius, uninterrupted save by my own banal animal life, declares so clearly the gap between its simple exaltation and my crawling haltness. For people who read all the time, reading has a quest to it and I appear to myself, for the time being, to have lost that quest. I do not understand what patterns to make mentally with a cast of books that, although generous, is undoubtedly finite and devoid of, for example, contemporary clutter and the chitter-chatter of magazines and newspapers. I can't look things up. I can't reach for the tail of a memory. So much for recalling all the poetry you have ever known when you are in prison.

I must have known that the hardest part of this story to relate would be that of my marriage to and with Fram. Many of the strands that we worked at together with real happiness and perfectionism were in themselves, it is now evident, not good for us. It is only looking back that I can see that where I thought I was doing the gentle, sweet, right thing, I was in fact harming him by feeding that trait he had derived from his mother; not sadism at all, but a cool distaste for weakness. To this day I take very few breaths that are independent of thought of Fram, I take very few decisions that I do not run past the idea of his mind, I feel no experience full or ratified until I have described it to him. He is without doubt the person who knows me best in the world and has the imagination to see in me and care for the fat, pigtailed child lost in books. He is my home. I am homeless.

How does one write about a marriage? I knew what he was thinking about by looking at his face. I found him beautiful, we had countless small overlaps, plots, jokes, habits. I mourn it so much that I do not seem without it to be able to live properly, as I understand it, giving and receiving love within a moral shelter. That there were deep flaws in our marriage we accepted and grew with, like a distorted tree, and I conducted the lightning strike that cleaved us. I loved to think of us as Philemon and Baucis. But I was watering the tree from underground with alcohol and this, while Fram did everything he could to stop it and to understand it, was never as known to him as it was to me. There were the many times I got away with it and if you think you've got away with anything you are digging yourself a pit, most especially in a marriage. I felt that if I were thin enough and obedient enough and accepting enough, that eventually my mother-in-law would come to see that I was gentle and trustworthy and good enough for her son. The 'surg' might retreat, 'surg' being distaste in Gujarati, distaste especially in this case for too-muchness, my nimiety, Fram calls it.

In fact, of course, perhaps because of the alcohol, perhaps because the situation was irredeemable, no good behaviour was ever enough for my mother-in-law. It was probably not even what she wanted. Of course she was right to feel that I was meretricious, because I was changing shape to suit her.

My steadying father-in-law died suddenly on Jersey in the winter of 1992 and Fram flew to be with his mother and sister. On his return after the funeral, he lay on our bed and recounted with clarity the wrapping of his father's body in white cloth, the holding steady of the chin with a band of white gauze and the days before the funeral during which my father-in-law seemed to exude a sweet scent. I could not have loved Fram more. I still today could not love him more. I love him more every day, as I do my children; it is a growing conversation.

Yet what cracked it? My insistence on surface perfection and my falling far from it? His insistence on surface perfection and my falling even further from that? Our tight closeness? I do not think that our marriage was airless and certainly we had many friends. I have far fewer now. Aloneness and blindness have seen to that. Fram built a beautiful and painterly garden, filled with striped roses, tree peonies and a special tree for the birth of Minoo. Indoors we had made an elegant flat, deeply inhabited by the spirit and works of his mother though it undoubtedly was. I liked that, solicited much of it. The thing is, I thought that I was helping my husband by going along with what his mother wanted of him, and in this I could not eventually have been more wrong.

So it was that I never fussed when my mother-in-law needed Fram at weekends or didn't include me in family matters. I understood completely that it was cosier for them to speak Gujarati on the telephone as well as being more discreet. I understood very well that it was I that was being excluded and I went along with that because I believed absolutely fundamentally in my own exclusion. I did not think I deserved a place at the table. I was a servant and not a very accomplished one, when it came to comparisons, at that. I suppose that I added to my own distaste for myself that of my now widowed mother-in-law who needed nothing more than her children at her side, and if one of those children were married, well, it was to me, who made a very good job of dismissing my own self. I rubbed myself out.

A healthy person would see that this was the very opposite of what everyone involved might require. During our marriage, I had three novels in my mind whose long period of gestation I was moving through. One, set in a hunting lodge in the Czech Republic, was about children, power and loneliness. It will never get written. One was to be about the consolatory and diverting place that a wife's girl-friends play in a marriage. I didn't subscribe to the Anita Brookner theory that no woman is loyal to other women when it comes to men, and I still don't; though I do believe that female institutions are nastier than male ones, very possibly on account of something like the Brookner-drag. The third novel, which perhaps I now may write since I have at hand what I never thought I would have, its termination, was to be about marriage, specifically about the happiness in marriage that is so far deeper than any I, at least, have found outside it.

Autumns were always difficult for Fram throughout our marriage. Not only was it the new academic year, but I would almost invari-ably, at some point around Remembrance Sunday or All Souls, get very drunk, mourning, or that was how I excused myself to myself, my dead. The boringness, the repetition of being married to an alco-holic and its frighteningness, are inexaggerable. Yet we went through long periods when I absolutely didn't drink and we felt unclouded. A logical person, a non-alcoholic, would say, 'Well then, don't drink.' But drink isn't like that. It tells you it won't hurt you and then it steals your love. One of these autumns, after both our fathers were dead, I dreamed that we were divorcing. It seems to me now that I fell on the floor. I felt like carcasses, hung upside down from their feet, split through, revealing all the purple and green and webbed gut and chipped ribbing within. I was not just one carcass, I was many. Fram comforted me and we went back to sleeping like spoons, which was how we slept. All along, throughout our marriage that was to me an intensely, intrinsically romantic one, where the romance lies in the heart of the marriage, not in assumed behaviour, Fram, who is rational, had said, 'We can never know the future. One of us may fall in love with someone else. It's more likely to be you.' I could not imagine anyone who answered my internal mental and spiritual detail as he did. I still cannot. Nonetheless it happened, and he was right and here I am now living my life, thirteen years after leaving Fram, still married to him and fortunate enough to be, as his new companion Claudia, says, 'His widow. You're his widow. But you're lucky because he's still alive.' What led us from there in our marriage, that several shrinks said was too close and we scoffed, to here?

It is hurtful but may be true that what led me here was nothing more, nor less, than alcoholism. I could not have behaved as I did behave had I not been, in addition to being unhappy, at a point in our marriage when Fram was intensely preoccupied with work, drunk. The children were fourteen, twelve and seven. I am a person who cannot bear mess, who is deeply invested in doing my best to be kind to other people at all times and who loves her children pre-eminently. I am a conventional woman and was at that juncture in my life not unhappy so much as caught in a web of behaviour that bewildered me and that I was not clear-sighted enough to see my way out of. So I hid from myself that I felt any resentment or pain at my unnatural obedience to my mother-in-law, because I really believed I was doing the right thing. Nonetheless, I left my marriage at the urging of someone I hardly knew who knew less than nothing about me.

Fuss is made about turning forty, particularly if you are female. People start muttering about hormone replacement therapy and diminishing quantities of eggs. In this last area of concern, I couldn't have been gifted with a more imaginative present than that which I received, driven over in person from Herefordshire, from my step-aunt Nicola Jannink. By then personal assistant and more to the head of an international security firm, Nicola was a compoundedly confident character. She parked her sporty roadster in the always rather controversial car park with allocated spaces in front of our flats, and pressed the doorbell, arriving unannounced on my fortieth birthday for which I had invited twelve friends to lunch. I was making complicated vegetable mousses in the shape of lobsters and was already attired in the size twelve knock-off of a Jasper Conran that came out on these occasions. We saw and did not recognise Nicola on the entryphone camera, but of course her voice was characteristic. I was at once aware that I could not invite her to lunch and that it was approximately quarter to one. I was going to have to be rude.

Luckily, she, according to some ways that one might interpret it, got in first. She entered our drawing room, which we had been titivating and filling with flowers, with a very large box, perhaps a yard wide and a foot deep. From it there came a smell that combined every single pong that makes you want to chuck. It was not a question of a light whiff of white truffle, or a little farmyard on her boots. It was everything that no Parsi – no, no *person* – would want in their house. She put my scented gift down on our sofa, which, as it happens, was cream. I looked into the box, expecting to find I really was not sure what but at the very least telly-dinner for Grendel. Within the box was my name, 'Candy', beautifully spelled out in many varieties of birds' eggs, from pheasant to goose to duck to Canada goose to hen to bantam to quail. So long must it have taken her to collate her generous gift, which comprised exactly forty eggs, that not all of them were barn-fresh. With them went a card that I opened to spread further this unique moment of coming of age. The card read, 'To Candy and her various children by different men, happy fortieth birthday.'

I think I left it to Fram, to whom that sort of thing comes naturally, to be clear, or at least so polite as to get rid of her, while I in my party dress took my ovarian future down to the furthest end of the garden, trying hard not to break any more eggs.

The day extended and no further social eggs broke, so that for once, I believe, I did not even get shaky or high or any of the infinite gradations of drunk that were legible to me and my poor husband who, by nature vigilant, was rendered hyperactively so by having to thole my hidden but evident alcoholism over those first ten years. And there was that one other thing hiding inside us, we two who were one, of which we were ignorant.

LENS II: Chapter 9

Sonnet CX

Alas! 'tis true, I have gone here and there,
And made my self a motley to the view,
Gor'd mine own thoughts, sold cheap what is most dear,
Made old offences of affections new;
Most true it is, that I have look'd on truth
Askance and strangely; but, by all above,
These blenches gave my heart another youth,
And worse essays prov'd thee my best of love.
Now all is done, have what shall have no end:
Mine appetite I never more will grind
On newer proof, to try an older friend,
A god in love, to whom I am confin'd.
    Then give me welcome, next my heaven the best,
    Even to thy pure and most most loving breast.

Perhaps I was at such a pitch of alcoholism, though I had kept it so well hidden, that Mark Fisher might have been anyone; he deserves a better life than the one I was not by any means sharing with him. Anyway it read more like a play than like a life, from this point on, for several years. The plays change in my mind but in the main it is *A Midsummer Night's Dream*.

For the first two years I made an ass of myself, dislocated my children's lives and misled another man as well as breaking Fram's heart. When told the news, Minoo, brought up on Narnia, said to Fram, 'It is all right for me because Mummy still loves me, but for you the golden chain is broken!' He was seven. He held to the faith that it

250

was not actually so, and he has been, a decade later, proven correct. For perhaps the next three years, I lived in a way that is familiar to anyone who lives on the streets. The only way that I can atone to my children for this is by never going near a drink again.

When I was alone, I simply drank, and I drank whatever I could get. This included household cleansers, disinfectant, a substance called Easy-Iron that lends smoothness to laundry but is not a smooth drink. I arranged to be alone as often as possible because I was so ashamed.

When you begin to drink, if you are a 'normal' person, you receive a faint heightenedness and a sense of confidence and permission. Very soon, and I do not know how, I realised that alcohol was my false friend; I think I knew it by my first term at university, but I chose to deny this to myself. I knew it changed me.

Alcohol utterly transforms my character. Very briefly, it used to give me a window of beauty and connection to that beauty, when I would see nature, people, children, all, as it might be, heightened in their own, as I thought, glow. I suppose it was nothing more aesthetically grand than having a sort of Martini-ad director inside my brain. During the years after I left Fram and was drinking, I must have humiliated Mark countless times and I am dead certain that I scared my children. How can a woman who has found her own mother out cold, actually dead, pass on to her beloved children the same experience in all but actual fact?

You can spot other middle-class alcoholics just as you might spot someone who belonged to the Masons. There are the big signs, such as being there before the Co-op opens, which it does, conveniently for alcoholics, at six in the morning, and the small signs, such as being far too polite and explaining exactly why, as you hand over the precise change in 1ps, you need a ready-made gin and tonic at nine in the morning. You learn to spread your custom thinly, so that the people who run Oddbins, Threshers, etc. won't know that you are an alcoholic, when your every gesture tells them as clearly as though you were wearing the T-shirt. Alcoholics know a good deal of secret information and will in any town be able to find the corner shop that does sell booze. Under my belt are Aberdeen, Middlesbrough, Wick, Cromarty, many districts of Edinburgh and Glasgow, Inverness, a comprehensive guide to Oxford and absolutely no experience of where to get drink in London at all, although I do buy it online for my friends and my children. That gives me not a pusher's pleasure, but answers the old need to feel connected to what is normal.

The rules by which alcohol makes you live are the instructions in how to live as though you were dead. Alcohol tells you not to answer the telephone, not to answer the door, not to open the curtains, not to eat, not to wash, not to clean your environment and to cover all mirrors as though after a death. Alcohol tells you to wear black and not to clean your teeth because your toothbrush will make you vomit. Alcohol tells you that you need a drink at four in the morning. It then tells you that you need to sick up that drink to get the way clear for the next drink. You obey it and you sick up blood. In the end your ears, nose, eyes and mouth are streaming blood. You shit blood. You piss blood.

I used to be visited by a bloke called Gary, who represented himself as being an ex-miner. He sold dusters, mops, oven-cleaner and the like, all smelling strongly of cigarettes. Every year of the ten or so I lived in my Oxford house, at the end of the cul-de-sac, Gary visited. In my, perhaps, fourth year of residence, he said, as I passed him a tenner, 'God, m'lady, you look bad. I've never seen you look so rough.' Oddly, I realised only a month ago that the honorific title was a tic widely used by Gary's brethren. Sober now, but quite as jumpy about the front-door bell, I picked up the entryphone here in London, at Tite Street, to be greeted by:

'Hello m'lady, it's Gary. You know, dusters, ex-miner.'

I don't think it was the same Gary and I'm not capable of seeing single, let alone double, but I was struck by the usage. The only other place where women are routinely addressed as 'm'lady' is, in my experience, Wiltons restaurant in Jermyn Street.

'Hello, big girl, who are you married to at the moment?' Peculiarly enough, I have been asked this question twice in my life and I take it ill. I forgive the first enquirer, who was drunk himself, unhappy and shy. He is now dry, handsome as all get out and back to his delightful manner that I've known since I was newly wed to Quentin. The other person should have known better. The occasion was a cocktail party for my older not-sister Jane's fiftieth birthday at Leighton House. Actually I like the man who asked the question; he is interesting and uses his fortune to good ends. Nonetheless, I explained to him why I did not want to be called 'big girl', even if I am one, and I could not credit his having reached over fifty without realising that women are unfond of the insult direct, let alone the implication that one shags like a stoat and marries frivolously. Evidently my voice was carrying, which was very lucky as the party was full of family, their voices raised in euphonious competition. One of the many pretty cousins called Kiloran, this one a whip of courage and loyalty, was bouncing up and down. She is tiny, very sexy and has a lisp. 'Thatth's it, Claude, thatth's it. You've toughened up at lathst.' Not in fact.

Speaking of toughening up, there is one, slightly solemn, point that I'd like to make about AA. Of course I love it and owe my sobriety, ergo my life, to it, but it cannot but be observable that as an institution it is, *and I'm not complaining*, made for men. The systems whereby it strips down the ego and squashes, filtrates and cleanses the superego are all very well for people who think a great deal of themselves in the first place. I know that I drank from fear and shame and I have heard the same from many other women. Fear of what? Of comprehensively everything, mainly of how and who to be. And shame? Well, you are a woman and to be a woman alcoholic is to be born to shame, which makes a fine foundation for the Rapunzel's tower of shame that will grow up on it as the woman drinker lives her eremitic life, and lets that lovely hair get so filthy she could never plait it to make a rope and escape from her tower of shameful habit. Her habit has become her habitat.

There is a point in alcoholism from which you cannot be brought back. This point is referred to by the nickname 'wet-brain'. When people have wet-brain they are simply gone and are allowed by the defeated carers, medical and familial, whatever spirit it is they wish to kill themselves with, since the only way is down.

I do not know why it is but the feet, that are so rich in nerve endings, are tremendously vulnerable to alcohol, increasing in size, turning blue, cracking, exuding pus, losing nails, prone to ulceration. At one point, it looked as though my left foot was going to have to come off. I may say that my family spotted my alcoholism long before my GP did and it was Quentin and Annabel and the children, with poor Mark Fisher, who at last confronted me, collected me, cherished me and delivered me to Clouds, a rehabilitation centre near Shaftesbury, about which and whose late inhabitants, I had, long before, written that architectural-cum-social review. Clouds was, with Taplow Court and Wilsford, the lost house that V.S. Naipaul describes so beautifully in *The Enigma of Arrival*, the residence of a family who were part of that poetic grouping known as the Souls.

Since I had, amateurishly and alone, attempted all the usual separation between myself and alcohol − not drinking at all by using willpower, only drinking one glass and that glass being Champagne/red wine/vodka/alcohol-free lager/White Lightning/Benylin, and so on and so forth ad infinitum or more properly ad nauseam, I knew that I had to ask another person to help me. I was enormously lucky in that, given my incapacity to take initiatives, except disastrous ones, my family, that is Quentin and Annabel and the children, did so. I was literally too drunk to notice that Fram had a hand in it too.

For some reason I had never been to a multiplex cinema and on the fourth or fifth day of being dried out in Hampshire, it was decided that Rose, her friend Viola and their mothers and I would go and watch *Shrek* at the Basingstoke multiplex. I was, from the first moment, certain that someone would arrest me for being with normal people. Rose then ordered a medium-sized popcorn and I knew that I was very unwell indeed. A thing the size of a filing cabinet was placed in

Rose's slender arms. I asked the person behind the counter what large looked like and there passed across his features the terrible boredom of having to explain things in the real world to leftovers from the dusty old world. We sat in ogre-seats, each the size of a small car. I had Rose next to me who explained to me the quotations from other, classic, movies. Later in the day Rose was kind enough to opine, 'I think you're getting better, Claude.' At that stage in her life her voice was very much like that of the Queen. Her part in my recovery is inexpressible because that child put her trust in me.

Of course no alcoholic is being honest if he or she denies that there were those radiant moments of connection with what felt like the truth and a clean vision deep down into it. William James catches it in *The Varieties of Religious Experience*:

The next step into mystical states carries us into a realm that public opinion and ethical philosophy have long-since branded as pathological, though private practice and certain lyric strains of poetry seem still to bear witness to its ideality. I refer to the consciousness produced by intoxicants and anaesthetics, especially by alcohol. The sway of alcohol over mankind is unquestionably due to its power to stimulate the mystical faculties of human nature, usually crushed to earth by the cold facts and dry criticisms of the sober hour. Sobriety diminishes, discriminates, and says no; drunkenness expands, unites and says yes. It is, in fact, the great exciter of the *yes* faculty in man. It brings its votary from the chill periphery of things to the radiant core. It makes him for the moment one with truth. Not through mere perversity do men run after it. To the poor and the unlettered it stands in the place of symphony concerts and of literature; and it is part of the deeper mystery and tragedy of life that whiffs and gleams of something that we immediately recognise as excellent should be vouchsafed to so many of us only in the fleeting earlier phases of what, in its totality, is so degrading a poisoning.

When I was about thirty-two I went on a book programme with Allan Massie and P.D. James in Glasgow; it was for telly, and I'm scared stiff of that. Each was asked to recommend a favourite book. I had just finished reading *The Drinker* by Hans Fallada. If I had obeyed it, I should not have had to live it to its dregs. It is the stony truth about drink for those who have alcoholism as I have it. It takes genius to write of altered states and how they feel, so that the sober reader may enter the state he has very probably never known. Are such passages ever written by non-alcoholics? One thinks of the writers of such sustained and convincing accounts as *The Lost Weekend* or *Under the Volcano*.

I wake up quite often in the night in white dread. Drunks are prone to what are called 'drinking dreams'. One of my worst drinking dreams reproduces an evening at a private house in Smith Square at which I entertained Simon Sebag-Montefiore and John Stefanidis on Simon's Anglicanism. He is, of course, a Jew. Neither of these men is crazy about fat mad enormous noisy women; they are used to the most groomed, elegant and pliant women the world may offer. The relief on waking to discover that at my bedside are no bottles of red wine, none of vodka, not a trail of sick, and no blood in the bed is great. I have as many gaucheries, madnesses and fugues as any other drunk. When I hear of some shit who has taken advantage of this looseness in my memory and suggested that we may have been intimate, I add it to my files. You will recall St Elizabeth who, when asked what she had in her basket by a superior who was growing weary of her good deeds, replied, 'Only roses', though in fact she was bearing bread rolls to distribute among the poor. So once, caught terribly short on Lexington Avenue, very late at night and unable to find the keys of my sweet old-fashioned hosts, I peed into my Accessorize evening bag. No trace at all in the morning; a miracle. The great thing I mind about having been drunk is the imprecision and boringness that descend and, should one sink further, the self-pity that is the worst of self, in the guise of a lament and in my case, at any rate, a keening for all the dead and all the living who will be dead.

Of course there were lovely funny things that felt like being fully alive, things like chatting with Jerry Hall, in her off the shoulder turquoise Chanel leather mini-dress and matching shoes, about our shared problems with long hair. I told her that, at her recommend-ation in *Vogue*, I'd put Hellmann's Mayonnaise on mine when I was at boarding school and she ratified my suspicion that models are bril-liant at teases when asked goofy questions by magazines.

A magazine carried a small intelligent piece on me in which I was described as a 'party-goer'. It was almost then that I folded up on going to parties, folding myself ever smaller and smaller as with the impossible origami trick, until I was so infolded that I went out not at all, my character as apparently hard but actually layered and latent as a tree peony's balled bud before it braves its own revelation. You can never prove that you don't go out; it's a self-defeater.

———◆◆◆———

I suspect that there is a certain amount of old-school-tie snobbery about which place dried you out and which place is tougher than the other. I am certainly prone to it when I hear that softies at The Priory have televisions or rooms to themselves, or are allowed out for unsupervised walks. That is, you could say I am thoroughly brain-washed and very easily institutionalised. Going to Clouds was more frightening than the first day at school, but with many similarities. If you break the smallest rule you are expelled; these rules seem arbitrary but are life-saving. If you hear of any substance being abused and do not shop the user, you are expelled. It goes against the grain. It goes, in fact, against all sorts of grains, both in soft privately educated people like me and in those who are taking the option of doing time at rehab rather than in Pentonville. There is something repellent, dishonourable, not to mention explicitly forbidden in the traditions of Narcotics and Alcoholics Anonymous, about telling 'war stories', as they are known, to civilians.

There is nowhere to hide. Those who find this most difficult are certainly the bulimics and anorexics, whose habit seems to have its teeth into them further even than methadone or alcohol. Heroin is jittery to come off; for about three days people sit around shaking, saying 'I'm clucking', which means 'I'm doing cold turkey.' Methadone is a dulling brute. Junkies pass a rumour that it was used in the Reich, and derives from the words 'Method One'; I just don't know, but it is a slow pig to get off for sure.

The drugs that tell you most sharply that you must have them the minute you've got out of the place that is protecting you from them appear to be methamphetamine sulphate and crack. Speedballs, once had, are never forgotten. Speedball bores are like orgasm bores. You can't convey it unless you can.

You have to have got to the bitter end of your using if you want to recover. Only desperation has the energy required in order to stay clean and dry, as the spooky, infantile words have it.

What I never got used to was that people were expelled or ran away with terrific expedition, so that the cast of characters in rehab – normally around thirty – changed all the time. Very few people lasted the whole six weeks and any of us who did were told that only one of us would be alive in five years' time from among the thirty or so.

I grew attached to a beautiful heroin addict called John who'd been a pimp and had found his sister self-garrotted when he was a small child. He said that on the outside he'd have rolled me in thirty seconds. He meant robbed, burgled, what have you. He was fascinated by what I ate, particularly salad and olives. He kept telling me that they'd be no good for me at all and what I needed was a Big Mac. He spoke of a Big Mac in terms of such descriptive brilliance that he might have been describing the Warwick Vase. One day I gave him a physalis fruit that my daughter had brought for me. Of course I didn't tell him its proper name or he'd have said, 'You're having me on; you can't call fruit after the pox.' I told him it was called a golden berry, which it sort of is in a merchandising way. There was one room where we were encouraged to mix, write our diaries of events throughout the day and hold meetings. It was the old drawing room of Clouds House, a long chunkily elegant room with desks and wipeable furniture. It was a visiting Sunday, deep into my stay at Clouds. The vicar really was circulating; it was teatime. I gave John my delicious golden berry to try.

'FUCK, FUCK, FUCK,' he screeched. 'FUCKING BITCH IS TRYING TO POISON ME. IT'S YOU THAT'S THE VILLAIN ROUND HERE.' Only a really big bar of Fruit and Nut went even half the way in convincing him that I was innocent.

In a rehabilitation centre, the currency is cigarettes and milk chocolate. Bizarrely, I met no regular user of heroin who didn't inveigh against putting white sugar in your tea or coffee, explaining that brown was much healthier. Nor was this an in-joke; it was in deadly earnest. Same with bread.

We slept in dormitories, rose to and were run by shaken hand-bells, and were allocated chores according to the length of our trembly new sobriety. To a person who hasn't washed for months, the sense of achievement in being promoted from dusting to cleaning up the hot drinks room is extraordinary. The first real faculty to return seems to be vanity and in its wake, not far afterwards, the instinct to, if not have sex, flirt a bit and find someone special among the crowd. This is entirely forbidden; when people are seen to be fraternising too much solely with one another it is systematically broken up, even at the level of friendship. During my time there were a few lightning conductors for all this loose lust, including a thrillingly tattooed Irish traveller who looked like a silver wolf, and a lap dancer whose loveliness was vitiated by the low price she put on herself. Hardly ever have I known a girl so in need of love and so incapable of understanding it save through the giving of sexual services. She could not remember a time before penetrative paternal abuse. She would sit at a table and one would wonder why all the boys were clustered round the table. She was, as it were, doing phone sex so that they could all then rush out of the room and wank. She had the face of a singing angel or a sex doll, mouth always open. She could not get my name right so she made me new ones every day, which pleased me. She was obviously used to the notion of confected names since her own was Benice, pronounced to rhyme with Denise; goodness alone knows what it was in fact.

She and I went together to church on the last Sunday in Lent. She asked me the meaning of many of the pictures in the stained glass. She had not heard the story of the crucifixion or of the resurrection. How had she avoided them? It was easy to imagine her in the garden, astonished by the man who was not the gardener. She had such space for belief and intelligence in her neglected life. She had a craving to be a mother because she had so much love to give and so much redress, she felt, to take; it was she who felt guilty at the abuse she'd suffered. She would plan how she would knit little outfits for her child – always a daughter – and she cooed over all the pictures of our children that those among us lucky enough to be mothers whipped out at any opportunity.

It was impossible not to be chuffed by attention from such a lovely being. She was being visited at weekends by an individual pretending to be a relation who was actually taking from her, repeatedly among the trees after Sunday tea, the thing she was used to giving. She hated him, but she gave him what he wanted: 'I went around the world, Italian, French, fucking Russian, the lot. Who cares?' she'd ask. He sent her children's clothes to wear while he was doing it. Crystal meth was her drug.

Only two of us didn't smoke and I am embarrassed to say that sometimes I took up smoking just to escape my fellow middle-class, healthy-lunged goody-goody. I think that what I could not bear in him is what I possessed so much of myself: the element of hysterical control. He was a high-achieving professional whose recourse to spirits had driven him to shove a knife through his wife. Each of us in that place was trying to find the reason why and how not to, not ever again. To deny the metaphysical aspect of this would be to deny the subconscious.

I'm trying to think what questions people ask about rehabilitation centres that I can usefully answer. If they are considering going to one the questions are all about what you are allowed to take in with you. I can only speak for myself. I was allowed to take no books, no personal sound system (not that I have one), no radio, no acrosols, no razor blades, no nail clippers, no scissors, and had to surrender to the nurses my scent and lotions in case I was moved to drink them. After a few weeks, I was allowed a squirt every morning of my scent and this luxury, having been withheld, became the morning's grand bouquet.

When you arrive at a rehabilitation clinic a photograph is taken of you, for which you prepare to pose by, on the whole, being completely blootered, off your face, since it is the addict's logic that if you are going to get clean, you might as well get truly dirty first. As it happened, I was only half intoxicated in my mugshot because of the good work my family had done, but I was still incapable of sitting still, incapable of walking, and drinking litres and litres of Diet Coke and water, and I was seeing things, scuttling, swarming, inbreeding. Five days after having had a drink, when my blood was taken, it was still well over the limit where it is legal to drive. I could have been used to start a fire.

There is nothing amateurish about the medical care at Clouds, and it is to the doctor there that I owe a blessed clarification he made for me. For years, doctors had been telling me that I was depressed and 'self-medicating' with alcohol. I knew I was not depressed. I was sad. Sad things had happened, one after the other. I did not fail to respond to beauty, I did not hate life, I did not want to be dead. Or, and it is the crucial golden 'or', I did not feel depressed unless I had been drinking. It was drinking that made me depressed, not drinking that 'cured' my depression. I was pleased that the doctor realised that matters were this way round because he could see that I was in good faith when I said that I could no longer drink and stay alive and that I wanted, more than anything, to be sober.

In my dormitory were a gorgeous pregnant crack-head, a sad girl who didn't think there was anything wrong with her, and a methadone addict who later duped me into lending her ten quid, which was an expellable offence, but the Board of Trustees agreed that I was so dopey that I was hardly culpable and had probably really just been doing her a kindness, as I thought. Clouds is not smart. It is run by a charitable foundation. Many of its inmates are not paying for themselves.

The beds are just beyond camp beds, the blankets are nylon, the sheets polycotton, the rooms are stuffed with addicts and there are never enough beds. Talking after lights out is discouraged. Fraternisation between the sexes is forbidden. The nursing station and the smoking room and the room where hot drinks are made remain open all night. Hot drinks acquire fetishistic significance. When you enter a rehabilitation facility you are given a mug on which, with your shaky hand and some nail varnish, you write your name. For us, this was perhaps to be the seed of a future responsibility for our own lives, looking after a single mug. Hot drinks become all that drugs and drink were. People try new combinations and on the coveted Saturday afternoon shopping hour in Shaftesbury that is allowed at the end of your stay, you see your peers looking crazily for new ginseng, apricot, strawberry, redcurrant and vanilla teas. My own great discovery was high-fat Horlicks with extra milk. I broke a rule and took it to bed with me. In order to encourage healthy eating, there was a bowl of fruit out at all times in the main room. The only fruit my peers liked was bananas. They did diverting rude dances with them and didn't think they were as disgusting as normal fruit, so I got my pick every week of apples, pithy oranges and tall, woody pears. The hero in the daily life of such a place is the cook. Day after day, with the help of whoever was on kitchen duty that day, the cook produced four or five options because, of course, there's nothing like an addict for saying he's allergic to gluten, nuts, chilli or what have you. As in, 'The smack never done me no harm, it was all the take-aways. I can't take rice.'

There was something beautiful, too, about seeing those who had been close to death regain, literally, an appetite. And God those skeletons ate. It was the crack addicts, the speedball users and the heroin addicts who just had to have puds, and every day our giant of a cook produced all the old-school favourites and then fruit salad for poofs like me. It was one of the shocks of body modification that I received when I was in Clouds, that probably half the girls in there had had boob jobs. But was it surprising to be able to abuse your body in this way (and who am I to be priggish about that?) when you had felt able to swallow fifteen condoms full of cocaine? When the girls got better, which took about three weeks – as short as that – each planned a new life, in almost every case, without the man inhabiting her old life. He would frequently be her dealer or pimp, often too the father of her children. The girls looked to a purer future, all except one who seemed already to be resigned completely to death. She was beautiful, loved, in her early twenties, affluent to boot, and very bored indeed. It is a sad reason to resign from life.

With the boys, it was the other way about; they'd got straight now and they wanted to get back to the old lady and straighten her out too. Invariably they wanted to stay in the relationships they found themselves in, unless, that is, they found new relationships in Clouds. We were attended by male nurses and male and female counsellors. The day began at 6.30, we hauled on the comfortable and loose-fitting clothes that the list of what to bring had recommended, and hurtled or hobbled down to whichever room was designated to our group. There was no doubt a more than quasi-religious element to the day. We would listen to a reading, go to breakfast, say grace. To be chosen to say grace was a privilege. Sometimes people would have gone in the night, having been found with gear or trying to escape.

We cleared away breakfast, a mysterious meal for me because the dying girl could put back a packet of Cheerios and one of Frosties, and still she looked like death. A slight rivalry grew up between myself and a really handsome blond junkie who said his legs were murder weapons and he could kick a man to death. He kept a place for me at breakfast every morning, which I loved him for, but I knew one reason why. Every week I would try to get my Sunday visitors to bring hotter and hotter mustards and Linton could always beat me when it came to either putting them up your nose or eating them off the spoon. So we were getting our capsaicin high. While he spoke to me often of the beauty of needles, I just couldn't be tempted to mainline mustard and I didn't see how we could get any works here. Anyway, I'm scared of needles, but, peculiarly, the really needle-fixated junkies will tell you that they are scared of needles too, just like alkies 'not liking the taste'. It is a complicated business that these poor counsellors are there to unknot. As a rule, they have 'been there', which creates trust and an ambition to emulate that is again – has to be – infantile. Counsellors go at it simply because what they seek is emotional truth, which is far plainer than all the distractions like class and milieu. After our morning's group work in which I hid and said nothing at all for some weeks, allowing the others to fill in questionnaires about my character which were pretty spot on ('this person is full of fear'), we had lunch and then optional creative work or exercise or other organised pastimes. I painted a bit but I saw at once that not my facility but the truth was required and that I was just making pretty marks on bits of paper. One of the sweetest inmates was a professional graphic artist who hoarded Marmite, since Marmite is famous for rehabilitating your liver. He shambled like a man with chains on his legs and his feet were too painful for shoes after all the superlager and methadone; yet every word he spoke was beautiful sense. He died shortly after leaving Clouds.

I abandoned myself to a masseuse who was using a technique called reiki. I was in a smallish room with two peers of whom I was categorically afraid, one a big talker from a family of nine sons in south London who teased me by stealing things from me; and the other, a displaced semi-posh boy with a heroin habit that had used up his mother's jewellery and his father's money. He was as proud as a knife out of a stone. In the background there was the customary uncommitted music that goes with massage and that makes me faintly cross in a Colin McWilliam-ish way. It was, nonetheless, in this company and within the aroma of a really cakey lemon-scented candle, reminding one of a lifetime's washing-up, that I unbuttoned sufficiently to shed tears, which is, for the counsellors, a place to start.

Each evening we had to fill in our diaries of the day and write how each day had struck us. Several hardy souls played Scrabble. John the pimp was fantastically intelligent and as beautiful as a cat; what a life he could have had, maybe is having. Quite soon I was hauled into the staffroom to talk about my diaries. 'What is this word "pulchritudinous", Candia?' I mumbled and said that it meant good looking.

'Well, we're going to have to change your diary keeping. You can write the diaries for the guys who don't know how to write as long as you let them use their own words, but you are to keep your diaries, which have already covered more than a hundred sheets of paper and said nothing at all about yourself, to eight lines a day, *only* about yourself.'

I felt very much like crying.

They had me caught.

But looking at it from now, I see what they mean. Reading and writing *were* a kind of drug to me.

In order for the message of total abstinence to stick, those clinics where it is practised recommend no reading at all that is not concerned with the programme of Narcotics Anonymous and/or Alcoholics

Anonymous. I was allowed my Christening Bible, King James, given me at Rosslyn by the Kuenssbergs four decades and more before.

It is true that I have consoled myself (the programmatical word might be 'medicated') with books and with reading and writing, but I am not prepared to accept that these are malign. I was, however, prepared to suspend them for those weeks during which I was, because I am, ultra obedient to our counsellors. The highlight of our week was a sing-song with the vicar, and the highlight of that – truly – was singing 'Angels' by Robbie Williams. I hadn't heard it before. I hadn't heard of *him* before. I was that disconnected.

For a start, there was the fact that almost without exception the counsellors were good looking (that's where the pulchritudinous slipped in). Many of the male peers hungered for the beautiful, Spanish, booted, stern lady who took us through our character flaws with practised discipline on a daily basis. They vied for her white smiles. Romances were led in the head and added to the already electric atmosphere which sometimes exploded into a fight or a shouting match of incredible vituperation between women, but for a lot of the time people just shook and said, 'I'm in bits, me, in bits, d'you hear, in little bits. I'm fucking fucked. I'm fucking FUCKing fucked.' One boy who arrived in a state like this, left having built upon the good he had found within himself. He could have got a job at the Foreign Office, so great was his ability with every level of equivocation.

I wish any government would dare to institutionalise NA and AA rehabilitation programmes in prisons.

There's a commonsensical and rather trite saying that goes around about addicts. The idea is that we are capable of enormous workloads because we in the past put so much effort into getting, using, recovering from, etc. our drug of choice. We are certainly obsessive, which is at its healthier end known as 'applied'. When I left Clouds, I felt as newly hatched addicts do, skinless and terrified that I would find myself taking a drink.

One Monday after Clouds my literary agent came to see me and suggested that I write about the experience of detoxification. The people at Clouds had said the same. This book is not it. I would like to address a book that might be of use to an addict who is not sure whether they are one, and I'm fairly sure this book will be, if useful, useful in a more diffuse psychological way.

I will tell quickly, because I am so ashamed, the fact that after my agent had gone I saw the migrainous aura in the air that tells me that I am going to have a drink. For the next two weeks I drank to die, to the despair of all who had invested love, patience and trust, not to say a large sum of money, in my sobriety. Entirely drunk and responding, no doubt, to what had been there all along, I ran from my isolated house at the end of the cul-de-sac to Fram's house that had been our marital home. Perhaps that is not true, perhaps Fram came and collected me. At any rate, after as many as five years without seeing each other in other than strainedly civil circumstances, we were together again. And there was Claudia. For, I think, two days, they nursed me. I stole two bottles of wine because I was having DTs. In front of Claudia, who is dry, witty, confident and intelligent, I was everything I had I thought managed not to be: maudlin, sentimental, snobbish, bitchy, envious of her solid yet elegantly raffish background, the lot. She took it all. Claudia is one of nine siblings from two marriages. I am one of one sibling from one marriage, really.

After that last bender, once more, and without complaint, the Farleigh household rallied around the woman who had never been its head. I was nursed for perhaps ten days in 'my' bedroom at Farleigh. Every day the sway of the trees made me a little less sick. Every day I could more easily fight off the racing thoughts of the urgent necessity of suicide. I could even see, in person at the bottom of my bed, my older two children, who were, if you can believe it, offering to drive me to meetings. The last drink I had in my life I could not finish. It was a can of Special Brew, taken from the refrigerator in my first husband's morning room. I poured the rest away, squashed the can and wrapped it up. Later when I was returned to Oxford and

having my second try at a sober life that has, so far, while under-
mined from many angles, not cracked, I threw the can away.

———◆———

What seems to have happened is this, and Fram will correct me if
I am wrong. When I left our marriage, Fram said his mother was
'on the verge of beginning to be able to contemplate thinking of
coming around to me'; Minoo insisted that she loved me. After I
left, I received a letter from my mother-in-law begging me to re-
consider and saying that she was sorry. I was very touched by this
letter and have hidden it somewhere so deep that I can't find it. I
know now that Fram dictated it, but my late mother-in-law was
willing to write it.

In a way, my departure was all my mother-in-law's fears and dreams
come true. She had her son back and she had her proof that I was
as delinquent as the culture that I represented. She cannot but have
been agonised by the pain in which she saw her son, but she also
knew that he blamed her in part for the catastrophe, and that blinded
her with fury. It was Avi and Minoo and, later, Claudia who got
Fram through.

During the years in which I had imagined Fram all-powerful, plot-
ting, arranging for my book to get bad reviews, talking the brilliant
streak of malice that he can, and always, always outflanking anyone in
argument, Minoo had made mention of Daddy's 'horizontality'. They
had taken holidays together in Greece, in Sansepolcro, in Menton, and
'Daddy has gardened and we did a lot of Gibbon/Plato/Donne together.'
Minoo would not be used as an informant and nor did I ever approach
him with the intention of so using him. It was Claudia who told me
later that Fram had, during these years that I was drunk, a nervous
collapse.

At once all feuding and all stiffly held positions melted for me and
I was struck at heart that this person with whom my mind was most

involved had been dealing with such pain over such time. I bought a quantity of books on bipolarity and read them properly. I wanted to know everything that retrospectively might mend him.

My mother-in-law's father, who looked very like Fram, died young driving home one evening on a road he knew very well. Mehroo's mother, Ratu, remarried quite soon. She was the first woman in India to get a pilot's licence. Home movies show her beauty but also shyness veiled to some degree by the fashions of the time – a cocktail or cigarette holder never too far away – and a Leonardo smile. Mehroo found it difficult to come to terms with her mother's remarriage, and though they remained close, there was a touchiness between them. After her mother died, Mehroo cried every morning for several years. When Eddie died she berated herself for having done so and her own widowhood was almost impenetrably sad. When Fram returned from weekends spent with his mother, it was often as though he needed draining of the gloom he had ingested. In fact his patient, tranquil sister, who lived with Mehroo and increasingly looked after her, protected him far more than he cared to admit.

When Fram introduced Claudia into his life, which was long after I left him, Mehroo said that 'even *that* one' (me) would be better than 'this one'. It is possible that she saw that Claudia (who hates me to say this, remarking that it makes her sound like a breakfast cereal) was authentic in ways where I, who had trained myself, in order, as I thought, to please my mother-in-law, seemed not to be.

The language of disgust came easily to my mother-in-law. It was the dark side of her noticing eye and impulse to order her surroundings to make them fresh, light and airy. It is a language perhaps available to women who have not allowed their sons to grow up. Fram was much more her construct than his father's. Perhaps I am still in a swoon of honeymoon with my sons, or perhaps I am smug, but I don't see why their loving other women should spell infidelity to me; I think it might even mean that they must like me, or some category to which I belong, that of being female.

It was Claudia who saw that Fram must choose between her and his mother and enabled him to make the necessary transition without any unnatural break. Throughout all this, Avi nursed her brother, took no sides, exhibited perfect tolerance and when the time came, with Fram, nursed their mother in her swift last illness right up till the end, which Minoo and I missed by a few hours. In her last weeks, she was allowed to remain at home, consumed by cancer and read to by her children. I sent her a short letter saying that I was sorry that she was ill, that I had loved her and that I was very sorry that I had hurt her.

Fram chose life. Claudia is life in the many. With her came Toby Buxton, father of her twins, and tutelary spirit of the household. I was lucky enough, and this is not invariable, to love their twins Xavier Buxton and Yvo FitzHerbert, on sight. They are dissimilar twins yet their sense of a shared life saturates their relationship. Tall strawberry roan Yvo has cornered climate-camp and chess, and blue-eyed auburn Xavier is that rare thing, a born classicist. By lucky chance, though his school offered no Greek, he attached himself to a retired don, Margaret Howatson, from whose private lessons he would return with shining, sharpened eyes. Curiously, through their father, Yvo and Xavier have, like my son Minoo, a brother seven years older, also named Olly and with a poll of red hair.

When first I heard of these domestic arrangements, my reaction was envious, I suspect, and petit bourgeois, I know. The truth is that it works very well. Toby does the cooking and lives in the coach-house. Fram does the gardening and emanates power from his elegant drawing room. Claudia does far more than she pretends to and emanates an equal power that contains Fram's own and protects him from it, from her large, wood-stoved study. Bysshe, the standard poodle, a redhead himself, has the best manners of any dog I know. Segolène the cat seldom settles save to scratch or to burrow into her fleecy manger next to Claudia's computer.

As you will imagine, I'm defensive when people ask the sort of questions you can conceive they might. On the whole I do not speak to people about it unless I'm fairly certain that they will understand, and the key to their understanding must be that I wholly accept all of this, since it is the source of Fram's happiness, and to love someone properly is to wish them that.

When eventually I went stone-blind and I was still too scared of Claudia and of her and Fram's felicity to go to their house (it made me shake since it was all I had failed to make with my husband), Claudia came round to my house with a bunch of flowers. Her colours are autumnal – warm Victorian reds, blues and browns. She also brought for me Antonia White's *Living with Minka and Curdy.* This was a perfect present. Claudia herself is a convent girl like Antonia White and clever and teasing in a similar way. The book was a pretty edition with its decorative dust-wrapper, and Minka and Curdy were, of course, cats. For good measure, Curdy was short for Coeur de Lion.

In February 2007, I received a letter from Claudia. Once we had seen one another plain, I believe we immediately trusted one another, but for ten years before that I feared the Claudia I had invented: ferocious, social, *branchée* and able to mobilise, I chippily thought, platoons of literati, wits and heart-struck young men bound to her frank beauty and disgusted at my putrid, tarty, fat, pretentious artifice. I used words to describe myself that hurt.

It occurred to Claudia, as I grew blinder, that I should come to live with her and Fram. This was brave. The first time I had visited their house I was wobbly with grief and envy, for what I saw was my own exact life, but relaxed. I felt shredded and like a fat ghost, an undisposed-of Rebecca. I do not think that Claudia has any Mrs de Winter feelings about me, nor need she have. She wrote:

Dear Candia
I felt that I should write to you directly about my reported suggestion that you think of Winchester Road as a base. I wondered if you felt you could not think of leaving Beaumont Buildings for as long as Minoo was Oxford based, and I thought that might seem an age

given how unhappy you are and have been there and how impossible it feels to turn things around from there. You know that I have thought often, in the last few months, that it was quite wrong for you to be stumbling around alone and wished that you could see a way of stumbling around Winchester Road until the eyes were brought under some sort of control. But I also saw that Winchester Road seemed no solution to you, and was in fact a sort of torture. 'I am alone', you say, 'that is the truth'. Well you are and you aren't. If you can bear to take a place in our loose family structure then you would be a strengthening rather than a straining element. I think you know this, perhaps you resent it, why should you prop up our structure? Only because in becoming a prop it would become your structure too. I don't know any other way, except to prop and be propped. But I also know, in some quarters, that this is regarded as a sick way forward. Still, I reiterate – we haven't anything cosy and nuclear for you to disrupt – you must see that. Toby and I failed as a partnership – now we are back on course. I have no doubt at all that Fram and I would have failed if we had tried for anything tighter or steppier than we have got. You say the place for you at the table is still an outsider place and that is the story of your life. I say it is as outsiderish as you choose to make it. There are bonds between you and Fram which make me the outsider and bonds between Toby and me which make Fram the outsider and I don't doubt that we too could grow some bonds of our own that would make outsiders of them both, not to mention all the bonds we have with our own and make with other people's children to pass the life. I know that Doctor X and Doctor O have both warned against what is on offer here, to which I can only say what do they know and what do I know. Well I know – sort of – what is on offer and why – but of course cannot be the judge of whether it is what you want or need. I have, I suppose because of my mother, a horror of endings. All sorts of mess and experiment seem to me preferable to losing sight of loved ones. But that is my wing, I cannot make it yours.

I have no sense of anything but gratitude for this letter, with its beautiful sense of 'passing the life', a phrase she has coined, and its generous reference to her own mother, a Margaret like my own, who died young in a road accident. But I am I think too old and conventional and under-confident to enter such a collegiate way of life. I know myself too well and that I would fit in around the edge of yet another family while significantly being in some sense dead or absent, as I felt it. Am I wrong? I don't know.

Most psychiatrists I have seen say keep off, keep off, he has two wives, his cake and his eating, and she has two husbands, and you have no one: face it. But how can I when they are my family and I love them? Much of me is from or in or with Fram, for I have known him for so long and am formed by much about him, that I have had to rip out, heal, remould and reform and solidify those traits or excise them, for I am a stand-alone doll now, unattached, what we are told all healthy personalities should be – or un-overattached may be fairer to the psychiatrists.

I feel that it is best to leave bits of myself behind at that house and leave it whole, and over time not to grow scar tissue or to harden, but to try to learn what it is to be a whole person, alone, a coloured-in letter 'O' rather than an incised and empty zero.

I think maybe it's anyway time for Claudia and Fram to get a rest from me. I have come to resemble Fram's mother in a way maddening for and to him. She was inconsolable after the death of his father. Why should he have to console me for my having left him? When first Claudia was with Fram, he was bruised by me, and no doubt talked about me a lot, never guessing that I was thinking about him all the time. Now both Fram and Claudia know that I love them, separately and together, why should they not forget about me?

Then I remember the words of Turner, when asked which was his favourite of his own works, 'What be the use of them, save all together?' and I do think again.

Earpiece II

Q: What do you call a no-eyed deer?
A: No idea.

For many years before I began writing this, I was thinking about it. I thought about it in terms of glimpses and of incidents showing the inner life of those who surround me and whom I love; above all I thought of it in terms of scenes depicted, conveying the evolution of this scattered human soul. Whom did I have in mind as a possible reader when writing it? In writing a novel I think it is important to have no one save the ideal reader in mind, as though you are writing a letter to life about life. This isn't a novel, but it is perhaps a bread-and-butter letter to life from someone who has loved it but not sufficiently belonged to it.

Which almost leads me, but not quite yet, to the subject of religion that has underlain my whole life. But first I must answer the question about who this book is for.

When I was sighted, it would undoubtedly have been for those few readers who are interested in the minds of writers. I have no celebrity and any success I have ever been close to, I have shrunk from, if not sabotaged.

Then there is the question that had already entered my mind a year or two after my stay at Clouds House, of how to write a book that is not merely an episodic story of the dreadful scrapes addiction has got you into (a genre that usually does well at the tills), but a book about addiction that somehow touches the addictive synapses of other addicts, as a novel touches the synapses of those who are addicted to fiction. In other words, I suppose I was keen to try to find the pleasure centres of the brain, those centres that keep people gobbling the sugar, glugging the caffeine, swallowing the delicious fiction. When I was an undergraduate, my friend Anthony Appiah and I used gently to tussle about whether or not it mattered if fiction was untrue. I thought it certainly didn't matter because, actually, fiction is true. At that time of his life, Anthony was already picked out for stardom in the philosophical world, editing a learned journal called *Theoria to Theory* with Elizabeth Anscombe and other distinguished philosophers. He is now not only a philosopher at the top of his powers and an expert on African-American studies, he is a poet and an extremely readable novelist, the old fibber. I think he has written more novels than I have, which wouldn't be hard.

I've been thinking of writing a memoir for some time or at least a long poetic visit through unearthed memory to Scotland. Now I think I'll do that next, because this book has not been that. Maybe I shall never be equipped to write it if I remain blind, so distorting is memory; otherwise readers of the putative book might accuse me of having invented Scotland.

That we each invent a world I do not deny. Mine feels unwhole to me at present, without sight and without a presence to give love to, though with many beloved absences, but I know that when I write fiction, I can make something external to myself that *is* whole. If one cannot daily build love, one must make something. I am digging a hole through the dark.

So, there I was contemplating an, as it were, if not curative, at least helpful book for other addicts. I don't think this is it.

Then came blindness and the knowledge that here was something I really could share with very many other sufferers. I also had the more self-interested thought that by writing about my blindness and the life that, some doctors hint, has brought it, I might lift it from my eyes.

I've never written a novel without having at the start a clear picture of its architectural shape in my mind. To cheer myself up and to give some sort of idea of how I work to my kind amanuensis, who was to type all this out as I spoke it, I thought to write this book in the shape of a pair of spectacles. There's no point forcing these metaphorical matters; they happen or they don't.

At this point I'll touch on religion, or rather, as it feels to me, on faith. To each of the psychiatrists I have seen in my blindness, none of whom has been a Christian (they include two Jews, a Muslim, a Hindu and some humanist atheists), I have made the tired comment that I was born, Darwinianly, with the gene for faith. I think that perhaps rather than calling it a gene for faith, I might more precisely call it an impulse to thank and a consciousness of the creation that, *and here's the rub,* I saw so vividly. It was almost in my eyes that my faith inhered and one of the reasons, I am sure, that I have been so unpersoned by my blindness is that I was my eyes, my eyes were how I got to being me. My eyes saw the edges of things and the insides of things and permitted me to write novels about these matters. My eyes gave me jokes that led me to friends who enjoyed my company. Without my eyes, did I still believe?

I still prayed, because I believe that the only way to eradicate a habit is to install a new one and for drink I substituted a different kind of praying from that I conducted while I howled to the dead in drink. It is interesting that in his novel *Greenvoe*, George Mackay Brown has a drunk woman who, when pixillated, puts herself in the dock and hurls accusations at herself from other personae who reside within her. That's me.

Over the last two and a half years I have been without independence but with the great gift of the reawakening of my bond with Fram. He said at one point that my faith had been, throughout my life, simply yet another means of punishing myself. He himself does not experience guilt, which is a marvellous lack to have. I subjected his theory about my faith to analysis, scepticism, prayer, conversation with an ex-monk, discussion with religious friends, but there it stuck and I thought, 'Yes that's it, I'm blind and I've lost my faith. I've achieved it, I've become a stone, the thing I most fear, the thing my poor maternal grandmother pretended to be, the thing my mother-in-law turned herself into, the thing that Liv's first name so extraordinarily, coincidentally, contradicts in her surname, a stone.'

Nonetheless, if this is true, why have I not enacted the instructions in the nasty little book I sent off for called *Final Exit*, an instruction book on how to kill yourself? You may ask how I read it and the answer is with difficulty, holding my eyelids up, *very slowly* and not fully. As an antidote to it I read the recently published and tremendously, as you would expect, sensible *Easeful Death* by the philosopher Dame Mary Warnock and a cancer specialist and lawyer, Elisabeth Macdonald.

I was alone, I was blind. Sometimes I felt 'like death'. Nonetheless, I did not feel like dying. I could not wrest from myself that thing that poets track, that we feel when we wake up on good mornings, that slippery thing that is not death at all but the light that comes before death and that we call life. I couldn't seem to shake off my faith just as I cannot seem to shake off a conviction that I shall see again, which is not to say that I am not frequently almost completely humanly reduced. It is often at points like this that Cousin Audrey, whose instincts are unerring, will call sometimes simply to say the words, 'We're lucky, darling. We're not in Auschwitz.' She rings many of my family with this message. It is an undeniable one. I had a glimpse of what the Great War did to Cousin Audrey's life when last week she told me that every day of her girlhood at Lochinver Lodge began with the raw sound at 5 a.m. of her father vomiting his guts up. It was the trenches he was remembering. His body sicked them up every single dawn until his dying day.

Le Ballon Rouge, a film shown to me repeatedly in childhood, is the story of a little boy who loses his balloon and who is found by many millions of balloons which carry him away and up into the sky. The film, I see now, is about death and loss, and it has stuck with me. I seem, in spite of Fram's suggestion that it is a punitive faith, still to have it and to understand it as not punitive. It is, if you like, the basket in which I put my few good eggs. I want nothing from it, it is simply my sense of attachedness to other minds, including those long dead, and to the created world. The punitive aspect of my life comes from something that happened to me that has made me mislike myself and agree with those who mislike me; I know it is wrong and a perversion, a bad habit, perhaps private, perhaps generational, perhaps inherited, possibly inflicted. I really don't know. All I know is that I refuse to pass it on to my children.

This morning on the radio I heard 'Thought for the Day', which my devout and commonsensical first husband calls 'Gutlift'. And yes it often does make you want to heave with the chumminess, the euphemism, the sidelong holy boasting and the presumption of familiarity. Today's crasher touched on 'the old lie: *dulce et decorum est pro patria mori.*' He referred to the Latin words as 'The poet Horace's jingoistic soundbite'.

While there is such bracing illiteracy available in daily life I am too cross and too exhilaratedly pedantic just to curl up and die. What is the man talking about? I hope his wife bet him that he couldn't get four solecisms into one duff phrase. Or perhaps there's a stupidity race with points for really dim anachronisms and super-thick conflations. Perhaps then I'm trying to say that my faith is in language. Certainly it is so that the very greatest writers, those who manage by suggestion to give shape to their silences and omissions, come closest to expressing what I am reduced to calling an insistent urge to acknowledge what is and has been beautiful in its wholest sense about life.

Now: the hook of the earpiece of these spectacles. I had written the first lens when one of my doctors suggested that, in sequences of bunched years, I have another go at telling my story and that I, as it were, should blow my clinical cover and at least try to explain to the reader where I am now.

He also wanted me to speculate as to how I might have acted differently when it came to repeated behaviour. By this, I understand him to mean that I have brought unhappy events to bear upon me because I think that in some profound way I deserve it. He is dead right. My system of thought has run along the 'it's my fault' tram-line since before my thought began. Of course, it bores and hampers me that when my brain is idling it is turning on itself. I have tried many antidotes to my obsessive gobbling up of blame, which, I don't need to be reminded, is in itself a form of egotism.

Perhaps it's my daughter who has taught me most. She has taught me that if I am imperfect then she doesn't have to be perfect and so, she tells me, she will now dare to be the mother of daughters, whereas before she had sworn it would only be sons.

My memoir, or so I had thought until I found myself writing it, odd little unwritten book that it has proven to be, was to have been a love letter to Edinburgh and Scotland itself. I was made and born there. I miss it more than I miss my sight. I did not realise that was true until I said those words to Liv.

There are some jokes about being blind. Liv – who by the way has a house of her own and a life to go to and is not with me for more than five hours a day – and I have just taken delivery of rather many blueberries, perhaps enough to constitute the entire five-a-day ruling and intake of Her Majesty's Government, if only they could get over the colour. We have had problems with Zoflora disinfectant too; you might almost think I drank it. I buy online and sometimes blindly whack in the wrong number. I have thirty packs of Sheba cat food in delicious jelly. If you get any of that jelly on your fingers, your hands smell for days as though you were a whale's midwife.

I will now try to implement what the cognitive behavioural therapist has asked of me, that is to say speculating on how I might have behaved in order to avert disaster. My mother's death was, I think, outside my own power to affect. I might have asked for love from, and shown more loyalty to, my father. I should have, as Claudia has done, said no to the perfectionisms by which Fram's mother was torturing him and he was involuntarily tormenting me. I should cease to collaborate with anyone who attacks me. I rushed too often to greet my literal or metaphorical attacker. I always argue against myself. I install routines that do me harm and I am unkind to myself because I think it somehow vulgar or American or wet to be kind to that person. I should have asked for help before I became completely blind instead of saying, 'I'm fine'. I would say that I hate attracting attention, but this is not completely true, because I absolutely love reading my stories to people and am masochistically conscious of publicity.

It is late in a life to install straightforwardness, especially, come to think of it, when pursuing the metaphor of a hook, but I am pledged by these doctors to being more direct – and it may be working. I have kept up the habit of buying books and last week I nearly dared pick up a book to read but I was afraid lest I miss the wave, the exactly right wave that will take me out into the blue open, where I shall be able to see. It was a book of verse called *The Lost Leader* by Mick Imlah. Even to hold it was proper physical pleasure. Soon, if I'm careful and straightforward, I may be able to do more with this book than just smell it and look forward to it.

There is one thing I have not told because I am so ashamed of it. I used to have a photograph, black and white of course, of Mummy and me in her bed. She looks about thirty-three and I look about six. My mother is rangy, her long hair is down her back, her big mouth isn't smiling, but it is relaxed. She had the cat face that Cate Blanchett has. I sometimes gasp when I see pictures of the actress, because I see Mummy. She was not anything like so beautiful but she had 'it', the cat thing and the mouth and the whirl of cheek and the poise and the sexy arms and angles.

In the photo, she is wrapped in a paisley shawl. She is easy, happy, at home in her marital bed. Presumably Daddy took the picture. I had not yet started to get fat and look like my mother save with a fringe and instead of her slanting eyes, large happy ones. I'm in a nightie from

Mrs Virtue's. When I moved to live with the Howards on Colonsay, I cut this photograph in half and put the little snap of me with their big professional photographs of their six children. God knows where it is now and I've lost the half with Mummy on too. I did not think I would be able to speak about this since I feel scissors at my heart when I do. Or 'when I do' because I never have before, not even at AA.

I went to an AA meeting in Aberdeen. There were four big men off the fishing boats. The cold on the boats, all that freezing salt fish, makes heroin a useful comforter, and drinking is forbidden at sea. There was a pretty little lady with black hair and there was the secretary of the meeting. I don't think it's breaking any rules to say that at the start of most AA meetings there is a talk which is called either the 'chair' or the 'share', I've never worked out which, so I allow it its bungy ambiguity. Quite frequently, a stranger is asked to do this part of the meeting, as everyone else is, or may be, familiar with the others' stories, though something new always comes out no matter how often you hear someone tell their tale. What I have just said is almost invariably true unless you have the bad luck to go to a meeting where a famed clown or someone with a well known 'terrific sense of humour' is anticipated; in these cases I've often felt the slippy clitter of used coin.

In that little hall in Aberdeen, with the sound of rain bouncing back six feet off the pavement in its thick strength, I told my story and everyone shared back, which means talking about their own lives and relating them to yours, having attention to 'the similarities, not the differences'. For a non-alcoholic the principles of AA are pretty useful. That one about similarities cannot but be, quite simply, right for civilian life too. It was what Ian McEwan said the day after the Twin Towers were struck, and he was spot on. Fiction is what takes us into the understanding of people who we are not. So it is with AA.

The wee lady with the black hair came up to me afterwards at the Aberdeen meeting and put her hand on my arm. AA is quite full of hugs, touches, taps, and, most terrifying, bear hugs. 'There is a higher power,' she said (the higher power is what it says it is – i.e. anything you want it to be, so as not to offend anyone, believer or unbeliever).

I must have looked interrogatively at her. She said, 'Well, I was praying to get X (another writer who is anonymous, who must remain anonymous); but I did say if X wasnae around, Candia McWilliam would do. I was just wondering, would you have time to have a wee look at these pages I've got on me?' She went on to tell me a story of recent and unremitting tragedy. But she hadn't had a drink.

In the underworld, or is it a labyrinth, of those of us who are unwell in whatever way we are unwell, there is a generous custom of passing on threads of hope. So it is that this afternoon, in a hotel room, dressed in what he has requested be 'loose clothing', I am to meet a total stranger who will touch me in ways I have never been touched before. For this I am to pay him in cash. I am innocent and ignorant of what the encounter will entail. The hook is trust, if not faith. The clincher was what I really loved. After I had explained the intricacies of my own name, he confided his own,

'Arthur Jaffe,' he said.

'I like Arthur,' I said.

'But Art is good,' he said

'In life,' I said.

Let's see.

PART TWO: SEE/SAW

Proud Maisie is in the wood,
    Walking so early;
Sweet Robin sits on the bush,
    Singing so rarely.

'Tell me, thou bonny bird,
    When shall I marry me?'
– 'When six braw gentleman
Kirkward shall carry ye.'

'Who make the bridal bed,
    Birdie, say truly?'
– 'The grey-headed sexton
That delves the grave duly.

'The glow-worm o'er grave and stone
    Shall light thee steady;
The owl from the steeple song
    Welcome, proud lady!'

Walter Scott

Chapter 1: The Seen in the Thaw

I spoke those words, 'Let's see', to Liv in the hope, if not the trust, of something happening that would cast me with the white pebbles of sight or the black stone of blindness.

It fell out less plainly, or less directly. There is a kind of resolution, but it's not white, or black, or even grey. It is black overlaid with a new variety of white, you might say. I shall try to explain. I wrote what follows in the late spring of 2009.

This is what actually happened next.

Art the masseur, I should say, broke me down into pieces and made me drink something that tasted of guavas and hot rubber. After any strenuous massage at the hands of those who know the body's connections with itself, I was given sometimes as much as an hour of seeing, and often a near-night of sleep. These things became, throughout that time, impossible to set a price on.

More than ten years ago in a suburban supermarket I bumped into a friend who paints on silk. She happens to be the second wife of an influential and lucid atheist. She is an actress as well as a painter, used to making something new where there was something else before.

I was bunging stuff into my trolley, being familiar with my own tastes and those of my children, my spirit dimmed yet excited by the anaesthetising greedy glare of the supermarket. She was taking more care, handling her purchases in a fashion more mannerly, like one not wholly familiar with some aspect of the chore, as though she might be undertaking it for someone else.

And so she was. Her shopping trip that day was executed for the woman who had been married to her husband before she was and who was now, in the last stages of mortal sickness, too unwell to shop for her own groceries.

God might have been let slip, seen off, even, from the declared, indeed renowned, intellectual orbit of the household. The graces of private moral consideration were however very likely reinforced rather than diminished by this large overmastering dismissal. Illness was making its demands upon family life and causing new domestic shapes to be made. A net was being set for safety, in a system acknowledged to be without certain consolations.

I was often to think of my friend doing her predecessor's messages in the months that were to come, and as my husbands' wives did much for me.

———◆◆◆———

Ten years or so later than that observation in the bright supermarket, in the late June of 2007, I finished dictating my short memoir, *What to Look for in Winter*. I didn't know what to make of it, when it was over. It didn't feel as it had when I finished the others, the books that had come down my arm and not out of my mouth.

I had little sense of its weight. Talk flies away, while words, written, are at least a bit more tethered. The silence left by words, uttered, is for the talker, in this circumstance perforce a monologist, often a self-disliking silence, sweetened only by relief at the falling away of the sound of one's own voice. The negotiations between thought and page are grosser, at any rate in my own case, when spoken, than those accommodated by the hands moving under silent orders that have not been confided even to the self, when the writer may have planned the journey but the mind may take detours or unpack maps of quite another route towards the posited destination. Is that the place, after all, where you want to end, let alone end up? It's perfectly possible that the mind has decided to travel by air, or water, or to the stars, and that it decides to travel beyond the planned destination, or to stop short of it.

The unconscious mind is more explicitly present in a room where a writer is working apparently alone (though almost certainly with one or more invisible collaborators) than when he is working with someone else, the typist, in the room, waiting to trap the spoken words.

Or so it has been for me during these years since I began to go blind in the spring of 2006. Let me remind you now, for fear of offending any more conventionally blind person who may by some means be reading these words, that I am 'functionally blind', that is my eyes work quite well but my brain has decided that they must be shut and that its self-allotted job is by no means to permit them to open. My own brain is powerfully good at its task of interdiction.

So, having become trapped in a sightless head, I decided to try to talk my way out of it by speaking my little memoir. A talking cure where the typist is the neutral presence and the reader the eventual listener or, perhaps, if he or she cannot read in the conventional way, or has come 'blind', to a recording of the work, its eventual hearer. A reader hears things in his head more than he listens to them, since the sound made is often silent though uttered in the reading mind, having been fed through the translating eyes.

In the carrying out of my project, I was as encrypted and self-subverting as I have learned to be from habit and by training, temperament and taste.

Fewer forces, or so it felt to me, were at work upon the spoken than had been upon the written words, when I had written my first books in the conventional way. The spoken words were less refined, more coarsely hatched, the pressures upon them all but social, the misgivings and selections temporary and local, necessarily predicated upon what I wrongly or rightly felt that the typist might endure, or even be entertained by.

The sense of invocation, paradoxically, was lacking, when the words were spoken. A fruitful uncertainty was seen off by the transaction. I was fairly certain that much of what I value and seek in fiction and attempt to transmit in my own writing could not have existed had

I tried to speak fiction as I spoke that memoir. I wasn't sure that this quality was present in the memoir.

Still, my agent sent it out, and I was happy when Jonathan Cape offered for it. I was fifty-two when I finished dictating it.

In the months and now years of compromised sight, what has borne me up now that I cannot read words from the page with any continuity has been the written word, spoken. I have listened to books. This is very far from reading them.

My gaze, like that of Actaeon upon the naked goddess Diana, is refused. Many of my new or fresh thoughts came, in the sighted past, to my brain through my eyes, in reaction to what I saw or to what I read. The thoughts that lay in the new dark within were in danger, without the eye-fed light from outwith my closed brain, of knotting up. My eyes had brought in the light that kept my mind open, or as open as it was. Now that my brain refuses my gaze to me (my brain absolutely will not open my eyes; I do it, when I can, manually. I would rather mention this blinkingly between the curving lids of parentheses), the thoughts can be like hunting dogs in my mind and tear and tear at my jittery gaze, my dear and dragged-low sight, tear at it constantly.

I sleep poorly. Inside my head carnage repeats itself daily; by night it is bloodier, since the vocabulary of image and event available to nightmare seems crudely vulgar and sensational. It is also predictable and banal. I may dream architecture and colonnaded freedoms, but my nightmares are of body parts, humiliation, fear and leakage.

I suppose we know so well what to scare ourselves with, having made the limited and powerful selection without words before we could speak much. Most of us saw before we spoke.

The most intimate consolations have been offered by two writers who did, as it happens, dictate much of their work, Henry James and Marcel Proust. The length of breath, the precision and extent of steer, the understanding of the pictorial and the want of illusion, that acceptance that we are very little but all in all to ourselves and all that we ourselves have, that breakage can be less sterile than some forms of wholeness, are in both cases such that each writer in his own fantastically atomised fashion does reflect the fabric of thought while seeming for the duration of one's immersion in his art, to hold up or to reveal the richest losses of time.

Each of these great consciousnesses could be said to have married itself and within this solitary generous hermaphroditic union to have fertilised its own internal world with a rich inward folding, with the apparent arrested liquidity, the look of layered softness, of some sea-rubbed rock. Retirement from the world, in the cases of these two more than sociable men, by all accounts matchless companions and talkers, superabundant writers of letters, was not a sterile fugue but a necessity in order for the travail of making to be protected, fostered, brought to multitudinous birth. Both teach compassion through clarity and that style, far from being extraneous embellishment, is the transmitting currency and current between reader and writer.

Both writers suffer from being smart names to dismiss. Rather, they do not suffer, being beyond existence, which *is* suffering, but potential readers are discouraged, which is a wanton deprivation in a diminished world. Eyes are voluntarily sealed in the name of clear-sightedness. Most dismissal of either writer takes place without the fatiguing commitment of investigation. A superstitious hope of ingested glory goes with the dismissing. Just as if you eat the heart of your gallant enemy you may be held by some onlookers to grow in courage, you may be accounted rather a stayer if you contemn the immensities of *In Search of Lost Time*, or something of an exalted spirit if you belittle the heights of the later James, decrying the rainbow-rich mist as wilful fog.

Thus you may bag the medal without enlisting, never mind getting anywhere near the heart of the engagement.

That is not to deny that the problem is there, the other way about, where the artists' names are not there in their full suggestive lightness and potential but mentioned with the thumping self-satisfaction and positioning of a name-drop, as though the adducing of one or other of these two, let alone both, settled something in this world instead of adding other worlds to it. You know the stakes are high when Proust or James is brought in to settle one of those questionnaires about the best works of the twentieth century. You also suspect that no one wants to talk about it much any more but rather to set a monument upon the question, adding a stone with the partisan reader's name upon it to the cairn at the top of what can be regarded, or so the implication is, as a mountain range unsusceptible of scaling save by, well, such people as that high-breathing cultural referee.

------◆·◆·◆------

It is now May 2009, almost a year since I thought I had 'finished' *What to Look for in Winter* and, if anything, the frost has taken a tighter grip on my eyes and upon my life.

I have abstracted myself from that life for two months in order to find a way of thawing it out.

How have I managed to get to where I am now from where I was then?

And which 'then' would that be?

And why should you care?

I will answer for the moment only the third question. The frost, in some form, is waiting there for us all. My account of how I failed to help myself, while trying as far as I could tell very hard to do so, may make you feel smug. In an age of self-help books, here is an account, to warn any reader, of almost exemplary self-unhelp. May it inoculate you against the same sickness, or against it in so acute a degree.

What connects my blindness, the atheist's wife and the living words of dead men? I have come to an island to find this out for us, you and me. I have fifty-six days left in which to do it.

During that time, I hope to finish this book, and to set in the ground that I roundly hope will be melted thereby the bulbs whose flowering will I also hope compose a short novel, as vivid as energy and compression under silence can have made it.

I have set aside the whole month of May, writing a minimum of eight hours a day, to write the first draft of this second layer of memoir.

At present, I can see when writing if I hoist my forehead up with the flat of my left hand as I laboriously and inaccurately type with my right, and when my eyelids get wise to this and clamp insistently down, I lift them with my thumb and little finger, dedicating the latter to my right eye, the thumb to my left. My eyes fight back and weep to be shut down and left in peace. They are hot and dry and hard. Their white goes to leather. They leak thick tears. These tears are ineffectual lubricant. They are so hot that sometimes they make you feel like crying.

Meanwhile the bottom of my face works and strains and munches and contorts as it reaches for some kind of comfort let alone rest. It is not pretty. Quite often I dribble. I swear (my condition, blepharospasm, has a contiguity with Tourette's Syndrome). I was never before a swearer. The features of my face have thickened, the skin over them coarsened as I pull at my mask in the attempt to free my thwarted struggling gaze that I know is in there somewhere. There are surprising batches of wrinkle and hard elbowy flesh on my face as though it were a long-used handbag or a tired dog. The dog likeness is made closer by a couple of twitches and a tremor that is worse in company or sunlight. My eyebrows are a tangle of argufying bristles, like moustaches. Along the crevices of my muzzle, where I grimace in the reach for settled sight, the skin is irritated, red, flaking and psoriatically itching. I bare my teeth such that strangers comment, and babies, after whose company I hanker, hide their faces from this witch. Those teeth clench and grind and gurn away, trying to find settlement for the reaching eyeballs lying above them, to catch the wind of sight and set aloft my eclipsed brain again.

I haven't seen what colour my eyes are for months. I know that they are green. I've looked into no eyes for years. Humans read one another with their eyes well beyond, within, through and behind words. I'm trying to find new ways of doing this deeper reading.

There is something wearyingly unimplicit about the social life where little can be left unstated and understood; understanding being, with the word's apparently negative start, a perfect example of what Keats called negative capability, the magnetically attractive force of what is felt to be present in the unadvertised, the swell of beauty lying within what is not bound or bounden.

As far as I could, I avoided contact. This can worry and upset the small number that remains of persons who can endure you, or who are bound by piety or affection to do so. I terribly regret that.

If you think like this, you are likely to be straddling a cruel gulf into which you will decisively fall, and from which I am typing these words to you.

So hard is my brain lobbying to shut down my eyes that it makes up a headache in protest at the wrenching I'm imposing on my eyelids. Something has gone wrong in High Command, up here in my head. When I ask my brain whether it would like to come to bed, it replies that it has a headache.

In fifty-six days, I am to be the subject of the second half of a procedure that is quite untried but that has led to some relief for fourteen possessors of my condition. The other one has died, not of the procedure, but in the way of things. Most people with blepharospasm are women, yes, and most are older than I am. Which isn't to say that I won't die.

To my shame I have far too often and too routinely consulted means of doing so undetected in these last three years. I don't like to mention it, as the thought of my children having to outlive such a step pains me for them in the way that perhaps only the child of a suicide can know. If I can help it, my children will never know that particular shape of loss.

The procedure is called a Crawford Brow Suspension. In January, the muscles around my eyes were cut and stripped out. The effect is to toughen up the eyelids. Mine don't feel tougher, actually: they hurt more than they did. They are thicker and mauver than normal eyelids.

They feel and look swollen. They are shiny as though I have painted them with nail varnish the colour of certain small hard purple turnips. Where many women might put eyeshadow, I have scar tissue. So powerful continues the brain's imperative to the lids to remain in spasm that they force themselves shut with muscles extraneous to the lids themselves, muscles that the brain conscripts to effect its strange censoring.

The second half of the operation happens six months later, and I thought, at the time seven months ago when I elected to have this operation, that it would be a good idea to have it the day before my fifty-fourth birthday, which is on the 1st of July. The secret notion I had was that I would wake up remade on my birthday. The plain surgical fact is that I shall wake up not capable of walking comfortably for the coming month or so. And blind.

The operation comes in two parts in case of vascular crisis during a macabre reallocation, since the second half of a Crawford Brow Suspension, six months or more after the first, harvests the tendons from behind the subject's knees and inserts them, umbrella-frame-wise, beneath the forehead and the thickened, stripped eyelids. Some subjects report a subsequent difficulty with closing their eyes. Eye masks, like those used on long plane journeys, have been mentioned as being useful, as have partners, who may assist the subjects at close of day by firmly shutting down the now staring eyes of the once blinkered loved one.

I was chary of making the first part of this memoir and now I find myself writing a second, further to expose the first. It isn't unlike that eyebrow-stripping procedure: phase one, the first bit of memoir, to toughen up and prepare for deeper digging; phase two, this bit, to do that deeper digging, in order perhaps to see more, and be on the move again. Or to prepare to do these things.

I very much didn't wish ever surgically to interfere with my face and now am committed to doing it twice in a single year. It wasn't particularly that I was vain, though I was, but that I didn't fancy that shared look of terror and conformity that declares cosmetic surgery's costly untruthful ghost to have passed. And I thought that I was interested by time and its effects upon a face. My children, too, had mentioned their misgivings about cosmetic surgery, the batched moms, the party lines of preservation. And it is expensive and self-necessitating; and I am a Scot and we don't do that like of thing.

I no longer physically recognise my face. My body is another matter that I would rather leave aside for the moment, which may have been something of the problem all along. Scotswomen make crack dualists; we are at odds with our bodies often, especially if we have early been fingered as being possessed of a brain.

⸺◆•◆•◆⸺

I took the train to Glasgow from King's Cross. Since not noticing that my own house was on fire till I was nearly smoked, I have been staying at various places in London.

At Glasgow, I was met by the husband of my sister who is not my sister. So many of the relationships in my life are this kind of double negative adding up to a positive. As has been true throughout my life, quite little is what it seems, though much feels straightforward. I think this not unusual for people who make things.

I described earlier how I subtracted myself from home in my teens and added myself to the Howards in the Hebrides. Each of these islands is geographically, culturally and linguistically identifiably its own place. Smallness does not wear away individuation; rather the opposite.

I am here now, on the island of Colonsay, the place in the world where I borrowed a second childhood. I just sort of sank out of one life and emerged into another. It was not a kind thing to do. It may have set a pattern of which I cannot be proud and that my blindness may have given me the insight to break at last.

I'm renting a flat in the big house where we were children and where

I learned, if I learned, to share and transmit. This flat is made from rooms that were once nursery bedrooms; the flat's sitting room was the bedroom where my not-sisters Caroline and Katie ate Eno's Fruit Salts off their fingers in bed, and on the wall as he ever was is an engraving of Sir Wm Hamilton, Bt, Professor of Logic at the University of Edinburgh, published, as it happens, on 4 May 1857. Today is 4 May. I began this chapter on the 1st.

Next to Sir William is a coloured map of the Western Isles of Scotland, done into the Latin as befits a Scots nursery: '*Aebudae Insulae, sive Hebrides, quae Scotiae ad occasum praetenduntur, illustratae et descriptae de Timotheo Pont*. Colonsay appears, lying on its side as is the whole of the West Coast, preserving the modesty of the usually incontrovertibly (though docile) phallic Mull of Kintyre, under the cursive word 'Collonsa'. The part of the island where this house would be built bears the label 'Killouran'. Oransay, the small island off Colonsay, appears to be designated 'Gruonsa', though that 'G' may be a ruptured 'O'.

The bathroom of the flat contains a small modern plastic bath that just holds me. Once, in its place, was a cast-iron bath that held all six of them and me, with a heavy steerable cylindrical contraption between the taps that was the plug. The bath (and all other) water in those days came off the hill and was the colour and flavour of peat. Now it is clear, though it still comes off the hill down from the loch above the house.

My brother Alexander who is not my brother is in charge here now, though his father, whom I call Papa, as all his children do, is completely alive. My not-sister Katie is Alexander's assistant and right hand and her husband William is woodman, dustman, playwright, diplomat, angle-grinder, freight-sorter, mandatory representative non-native at community meetings, and maker of vital connection. That is he takes life and rebags its stuff into packets that people can enjoy and be fed by. The blindworm boredom dare not come near him.

I have come here to recuperate in advance of whatever comes next and to allow to settle the furious ineffectual seething of my inward life of this last year, and of too many of those years that preceded it. To some extent, too, I am getting myself, and the problem I constitute, out of the way. Where do you put a blind mother who falls over quite a lot and is not yet old enough to fold away for the winter with the barbecue and the swimming towels? It is I, not the children, who think like that, I know, and it's no help to anyone.

Upstairs a family who have rented a flat in what used when we were young women to be called the bachelors' corridor are preparing their tea. The father is talking. I cannot hear his words. It is not unusual for families to rent an annual holiday on the island over the whole transit of the raising of a family, whose progress may be followed through those irresistibly voyeuristic and eventually shaming comments books that are a feature of rental property. One is ashamed because one hasn't recreated the idyll recorded by some family more ideal, better at spotting otters, happier within itself, than one's own.

Or maybe that's me, who have been playing at families all along, with deadly seriousness and an eye on the competition because I've so little idea of how it works, my darling mother's surprising disembarkation having left me to improvise.

It is bath time upstairs. A tired young child is grizzling without commitment, nothing that a story will not sort. A radio is on. Water carries radio waves and I can hear enacted conversation, perhaps *The Archers*, under the living voices with their more convincing scoring for rests.

Outside, after a day of rain, the light is glittery. Through one window of the room where I am slowly typing may be seen the deep garden over and beyond a stream that is itself well beyond three swooping levels of lawn. Two huge trees, *Cupressus macrocarpa*, twisted by wind and time, hold the last evening sun till late (this is the North). Daisies and blossom smutch, sparkle and powder all the green lawn. Several surprising palm trees announce the passage of Victorian plant-hunters through this lush declivity, actually a geological fault, through Colonsay, this old small rock, nine miles by three, covered with green and surrounded by that light-reflecting north-western sea. I know these sights because my memory provides them, though I can with discomfort and a certain stiff pincering address hold my eyeballs bare to take them in, even if it is not the same as the absorptive wash that soaks all-gathering sight. But it's something, and I do count my blessings.

I am unsure how good blessings-counting is for the character, or am I the only person who resents it when others tally your reasons to be cheerful for you? It's hard not to observe that they are finding coloured veins in the rock that sparkle best in rain. Also, don't lists with an uplifting undertow almost mandatorily make one gloomy?

A less negative aspect of blessings-counting came to me. Two electronic benefits occurred. I turned on a kettle, with whose product, hot water, I made a cup of Scottish Blend ferocious strong tea, with milk, and I received a text message from Claudia telling me of her doings today, and those of my son and Fram. I read the message by feeling my eyes and holding them bare, open.

Annabel and I also exchange texts most mornings. We have communicated daily for years. After all there are children in common. We are close friends who lead widely different days and may think we hanker for the other's way of life, but actually probably favour our own. I like the detail of her day; she accompanies the emptiness of mine and does much spiritually to fill it.

When we count blessings as they occur, we have a greater chance of valuing them. I cannot remember when I have not, having lived at certain times of my life without one or other of them, been grateful for plumbing and electricity. Hot water almost demands a deity of its own before which to lay oblations of scented soap and rough dry towels.

Which leads me to the pattern revealed in sleep to me, not for the first time, but with the soothing power of pain relief. My actual father, the man who with his short-lived first wife, my mother, conceived me, liked to ask me when I was small, 'Do you know how to make a fishing net?'

The answer is that you find a lot of holes and tie them together.

Upstairs the toddler is gurgling. Voices through pipes make of the largest house a shared familial linked system, those rooms of space connected by the web of piping, the moving webs of water telling their message through the darker parts of the whole constructed system. Water is making comment throughout the pipes of the old house. A hum, the inception of warmth, accompanies the low hint of heated water through them. Flushes fall back and rise again within the white bathroom walls.

The best way to tell it is perhaps to try to thaw out that declared winter and to attempt to capture now what may be the actual, not the fancied, scene in the thaw. It is time to see that what felt like a sentence to emptiness may be an offer of air.

Chapter 2: Saw/See

I thought that I would take two lenses of time, one from after finishing the first part of this memoir, and one from now, here on Colonsay, this place that combines the present with the far personal past, and try to adjust them so as to see through or even catch some light to partly melt the snowy cover that lay across some of the bleaker branches or wider wastes of the earlier chapters.

There is a newish convention, that goes against any observation or experience of life that I have, that characteristics and narrative must not be ambivalent or ambiguous, or the reader will be confused. Since this is the condition of language itself, we are talking here about books brought to the level of nursery school reports, or of bad film synopses.

Ambiguity is there at all times. Tolstoy and Proust catch it. In triumph lies defeat, in consummation boredom, in despair self-watchfulness and the resurrection of attention. When I was told that I would never see my mother again, I felt not one but many things. As well as the confirmation that I was now unaccompanied, as well as the questions as to the cause of her death, that might not be asked, there was the unpleasant gratification of the event, that could not be admitted, but was nonetheless an attribute of that time. I knew that, for this probably very short time to come, no one would be unpleasant to me for being peculiar or showing off, or being fat, and that I would for a time be at the focus of something. In neither case was I in fact especially rewarded along the lines I had envisaged as parallel to feeling that harsh deep abandonedness. But I certainly knew that there was never going to be the simplicity and clarity I had previously imagined went along with growing up.

And surely it must grow one up remarkably, becoming motherless as quite a small child? Yes and no, of course. I have always tried to think how another person would behave, given my circumstances. I may think I can imagine this, but I cannot. Can I? Can you? I can think how a character taken from a book would behave with more success than I might think how a friend or a member of my family might behave. I can guess, and I may be right, or I might be confounded, I cannot even imagine how I might behave. I just behave.

I may think that I have taken stock, but what will most likely have happened is that curdling mixture of inanition and violence that have characterised my life and that are more usual than either literature or our understanding of life conventionally allow. For if we were fully conscious of this catch all the time, it would be as impossible to live as if we were able continually to look at that glaring fact of mortality against which we have to fold our time away, and from which we must avert healthy eyes.

Our character and our personalities lie in the torsions between ambiguities, no matter how Romanly straight our apparent, enacted, nature. In fiction too it is these electrifyingly unsmoothed characters who most live, as against characters taken from stock. In life we are drawn often to people as unlike ourselves as possible. That compensating attraction means we outsource traits we do not possess but require. I twine like a convolvulus about people who apparently know their own minds. In very few, but how beloved, cases, have I been right.

As for such people as pride themselves on self-knowledge, it is as with those who admit with sheepish self-tenderness that they pride themselves upon their honesty. They are playing to their own gallery.

Some people do act without reflecting. They may be stupid, very brave or extremely well trained. Almost without exception there will be a sadness about them at the weight of those closed chambers and tightly stifled reflective surfaces within. Unless they are beyond privilege naïve, they are made jumpy by the untested and will not allow of the unknown. They curtail their vision with the red denial of a butcher insisting that his bloody crib is not an ox's carcass.

It is still raining in the Inner Hebrides in early May 2009. Through the water pipes I hear the upstairs toddler and through the window that is opposite the one that steams with garden green, I am aware – the window is at my back – of a conflict of rooftops, one curving over an arm of the house, the others sheltering its kitchen and offices, finished with softly bent pale lead and tiled with slate as deeply purple as pigeons. Everything is wet, the window as well. I am conscious of this sight because I have in my life seen it so often, so often that I am not sure that I need to see it now, such that I am saving my eyes for this screen rather than for the window whose view I am describing as I tap laboriously trying to elicit some scene from the past in order more clearly to stalk the truth like a white hare through the thaw, although I am pledged to the idea that truth about one's own life melts, or flits, again and again just as you breathe on it.

Not long after I spoke the words 'Let's see', just after my birthday, I had the first and so far only grand mal fit of my life. It felt as though I were an old-fashioned camera, into which innumerable heavy lenses were being inserted one after another, each at a different and more acute setting, and then as quickly and clatteringly taken out. The world weighed heavy, shivered, fluctuated, jerked, grew too heavy utterly and fell to the ground in pieces as though my limbs were dud and chopped like fallen empty armour.

It felt not unlike the aftermath of drinking till blackout and indeed Fram, who saw me in hospital, at first wondered if I had been. For me the consequence of taking one drink is that I cannot stop for ever longer and more deeply degrading periods afterwards. If only it had been that simple. I do not know why my brain took this great insult and gave me a fit. I know that I was saved from something worse by my god-daughter, who was with me, and who rang an ambulance because she was afraid for both of us. She told me later, doing an imitation, that I hid from the ambulance men, and questioned their choice of shoes for hospital. I can remember nothing, just as after a blackout.

It was in A & E that I came to. I felt as though I was in the middle of a painting of a deathbed. I lay on a foreshortened bed off which I hung in a curtained space, with, to one side, a slim young man with striped hair in a stream like Beethoven running, and at the foot a group of young people in summery motley, cotton, stripes, lace, shawls, hoods. Two of them were blond and one had the dark hair and eyes of a young knight in a painting from the Renaissance. I remember thinking all that, the Beethoven, the clothes, the similarity to a painting, and I thought at that same moment that if I had had a stroke I was still myself within. I was frightened. I was worried that I had disrupted a number of people's days. I was embarrassed. I wondered how I could ever make it up to the children. There was also the startling fact that I could see.

I knew that I could not simply be polite and get out of this one. Something had occurred and the event, whatever it was, would not go away. I could not pretend that it had not happened. I was unable to remember that morning save for two detailed things. My first visitor that Sunday morning had been my daughter's friend Edward Behrens, later to be the Italian Renaissance figure at the foot of the bed in A & E. We had discussed the mushrooming scene in *Anna Karenina*, the moment when Tolstoy says that you could almost hear the grass growing, and describes a blade of grass that has pierced its way through a grey-green leaf of, I think, aspen. I said that I wanted to learn Russian and we discussed audio systems of teaching oneself a language. I suspected that I would be too passive to compensate for the absence of a teacher. Something was wrong that morning and I sent Behr on his way. It was a sunny day in Chelsea. He was off to lunch with friends. I felt as though the inside of my body were heating up and going to split my skin. I was afraid that I might be sick or worse in front of this clean young man who has been so good to me over these blind years.

The next thing I remember is that my god-daughter Flora appeared in the dark of the hall at that flat. Its lighting was faint, its mood brown. The hall featured several subfusc contemporary oil paintings of Italian street scenes and a large bronze sculpture of a multiple demonic head that cast a horned shadow. When Flora arrived, over six foot two and thin as grasses in wind, she stood in the light of the front door and I saw her in the kind of intense detail that came to me often when I was very drunk and that was one of the reasons why I continued to explain my drinking to myself – that crack of clear high vision before passing out. It felt a bit like some kind of love, or doting.

I saw Flora heightened, as even more porelessly exquisite than her genes and mien have made her. She might have been the last thing I ever saw. For all she knew, she was. I scared her terribly. My last mortal sight before the new, fitting, world was a young woman of disproportionate height and slenderness in the lace and pinny of a Victorian child, complete with bloomers and smock. Below this stretched her long white legs, ending with ballet pumps. Her chiselled pale blonde head is perhaps a ninth of the length of the rest of her. Her hands waved like white cloth under water. She looks at the world through specs. God knows what she saw.

And then, for me, nothing. For poor Flora, panic and telephone calls, chasing to ground diverse family members, keys, messages, toothbrush, the intimate chores of sudden event. We get no rehearsal. She did it all with the kind of competence that can come only naturally.

I knew that something had happened and was possessed by the idea that it was a stroke. McWilliams die young of strokes, especially fat McWilliams. Thin ones die young of heart attack.

In the hospital Flora said, 'Fram and Minoo are coming. Fram says everything will be all right.' Fram is the human whom I always believe. I hand to him inappropriately profound knowledge and sagacity, authority. It is burdensome for any mortal and worse for one as sceptical and intelligent. Nonetheless, all I wanted was Fram's assurance and he will have known that. The same goes for our son Minoo.

Beethoven said, 'You are in the best place, Candia. We do not think it is a stroke. As far as we can see, you seem to have had a grand mal fit.'

He knew what to say. He saw the main fear, addressed and dismissed it, and supplied as much fact as he was able. He also, with some generosity, said something sensible and kind about the ever higher doses of antipsychotic drugs I had been prescribed with a view to causing my brain to have some sort of benevolent convulsion that might, as had sometimes been suggested by certain controlled cases and had been written about in a couple of academic papers, alleviate my blepharospasm. What Beethoven said was mild, intelligent and noncommittal.

By now I realised Beethoven was in fact my GP and he knew me well enough to tell me the truth. It was a relief to be understood, to be treated as myself. He spoke sanely and the relief, that of finding myself in a sane, if frightening, world, was great. It is Beethoven, of all the first wave of doctors, who has helped the most. How frustrating then that his skills – common sense, empathy, compassion, practical doctoring – are undervalued in an NHS crippled by bureaucratic failure to communicate from the most basic to the most elevated levels and awash with specialisms that take no account of one another.

'I'll tell you what,' said my GP. 'You must go to *Don Carlos*.'

I heard it with gratitude as a sentence from the lost world, from which I had been cut off by a mixture of illness and my own self-isolation. Long before I had become ill, I had become almost incapable of going out. But this was a healthy sentence and I heard it gratefully. I also realised that very few people knew how odd and shy I now was and that the thought of going out at all was nearly impossible, that my automatic response to any invitation or suggestion was 'No'. I wanted to be connected, but had forgotten the flags to hoist to make the right signals.

I love *Don Carlos*, the darkness of the bass voices, the problems of conscience and power, the fear that fills it, the intractable love-muddle. All the stuff that my father disliked about it, I love. It makes me feel that nothing cannot be thought through to the sound of it, though actually my father might have said one is feeling rather than thinking. It thickens the air and my father liked his mental air clear although he could do turbid domestic silences and was a retired master of brooding absence. He did these for my mother, not my stepmother, who was certainly a better wife for him. I wonder how often in a day I think, in three contexts, that last phrase? So much so that the ease with which I use it to hurt myself bears reining in. Since my husbands' wives are not there to hurt me, why do I sink to using the thought of them to do so?

Because, perhaps, it feels familiar.

The days that followed in hospital I still cannot make out. I felt like an animal and I knew that I was dying. I could not explain this to people. I was acutely worried about my daughter, who was already in a bad way as her ex-boyfriend had recently died in his early twenties of anoxia. When I got to a ward, my diagnosis was posted on my bed. It said that I had anoxia. Clem was wobbly and I couldn't properly help. I was rigged up to tubes and looked unconvincing as a comforter. In American English a comforter is what we in Britain call an eiderdown or quilt or in Scotland it's a downy. In the Prayer Book, the Comforter is the Holy Ghost. I looked more like an eiderdown.

I kept trying to make things better for people and failing. I had the powerful sense that I was being a nuisance. It seemed that I could not make things clear to anybody.

I am absolutely certain that none of this is unusual when you find yourself in hospital. When it comes to hospital *Omne ignotum pro terrore* says it all. Why was I so sure I was going to die? Was I attention-seeking? At first I feared I might be. I determined to be as mouselike as I could. It is a thing I do, a McWilliamish habit. We go humble and invisible. It drives Fram mad. I see why. But it's what fear brings out in me.

I didn't think precisely that Death would pass me over on his ward calls if I were polite and self-effacing enough. I thought that the nurses wouldn't resent me. It was as pathetic as that. And why should nurses resent their patients? Why are they nurses if they do that? I don't know, but these ones, or so I thought, did. I have reason now to think that I wasn't wrong, but let that come later.

It was a high-dependency ward, intensive care. The standard of care was considerable given the intensity of demand. Cleanliness was rigorously observed. My older son came in, his beauty like a bonfire. He loved washing his hands with the antibacterial gel at the end of the bed. It made him smile the naughty smile that I had forgotten till my children restarted it: it was my mother's. His green eyes went slanty and flashed jokes to me. I loved looking at him.

I loved looking at him.

In that ward, after that fit, for some days, I could see. It was as though lightning had struck with the fit and released me from the dark wooden trunk that had grown round me, blinding and stiffening me. I was shocked back to seeing for a bit.

It was lucky that I could see at the start as there is no point being unable to in an intensive care ward; there is such a lot to fall over, much of it affixed to or into people.

It was a mixed ward. It was arranged around death, of course, but more explicitly than usual in wards that are less acute. Beds did come free while I was there, if I can put it like that. Curtains and pulleys were used with seamanlike efficiency and speed. Two of us could not die in spite of efforts in that direction. Each was fighting according, I suppose, to their habit. To my right lay an elderly physician called Michael. He was very ill, handsome still, and over eighty-five. He asked for very little though one time in the night he asked for something for the pain. It did not come for a long time. He had been a consultant. He did not once use swagger or bullying or any of the tricks we saw daily put to good use by the young, fit, consultants on their ward rounds.

Why cannot doctors be kinder to doctors? What is it that makes them forget that to know what is happening to you is not to be relieved of pain or of fear? Michael had a younger wife and a son who was still in the sixth form at his Central London school. Not long ago he must have known the comforts of love, the warmth of talk.

Necessarily, the visiting hours were strict. He saw his wife most evenings for a short while. She was attractive, blonde, cool, American; an academic or even a doctor? They had no privacy. He was dying. She was losing her husband, her son's father. You do not marry a man far older than yourself without thinking of these things.

Nor do you marry a much older man unless you want the support of his seniority. Even sick to death, he was not reduced. Unlike many strong personalities close to death, he had not become pure will. He declared no faith and spoke little. We had one stilted conversation about schools for boys in London, which was how I learned about his son. We were sleeping not four feet apart.

I spent some of the nights planning a short story set in a ward like this. I was inspected by a serious, gentle Middle-European neurologist from time to time. A charismatic professor swooped sexily through but hardly stopped at me. The comely trainee doctors might have been his due. A hierarchy of desire was evident in the doctoring and nursing staff. After certain visits, the air was left with that sense that a personage has passed, a star shed its starry dust.

We lay in our beds beyond desire.

The other person who was dying was taking it another way, not with Michael's enduring silentness. She was opposite me and I feared her and feared for her. She was afraid of her own bowels with which she was locked in mortal wrangle. She wanted to catch them before they betrayed her. I had now seen this in two people I loved as they died, my grandmother and my friend Rosa, another uncomforted doctor.

Vi was dying like a little child unjustly shut in a cupboard. She howled to be let out. The cupboard wasn't her dying, it was her own body. Every few minutes she howled out, 'It's me bahls.' She was as afraid of her shit as of her end.

She called for a nurse at regular intervals all night in the slack light of the dimmed ward. A disdainful call would come over to her from the nursing station. I didn't realise it yet, but almost every high dependency ward has a lady like Vi, an old-fashioned old woman become a stranded little girl again, howling across to the other shore. It's the reaction to such women that varies, I was to learn later. But Vi was a nuisance and a bore and because she was reduced to an animal there was no chance for her to change; or that's how she was dealt with on that ward.

I mentioned her to Fram and he told me just to think about something else, to tune it out. He had misunderstood me. It wasn't that I was upset by her, I was upset for her. That made him crosser. Why did I have these fantasies of helpfulness when I myself was quite clearly helpless?

I did indeed mismanage that visit to hospital. I don't know quite how I got it so wrong, but I did. I was full of fear continually. I wasn't too afraid of dying because I almost thought that I had. From time to time I was put on a trolley or into a chair and taken for tests.

These were various and not uninteresting. Some I had been subject to before during the early days of hunting down my blepharospasm. Electrodes were glued into my long hair as close to the scalp as they could go. My brain answered various questions. My body got heavier and heavier. It became like a stone upon my spirit. I've always been prone to treat my body like a stranger into whom I'm surprised to have bumped. During this stay in hospital it became a bit like an uninvited guest.

———◆◆◆———

In the window of my workroom here on Colonsay, my small travelling radio, which I had turned off earlier because the rain was making its sound crunchy, has burst spontaneously into pure uncompromised sound. It is – I know it at once – the Adagio of Brahms's Violin Concerto. The tune goes sinuously and excruciatingly lovingly to its quiet end.

It's the first outing of a new recording by Valery Gergiev, so new, says, the radio, that it's 'still quivering'.

The Brahms Violin Concerto is for me a Colonsay piece of music. When we were almost still children, and the youngest children were properly small, we listened to it on Sunday mornings in summer. Electricity was trembly and contingent and the recording was on a long-playing record, played on a gramophone of home-made construction. To me, then, it was music of potential, of how my life would be, and of the present, new, familial, romance, the children, the parents, the smell of cooking meat, Papa sipping Madeira from a silver cup, so the drink smelt of damsons and tarnish, quite often a fire in spite of the bright summer light, the fire deep in the grate, its flames pale pink and blue, and a scent of spicy rose petals, never in this soft air completely crisp, in a thin deep bowl from China, and of rich dampness from unstopping rain that washed and washed the sky so that you could not believe its whiteness when eventually the rain was drawn aside. The books in Colonsay House hold water, sweet water unlike that salt library in the West Indies when I was twenty-one and could see though was blind to so much.

Of course I was perfecting things, turning them into scenes or tableaux or stories from a tale of happy families, and by so doing making them fragile; but the memory is not frangible. Later the parents parted and we have all grown older and too many and too few words have in some cases been spoken, but it is not nothing that, in a week or so, two of the sisters and Alexander and I will be here in the house, Alexander and Katie and Caroline with their marriages intact and their children growing, and all of us no doubt would be struck like damp matches in a different phosphoric way by those long notes on the violin, after one or two or three strikes of the soft tight bow.

What I suppose I should take from this gift in sound and the light it has lent to the story I was telling about this last year's first un-illuminating brush with hospital fear is that all my life I have been far too ready to leave, irreversibly.

I was ready to die during that time in hospital, pushing forward to volunteer for it, to get it over with although we may be fairly sure that nothing comes after that last crazily obliging rush to self-effacement if we succumb to enacting it. I just didn't want to be in the way. No wonder I exasperated my family.

I was so afraid of small things that I was ready to jettison the great ones. On account of not wanting to be in the way, of not wanting to present a problem that could not be solved by these intelligent doctors, I wanted to tidy myself away.

On account of not understanding what was happening within my father's mind, I decided to leave his house as though I had never been, because I knew, as I understood it, that things would be better without me and was then resentful that it was as though I had never been.

———◆◆◆———

What does the Brahms Adagio mean now?

It means itself. And after it has passed there comes that formal silence full of promise in which one lies refined and maybe hopeful.

Tomorrow, on the island, there is to be the funeral of a man who died, full of years, on Sunday. There is nowhere to die here but at home.

You are cared for in your house. There is a hospital, but it is a flight away, on the mainland.

Katie has been to say goodnight to me. She has been working in Papa's old workshop. It is now, on Wednesdays and Fridays, to fit in with boat times and the open days of the big house garden, a cafeteria, offering home-made lunch and tea. Today she made rhubarb and ginger jam before her office day began. Her office days are never alike. Many of them are spent fixing things, making things from other things. She and her siblings are good with orphaned objects. They can darn and weld and splice. They have learned never to waste. You don't when everything has to come from outside. You adapt. Katie still dances in a red velvet skirt that she made as a schoolgirl from curtains. The boys wear Papa's kilts that were his father's. Papa wears his father's suits.

The drying-up cloths to the right of the stove hang from struts in the shape of goosenecks made by Papa from inboard struts of wooden boats. Katie keeps the kindling William splits in a fish box the sea washed up and grows her tomatoes in others like it. Colonsay gets the afterwash of the world's wastefulness. One year it was hundreds and hundreds of pastel toothbrushes washed up on the white sand with the gummy wrack. This flat is full of things my not-siblings made as children, displays of collected shells under glass, glued scraps of botanical prints, a wicker stool.

In the laundry cupboard rag store are the remains of nursery bath-mats with reversible silhouetted scenes of blue geese, pink bears, from the 1930s. The linen is stitched with laundry-marks from the 1950s. My favourite shirt is made of Aertex and was bought at Eton for Papa's father to play fives in; it is laundry-marked at the neck '1921'. It is made of holes, held together, right enough.

I wasn't handy, but I was visual. Papa gave me small jobs such as the making of nameplates for Alexander's model steamship, powered by the purple spirits you used to have to sign the poison-book for. I could choose the name. It was *Methalina*. For several school holidays, I restored some mustard-coloured pâpier-maché globes, one sidereal, one terrestrial, and did it so badly that the earth stuck in its axis because I had wodged on so much layered papery weight on one side over the split in the tropics. I spoiled its first eggy smoothness with my damaging mending. Still Papa kept on entrusting things to me.

The constructive refusal to accept that anything is ready to be thrown out makes for transmission of what feels like memory because things stay around. How good is consumerism for memory? Part of its point is that it makes you think that the next set of memories will be better if only you buy the things with which to make them. But you cannot arrange for memory like that.

Papa's father had a routine that breaks the heart. It is surprising that it did not break his back. He carried a sack of cement daily miles over bog and briar down to the sea where there is a very small island close into the shore, the size of, say, a garden shed, called Eilean Olmsa. There he poured his sack into the sea. Was the idea to form an attachment? What was the purpose? Did he feel that days spent thus must add up to something in the face of the assured erosion that awaits us all?

In a romantically pragmatic family, that is in a family whose romance is with pragmatism, is that not a sad thing to do, a quest defeated at its inception? Did he plan it or did it just become a habit? What, beyond his wife, was he wishing not to be with?

Just before the sky grew its evening grey over the last twenty minutes, there was a pallid but clear and warm ten minutes of pure light.

The two big cedars that catch light were wet with the rain of three days and nights, wettest where the trunks cleave inwards, paler on the convexities, their chiffony bark clinging like drapery to legs. The trees seemed – I can see more clearly as the light goes; something stops hurting in my eyes – to be holding tall twisting dancers within themselves.

The lamb William found orphaned on the north of the island has been accepted, dressed in the fleece of her dead offspring, by its foster mother. The ewe whose eyes were taken by a raven has been destroyed.

Just after extreme events, I see as I peer at these alignments of experience, I feel that something may be about to come, at last, under my control. That formal feeling comes. But I couldn't stick even a paper world together.

———◆————

It is the next morning. The sky in the north has light until the stars can be seen. The moon was up in a lilac sky pale as day after the rain clouds cleared during the night. I got up twice from excitement at the lightness and could look the pink moon in the face the first clear time. The second time the winds were fighting it out while I waited for the kettle to boil and the sky had thickened to a duskier blue.

My machine for listening to talking books hasn't yet arrived, so I was reduced to my own company. I tried to practise the emptying of mind – known trickily as 'mindfulness' – that many doctors and their professional substrates have recommended. It's easier here than in London. I listened to the water rushing together, the stream below the lawns, the rain, the burns in spate that could only just not be heard at the edge of my consciousness. I like to listen to what isn't stated. It's one of the great pleasures of reading.

Katie has just come in to where I am working. She starts in the office at 8.30, does her email and her mail (when there's been a boat) and does what the day asks of her, from ironing sixty sheets and walking dogs to double-entry bookkeeping and arguing with the state about heating for pensioners or school meals for the island's nine schoolchildren.

She comes, it seems, sideways on into a room. This is what it looks like because she is narrow and stands with her head on one side. She is still but hardly ever at rest. She carries her knife on its lanyard around her waist. Her plait is silvering. She is going out into the garden to cut white flowers for the funeral, but, she enquires, do I think that colour would be disrespectful? The red and pink rhododendrons are at their best now.

We agree that green and white, and blue and purple, if she can find any, should form the mass of flowers that she will leave at the church for the ladies of the family bereaved to set about it as they wish. Bluebells are the right colour, we decide, but they are not sufficiently respectful. They are the juicy flowers of childhood, abundant, scented, profligate and wild. They do not look like trouble taken when they are massed, and they are at their massed best when left alone to smoke up a wood with their heavy blue.

There is a jar of bluebells on my dressing table, put there by Katie's son and his Iranian fiancée. He is a boy and doesn't read the language of flowers. She, being Persian, like my younger son and his father, well understands some languages beyond the spoken, of which she has English, Arabic and a little Farsi. She knows the good luck in a mango, the transportable nourishment in a coconut, the relation of sugar to good words.

———◆◆◆◆———

The men on Colonsay leave a funeral halfway through for the committal of the body to the earth. A dram of whisky for each man is passed around, and a bit of cheese.

The women remain in the kirk and weep.

Chapter 3: Milk Money

A book containing some of Chekhov's plays arrived here on the boat last night. It came from a dealer in New South Wales. I hadn't *seen* when I was buying it online that it was on the other side of the world. I was interested by the translation and the edition. Reassuringly, the edition at least is a properly Chekhovian disappointment. How can I have missed that the reason for the rock-bottom price was that the publisher is something called The Franklin Library, at the Franklin Center, Pennsylvania? The translation is by Elisaveta Fen, and copyrighted to her in 1951 and 1954. The edition is copyrighted to the Franklin Mint Corporation.

Do you remember the Franklin Mint? Do they still exist? I think that I once actually did write advertising copy for them, or have I invented that? Certainly I have not invented that they specialised in 'Collectables', ranging from themed thimbles with an ornamental display unit to show them off to best advantage, and poseable figurines of the late Diana Spencer in occasionwear with fully styleable 'natural' hair. In the early days of Sunday colour supplements, I enjoyed playing with the sorts of advertisement the slippy magazines carried on their back page. It was only in these ads that I ever did read the actual word 'Skivertex'.

My father and I would ask one another, in a special advertising voice, 'Have you ever longed to caress a book?' This was the head-line of a certain ad that offered classics of world literature for now and for all time in luxurious gold-tooled Skiblon, duchess green or cardinal red. I was absorbed by parallel idioms and by what you could do with words, and how words caught you out and showed you up, tickled you and took you in or left you out.

This not merely indoor but interior habit was not interpretable as much other than showing-off and time-wasting by my poor stepmother, who preferred her jokes less silly and whose ratio of meaning to word is a clear one-to-one. She was right to be suspicious of me. She thought I was a liar but actually I was something less direct: an ambiguity obsessive.

She was right that I was having a stab at making a shared world with my father, in the language we both spoke, but, to his matrimonial credit, he soon ceased to meet me on those borders and one sort of atmosphere lifted. While I love Greek and Latin, he never thought me much good at them and couldn't understand why I had not a grip on Greek accents. In the 'girls' Greek' taught at that time, accents were not included.

My stepmother to this day speaks a pure English that delighted him. English is a corrupt old tongue but in her words, spoken and written, it says what it means like a tread of precise hemming settling a margin of cloth. I listen to her talk with pleasure, and, freed from hot adolescence and respectful of her long widowhood, I realise that her speech must have been to him both a relief from his own subtlety and a line to clarity at an obscure time.

There is a line of thought that maintains that all writers of fiction are liars because they make things up. This coincides frequently with the other line of thought, which also thinks itself interestingly robust, that it is women who read fiction. And, moreover, that they do so to escape.

Proper fiction tells the truth by a means that, far from producing pain as untruth does, gives pleasure; this doesn't mean that it fails to reproduce or convey pain. The transformative element is not lies but art. Human truth is caught in translation, such that we may briefly be as close to not being ourselves while we read as we shall ever be. It's not a promise, but there is always the promise of a promise.

As for women reading escapist fiction, why would women wish to escape, if not from a nonsense world of material fact and of drudgery that is there, often, to free men?

And here I am in the autumn of my days, privileged at last to caress a book, gold-tooled for my handling pleasure, though the hide-type spine is not duchess green nor cardinal red but buckram brown.

Still, the book, whatever the cover, held its transmissible voltage. I am, of course, in a flat that has been made from the nursery bedrooms of a beloved old house in which a number of generations have lived. I've never known a time when things were at all fat on the estate. Twice at least in my time of being almost in the family it has been put on the market. Most of the children's lives are formed by the place. William, who was an art dealer, makes his living from chopping down trees, carrying coal and emptying dustbins. The sound of an axe is rarely far off from the house. He walks around with an axe as easily as with a book.

It is May. In the walled garden lies a cold dew between the fruit trees.

<hr />

I held open my eyes on this chilly early morning in May where outside the many greens under the cold wind are shivery with blossom and read the opening of *The Cherry Orchard*:

ACT ONE

A room, which used to be the children's bedroom and is still referred to as the nursery. There are several doors: one of them leads into Anya's room. It is early morning: the sun is just coming up. The windows of the room are shut, but through them the cherry trees can be seen in blossom. It is May, but in the orchard there is morning frost.

The last play I saw in the company of my mother was *The Cherry Orchard*. I had forgotten this till now, or so I think. I must I suppose have remembered it every time I've read the play since then, or when it's been mentioned. I've not seen it again, which is a bit peculiar. At that first, that only, visit, I was painfully bored until the end, when I couldn't bear it to stop in the way it did. Perhaps that's what they mean when they say Chekhov is like life? Unbearably boring, then you don't want it over with. Or, please, not like that. Boring isn't the word, is it? The word is . . . like life.

Not 'lifelike'. Which is for inanimate things that imitate life. The plays of Chekhov breathe. They summon life. They are . . . like life.

After she died the first play I was taken to was the *Alcestis* of Euripides. It was in English. Alcestis, Queen of Thessaly, vows to die in the place of her king, Admetus. Admetus, aghast with grief, nevertheless proves a noble and generous host to the man-god Heracles when he visits. In acknowledgement of this, Heracles descends to Hades, wrestles Death, and returns with a veiled woman whom the King will entertain in his halls only as a courtesy to his guest. Heracles persuades Admetus entirely against his will and protesting to lead the woman to his own chambers – and the woman turns out to be his dead queen, whose absence had made the palace a grave, restored to him.

Perhaps it was a consolation. Given my parents' milieu it may even have been a consolation that had been dreamed up. For which I thank any of them who survive, who may read this. I know I enjoyed it though Queen Alcestis herself was too short to convince in her part as my mother.

Art did some of its work then. I thought of this theatre outing with shame when my younger son and I went to Britten's *Rape of Lucretia* together. Better at seeing into life at twelve than I at any age, he sat holding my hand in the airy Maltings at Snape in Suffolk. We were there in the company of Mark Fisher. It does not do to think that we will not pass on to those we love pain that we have ourselves sustained. So many kinds of blindness are involved in love that can in its turn bedizen us with sugared illusions.

We watched Tarquin sucking up to Lucretia, making his case in frontal fashion, warrior without and weasel not far within, and we watched her piteous shame. My father's deep attachment to the work of Britten and his taste for the composer's summoning of pity and fear without grandiosity has come straight down to me and Minoo.

It was as much the fault of the woman's vanity, the music made it plain. Yet Minoo never let my hand go. He is a realist and a natural writer who saw it all before I did, and waited, a seasoned reader of Greek, accents and all, for the consequences of the actions and in-actions that might have made his life unrecognisable to him, had he not decided that, being life, it was to be royally respected and stuffed with jokes. And taken at an angle when it was sore.

———◆◆◆◆◆———

It is my lunch hour in my nursery-study on the Isle of Colonsay. The reason why I cannot hear an axe is that William is in church for the funeral. I decided that I should not go because although I knew the dead man I look so odd at the moment that I might be a distraction. Then I wondered if that was not vain. Where is the proper place to be? In church, I suspect, now the funeral is under way. What does it matter that I bore myself explaining why my face is screwed up and I am twice the size I was as a girl? No one is looking and probably the ideal place to be to avoid explanation is here, where all is known anyway. You don't keep a secret long on an island with 120 souls.

I allow myself to listen to the radio during my lunch hour. I switched it on and there came the sigh and rush sound of an amplified seashell. 'Ah,' I thought, 'that's interference. The reception is bad here.'

It wasn't. It was applause. A different kind of reception. It can be hard to tell what's what in the world of sounds as well as in the world of seeing.

I had a short blast of sight earlier and looked out on the pair of tall cedars I seem always to have known. There are in fact three of them.

———◆◆◆◆◆———

After my time in hospital that was in order to observe and catch me should I have another fit, I was allowed home. None of us knew what had happened. During the preceding two years, several highly qualified neurologists and neurosurgeons had taken a squint at my brain and its nervous system. A neuropsychiatrist of penetrating if iterative intelligence had reminded me weekly in a slow crisp intelligent manner of the inception and progress of my complaint, at the price of a . . . I can't actually think of anything that costs as much as private medicine at those reaches of obscurity. And there was no one in the National Health, apparently, who could address my brain's particular problem of function after the failure of botulinum toxin injections.

I have thought of a measure of cost. During my years of reclusion and then of blindness, I reverted to stereotype. Female novelists are caricatured as troubled, often overweight beings accompanied by at least one cat. As readers may remember, I had two, by the time of the fit, a Blue Russian cat called Rita and a creamy soft British cat with lilac edges and a butch glare, whose name was Ormiston, a name given to male McWilliams for hundreds of years.

If you don't like cats, skip this paragraph. Rita came to us when our first Russian cat Sigismond was run over. She is his sister. Her first owners had not been able to care for her and her second owners became allergic. She is nervy, possessive, controlling, man-mad and clever, a bossy animal devoted to Parmesan and small warm places. Her eyes are green with a turquoise depth and she has the incomparable limbs and head of a Russian. Her middle is soft. Ormiston's breed is meant neither to be fluffy nor intelligent. In both regards he failed, if it is a failure to be fluffy and clever. He showed from a kitten, when he was the size of a meringue with whipped cream, preposterous bravery, devotion, ball skills and single-mindedness. Prawns and human love have been his areas of study. Between the cats lay the vexed questions of all shared private lives, power and influence. Our family divided just about fairly around the cats, my older son keeping a good balance by liking neither. These animals, who comforted my nights and conversed with me through the days, who knew my goings out and my comings in, who petted me and fed my

need for contact, who were the differences between the often slug-
gish days, cost £350 each. It is a great deal of money, but one visit
to the doctor who recapitulated to me each week my illness's symptoms and progress was two cats per hour or every part thereof.

Not one cat, or part of a cat for a part of an hour, two full cats.

Not that sight isn't priceless, but I was being prescribed drugs.
These drugs came to about two cats a month. I saw, or attended, in
addition, during that time, at least two other doctors per week, at a
combined cost of two cats. The cats added up.

By the time of my fit, I was ingesting multiple high doses of venlafaxine,
mirtazapine, levetiracetam, and had been through exceedingly high doses
of citalopram and lamotrigine. Zopiclone had wended its powerfully
stupefying way among them like a thug whom you fancy. I'd abandoned
beta-blockers because they scared me. I preferred the panic they were
meant to stop to the nasty medicinal panic they created.

The drugs bothered the children. A number of these drugs are
powerful antidepressants. When first I was blind, no one suggested
that I was depressed. I was not happy, but my circumstances had
been peculiar for years, and now I seemed to have gone blind.
Happiness of any marked sort at such a time might have been
surprising. After I was first put on these drugs, with the primary
purpose always being that they might in sufficient doses cause my
brain to release my closed eyes, it was opined that I was indeed
by now depressed. I was still sad, maybe sadder, but all my own
observation of depressed people, and I have had a good deal of it,
told me that I wasn't depressed as they had been. I was, since
becoming sober, never unable to create a pretext to enter the day.
I could spur myself yet.

However, the insistence was by then that, having taken so many
antidepressants, I was depressed. I was taking sufficient antidepressants
to cheer up a cow by the time I fell down thwack in a grand mal fit
in that shaded summer last year, just after speaking my first book for
more than ten years.

After the fit, the children arranged a rota. They, or their friends, babysat me for a time, day and night. The cats and I loved it, when we were conscious. I couldn't any longer recognise myself, even from within.

I'd grown used to my swollen and unfamiliar body, but now my mind was loosening and, it seemed, hardening too. I was returned to the same thoughts with a repetitiveness that grew tighter and tighter. I couldn't challenge my own poisonous logic as ably as I once had. I had aged suddenly, become a dead weight on those I cared for, a bore, ugly, terrified and alone; and I deserved it.

Perhaps the antidepressants had at last, as one doctor hazarded, summoned their customary foe. During these sweaty nights I longed for the unabridged *In Search of Lost Time* but listened over twenty-five times to the Naxos abridged version, read by Neville Jason. I have now, by May 2009, heard it thirty-seven times. At the end of the last uninterrupted run, I turned to *War and Peace*, unabridged this time. It too is read by Neville Jason. Not one of the voices he does for each character in either book is the same as any other. I cannot sufficiently thank this stupendous actor and enthusiast. I hope he already has the *Légion d'honneur*. By abandoning myself one at a time to the sentences of Proust, albeit translated, I saw off zopiclone, even if I did not see off nightmares. The cats came and went happily in the garden of the borrowed flat. Rita lay on the hot terrace under the olive tree and Ormy fuzzed around under the spilling hostas and catmint playing ping-pong with bumblebees. From time to time he tried to kiss Rita, holding her precise head in his feathery paws, but she cuffed him. Early in the mornings, between five and five-thirty, he would come to me. The drugs made me sweat heavily. Sometimes it was tears, sometimes it was sweat, but my cat Ormiston made as though to pat my face dry with his front paws. He held his claws quite in, and laid his pads on my eyes.

In July the builders were to arrive. They wanted to work over the whole place. They started the day prompt at six-thirty. They were drilling out a whole new basement room. Every bit of rubbish, masonry or earth or mortar, plaster or lath, had to be carried back through the building in sacks and into a lorry for deposit at a yard. Hundreds of designated sacks were filled and hoisted daily. One can only hope that the fate of these sacks of building materials was something less sad than to be tipped into the sea between islands as a metaphor for loss, like those daily sackfuls of cement on Colonsay.

I moved into the flat on the floor above; it was less dramatic and atmospheric than Sargent's former studio, but more practical too for a blind woman prone to fits. I was very confused. My friend Nicky found me weeping outside Tesco because I couldn't find the hospital where I was due for an MRI scan. She cancelled her whole day and took me, holding on to me and steering me and taking me for the scan, then taking me home. I could have done nothing without her. I could not put one thought in front of the other. Not. One. Thought.

In May, in Colonsay, the weather is prevailing. Rain is pouring through and down all the guttering and downpipes, what in Scotland are called the rones, and hail is tittering down the chimneys and on to the sills. The air is full of long brushes of rain, the wind whisking them. My radio, responsive to something electric in the weather, perhaps a storm to come, has become impossible to turn off. It's desperate to tell me something. I've taken out its batteries: that'll settle its hash.

There must have been times when my family, most particularly Fram, must have wanted to do something like that to me, just shut me up, turning me over, sliding open the panel and slotting out whatever it is that keeps me transmitting. At the worst times I have only one frequency, that of guilt and shame. Self-pity is the one I fear. It's what I'm worried would be on default, on my pilot light.

This silence after the rain's battering is delicious. Though it isn't complete. Don't say the radio can broadcast without power. Don't say the radio is in my head.

I moved to the upstairs flat in London, and settled there but for one thing. Two things. Rita and Ormiston. I realised that it had to be done. It was a smaller flat, with no outdoors. I was blind and might fall down unconscious in a fit, and then who would care for them? Rita went to be with an artist's widow. Ormy went to be where he was always ecstatic, with our friends Leander and Rachel in Oxford. They reported on him constantly and in short order he had become Rachel's slave, which in cat terms is master. Leander said that he chased butterflies but released them. I suppose he never caught them. He was the indulged new boy in a house with four other cats. At first uppish, he became the lieutenant of their top cat Elvis. He gardened and grew fat on tuna and prawns. To the children in their street, he was known as Warburton, a name as pleasingly Britishly pompous as his own. He got a bad scratch on one bulbous blue eyeball and had to wear a bonnet and have twice daily antibiotic shots over the summer. Rachel made their sitting room his sickroom and gave him love all day. She was looking for work at the time and awaiting the results of interviews. The artist's widow has not said anything about Rita, herself a companionate but discreet cat never much given to getting in touch.

July dwindled into August, which has all his life been the time when Minoo and I go to the Edinburgh International Book Festival, and then, most likely, over to Colonsay.

I had a plan too for our stay in Edinburgh. I was hoping to visit the shaman who had helped the friend of a friend, as she understood, to see off grave illness from the very heart of her family.

A shaman?

Why not? I had by this point seen seven professors of neurology, one neuropsychiatrist, two consultant neurologists, two cognitive therapists, four ophthalmologists, one psychoanalyst, one counsellor, two general practitioners, a cranial osteopath and a beautiful octogenarian acupuncture-practising ex-nun named Oonagh Shanley Toffolo, who had modelled for Issey Miyake and to whom I was recommended by the owner of a clothes shop who saw me blindly patting her lurchers under the counter. Oonagh was very good. She was a great reader of Thomas Merton and was as certain of heaven as of the ground beneath her slender feet.

I am not on the attack against conventional medicine. I just think that no one knows much about the relation of mind to body, while, it is to be hoped, learning more constantly about the relation of brain to body, though even that science is in its infancy. I have wondered, for example, whether my compromised dopamine system (which is what alcoholics have; we retrain our poor pleasure centres into thinking that a drink is what they want because once, just once, and once upon a time, it felt good) has not some relation to the closure of my sight. I do not know, and I am, or thought I was, resistant to barmy science.

I am aware that the dopamine theory could just as well be the punishment theory in modern dress. I cannot bear to think that maybe the enormous pleasure that has for me been in looking has to be taken from me precisely because it was a pleasure and that for me all pleasure is bad, being analogous to alcohol. Can that be so? Or has some Calvinism crept in there?

I am pretty sure that if I had ever understood – and practised – relaxation, and in that I would include dancing and some kinds of exercise as well as I understand willpower and self-punishment, I wouldn't be in this tight spot.

I am fairly certain too that an operation is a crude and mechanistic approach to something that maybe I should have tried to charm down out of the tree of my nerves and brain, a bad black snake I might really have induced to let go its grip, with talk and ease and music. Instead, full of fear, and keen to show those I love I have the will to fight, I have done the thing that Fram was the second person to tell me that I will insist on doing, which is to go out into the dark alone with a knife, and cast about me till I am bloody and on my own. Fram is far from the only person I love who is resistant to the idea of this operation.

The first person who told me that I do this blind casting about was me. But I don't listen to her. Or not when she talks sense.

Or I hadn't till recently, and am attempting to now.

We set off for Edinburgh, where Minoo and I have been the consistently happiest over the years of internal exile, but not before I had had a terrible unseemly fight with Fram and Claudia.

It started with two pints of semi-skimmed milk and two one-pound coins. I cannot write about it while the rain outside is falling. If I feel tearful when there is rain, the rain allows me to cry with its tears. I have learned this through a lifetime of living in a rainy country and seldom actually crying, though sometimes feeling that I will burst if I do not, by the use of one of my bluntest tools from the kit of self-damage, unnecessary control. I boil my tears dry on the nasty internal burner of my sense of injustice, and my hot stone of loneliness.

Jealousy pains more than bare bones through skin. That's not a figure of speech. I've had both in this last year and there isn't a comparison. Jealousy is greener than those old sharp white bones I saw, though they were my own and sticking out sharp and splintered through my own flesh and skin.

But that's to come.

I am daily working on its cure, the slaking of that thirsty rootless jealousy. If love is blind, jealousy is sharp of sight, even in the blind. Maybe it seethes more in the blind, who create evidence where it cannot be seen?

I will save any account of that row till the sky is empty. It was my fault. By the pitchy light of my jealous nature I will perhaps see the sequence of my, always congruent, mistakes. I always slope off and never ask for help. I think I can mend myself on my own by thinking and instead I make the same mistake. I do not see it as being the same mistake in my own life because I treat myself with less care than I would treat a character in a book I was either reading or writing. I always think, however extreme the circumstances, 'This doesn't matter. The only person who is being hurt is me.'

This idiotic yet evidently lifelong feeling for some reason does not allow itself to be supplanted by my expressed and fully conscious certainty that, however secret we are to one another, we are also connected in more ways than we can know.

I think the word for it is dissociation, and I wouldn't recommend it to an atom. Especially not to an atom, since the consequence might be annihilation.

———◆◆◆◆———

Minoo and I set off for Edinburgh. My Edinburgh friend Amanda had made an appointment with the shaman, in a suburb of the city called Portobello, a suburb that is something of a hydro, which is the Scotticism for spa, that is a fancy place you go for sea-bathing and the taking of the waters.

Plural water! And I'm that big a drinker!

(I recall participating in a blind water-tasting with the son of Hugh MacDiarmid, Michael Grieve, and his wife, for the *Glasgow Herald*, in the house of two Highland friends. Apollinaris and Perrier were too strong. Later, we watered the water down.)

Amanda, who, like all my friends who properly like me, likes Claudia, said, 'You've to guess the shaman's name. It's auspicious. It's what everyone's called, Claude.'

The shaman's name was Claudia.

During that time when the fit held the summer thick and dim to me and I felt ever more cut off and adrift, I didn't say so until things became so desperate that I burned with disgust and anger at myself. The only person to whom I dared show it is the person for whom, with the children, I want to be best, as though I hadn't yet understood that he knows me at my worst.

All the things I miss doing for someone, the things that I thought were the accumulating point of me, cooking, cleaning, tidying, arranging, thinking together, sharing silence and words as Pierre and Natasha do at the end of *War and Peace*, all the setting forth in the vessel of home, I blew into the air with one neglected cinder of resentment allowed to smoulder over years because I accepted to be tidied away. Was *that* the pilot light? Resentment?

I didn't accept it, only, to be tidied away. I folded myself up like an unwanted sail and locked the sail-bin door from the inside, not having forgotten to make sure I was dry with exhaustion yet drenched with alcohol to the point of double flammability.

The rain has gone and I shall rush at the story of the row and the milk and the money, which is about jealousy and left-outness.

So Fram and Claudia visited me one evening in the upstairs flat in London. They were going on, out to dinner, or the theatre. I was overexcited and had saved up a selection of thoughts, of notes and queries. Thus the lonely blight the contact they do have. Punctuality exercises me. It is part of my tense need to be prepared and hospitable. It has always been my failing and it is made worse by not seeing because I have to try to make things, and myself, look OK. Or I think I do. After the time that was due to be crowned by company has passed away, a dismantling takes place as though an actor has been taken ill before the performance can be begun.

Claudia rang from a supermarket. I am afraid that I can remember that it was Waitrose and not Tesco. Waitrose is more lavish and metropolitan than Tesco. Such is the ugly smallness of jealousy.

She was ringing to say, 'We're in Waitrose. Can we get you anything?' I replied, 'I'd like two pints of semi-skimmed milk please, and don't worry, I will pay you back.'

As cheap as that. A world of love, flung aside from jealousy because it is one who has fallen short of it. I knew I was old and past it all then and that Fram and Claudia were like my social workers, fitting in a cup of tea with the old bitch who can't get out before they returned to their real world of intimacy, the first-person plural, litres not smaller units, love, the theatre, seeing things . . . and Waitrose.

Actually I can't, yet, bear to go on. Jealousy is hard to abide in the feeling, the telling, the reading. It is witness to our worst selves. It is mad and hungry and it tells us lies. Which to our shame, we half want to hear.

I have for the moment to hold the frame there. I typed 'Fram' in the middle of that word 'frame'. There is nowhere jealousy doesn't reach, nothing it doesn't sour. It tears the kindly milk.

This is the frame, held. They entered the flat. Claudia had on a new coat. I couldn't see it properly of course, but it was embroidered with pink and green flowers. She is of normal size. I have always been tall for a woman and am now fat. She held the milk out to me. I held out two pounds in return for the milk.

I could feel Fram's anger as close as my own bile.

That is the frame, held, to which I shall return when I have found a way of not crying over spilt milk.

Now, for the company, I am listening to a concert from the Wigmore Hall in London and the main noise is interference, but it's not unfriendly. It sounds like not the sea of faith but the sea of electricity; something that is a context, and one from which something clear may emerge. In the one case, a poem, in the other, music or light.

<hr />

Katie and I this morning bunched up the wet branches of flowers that she had gathered, rhododendrons and azaleas for the funeral that was today at two in the afternoon.

It's been a brute of a day for weather and the boat was not going to come alongside at the pier, but it did, for it was full of mourners, maybe twenty-five of them. Miss Angell, the aeroplane pilot from Oban, who works this route on a Thursday, flew in four more mourners in the teeth of the wind. The dead man leaves three daughters. A small granddaughter spoke in the church. Katie said that everyone was breathing with her to get her through. There was also a baby.

The lady lay preacher spoke.

There was a tribute from the dead man's son-in-law, a big man on the island. The helpful breathing started again at the end of his words, when he described saying goodnight, every night (save the winters, when the dead man had annually gone down to Guildford to sleeve up and sell Christmas fir trees outside B & Q), so, saying goodnight, every night, with the same words, and that had gone on until this last Saturday, when there had not been the same exchange of good-nights, nor would be again.

The graveside, in the wind's teeth, was well attended. Poems were read; Auden, Katie thought, and Keats and Wordsworth.

'No,' said her husband. 'It was Auden. Keats, I think. Wordsworth, certainly.'

Katie made her face that signifies 'Am I married to a man or an old deaf dog?' and turned to her stove to poke at the lentils. She then asked a question that she didn't need answered, 'Why do people always say, when they know it can't literally be true, that at least the widowed one will be back with the other now, at least they'll be together?'

That terse code for attachment to her spouse, and the old van she drove earlier to the church before the service, its windows blind with gathered creaking sappy boughs of flowers, cream and purple, cream and white, pink and cream, creamy pink and splashingly scented, cut from the dripping flowering lichen-armed rhododendrons that crown this garden, boughs shining after all that soaking rain, short-lived wet falling caps of coloured flowers more than six men could carry, those are her way to catch life's fitfulness.

Chapter 4: The Shaman in the Basement

In the afternoons since my eyes shut, I have slept densely for two hours if the day permits. When I begin the sleep, I cannot endure that I shall wake up and know I am alone. When I wake up, I know that I am alone and that I have to be on with it. Thus sleep accommodates.

There are several tricks writers use to get themselves moving along in a book when they are stuck: some use a walk; some a swim; some do chores; others either go to bed for the night on it or steal a short daytime sleep. I don't have these sleeps nowadays because I'm stuck in my writing, but because I get stuck, at that point in the day, around two o'clock, in my life.

An ebb so low is reached that I feel my thoughts dwindled to just the one thought trawling empty along the stony repetitious levels and approaching the underwater cave mouth I do not want to look into, covetable extinctness. Not extinction, extinctness. It is a wanting to be dead, not, emphatically, a wanting to die. Moreover I can see it off with various forms of everyday magic, from folding sheets to washing my hands with welcome soap. It's just not practical, though, routinely to address low-grade thoughts of suicide early every afternoon if you can avoid it. It leaves a banal plaque on the mind and is no doubt antisocial, like bad breath. That is what it is, bad breath. The breath so bad, it stops at nothing.

Not that I believe that we do not, or should not, live with the present consciousness of death. Or try to, since of course we cannot. It's one of the blessings my mother passed to me, that appetite for life in the face of death. And she did nothing but make the gift greater by her own sudden departure. I have often worried for friends who haven't yet known death so close that it will break them. My mother in her dying gave me every single thing she had and turned a morbid child to life for life. I won't take my own life unless its prolongation is causing distress to my children. By when I will be incapable . . . Ah no, there are ways and means. We must talk, my darlings, when the exact, the precise, moment presents itself.

As a child, I used to wish that you could, as you can with many things, do 'nasties before nicies' and get death over with, buy it off by volunteering to do it first. But it's like washing up before you serve the food. The abundance will have its toll and leave its trace, and must be made as though it had not been. I cannot remember a time when I was unaware that those I loved could die at any moment.

I don't think that innocence is the unawareness of death. I think it is, at its truest meaning, want of self-interest, an incapacity to receive pleasure from hurting another, and, at its least true extension, a sort of blindness willed by others. Although it was I who left him (something I think of and repent of maybe sixty times a waking day) I hanker for the innocence that was the world Fram and I had. Maybe it is just that it is available to regret the time before a catastrophe as prelapsarian. But that long mutuality feels like a close-sown flower meadow to me, a meadow that I harrowed up. Anyone raised with hymn-singing will hear the tone, the heart's field red and torn, the foolish ways, the still small voice, the pity that dwells with the Peace of God.

My afternoon sleep is longer than is usual for a siesta and I feel a bit guilty about it, but if I don't go to bed by three at the latest there will be the equivalent of tears before bedtime.

If I push on through the afternoon I unravel at the least thing. I don't show it, but I direct at myself a regular stent of internal poison when I am tired and blindish, that can result in inelegant over-reaction to other people, extravagant concessiveness and really implausible self-sidelining or peculiar self-directed violence that is I suppose directed at the world.

It is like having been eaten by a gigantic menaced two-year-old and not being able to escape from her body. Since I am most often alone, these reactions may be to the radio or to an idea. If I don't have those two hours of sleep, I start to disintegrate, to lose and cease to recognise myself.

It's not, I don't think, an Alzheimer's-like cessation of recognition. I recognise my monster self, the self in whom the black humours run high, and I wish to bring it out into the light and scotch it like a snake. I tempt it out with a big bowl of rancour, watch it approach to drink, and wait to set about it with that knife of self-contempt. Failing the knife there is the cudgel of bleakness.

The bleakness involves taking a close look at what my actual situation is and turning away every time I offer myself some hope. It does not improve things that by this time in my unsighted day I shall have put blinkers on inside my head as well as the compromised sight beyond it, unless I keep things calmer with those two hours in the afternoon.

My dreams are still sighted in the way I used to be.

Perhaps now is the time to address any bright side of my not-seeing. I am used to looking for bright sides. Usually, though, being bright, they will have shown up if they are going to.

<hr />

Long ago, when I was well inside my marriage's shelter and could see, with no thought of either safety or sight being in question, I was much interested by the writing of Ved Mehta. His blindness, his Indianness, his dwelling in the reading world, his insistent intellectuality and his pursuit of love, his utter failure to accept that one mustn't grumble, his want of need to camouflage within consensus, all appealed to me. Try as I might, I cannot find his work in recorded form. All these traits but blindness are shared by Fram, I see.

Why was I interested in blindness, so interested that throughout my reading life I sought out books about it? I think that it was simply an impossibly difficult state to imagine, and probably among the worst routine bad things that can happen. I think that I returned repeatedly to the matter of blindness because I believed, and do believe, that we are all to some extent metaphorically blind and this is something at which I have squinted, more or less blind-sidedly, in my work.

Or rather, I think that the gift is rarely given us to see ourselves as others see us, that we do not see others as they see themselves, or if we do they might have preferred that we had not, and I am sure that the whole event is but half glimpsed, if that.

I do not believe that when I was reading books about blindness, metaphorical or not, or by blind writers, by Stephen Kuusisto or José Saramago or Henry Green, let alone by Homer or Milton or Borges, I was stocking up in advance on works that would come to my rescue in my later darkness.

If a person who goes to prison happens to have by heart a good deal of verse, that is an arbitrary blessing, although a great one. We cannot prepare for these blows. All we can do is our best.

———————◆•◆•◆———————

The shaman of Portobello had her pitch in the sort of set-up that is familiar if you have visited the fringes of alternative cure. Outside, it was an unexceptional shopfront in a small red Dumfries sandstone terrace of businesses, a tiler, a greengrocer, a Londis. To the left of the terrace a narrow close led down to the North Sea and its sandy shore, grey cockle and sea-glass sand crunching over and again under low waves that day.

I was early and had left my son to listen to his chosen writers at the Book Festival. He knew about the shaman and would have been happy to come along. In the event, I was glad he hadn't so that the idea might remain in his mind's tropical zone. At first, the impression was of an entranced and definitely decommissioned beauty parlour, with just a hint of those therapy rooms that induce a special claustrophobia relating to fruit tea and uncleanliness, lost hopes and women beyond romance having that new, fairly frugal, fling – with themselves.

I held open my eyes and peered through plate glass into the little carpeted shop beyond. The keynote shades were from the calming gamut. I am unsuited to alternative medicine. I do not like yellow on walls (or on book covers; the how-to-commit-suicide-and-not-be-found-out book is actually yellow, in a bossy life-affirming way). I am afraid that I will break wicker furniture. That said, I'm always curious about what is on people's mugs. And if there is a mug tree, I learn something. Mugs don't grow on trees.

On the wall behind the door, there were leaflets about hypnotherapy that had gone stiff on the noticeboard where rain had forced entry. There was an old and duly respected kettle, with a tray to catch its spillage, and a cloth for the handle. There were head massages on offer in the window from a young woman with a surname from deep in the Scots nobility; a novel in that, as in all disjointedness? She was also offering journeys into past lives at reasonable rates. There were long-overdry dried flowers.

Because I have lost the notes I made that day, I am collecting detail up from my memory-beach where things are ground down and worn away by the days coming in over one another like waves.

How can I see detail and have as my illness that I cannot see? It is one of the peculiar things about blepharospasm that sometimes the twitch and tremor leave you in peace and you can see. But if you badly need them to do so, they take a tighter grip and blind you. I remain observant although, as I am now, I need guiding around this house that I have known for over forty years. It's hard to explain to those you know, and impossible to explain to strangers without boring them.

Claudia the shaman appeared. I knew it must be Claudia because she practically made the car's bumper curve upwards, she was so smiley and dainty. She parked her Mini and hopped out, a small

Latin woman of perhaps twenty and pretty as a picture, long black hair, gold skin, smile to make a morning, lots of jerseys and a poncho. She had a soft raffia basket, which she put over her elbow.

She asked, 'Are you Candia? I am Claudia', which always strikes me as an almost palindromic and certainly confusing thing to have to say, and unlocked her premises just like any shopkeeper. There was no alarm system. That was a good sign. Spirits worth their salt can protect their premises.

She had the glow and pace that make normal gestures feel like bestowed privileges. We settled with our mugs of fruit tea. After many years I have not worked out which blend is the least nasty.

She was undoubtedly a hibiscus flower along this cold shore. She took off her sensible boots and some of her thicker woollens. It was, after all, August. Settled at her desk, she took a look at me over it. She was tiny, and perhaps not even twenty. I was sure that I was growing.

Soon I would fill the shop.

She started to ask the questions and I began to bore myself, retelling my much-handled story. Often, when I am telling medical people or other putative therapists about it, I start to think, 'Oh it's not that bad really. Why don't I stop troubling you this minute?'

Shaman-Claudia sat on her chair like a sprite, not in it like a weighted person. I noticed a tall thing in the corner that looked as if it might be a rainmaker, one of those hollow stalks full of seeds that fall with a sound like sudden rain on big leaves. I was sure there were maracas somewhere about.

There is no point doing these things with half a heart.

We went down to the basement; it was clean and fresh. It might have been in a modest East Coast B & B, before the Scottish Tourist Board fell to the torrid charms of air freshener and full-strength potpourri.

I lay down as I was told, Shaman-Claudia dimmed the lights and lit a candle, passed a number of large feathers, could they have been from a condor? over me, rattled her various instruments, and settled, with a gravity that made her small form intensify, to calling down the relevant spirits.

At no point did I even feel like laughing. I am not unusual I'm sure in testing myself in these circumstances. As a rule I can get through with manners and going deep within not to retrieve past selves but to avoid being hurtful. At no point at all did I not take literally all Shaman-Claudia said. That was her achievement. The bogus couldn't get a grip on her anywhere, possibly on account of her wholesome physical person. We entered the spirit world.

That, in a basement in Portobello on the East Coast of Scotland, takes some strength of being, when a complete stranger is rattling and chanting over an old Scots body, calling up its animal familiars. Mine arrived at once, punctual as their keeper, or whatever one is to one's animal familiar. One was a small tiger not through the kitten stage and with very large feet and the other was a whippy and talkative snake.

There is no surprise for the reader there at all. They come straight from my library of predictable attachments and concerns, my usual wardrobe of metaphors. Maybe the tiger was related to Ormiston, maybe the snake to our first mother, Eve.

The tiger told me to walk towards Fram and Claudia and to say to them what was in my heart. My normally rather distanced way of speech, at least with strangers, became direct.

I spoke the plain words of affection.

The headache that I carry which combines the strain of my condition with the puzzle of my situation became acute.

When any physical sensation occurred, Shaman-Claudia identified it well before I had expressed it to myself. She told the headache to be off. It did as it was told.

I explained to Fram and Claudia all that I wanted for them and their happiness. It came out without the administering of blows to myself.

The snake was a subtle customer, as tradition dictates. In a gesture of elegant animistic diplomacy from beyond both rationality and the grave, it turned out that the snake was my late mother-in-law who had in life feared snakes terribly. It was a nice snake and full of excellent advice, all of which I was anxious to remember in that way you are in dreams, because you know that this is it, the last, the only chance, before . . .

You wake up.

There is, when you come round after these things have gone well, or reached something important, a sense, I know now after several brushes with these other angles to healing, that you are on the edge of flu. You have come down with something.

We had been over an hour in the basement with the small tiger and the snake. I checked all the graphic works on the walls to see if I had glimpsed a picture of either creature before going under. Irreproachably nebulous images or nice Scots scenes hung on the walls. My eyes were fairly open, and did not insist on closing.

I was rather competitive about my familiars and asked, 'I s'pose everyone has tigers and snakes?'

Shaman-Claudia was wise to all levels of the question and avoided it. Like all convincing practitioners of creeds, she had no exotic manner to her although her flowerlike head and tininess made her exotic. She was tired after her exertion, like a dancer or a hod carrier.

We had more tea, and chatted about the usual ice-breakers. You get used to this upside-down intimacy, drawing people out about themselves after they have seen you weeping in the foetal position. I am unable to say how this rhythm lies in relation to paid sex though the thought of the parallel has crossed my mind.

I have sometimes wondered how many women like me pay to be touched, completely innocently, by strangers, just for the specific it may offer against loneliness? I have even resorted to manicurists during a bad three weeks this January, but I couldn't keep it up. They spotted me for a first-timer at the salon in the Gloucester Road and I was shy to go back after I realised that I was too guilty and not rude enough and don't like coloured fingernails. But I did love the tender Polish touch of the girls with their cream and patting and the little bath of wax for your fingers' tips.

Shaman-Claudia told me a bit about herself now. She was, despite appearances, rather more than twenty. She had two children with her Brazilian ex-husband, one nearly grown up, and she had recently remarried, a Scotsman, an ex-minister of the Kirk. Her personal tone was calm, amused, taken at a magnificently easy pace. It is unusual for the very small to be magnificent. Her own magnificence lay in this: that, like a creature, she was at once serious and weightless. She was one of those rare people from whom you get the strong sense of what the world is to them and how it would be to be loved by them. She was both unstrained and entertaining. It was hard to be defended or harsh near her. She had shown me at the very least that it would be by ceasing to struggle and writhe and try to exorcise my grief about it all that I would take the hook out of my heart and stop re-impaling myself on it as I had been doing for months to no one's benefit.

She was one of the beings graceful beyond words amid this year's, literally, unsettling thaw. In a thaw, things rooted are induced to shift.

I began that day to try to go limp against unhappiness, though I have to this day far from succeeded.

She zipped up her boots and put on some of the August jumpers, greeted her friend Amy the film director whose illness Amy firmly knows Shaman-Claudia dispelled, and gave me a hug. She had the matter-of-factness of the seer, which is like being teased by a clever child. I liked her a lot.

It is very competitively priced, as far as I can see, the shaman world of East Scotland, and worth every silver bawbee.

Amy and I went paddling in the shiny grey sea not even a block from the shaman's shop. We got sandy toes and walked to Amy's car in bare feet along the pavement. I cannot remember if we did buy the ice lollies that false memory supplies, as I would have in Portobello with Mummy after swimming.

When I got back to Minoo, he had been listening to Will Self. He was particularly charmed by Will's family-man graces in the authors' yurt, and how he put on his cadaverous churlishness so as not to disappoint his fans, who were queuing two and a half times around the square where the Book Festival is held. Minoo was delighted because he was pretty sure that Will had his mother-in-law with him. Not surprisingly, Minoo is a devoted proponent of the extended family. I hope this doesn't embarrass Will, who maximises the stretch of his alarming outer gifts while cultivating his inner delicacies of grasp and attachment. A very tall man, he has been unafraid, in the metaphorical sense, to grow right up.

I told Minoo over his teacake and butter about the companion-animals. I didn't say what kind.

'Yes,' he said, 'a tiger and a snake. That was me and Granny, looking after you.'

It is very seldom that his grammar falters.

'Granny and I,' he said, before I'd breathed.

Chapter 5: Mine Eyes Dazzle

After a first fit of the grand mal type, if that is what it was, a number of precautionary measures can be taken. They do not conventionally include a seaside trip to a newlywed shaman, but of those offered at a time when things had fallen apart, that seemed the most practical and effective. The consultant neurologist with whom an appointment had been made automatically by the hospital cancelled it on the day, even though by the time of this appointment, four months on, I had managed to be once more in that same hospital. But that's to come, and hospital doctors are horribly stretched.

No one could work out why I had had a fit, so, or and, they stopped trying to. The consoling phrase used to me, as a layperson, by several doctors, was that I had 'boiled over' and that this is more common than one might suppose. I don't doubt that. It's a safe statement. There are a jolly good number of folk out there and you don't want to go running away with the idea that you're any different.

The only serious biochemical theory advanced for my fit was that I had given myself, in that careless way patients will, hyponatraemia. I mentioned this to a handsome wild boy who does much clubbing and who enjoys the attendant refreshments. Hyponatraemia is well known to him. It is the consequence of drinking an enormous quantity of water. Disco biscuits give you a thirst like a gravel pit. As a consequence of hyponatraemia, death is not unusual, the salts in the brain and blood having become drastically diluted.

I do drink a lot of water, but not that much. When I told the doctor who proffered this theory how much water I drink, I translated the imperial measures wrongly into metric, probably a mistake hardly any except the very oldest clubbers make, so I said litres for pints.

Like an alcohol counsellor, he doubled the number of units the client had actually offered as the amount imbibed and arrived at the conclusion that I drank eight litres of water daily. He had been seeing me almost fortnightly for a year and I had shown no symptoms of water damage before. Though I had put on several stones in weight, which might relate to some of the drugs, now that I mentioned it.

I wasn't able any longer to walk around energetically as I had before I was blind, so I took account of that and ate carefully. I had fluctuated in size all my life but this fat felt doomy. It was solid and already old; it was hard like lamb fat. I could imagine it white and solid over the cold grey stew of my inner life. My limbs were no longer of any shape. They fell like sacks and settled oddly; sometimes I had to pull my legs across one another with my hands. I had been used to sitting with my longish legs crossed twice, at knee and ankle, for comfort.

I couldn't sit in normal chairs without worrying that I might stand up with the chair stuck to my uncontrolledly voluminous arse. Yet at the start of 2008, when I went to my uncle Clem's memorial service, before starting on all those high-dose prescription drugs, I had been able that morning to touch my forearms to the floor when I touched my toes, meet my hands behind across my back, and stretch so that my head lay on my calf when I sat on the floor with my legs in a V. I had had long slimmish legs and feet that I could fit into proper shoes. I had had flexible arms, not legs of mutton. I wanted to look nice for my surprisingly dead handsome uncle and his great-nephews and niece, my children.

Something was rebelling, now, only a few months on. I looked out of my body as does Winnie the buried woman from the pile of rubbish in Beckett's *Happy Days*. My head came through, but even it was thicker, to look at.

I was not asking for the old ranginess in my fifties. I was just baffled by yet another thing gone quite so quick, another lost identifier. Fram is right to say that it is vain to mind the loss of what was never certainly mine in my appearance.

But the loss of usability, on a sudden, is a blow. I now had mass of a sort I felt unable to control, and was absurdly weak, for a woman who has lifted, carried and walked all her life. I was moving with the slow barging diffidence of a learner lorry driver who can't yet work his mirrors. I knocked into people.

They did not always like it.

I got called names, or whistled at, ironically. I was twice asked in the street if I wanted a fuck. That makes you jump if you can't see.

I avoided going out as much as I could.

On sunny days I saw less, after all, and I was ashamed of exposing even my clothed physical self.

I began to treat myself, as I have done periodically throughout my life, as the ugly person I had often felt like. I did it with practised dissociative skill.

I spared friend and stranger the sight of me.

I worried especially about this for my daughter. A pretty girl may not want a raging corker for a mother; but nor does she want a tired sow with lost eyes, who holds the wall when she feels her way along and appears to have shrunk from six feet down to five and a bit as she bends over her stick.

⸺◆◆◆⸺

After the tentative suggestion of internal flooding after my fit, the judicious doctor wrote a prescription, which I took round the corner, paid several pedigree cats for, remembering that blepharospasm is a private matter medically (and drugs for its treatment therefore need a private prescription), and kept on obediently putting them into my mouth twenty-four times a day. I never less than liked this doctor. I never wasn't interested by his method and levelness. I would say that I had perhaps wasted his time, to the tune of many cats. I have time too, though I have been conspicuously less good at selling it.

That August after the fit, Fram shook away the end of that academic year to tend his garden. Our son and I were at first in Edinburgh, at the Book Festival, fitting as many authors as we could into a day. It's a pursuit that baffles me and makes me shy until I am in my son's company when it feels just right. I suggest this is because he is an author born, whatever he chooses to do with it, and certainly he is a born reader, and to see with his ears or hear with his eyes has become one of my most reliable forms of escape from myself and the forms of thought that ambush me when the world's sap sinks.

After Edinburgh, we went through to Glasgow and on to Oban, with a man named David from a local car firm. He heard our voices, kindly assumed it must be a first visit north and made a special stop to let us pet a Highland bullock, having explained to us that the haggis were all roosting indoors at this time of day.

Hamish the flamboyantly hairy orange bullock lived outside a teashop. He stood at the edge of his paddock, head over the fence, asking for sweeties. He had that look animals do have when every bit of them is fluffy. Just his wet rubbery nose and his pink tongue weren't; and his strict galosh-like hooves. He was stroppy but inert and wanted something sugary before putting out. Under his long fringe, below his shaggy orange poncho, his forehead was fluffy, his shanks were fluffy. His orange pelt was backed by orange fluff, felted itself in orange fuzz. He glowed in his wet green paddock under the purple hill. How many hotels and provincial galleries hold paintings developed around that Scottish field of colour?

Hamish was apparently silly and actually indulgent, a creature-witness to the daftness of people, a sharer of the joke that it is to be shut up inside a body.

Like Ormiston my cat, who will lie on his back in his cat-suit of creamy fluff and display the centre parting through his foggy fur from chest to prettily lilac but now podded scrotum, and observe one with an expression that defies anyone to assert the dignity of their own embodiment, Hamish had the look of affront that goes with being of cuddly aspect.

Fram knew early in our time together that I was as much an animal familiar as a socialised person. I don't mean that we related to one another through animal names like the disturbing couple from *Look Back In Anger*, but he recognised me at once for a companionate moth-eaten lion, with big paws twitching in its sleep, in the corner maybe of St Jerome's study in a painting, or on a deserted gatepost in Scotland, tiredly rampant as though missing only the drinks tray or trolley from her front paws, or toothless but dancing and shaggily maned at a sooty stone fountain in Italy, moss clothing her where the water has for so long fallen. There are elements of St Jerome to Fram, the care for books, the asceticism, the poring close over text, the burned thinness as breakable as charcoal.

Part of being safe in love is being known and fully seen. The urge not to be known is superficial as well as primitive; facile and destructive compared with the need to be known, that increases as friends die and the world changes, that makes of the loved one an environment in which to root and come into leaf. The urge not fully to be known is the urge to recreate oneself and that is the urge to escape, as dangerous as a rip tide and as hard to harness or control. I lost worlds in their firm orbits when I left him, and now am trying to make on the wheel just a thin bowl to hold myself level within. I see this in the thaw, as I look at the true story of my life, which I thought I could leave resting under the chill light of a protective, eventually weighty, snow.

———◆◆◆———

The mower is moving to and fro along the terraced levels of lawn at the back of the big house here on Colonsay. It has been too wet to mow for more than ten days but today the sun has been bright since six. Last night it was still light at ten and there is more than a month to go of lightening evenings and light nights.

After the fit but before the next failure of the body, I received a visit from a friend. Many friends we made when we were very young we would not make now. She and I are close but we leave views aside, or I prefer to. She does not so prefer, which is in itself a view. My own view has calmed, intensified, deepened since I have seen less. I've always been chary of views, in the plural. I think of them often as places in which to position yourself, to be seen to be positioned, places in which to stand still and get stiff not seeing very much and not thinking about what may be perfectly visible from the inward eye without so much fuss and noise and sending of highly opinionated postcards from the car park of the view.

My friend's life has spun her compass in ways I am too sceptical, too off-put by solutions, to embrace. Of course, knowing me, she can read my tired eyeless if not toothless liony head when she lays out her brand-new views, that are working well enough for her.

She voiced an idea that is a common one but whose truth inheres, or so I think that I deeply believe, in its opposite, that she was glad I was doing a memoir as that is where truth lies, not in fiction.

Well, exactly so. It is in a memoir that truth will, if not lie, tell as many versions of itself as there are drops of water in a river. Does anyone who has lived feel that there is one version of their life? There is only the frozen water of story that will melt and retell itself in another shape, there are only the tides and storms, whose drift will be countered, whose wreckage will be rebuilt, in countless ways by the survivor, and the survivors of that survivor.

I was cross because I thought that she was doing two silly things. The first was attacking fiction and the second was losing out on all that fiction by an attachment to biography, as though felt life were confined to a recorded life. This attachment is fashionable. It is based on the idea that 'life-writing' is real, where fiction is not. That notion is perilously close to the idea that fiction is interesting only when we find ourselves in it, that identification is more essential than recognition and compassion and the acknowledgement of otherness. Not all biography is gossip, of course, but to assert that you prefer biography to fiction is not, as many now understand it to be, to reveal yourself as a person concerned only with what matters. It is to reveal yourself as a person who enjoys biography. (I'm one, emphatically, by the way.)

My friend will be looking for a trajectory in my memoir, a plot, a lesson learned, a message that can be extracted from the thousands of bottles.

She has as much chance of finding one as I have of returning to their stems the hundreds of cut daisies that lie now among the lines of clippings on the scented close-mown lawn under my window. Some of the clippings have been caught in the bin of the old mower, some have not. It's over, it was grass, it will be compost, the flowers fall.

I can say nothing more to my friend with her firm view than that it was my life, that it sometimes went too slowly but was over too fast, now that I look back at it. It was all I had. The miracle would be to convey a breath of how it was.

Yesterday . . . now, yesterday is good and close, perhaps it may be tickled up to life, taken from the stream, and caught before its freckles and the blue shine on it go?

Yesterday was Sunday. It began bright at before six. Yet it did not decline into rain. It grew brighter all day, till by the evening the sea around the island was bright like polished blue metal, and the lochs inshore had the path of the sun across them, blazing.

Katie had promised her mother that we would go to look at the grave of the newly buried man, who had come all those years ago to collect seaweed to fertilise the fields, and who had stayed to live on the island.

The graveyard lies close by a ragged coast to the south-west of the island, away down from the school, where seven children are at present seniors, and two juniors. Katie met the juniors doing a project in the garden at the house, doing a project by the fruit cage. The project was, according to Seumas, who is three, 'Counting strawberries'.

A skill it seems prudent to master as early as possible in life.

> The man in the wilderness said to me,
> How many strawberries grow in the sea?
> I answered him as I thought good.
> As many red herrings as grow in the wood.

The school on the island attains unbroken high standards. It is hard to think of a more concentrated or rich education for small children or of a school more ideally located or staffed to inspire application and initiative or develop native wit. These pupils are as surely made by their teacher, Carol, as are the tutees of an influential don. There has to be nothing she cannot do. This must literally be true, from the more conventional curriculum to the setting of a willow bower, playing the fiddle, telling otter pugs from cat's paws, and sowing nine bean-rows. Three people from that school have recently graduated from Cambridge.

The closest mainland over that compass point out to sea beyond the rocks beyond the graveyard beyond the school is Canada. The graveyard at Kilchattan is exposed, but very green. The graves are set in two turfy yards, within dry-stone walls. A man came two years ago to repair these walls, and Katie and William and their older daughter, my god-daughter Flora, built a section of the wall under his guidance. He sees the compatibilities in the stones and sets them together so that together they will remain. Katie said that he did it as fast as a man laying out cards, and his stones lay immoveable in the places he had ordained for them, while her wall shoogled. Less, she said, though, than her husband William's wall.

Because the day was bright and there was little wind, the small inland lochs were blue and bright over their brown as we drove to the graveyard, slowly. You must drive slowly. There are cows and their calves sitting across the road, and lambs taking a rest on knuckly legs, to feel the warmth of the asphalt through their fleece. The tar warms through quicker than the turf.

There are people out for a Sunday drive; there are churchgoers, and tourists. There is the shepherd, on her quad bike, and Angus, the special constable, in his crime-fighting vehicle.

Car accidents do happen, and the nearest hospital for a broken bone is either a ferry journey away, for which you may have to wait for two or more days, or a helicopter dash, with all the drama, expense and interruption that involves, calling the emergency people from the mainland and soothing and loading the stricken soul.

The graveyard is not at the church, which stands on the hill opposite the hotel and bar, looking down at the pier.

The graveyard is a pair of fields of marked places where human beings lie in earth. The stones number perhaps two and a half hundred. Katie and I read every one that afternoon unless the salty wind had worn it back to plain thin stone. The new grave was to our surprise covered with neatly placed flowers, none in cellophane or paper. Whether they had been tidied by a loving hand after the wind or whether the wind had spared them, I don't know. I feel peculiar about reading the letters and notes that go with flowers for a grave as a rule, in case there be something sticky-beaked about the motive, but we did read until Katie found the flowers from her mum.

A proper measure was returned to friendship and familial ties at that grave. You cannot fret away the ties that exist in a place as small as this. Friendships cannot be consumed at whim or jettisoned as things move along. They must adapt to contiguity. This citiless place makes the true demands of civilisation.

We walked the graves, many of them crowned with the family name of the person below, MacNeill, McFadyen, McConnell, Titterton, McPhee, the beautiful strange surnames Buie and Blue. The Archibalds and Ians, the Hesters, Floras and Euphemias, the one Annabella, the many lost children, the two young men perished in accidents in the late nineteenth century, the gardener at the big house who worked here for fifty-eight years, are joined by many people now whom Katie and I remember, three handsome young men with whom we once danced, dead in their twenties and thirties, a heartbroken father, a man with a hole in his heart whom we hero-worshipped for his glamour and whose grave bears the name of his house and its aspect, 'Seaview'. He was thirty-four when he died.

To one side lie the drowned, torpedoed in war, some from the MV *Transylvania*, one an Italian from an unknown vessel, 'Morto Per La Patria'. There are able seamen, a donkeyman, a wife come alongside her husband decades on from his death alone at sea and his eventual rest in a place she may well not have known existed before he washed up drowned on its shore. Two young men were washed up just a day apart. Imagine the shock of those two days in 1946, the dreadful practicalities.

Fresh flowers lay on a couple of other graves than the new one, wooden crosses with a paper poppy on some of the servicemen's graves, with their name and rank, or the bleak admission, 'Known Unto God'.

It was sad but it was not false. We were walking among the dead, many of whom we could see in our heads. Some of the words on the graves we were stirred by, even those in the Gaelic we could not understand. The graveyard is not there for us, it is there for those who dwell in it. Or it may be there for us, when our time comes, that we cannot know. And then it will be there for our descendants or for those who miss us. The stones are temporary but longer lived than we are. The lovelier stones are to me those that fall more swiftly into decline, that are friendly to the kiss or clasp of lichen, that bloom into defacement.

Loneliest, it seems, monumental and unmodified, are the stones of Katie's grandparents, her grandfather who carried those hard sacks to his melting jetty to nowhere, and his estranged wife. They lie together in the lee of a low wall, but as it were in single beds, each under one large stone like a lintel, with another granite stone on top. He died more than two decades before her.

I came to love her and she came to tolerate me, perhaps merely because I had graduated from being that 'awful common girl who is always around' to marrying the heir to an earldom. She was an indefatigable giver of recycled and mysterious presents with her name crossed out. She once gave Katie the hem of a kilt. She gave Quentin and me a history of the button, that had already been twice around the family tree. She painted and embroidered with a sense of colour that demonstrates her love of the island her spouse latterly forbade her by force of law to set foot upon. She was talented, rude, stylish, beastly and brave. I liked her, though perhaps it should be put on record that Papa, when asked how he could tell his mother and her identical twin apart, said, 'Oh Aunt Va was the one who loved me.' His mother covered surfaces all over this house with her painting, the laundry bathroom window with furling seaweed, the shutters with beavers, rhododendrons, shags, black-headed gulls. Her lively decorative spirit lives on in her handsome grandchildren; her dreadful trenchancy has entered my world of dead voices. When I took my firstborn to visit her, she told me that anything can happen if you let a workman near your freezer. They could for example take all your frozen herring roes. In which you will, naturally, have put your good jewels. I own neither freezer nor gems to place therein.

Oma's grave is sad, and so is that of her husband, by many accounts a gentle interesting man. His bears his title. Hers bears her role, that of his wife, and his title. All else gone.

'Known unto God' tells as much as those two graves of any private self, though not to the biographer. The stories told upon the graves at Kilchattan are mostly poems. The sea that can look savage or ravenous beyond those graves was purring under the sun yesterday, creaming in repeatedly with its soothing repetitions close by all the recently undone of this place.

I have since leaving Fram feared that I will not be able to be with him after I die. Now I know that I cannot because it would no longer be right. I used to think it selfish that I wanted to go first, but now it is unselfish, because it tidies me up. Not only is this not his way of thinking, but he thinks it pointless and somewhat manipulative in me that it is mine. At last I will not only cease to be a worry, but I shall have a place to be, and a place where I am snug and quiet and feel nothing. There is something inconsiderate and clamorous in a person bleating unstoppingly for the other to whom all is referred. Get on, he says, stand up. I cannot be the person who is your shepherd, I least of all. You must tie another fleece to yourself and set out on the hill. You will not find a new mother, you may not find a mate, but you will do what innumerable women and men have done before you. You will carry on, as you are bound to do, the expedient fleece bound to you.

That is what truth to life is. The way to be true to life is to remain alive.

———— ◆◆◆ ————

Later on Sunday, William took me to have a drink with our friend whose big window looks out over to Jura, whose raised beaches looked close enough to touch in the evening light across the blue sea. She has multiple sclerosis, is badly compromised physically, and frisky and busy mentally, running a bookshop, the community online newsletter, and belonging to many boards and committees. She told us about a recipe for cormorant pie; skart is the word in the Gaelic for cormorant and for shag, that the old harbourmaster, Big Peter, Para Mhor, used to enjoy in a pie. I remembered Peter, with his white sea-boots and his wide beard, his deep chest and his rosy cheeks. I had remembered him at his grave that morning. He held the old ferry in at the bow with a rope around a stanchion, balancing another rope sprung in tension at the stern. He slung sacks beneath the tyres of cars before they were wound out of the ferry by davits, when the ferry was not yet ro-ro (roll-on, roll-off). He wore petrol blue overalls that grew paler throughout the year and were replaced when they had reached a blue as thin as the last shallow sea over sand.

While we were taking a drink with our friend, a small red cruise ship came close to the island, and moored in the flat calm. Almost as soon as its anchor was set, the black ferry, twice its size, hauled through the silky water, with the large declaratory words Caledonian MacBrayne along the hull. For a moment it looked as though man had mastery over land and sea. We might have been looking, through our friend's picture window, at a poster from the nineteen-sixties about advances in travel by sea. The scene might have been posed by models in a tank of moodless blue water, that same sea though that will ensure that not the drowned of this place alone are in time known only unto God.

On the way back from our drink, we drove into a sun so bright that it wasn't just me who couldn't see. William drove slowly by feel into the sun past stretches of water that pulled its white light down in stripes of glitter into themselves, wild flag iris leaves like knives at the lochans' margins. At each passing-place we pulled in to let another car pass. We stopped for lambs. Why race to the end of a day so full of light?

Chapter 6: Goosey, Goosey Gander

Goosey, Goosey Gander,
Whither shall I wander?
Upstairs and downstairs,
And in my lady's chamber.
There I met an old man
Who would not say his prayers,
Took him by his left leg
And threw him down the stairs.

My computer has just offered to me, within its menu of formatting, the information that 'Widow/orphan control' is already in place. This means that no lone word will be left to stand unprotected by the words with which it has been conjoined, or with which it has grown up on to the page.

When I worked at *Vogue*, laying out copy, we hunted these widows with our scalpels, taking out antecedent text in order to bring the widowed word up into a warm paragraph away from the cold of white space.

Today the weather on Colonsay is so clear so calm so bright that I am afraid to use it up by mentioning it. I feel that by staying indoors in my apron trying to catch words and put them down, I am buying a day in the sun for someone else. If I have a dark indoor day, will that not equalise things somewhere? Won't the weather keep itself for the weekend, when we have our sister Caroline visiting, and Katie's daughter Hannah and a pair of newly married friends, Rupert and Ellis?

If you fly an aeroplane, you cannot think in such ways. You read for what is actually going on. You do not navigate by magic.

Alexander reads bodies of water, for the direction of their spume, the energy of their choppiness. If the loch that is full of brown trout is spilling over its dam on to the traces of the old road, he knows that the ferry will not be able to get into the harbour. He lands his small plane no distance from meadows where corncrakes nest and ragwort grows, the one a protected, the other a notifiable, species. He can't make provisional bargains such as mine with nature. His life, and the lives of those whom he flies, depend upon his reading its actual intent from its present state. Before the tsunami of Boxing Day 2006 struck, a teenaged girl who had learned in her geography class that, if the sea suddenly sucks in its breath so that beach is exposed where it has not been before, there is going to be a great tidal wave, ran about a beach in Sri Lanka, telling people to run for their lives.

Would you obey such a command? Some did, and escaped with their lives. She cannot have had time to explain her urgent order. Her listeners must simply have trusted and acted in the same breath. Knowledge gave her authority.

What interrupted her holiday distraction sufficiently to persuade her that the sea was holding its breath before it roared inland for devastating miles? There must have been a sound, or a silence, some sea change; possibly a melancholy long withdrawing roar. Or did she see the bed of the sea, exposed and appallingly dry, every bit of water sucked back into itself to reinforce the giant wave?

That girl was doing what we are told is the only way to live, now that an afterlife is all but discounted by rationalists, that is to live in the moment. Her moment gave what must have felt like an afterlife to those who survived.

Who, fully conscious, lives in the moment, actually? I have met some who think they do, or even appear to. The first are often intolerably selfish, the second usually very old and of apparently high principle, or very young indeed.

But can we know that even infants really do live in the moment? Anyone who has looked into the eyes of a baby knows that its soul is preoccupied. Those who try to live in the moment fail, since consciousness of the attempt occludes the purity of its essence. It is far easier to accept existential discomfort and accommodate oneself to it than to live existentially.

Aren't we more like the goose in the nursery rhyme, wandering upstairs and downstairs and from room to room in a house we cannot envisage as a whole?

Although Fram thinks of me as that sleepy lion, it is the goose who has lately predominated, and he would, when exasperated, call me a goose. In plenty of ways he is right. Like a goose, I hatched and fixed upon him, making of him my parents as well as a focus for my thoughts and days, just as a gosling will, of whoever brings its enclosing egg to term.

Like a goose, I would be rewarding to render down to fat, like a goose I hiss if my idea of home is attacked. I panic in advance just as did the Roman geese sacred to Juno, herself an intensely feminine and domestically petty older goddess, who suffered from jealousy incidentally, and was, while we are about it, unattractively insecure about her appearance. Also, like a goose, at the moment, and this is where the rest of the nursery rhyme comes in, I waddle.

And 'gander' is a word for a verb of looking, in which English is demonstrating to me its richness the less I am able to see. In English slang, to 'have a gander' is to take a look.

Last autumn, I moved from the upstairs flat in Tite Street to my older son's house, still in London. He was twenty-six at the time, with a demanding job, a girlfriend and a busy social life. He moved out of his own room for me and put himself in the small spare room which he had previously rented to a nice, very tidy, girl lodger. He is six foot six and a bit tall, and very tidy himself.

He opened his house to me and my clutter, my too many grey cardigans and my unnecessarily growing number of books, my large out-of-date CD player, the clattering heaps of talking books, my stocks of ballet pumps in silly colours, my eighteenth-century Scots-Napoleonic child's chair that I have had since I was two, and my chunk of lettered stone – the design for my father's grave – my fading watercolours of fish, executed in Macao by a painter, 'almost certainly of Chinese origin', and my painting in oils of a jug of pink roses made by Henry Lamb for my grandfather Ormiston Galloway Edgar McWilliam. The piece of funerary inscription says UTILITAS incised in grey Scots stone. Usefulness is one of the three essentials for architecture, according to Vitruvius. The others are FIRMITAS, strength, VENUSTAS, beauty. My father had these characteristics. The stone in the Flodden Wall of Scottish Heroes declares them together with his span 1928–1989.

My son has a thin television. His ironing is immaculate. He looks new. Even when I was more presentable, the way I look did not come naturally into his view of the world. No sooner had I begun to live in his house than it started filling up. He does not like stuff. His tolerance of my way of being has been gentle.

It's more graceful than tolerance in fact. He has twice alluded to something he has called 'homeliness' starting to happen in his house. But I don't think that he is being satirical. He is never snide. His face was open when he used the term.

◆••◆

It was a fine day further on into the autumn, and I had a doctor's appointment. I decided to make an effort with my goosey appearance.

It was a grey jumper I lit upon, instead, for once, of a cardigan, and black skirt and ballet pumps. I was running not as punctually as usual. My son's house is arranged around a steep but solid staircase, fitly carpeted, firmly banistered.

I keep my white sticks in a bowl by the stove, like the utensils they are. My mobile telephone was charging by my bed upstairs in my womanish bedroom; no old man, reluctant or not to pray, was up there in my lady's chamber. I was on the last flight downstairs when I fell in a way that struck me as new, and then as very new.

I saw what I was made of, clearly. Two white bones stuck out through the now surprisingly blue and white skin of my left leg. There was something pinkish like veal.

I remembered what my friend Robert had done when he had a stroke years before, as a young man. He took over twenty-four hours to do it, but he rolled and dragged his literally half-dead body to reach the telephone. Now, Robert was even taller than I, and in worse trouble, and telephones were immobile in those days, so I was lucky. These were my first thoughts.

I remembered that my son wouldn't be home for two days. I vehemently wanted to get out of this pickle before two days had passed as I did not want Oliver to find me broken and filling his front hall in a spill of handbag contents. I had resolved that he must never again find me wrecked.

I did pray then, simply and aloud. Praying for oneself is discouraged by every friend I have who is serious about prayer. I prayed for something I lack, whose lack has contributed to Fram calling me a goose. I asked my guardian angel to tune me in to the frequency some people are on all the time, common sense.

I was apparently stuck. It must only be apparent. I thought. I made three steps upstairs on my bottom and arms, backwards, towards the mobile telephone plugged into the wall two flights up, and saw that I was already late for my doctor's appointment that had before I fell been due in an hour and forty minutes. I thought that it would be a bore to pass out.

It might also be quite pleasant to pass out if I was going to spend forty-eight hours alone with my odd leg.

What was wrong with it?

The foot was pointing the other way. It was pointing backwards. I took it in both my hands, pulled my foot away from its leg and did my best to turn it round, so that the toes would point forwards. Nothing hurt because I held all my thinking away from my left leg. I cut off its messages.

It was the look of the thing I didn't like, so that proved that my trusty body, just as when I had my fit, was allowing me my eyes now that I was, in anatomical equipment terms, a leg down.

I was apprehensive about my family. They would not like this.

I thought of Robert, inching towards that telephone years ago to call his mum. I asked my mother for help. I neither cried nor shouted.

Not many people are around in the day in a small London street.

I was going to have to risk embarrassment. I did not want to shout. Noise makes me panic. It is seldom necessary.

I could go no further up the stairs. The line of least resistance exerted its to me inexorable sway and I was, not soon, but at some point after taking the decision to do so, making some sort of progress back down the stairs and towards the front hall.

Both Oliver and I had heard what may have been an urban myth about fishing rods with magnets on the end used to burgle the houses of people of methodical habit who keep keys close to the front door. We fondly feel we have another method.

I lock myself in when I am alone, almost automatically, having for over a decade before I moved to London lived next to an individual of whom I was afraid.

That once prudent habit might be, if not the death of me, a nuisance now, I reflected.

My son likes big umbrellas. I saw one, hanging behind my untidily many voluminous coats on that gloriously orderly boy's coat hooks in his front hall.

I prayed again, this time for as much stretch as I had had before I began to fall in towards myself, for my young stretch that had fled only in the last pair of years.

I reached Oliver's umbrella. I wasn't in pain, but I was high as a kite, observant in the way I am when in a chemically altered state. If only I didn't have to fall down in a fit or break myself to get my eyesight back at its former pitch and heightenedness.

Oliver's umbrella was naturally perfectly furled. He is a man of action who understands the importance of small things. He is the man who stows the parachute correctly every time.

I held the ferrule of the umbrella and moved its hook towards the door, not hopeful, but trying to implement the care of a burglar with his fishing rod, the other way about.

My earlier inattention to detail might just be going to save me from my flying slipshod fall, for I had not closed the front door on its intractable deadlock as I think that I almost always do.

I opened the front door, which was one astounding stroke of luck.

I began, quietly and not convincingly, to say, 'Is any one around?'

I had grown used to hearing no one pass the windows of the house in the day except to set off for work or come back. It was late lunchtime.

I did not want my upsetting left leg to be visible, were anyone to come. I tried to bend my knee back and conceal my shattered ankle within my black skirt with stars in its weave.

I'd not noticed the stars before.

I was seeing stars, like in a comic. I missed having someone to tell my thoughts to.

It was bright sun outside, low autumn sun.

I saw two angels, male of course as angels may be, one shorter than the other.

It was two weeks since the crash in the markets of 18 September 2008.

My rescuers had the sort of manners that occur only in romances. One was Greek, the other German.

When the paramedic who was driving turned on the siren of the ambulance in which I found myself I remembered that I'd been in the hands of these vigilant kind people before. They put a line in me and started with the morphine, managing at the same time to talk soothingly and to obey the bureaucracy that surrounds the administration of Class A drugs, while listening to my chief worry, which was that Oliver might find his house imperfectly tidy. They talked down their radios into the emergency bay.

It was the same hospital.

I had dreaded that.

The hospital had become my place of fear of dying alone.

Hospital had been till that fit the place where the children had been born. I was that lucky a woman.

Now, though, I belonged to that major part of the population whose knowledge lay with their fear; that it is our modern lot to die away from home and away from those we love.

In some ways, though, this was like another place, so different was the atmosphere of this ward from that of the first ward where I had lain with the silent doctor quietly dying and opposite the stark shrieking old woman reduced to open bowels and mouth.

It was during the following days and nights that I discovered that I do not get on with morphine, which I had been keeping as a treat for the rainy day when an addict knows her number is up and so she can accept pain relief without fear of dependency.

Morphine makes me itchy. Junkies often scratch, I remembered now, from gatherings I used to attend under the shared delusion that we were at a party, when gear was another way to spend money with nothing good to show for it. Not, ever, my bag. Too scared, too broke, too oral.

This time the dying old woman on the ward had a name that was lovingly used.

I was barely coherent and about to be taken to the operating table (the surgeons work all night in that place) when one of the angels arrived with orange roses in his hand, 'For the lovely Mrs Dinshaw'. People remember their first kiss. I will remember my last gallant bunch, and that courtly untruthful adjective. This was not flirtation. It was the completion of a certain form of gentle behaviour. What flowers these were, a disinterested, foreign, correct bouquet. I felt as fortunate as a researcher coming upon an unknown primary source.

Hospital gowns are made for people of average size. I had hardly been so unlovely, immodest in my gown, spotty with opioids, haywire with anxiety about the children. I asked him to put the flowers so they were for all of us women in that ward, in a jar on the ledge of the big window where pigeons panicked, settled, tapped with their bills on the other side of the glass through which lay London.

It is such things as my rescue by the two angels that make me in life believe more in E. M. Forster's and Elizabeth Bowen's sort of plot, that intersperses literally incredible melodrama with lulls where the shifts are apparently minimal, rather than in the steady organised tempo offered by more evenly plotted novels. Elizabeth Bowen says this in her notes on writing a novel: 'Chance is better than choice, it is more lordly. Chance is God. Choice is man.'

I'd say, chance is fiction at the top of its reach, choice is comfort reading.

Tolstoy feels like life, as you read him, with all the never irrelevant extraneousness, and the fullness of it all. But life, to me, seldom is Tolstoy. He improves on it, at any rate, for this reader. To read him is more fully and steadily to live. One calms down, daring to be tranquil within his fields of power. He is like life, if we were fully able to remember it outside the bias of our own temperament.

The ward was full. It contained only women, six of us. We might have been the cast of a soap opera, so neatly did we fill all the roles. Everyone was really quite ill, which achieved an unusual thing. Instead of sinking into solitariness and dislike, we looked after one another. The two youngest were particularly gentle. Each was gravely ill, one a blonde firecracker whose lover had killed himself exactly a year before and who was experiencing bouts of unidentifiable but excruciating pain, and one a young mother whose jaundice made her skin Vaseline yellow against her dark hair. She had a proper bust and lovely ankles and wrists and her whole family, mum, dad, husband and two little boys with crew cuts came in to watch telly with her in the evenings. Her father-in-law had been murdered in west Fulham the year before. 'Bastard said it was for his jacket,' she said. 'Leather.' Her eyes filled up as she spoke. Heart matched well-screwed-on head.

There was the other faintly shaggy person like me, an artistic and witty woman who raised her young grandson herself and had undergone a terribly botched operation, and whose ex-husband was slowly dying in a hospice near the hospital. There was the nice Chelsea widow lady who was afraid to go home and whose signal gallantry took the form of grooming. At all times, Betty's hair was perfect.

And in the corner there was Ethel. Ethel was very old, and terrified. She whimpered like a dog and moaned horribly and regularly. Her guts made awful noises. She stank of shit unless her nappy was changed, because she had bad diarrhoea. She fiddled all night with her catheter and cried out at the sharp pain. You could tell the type of pain by the outraged hymeneal cry. All night she did it, sleeping sometimes by day. She was lost and wretched and might have been ignored or sighed at by these other sick women.

It was the young ones who took the lead, the opposite of a pack turning on the weak.

Each of these young women had herself a lot to bear. Each was seriously ill, without knowing what that illness might be. The blonde, who put on her extra eyelashes daily and always looked a treat, had a mother in the last stages of Alzheimer's. On about my fifth night in hospital, the dark young woman received a message from her husband, who worked in a timber yard. A load had fallen on to him. He was in hospital with a cracked skull. She slipped out of our hospital, coat over gown, and went to see him in his hospital. By then our nurses loved her. They made no fuss when she returned.

'I give 'im a piece of my mind,' she said. Lucky man. She was a clever girl.

She was what tabloid papers call 'a fighter'. Things were clear in her head. She was affectionate, brusque, tender, direct.

We were nursed with discipline, which feels good when you are that sick. There was little unkindness, unlike on the first ward. Agency nurses caused real tensions, about pay and about relationships with patients. They may not have intended to do this, but it made the staff belonging to the hospital sore. They were jumped by absence of warning and by different nursing techniques. Agency nurses also earn more. I heard not one mention of this. It was the style of nursing that was the chafe. We patients unionised if there was a sense that Ethel wasn't being properly cared for. She was, being lost in her mind, demanding. If a nurse couldn't come to her, one of the beauties held her hand and kissed and soothed her, just as though she were one of their own. Ethel was in hospital, she was demented, and afraid, but she wasn't alone. It was a delicately managed thing, and took grace on the part of the nurses. They were fussy about hand hygiene and they shooed the girls to their own beds to rest. What kept the whole strained and frightening place from driving us into our lost selves was simply human connection.

I was blind and on a Zimmer, so they directed me as though I was driving a dodgem when I was allowed my first trip to the bathroom to go and wash. The bathroom was shared with men, who were quite as bothered by bumping into women half naked themselves as we were at being seen unwomanned. When first I was washed down with mean soap and an institutional paper towel, I felt remade by pampering luxury. It is hard to find yourself in dirt. You find yourself in water, or in being clean. Cleanliness is next to some exaltation if not godliness.

The nurses would shout across beds while they made them about why their parts of Africa were best. There was tough barracking and teasing. The main hero was Jesus. Very often in the night, a nurse would praise his name, or thank him. I wondered whether the two Muslim nurses seemed left out. It did not feel as though the deities were in battle. They were each so desperately required.

We were there long enough for a shimmer to go around the ward, a shimmer of secret delight when we were allowed to know that the pretty staff nurse was expecting her first baby. We began to mother and boss her.

The blonde beauty had many visitors, pretty girls and elegant men bringing gifts from the shops they worked in.

Ethel turned some corner into serenity. We discovered that she loved sweet things and would smile and babble like a little girl if you gave her soft sweeties. There was consternation that she might be going to have to enter a home, in effect to die. She had a daughter, but she couldn't remember this. An equal heartbreak. She had a voice as rough as a herring-wife from my childhood. It was lovely to hear her when her shouted news from wherever she was sounded happy.

'Aw, Vat's laaavely,' she would yell while she was washed down after having her nappy changed. 'Vat's laavely. Aintcher good ter me?'

I couldn't go home to Oliver's house. I was now a person who couldn't walk, as well as one who could not see. My eyes had shut down again when the blind panic of adrenalin ceased. My blind panic, so it seems, gives me sight.

In hospital, I had received flowers from my agent.

This was both to say, 'Well, you are in hospital again' and to mark the broadcast of my most recent short story on Radio 4. The story was a nasty jab at the consultants and junior doctors in the previous ward I had been in, in that very hospital. Of course, it was all transmuted into fiction, but I'd been so sad about the old doctor lying there politely dying next to me, that I made up a story where, although he died, he won honour from the teeth of humiliation.

Two things: the consultant whom I had had in my sights in that story on that day cancelled the appointment that had been made to investigate my fit further, and, thing two, although the radio was on in the ward, and there was my name, and my story, nobody but the author listened, very quietly. Fiction makes a low noise, well below a hum, in the life of a hospital. Books and writing are of interest only to those to whom they are of interest. This is a depressing truth, in itself of interest to fewer and fewer.

I had to go somewhere when the hospital released me, and it had to be where I could live without stairs for a minimum of six weeks. Annabel and Quentin invited me to Hampshire, for as long as it took me to start to walk again. They had dried me out and now they were again taking me in.

———◆◆◆◆◆———

In Hampshire, I humped upstairs with my metal frame from the car to the room I was hardly to leave for six weeks, watched as I lurched and wobbled with kind attention by my first husband, with the practised eye of a horseman-yachtsman. He's used to big animals and metal spars. He was also the encouraging kind of father who allowed the children to tackle stairs but kept a gate there too, a sensible facilitator. I toddlered my way up the familiar wide stair on my bum, hauling the Zimmer after.

I went to what has become my bedroom, that has seen us through many Christmas-stocking openings and two comings of age, washed with real soap for the first time since hospital, and entered a bed I got out of hardly at all for over a month.

Three busy adults, my older children's father and his wife, and my older son, made time to visit me in the slits of their crammed days and evenings. They brought me stories of the world beyond and set up a routine that gave me a triumph of time and enlightenment, you might call it, an understanding of how they spend their days.

Land defines its rhythms: one lot for farming, its own; quite another for people. They moot the lot, divide the tasks, split them, and do it as it comes, which is naturally. The life of books, or whatever life I thought I led, seems by contrast inward and unevidenced. But it's what I have to offer.

The separate personalities engaged upon the enterprise of the place made riper sense to me daily. I heard mowing, and hooves, and raking of gravel, gunshots, roomfuls of men, roomfuls of women, roomsful of both. I asked Annabel what she was wearing so that I could imagine her. I could hear when Quentin had been hunting because he would be in stockinged feet, having taken his boots off in the hall. I smelt bath oil in the early morning, then tea and cleaning products, then nothing till dinner unless there was a shoot. I could tell the doors of the visitors' cars apart.

It was a happy time in the knitting together of family routine and of bone. I made laps of the landing on my Zimmer. They did not let me get away with moping. I was never alone in the house. The kindness was such that I was shy. It doesn't do as a way to be among your own. I haven't ever managed not to be.

During these, I think, six weeks, my older son inspired me to stop taking all those drugs. The bag of drugs I had with me was greater in volume than my bag of clothes, and it was after all autumn, time of big woollens and greatcoats. Over the six weeks, I cut down incrementally, until all I was taking were mild sleeping pills of an accreditedly non-addictive type. I'd asked for these after getting so hooked on Zopiclone that I panicked if I didn't know I had substantial stashes and was upping the dose yet achieving less, thicker, harder, sleep.

Oliver's reasoning was twofold. None of the family could see that things were getting better under the regime of all those drugs. If anything, they were getting worse, though no one was so ungentle as to say it but me.

And if, as the doctors warned I might well do if I stopped taking all the drugs, I had another fit, I would be in a place where I might be caught if I fell.

Just before Christmas 2008, I was almost drug-free. I was so blind that I had to rely on others to write my letters, and hot flesh was growing like silt around an anchor over my metal-bolted leg, but I was starting to have some clarity of thought.

That thinking wasn't perfect, being tainted by solitude and fear, but it was less wholly reactive and fogged. I would wake in the night imagining that I had at last found the formula for being a wife who wasn't and then go back to what shames and pains me, I think because it reminds me of being a child, the staring into the dark with hot eyes and a wet face, with the sense that there is nowhere to go where you are not a nuisance. I carry it like typhoid.

The most useful formula that offered itself was from a book I have not properly, that is not unblindly, read. It is by Emily Wilson. *Mocked with Death: Tragic Overliving from Sophocles to Milton.* I've dipped into, and liked, it, throughout the last blind year, though I'm aware that such dipping is unsatisfactory. Minoo has been my deeper pilot fish with the book. I started to believe that I had presumptuously over-lived, and that it was in reading Shakespeare and Greek tragedy that I would find an answer, were there one. Not a surprise, but a map.

The sad jingle that Dora Carrington used as her farewell stuck in my head. She took it from Sir Henry Wotton, though it now turns out to have been written by George Herbert. She couldn't continue after the death by cancer of her beloved companion Lytton Strachey and wrote down the words:

> He first deceas'd; she for a little tried
> To live without him, liked it not; and died.

I knew I wouldn't do it but the words were there offering their clean comforting specific inside my clearing head as the drugs receded. I'm told, as people say before they adduce crackpot theories, that it will take two years to get all those drugs out of my system.

Is it not curious that the doctor who prescribed these drugs never got in touch with me again, when I had been told that any reduction in, let alone cessation of, dosage, could be perilous? What can he have thought was going on? I suppose it never came up in the life of one so busy. We wreck once more against the rock of comparative values placed on time.

The couplet remains inside my head but I think it is there more on account of its balance and structure than its message. Rhythm injects it deep into the head.

I couldn't work out what my point was. I saw myself as a tied-down giant, and Fram and Claudia as normal-sized beings who had worked out how to live, dancing free, in their triumph of enlightenment.

Why did I mind so much about the world, since I entered it almost never? Certainly, when people see a middle-aged woman whom they don't know, they try to place her within the customary grids, and marriage is one of these.

I must make myself whole by work. After all, I am old enough. I am at an age when I might not long at all ago have expected to be dead, or at least widowed.

Those things of which I am unpleasantly jealous reflect ill upon me and are to do with her having been born into a context, rather than into my little family where the hotter personality evanesced and the cooler one thought personal conversation all but contemptible. Or so I surmise. I just don't know. As must by now be clear, I've collected myself from here and there which may be the best I can do. In the middle are words and a capacity for recognition.

There is a particular formal stance of heartlessness that is a certain English way of protecting the heart, the elegant sternness that is one mode and often goes with the throwaway unadvertised, indeed denied, deep sensibility that sees off the vain and fake. It may be found at a peak of comedy and sadness in the work of Evelyn Waugh. It has been a tone congenial to Fram all along and now he inhabits it.

He is an alert reader. He grasped just as well too the empty dove-cote that is the McWilliam tone. Scots say doocot, and so do I, but I thought I should spell it out. It's only by a feather that I didn't say columbarium, which is the word that first came to me; but that word is too full and successful and plump, though hardly too classical, for my father, who mentions in one of his books the fine columbarium kept by Drummond of Hawthornden.

<hr />

I left Hampshire just in time to return there for our customary family Christmas.

I travelled by train from London carrying nothing but the stockings for the younger children. Standing room only on the train.

'You are joking?' said the woman who stood bumpily next to me in the vestibule when I told her I couldn't see very well, which was why I was peering around and craning, 'I had you down for different, but not blind. You've got lipstick on.'

We talked about Christmas plans.

Her son-in-law made sure the family had a tree that wasn't just thrown away. They had one tree outdoors with lights and real roots in the ground, and an artificial tree indoors with a long string of bud lights that also came in useful at birthdays. This was the first year she wasn't taking her cat, Graham, to the family over Christmas. The neighbour had a key and was going into her flat on the day itself, with Graham's stocking.

'Nothing fancy, though. Toys, biscuits, a card and that. Just what he'd expect.'

Chapter 7: Snowdropped In

On 8 January, my cat Ormiston was run over, the first time ever he had strayed from the girls' garden, where all summer he chewed grass and flew up to pat the air inaccurately over the spread purple buddleia tassels where a butterfly had been. Killed instantly, no marks. I still don't think about it. I skirt it in my mind because I am afraid to start, and, if he was only a cat, what do I do with all the other grief? Crying helps the sight after all.

Or it did, before I had the first operation for the Crawford Brow Suspension, on the 21st of January of this year, 2009. My eyes are different since that operation. Crying is hotter and tighter. I'll come to that.

Leander and Rachel were wretched. They had a haunted sense that if he had stayed with me he would have been alive. If he'd stayed with me, though, he wouldn't have had such a life, with companions, butterfly-attracting plants put in at his request, and fresh fish. He would not have had his summer of being Warburton and exploring the uncatty group ethic he enjoyed. He was a team player; an unusual characteristic in a cat.

After Ormy was buried, Minoo went round to the house in Oxford. He prefers his cats disdainful, sardonic and free, but he ate an entire lemon drizzle cake in memory of Ormy and reported the handsome location of my people-pleasing cat's remains.

Something of Ormy's appeal for me was that slight dogginess. He was in on the joke and played up to it, sometimes allowing himself to retrieve a ball if we were alone and unobserved.

He was funny, and you laugh aloud less often if you live on your own and don't really read. I didn't think I would ever say that about myself. It's always been a sentence that puzzled me: 'I don't really read.' I see it now. It means, 'I read what I have to, like instructions on dangerous machinery or in lifts.'

My first blind summer, two friends, married to one another, had sat with me at Tite Street. They'd brought a rhubarb tart with crème patissière. He had glancingly said that he had counselled a mutual friend not to buy puppy as it would be just another thing to grow fond of and eventually to lose. Rita the blue cat had fallen in love with him.

Now, a year and a half on, he, I and Rita remained above the earth. Ormiston had been an inch of air, a pinch of fluff. My friend's wife had been his response and crown of life. Who can plumb her loss? Nothing took her away. Nothing had her. Nothing had its victory. Nothing endures.

I now missed the foolish flat face of my cat up against my neck, telling me that it was time to get up at five-thirty in the morning. Even though he had been doing it in another house, with other people, I had known he was on earth and cared for. What comic strands have emerged throughout these years of eye-time (well? There is much talk of me-time). Ormy had been a guileless occasion of laughter.

Others went some way to providing other forms of diversion. Some have to be buried for discretion, or transmuted.

My favourite fun theme has been the silent wager I make with myself about the literary ambitions of the medically distinguished, and of quacks, too, now that I think about it.

It's my limited understanding that I have been visiting doctors so regularly for thirty-six months because I am decreasingly able to see. With my eyes, that is. My, admittedly subjective, sense has been that reading, by which I not only made to some extent my living, and by which I live, has become difficult. I'll put it simply. Very often I can't see. I'm blind.

You will be aware of this. You are a reader.

However, not invariably, but often enough to give reality a firm shake, a doctor will say to me as I leave his consulting rooms, very possibly having written a cheque (is that where I go wrong? They see that I can write, after all?), 'Ah, Mrs Dinshaw, Candia, did you say you were a writer? Books, is that?'

A bit. Once. Things a bit challenging at present. My eyes, you see. Cranking the odd thing out for friends. Scottish literary papers. Things like that (thinking, 'That'll put him off. Surely he will realise that it's a polite rebuttal of what he doesn't know I know he's going to say?')

Women practitioners are as liable to do this as men. Let me be fair.

'Ah yes. I must ask my wife to look you up. I don't get much time to read. Other than for work. Papers, you know.'

Indeed so.

'But you meet all sorts doing this job. It's taken me all over the world. Some pretty amazing places. You wouldn't believe. And I've often thought.'

If you had the time.

'If I had a moment, that it would make a book. An interesting one.'

Not a novel, then.

'I often think that real life reaches places, well, you won't mind my saying this, but truth is, it's not just a cliché, stranger than fiction. And you don't make anything up. It's all true.'

This is getting in deep. Ask it, do.

'Would you know of who I should talk to about getting it published?'

And then, a little carried away by the different glories attendant upon the idea of being a writer as well as a doctor, 'Would you mind having a look at it for me? I've actually had time to get something down. It's typed, you know. No doctor's writing!'

I am really interested by doctors. I wanted to be one. My mother and I, retrospect tells me, both go, or went, for tall men in old-fashioned clothes and good overcoats, which was, in Edinburgh terms in her young womanhood, doctors. We visited a doctor with

pinstriped long legs and a watch chain quite a lot. I sat on his knee
and he gave me boiled sweets from a jar with no top. His height
and expertise and silver hair imprinted me for life with one way of
being a glamorous man. I've no idea who prescribed her sleepers.

I would happily write about doctors in fiction. Or write fiction
about doctors, or help a doctor friend write a paper. I might easily
ghost a doctor's memoir, should he want me to, were he to find my
sight. A fair swap, words for seeing?

I except from all this my GP, whose understanding, he has self-
deprecatingly said to me, falls short of words. It doesn't. It goes beneath
them and into music. His kind of doctoring has that human affinity
that used to be called compassion.

As well as the doctor-autobiographers to whom I felt I couldn't at
that time give the assistance required, there was new and much more
interesting comedy in the form of the surgeon who has come to the
salvation of blepharospastics with his two-part operation. When people
keep saying to you, 'Of course, he is brilliant', you know that you
are going to be handed a sharp spray of human traits.

His name is Alexander Foss. I heard of him because a fellow sufferer
from blepharospasm, Marion Bailey, had written to me after reading
a piece that *The Times* reprinted from *The Scottish Review of Books*
that I wrote about being blind and not blind. She and her husband
have become as godparents to my eyes; they are the chief kind
strangers in our family's recent history. Alexander Foss gave Marion
back her sight. She understands exactly the trap and paradox of the
maddening condition that is blepharospasm. Her courage and
generosity have kept me upright. She wrote to me, enclosing photographs, about the operations with which Alexander Foss had given
her back her sight.

John and Marion Bailey came to meet Olly and me. Her story
was my own, baffling, alarming, frustrating, frightening, intractable.
But she had found some kind of redress, and now, if she husbanded
it attentively, had a good measure of sight. We decided to follow her

generous example. Words, their publication, and their being read, passed sight through the hands of Alexander Foss from Marion Bailey's eyes to my own. How can I thank them all enough?

———◆•◆◆•———

Annabel and I had made an appointment to meet Mr Foss in the Midlands, where he practises, before Christmas. We drove up in December snow, late one Monday. Our treat was a boutique hotel in Nottingham. I had a disabled room with a red cord to tug in case of falling. I was in a pneumatic boot by this time, and as ever used my white stick, not to feel my way, but to tell people not to be upset if I crashed into things, and that I was best avoided. The plumbing and electricity in the hotel were of that unexplained hidden kind that only those born to mobile phones can operate without fiddling and splash. The comfort was practical, the welcome warm.

Mr Foss works within swifter time passages than the rest of the race. His supreme charm as a doctor is that he does no prologue, no soothing, no explanation, no awful chat. I could tell at once that he was a surgeon, *tout court*, pure brain and action. We arrived, we asked questions from our careful list, then we were out. We tried in the coming weeks to work out what this acute man had said. We had fun thinking of things that he would be least likely to say. These included:

How was your journey?

Are you staying locally?

And the family, how are they taking it?

Christmas plans, at all?

What a relief it was. Does the mutton roast want to be asked about its native pastures by the man with the whetstone and the blade?

We took against him for about two minutes each and then without knowing it we turned him into a hero. I suppose he had been auditioning us too. Luckily Annabel is a doctor's daughter and managed a direct question.

Would it hurt for a long time afterwards?

I, sitting down, am about up to his chest when he is standing. He is nonetheless a formidable presence. His words come out at the speed of a lizard's tongue, where the fly is your attention. Only much later do you realise what's happened or been said. He smiles when he says the worst things, but not unkindly, at all. More like a true wit. I think he may be one. My guess is that he will not linger because what he does is of such intense moment. You can with ease imagine him seeing off death, around which he is often, as he is around the dark of blindness. His specialism is cancer of the eyes. He clicks and pops like an indoor firework.

What he told us was that I had one of the two worst cases of blepharospasm he had seen, and that I was lucky, as twenty years ago I would've been sectioned, that if I disliked him now I would hate him after the first operation, after the second it would be curtains for us, it would hurt so much.

Annabel and I returned south through the snow with a new person to develop inside the story. We each kept remembering delightfully, in a slow conventional world, rude, actually terrific, things he had said.

We started inventing them.

That leg'll have to come off too; no point holding on to a duff limb.

Prepare yourself for complete failure; no operation is more than a good try.

Only one thing's ever certain.

We imagined him paying compliments:

That hat has got to come off.

Ordering a meal:

Where's the bill?

Proposing:

It's shortly our tenth anniversary.

We liked Mr Foss.

For my first operation, it was again Annabel who took me. We tried to imagine, in hospital that January morning before I went down to the theatre, what he might say when he came on his visit to me before I was knocked out and wheeled in for his attention.

Mr Foss came into the clean little hospital room where I was too big for everything, chairs, bed, gown, slippers, paper knickers.

He had a form.

We'd been surmising and practising reassuringly feel-bad things he might be moved, or, admit it, induced, to say.

Annabel was in the lead with, 'I'm dispensing with time-wasting anaesthesia.'

She had also scored highly with, 'Look here, I'm busy today.'

He raced through the form. It was the usual. Next of kin, religion, etc.

He filled in the name of the operation: Crawford Brow Suspension. Then he spluttered boyishly, 'Benefits of operation?'

We waited. It was, after all, his field.

'None. No benefits. None at all. Not that I can honestly say,' he said, and was gone, leaving us in the highest possible spirits. That man could be a general. One would lose a limb for him with his surgical high spirits.

There used to be a phrase, used of certain drinks, 'A meal in itself'.

Mr Foss is the life force in itself.

This is not in my experience true of most doctors.

Annabel set off for the South; she drives with mettle. She is the sort of ladylike quiet person with quick reactions whom you will find calmly running things when flashier ones have decamped. Accomplished, brave, capable, dutiful, her alphabet might begin. She can name most popular music tracks of the last forty years, and keep a poker face.

It's odd. I am afraid of blue eyes, yet both Annabel and Claudia have them, markedly so, each in her way. Annabel's are pale blue, really like aquamarines, and give you a shiver with their bright chill and almost pure colour, no black but for a pierced dot. If she weren't smiling below them, they would be icy, and can look uninhabited. Claudia's too can alarm because they inhabit a face that will not play along with anything that discomfits.

Both Annabel and Claudia have a gaze of pinning intentness. Each is a contact-lens wearer of long standing, and short-sighted. Both shake themselves when their eyes are tired, as though to refocus. Each pushes her fringe up with a hand to catch and ingest light through her pair of blue irises.

My own pair of green eyes woke up in the afternoon that January with bloody blinkers made of gauze strapped over them. My whole face, when I patted it, was strapped, like a mummy in a horror film.

I was ridiculously anxious that no nurse should think that I had had a cosmetic procedure. I knew these were going on around me in that hospital.

When I came round in the post-operative room, a nice young male anaesthetist asked, 'Are you married?'

I replied that I was but that as I understood it, it was complicated and the terms hadn't been invented yet and that my husband lived with someone else whom I was fond of.

I thought that this was a good opportunity to start as I meant to go on, naming things as I awoke into this new post-operative world.

Poor young man. He probably wanted only to see if I was sufficiently unwoozy to recall elementary facts, like the name of the Prime Minister. He got an essay. I don't even know how to fill in forms. I alternate between 'Married' and 'Separated'. I think I want to put what our son wants me to put. I must ask him.

I asked the young man his own marital status. He had a wife, he said, from Edinburgh, actually, away at the moment with his brother's wife, also from that city, also a nurse. You couldn't keep those Edinburgh girls away from home, he said. At least he supposed they were going home because they were homesick and it was nothing worse.

He spoke with healthy confidence.

'I'm getting so I miss the place too, actually,' he said, and patted me in an encouraging way. 'You should go there one time when your eyes are better. It's gorgeous.'

Later in that day with my stitched eyes behind their blinkers, there was another conversation that pushed plausibility to its limits.

As far as I could tell, it was evening. A woman's voice, South African, almost social in its willingness to interact, reached me, enquiring about various practical matters. I replied.

I had had supper, insofar as I wanted it. I had found the toilet. Yes, I was used to finding my way by feel around the place, it was one of the upsides of not having been able to see that much before. Might I have a sleeping pill?

I might indeed not have a sleeping pill. I had just had a general anaesthetic. Did I know the inadvisability of risking it?

Silly me. I'm sorry.

Do you usually have sleeping pills? Are you aware of the dangers of dependency on prescription drugs?

Yup, I bullyingly said from inside my bandages, I'm a twelve-stepped alcoholic committed to rooting out addiction wherever I encounter it day and night.

How many years' sobriety?

Oh God, she had the lingo. Medical people on the whole absolutely do not speak AA talk, unless they are 'in the Fellowship'.

Oh, what had I done? Were we going to swap drunkalogues, as they are chattily known, deep into the hospital night?

But it didn't go that way.

I said, modestly, or rudely, 'A few', which is a sort of signal to be released that only the sensitive take in. It means, 'I haven't had a drink for quite a long time. Years, probably nearer ten than five.'

It is a way of not making newly sober people, who may have achieved those first, literally miraculous, few un-drunk days, feel small. It is a way of not bullying.

Her next question quite baffled me. 'Are you privatised?' she asked.

I thought I could hear earrings. So, not a nurse, if allowed to wear tinkly jewellery at work.

'I'm paying for this procedure. Do you mean that?'

'No', she replied, 'I meant, are you married?'

I had never heard the expression.

I told her what I had told the nice young man with the wife from Edinburgh. Life was offering me exactly what was required, an opportunity to be plain and clear about what remained obscure – at any rate in words – to me.

'Well, if you were a writer, you could write about it,' she said.

I couldn't engage with that. I was barely sure any more that I was anything, let alone a writer. I did the interviewee trick, and turned the tables.

'Are you privatised?' I asked. I wish now that I'd asked her where this odd term comes from. Can it make the husband feel nice, this microeconomic form of expression?

'I,' she announced, 'am very happily privatised.'

She too has a terrific name. I will call her Theophania Droptangler.

The spirit of the woman, whose bright clothes I could hear and whose warmth was toasting me merrily through the anaesthetic and bandages and darkness, suggested there might be something well worth chasing on to the page. The next morning she was the first to come to me, at the sort of time my cat might have begun the day.

She was more than a chatty woman used to talking to zombies. In the intervals of her night watch, she had done a lot of background research.

'So you weren't bullshitting,' she said. 'You had it right you're a writer.'

I said, 'What?'

'I found you. It was that unusual first name. We're sitting ducks for stalkers, darling. And I've decided you can have seven sleepers to take away because I trust you.'

Useful being called Candia if it procures you sleep medication and binds you to other people with funny names.

I asked the nurses what this earring-loud lady looked like. I wanted to see if it matched my picture. She had told me her age, which was more than sixty. They confirmed all of it, sunshine colours usually reds, pinks, turquoise, lovely dark skin they said, henna through her hair, tiny like a bird, lots of kids, must be around fifty, looks about forty, and earrings like you would not find in a shop. Earrings in the shape of things, parrots on perches, ice creams in soda glasses with two straws, cactuses.

'She's exotic. Not like a doctor, more like a writer.'

The next stretch of time was like no other in my life. The closest I have come to it is V.S. Naipaul's *Enigma of Arrival*, a book I have loved more on each rereading.

As I recall the book, it is an account of the writer's time at a small house on an estate that had belonged to the Tennants, part of the set that included Ettie Desborough and the family who had lived at Clouds House, known to me for its architecture, its inhabitants the Souls, and its efficacy at drying me out. The estate was in fact Wilsford, to whose melancholy sale of contents Fram and I had been just after the death of its owner, Stephen Tennant, the lover of Siegfried Sassoon and later recluse, who dwelt alone indoors making bulgy drawings of matelots in many colours of biro, seldom leaving his bed and wearing powder and lipstick, in rooms upon which were drawn white satin curtains full of dust and in which vases of white ostrich plumes fussed up into the heavy air. Those impressions were gained from the sale and the house's interior, the sad boxes of stuff that were having a harsh time of it in daylight, props as they were for a life of delectable tackiness and gimcrack fun, all, no doubt, in revolt against the stout Lowland virtues of solidity, bleach and no jokes, against which Tennants, beneficiaries of a chemical fortune, have for the last few generations so incandescently, sometimes chemically, rebelled.

The Enigma of Arrival, as I remember it, a recall of reading through blindness and forgetting, which seems in itself the sort of distancing such a monument to passing might rather enjoy having inspired, grows like moss upon the rapt reader, who perfectly enters its mood and is made part of it as he proceeds. Naipaul conveys the oldness of the landscape and the paths worn upon it, the ingrownness of the community and the dreams that make us who we are and what we might have hoped to have been. It is about hope and disappointment, dreams and death, and how worlds meet. It shows the absorptive power of the famously self-defining Naipaul. It is a great book. I can envisage its being read for many years beyond the time of our grandchildren because it is apparently clear yet it takes you into itself and shows you things there in the dimness for which you did not have words. It offers an England that isn't 'literary'. It's geographical and spiritual. With words, it goes beyond words. Just as the artist is rare who can write drunkenness, the artist is rare who can describe our pre-verbal sensations and thoughts.

❖

Not far from the hospital where my eyes were first cut, about forty minutes away maybe, stands an enormous house with a stony name, in woods famed for their many snowdrops.

What follows is not to do with the actual lineaments of anything that happened. My eyes could not see, I could barely walk, I was alone for long periods. The spring of 2009 was held in the grip of the most sudden and extreme snowfall in Britain since 1964.

The prevailing colour of my time up there is a white that fluctuates between being the blurry edges of my stitched-up eyes, with long filaments or tresses of light, the white of the snow-laden sky pressing down on the snow-covered earth, the fallen white of snowdrops beginning over one weekend to make shivery pools under black trees, the white stillness of the frozen lake, and the long white bath which I could not make hot, mainly because I was too passive to mention that the water ran at a heat that met the cold air without steaming. The big house was beyond the garden of the large Georgian vicarage that I had rented in a fantasy of recuperative entertaining and a mistaken certainty that I needed to be near the hospital. I believe that I was in this commodious house for six weeks. It was not unusual in me that I felt like an interloper. This was made worse because I was bed-bound, so couldn't fall into my usual pattern of cooking and cleaning in order to feel less guilty. I had to lie still. I couldn't afford this sojourn in any sense.

My eyes were prickly with big stitches of black thread holding them together. I was told the thread would melt and it did. My face was all bruise which became it rather if you forgot that it had been a face. It looked like those potatoes that are blue all through with a thin skin.

I had brought with me a Dictaphone, with an idea of dictating a novel into twenty-four one-hour-long tapes as small as eyeshadow pans. At first, I ignored it and then I realised that I must make a routine or I would . . . I don't know what.

And that's it. I don't know why it was as it was. I felt as though I had fallen through time and into the lives of other people who did not know me. I felt as though I were being kept on ice to be unfrozen and eaten later.

I was melting through the money my house had fetched.

The vicarage had seen unhappiness, perhaps, but what house has not? I had no telephone reception, but that is not unusual in my life. I have quite little here on Colonsay.

I was clean, warm, and cared for with more than kindness by a man of unimpeachable cooking and organisational skills, with elegant grooming and a perfect memory for tractor models and railway time-tables. These last composed much of our conversation as he took me through the snowbound village, re-teaching me how to walk with the patience of a mother. He had worked on the railways and then his smouldering good looks had brought him to the attention of the local squire, and a golden age of triangular emotional tolerance had commenced in the stone pile by the lake, a golden age that had come to a close only with the passing of the squire, lamented, celebrated and beloved right through from Eton, where he had Wilfred Thesiger as his fagmaster, the Army, the war, and the long reign as squire, with his fond family and attachments around him up to his fairly recent death, which was crowned with posthumous literary plaudits and rich memory.

I was twice as cut off by the snow re-bandaging the world as I was by my not-seeing eyes. The world seemed to be slipping, as though I were carrying sheets of sharp but melting ice and trying to slot them into sash windows. Nothing was solid, nothing stayed in its place, only the white felt firm. The safest place to be was in the bath under water or in bed under sheets.

I will not forget the silent arrival of my hot-water bottles, each covered like a piglet in a coat, carried by my handsome carer as he padded in three times a day with them. Their heat was my emotional life.

For the last ten days, I kept up a sort of routine, which involved spending the day in the part of the house that had once been its nursery, and spoke words into my Dictaphone. I did twenty hours. It wasn't as shapely as a novel, it was far too deep in snow, and I was able to see, when my last stitch had melted and my swollen drifts of cheek settled back down, that not one of the tiny cassettes had failed to snarl up on itself with the discretion of a wormcast in sand. So much for my novel written in snow.

I learned later that friends of mine had decorated the house, friends who had decorated the house in which Quentin and I had lived when our daughter was born. Perhaps that simple graphic explanation was a key to the locked sense of being doubly not present, of being a ghost in whiteness in a place that had been happy but was – at any rate not so that it coincided with my flickering passage through it – not so happy now? I had the sense throughout my visit that I had been cut back so that I might regrow, and that the cut was speculative.

Like many things that are over though it seems at the time that they will never be, that period has struck deep roots in memory. It is on the turn inside my head. For all its white silence, that month and a half almost wholly under snow in the North-East, just up to the time of snowdrops, is expanding still and turning itself over under its quiet, like a sleeper, becoming something, perhaps.

I suppose that the person whom I met again and again day over day who wasn't there upon the stair was myself, and that I did not like being snowed in with her. By the end, I was talking to the hot-water bottles and giving names to the taps. My bar of translucent pink soap had become the emblem of my time there and I washed with it angrily so as to wear away the hours of day to a sliver over the white cloudy lukewarm bathwater, in the house in the white silencing snow.

The snow did bear light within its reign though not the light that I had projected when I thought in advance of that sequestration in the North-East. I had thought that the post-operative period alone in the unknown countryside would cause things to settle and to calm, showing me thereby what I should do next in my life.

The phosphorescent snow bore some kind of reveal in its soft train when it melted, showing me that yet again what I had done was take an artificial position, in some pain, attempted to deal with it alone, got frozen in, waited for a rainy day and then – seen no option but flight.

Chapter 8: Eyes Half-cut

A kind friend drove me south to Fram and Claudia's house, where I was due to spend a week or so over Minoo's birthday.

We all wanted the idea of spring, no, more than that, the reality of spring. I had frozen my life so capably for so long while they were living through normal, seasonal, you might reasonably say seasoned, time.

They extended another chance to me. If it were a children's game, it might be thought of as another 'life'. Those reprieves feel like new breath in the playground, a fair portion of offered hope.

Fram tried to coax me into liking, even loving, myself again. The very notion of self-loving brings me out in an allergic unthinking nettle rash – we Scots may be prickly but we're also dead allergic, and often to ourselves. I have made a fair job of burning up what was ostensibly loveable and now I'm left with what remains. There's not much to love, while there is all too much of me. It's not a new story. The phlogiston has burned off – the mothering, any glamour, the cooking, the social fun, the jokes, the pretty ways in a house, the observantness – which were all but mothering, fair tosh anyhow – and we're left with the calx, which feels as reduced as it sounds, a shrivelled residue. How can I love that?

The answer is further in. Love in yourself what you would love in anyone, anyone at all, certainly in a sick person no matter how repulsive their illness, just because they are human and still retain life, or the vestige of it.

So, treat yourself as you would an employee. That's what shrinks say, because they know that I can't imagine treating another person as I treat myself, which is with automatic torrents of abuse that Fram thinks come from having experienced their like too early on. He also says they are part of a longing to have someone silence them by saying nice things.

The row over ransomed milk was so bad that I thought that was that. I had seen how exasperated they were by my incapacity to be helped and just to accept that this was now; they were there; I was here; and that life is not fair.

Gestures are often insincere and lead almost always to regret. The two pounds for the milk was a gesture. Gestures may be staged for the notional watcher, who is the spirit of Punch and Judy, and, worse, of the Colosseum. Gestures may be lies, waiting for their big fat bluff to be called.

I will not forget the one time I slapped a young man for kissing me, in the dark after a dance here on Colonsay. The slap was pure gesture as the kiss was not. I was showing off to whoever was watching the film of my romantic life; that is no one at all. Or, at most, just me. Unforgivable. I apologised to this young man's grave this week (he never grew old but lost his life to a knife in a city), but I did not say so to Katie. That would have been gestural. Whether or not it's gestural to mention it here, I am attempting to discern as I write. Writing about private things can be gestural, and it can not be. The reader will have to decide.

I arrived at their house in Oxford from the North and, not meaning to but not knowing how else to be, set about being as tiresome as possible almost before I was through the door. I could see very little, and just wanted to hide. I went to Minoo's room, which is my room when I am there, and although I couldn't see, I scraped my bruised newly stitched eyes open so as to ingest anything new that might hurt about the room, packed as it is with memories of our marriage and of Minoo's childhood, photographs of the other children, the cats, the poem written for our wedding by Peter Levi, framed, the sparmannia cuttings from our drawing room, the pink Roberts radio, Minoo's soft tiger Siberia and his wife and son, Blanche and Albert, the various sketches of the house in Italy Fram's mother made, Minoo's clothes, many of which are clothes I bought for his father, my father's furniture, my own, the painting of a Roman street vendor with buck teeth that once belonged to Henry James. So what? It is all Minoo's life.

He is the wholeness that emerges and it is fitting that his life should be whole around him and his home also.

To fuss about things at all is symptom of nothing more than the awful 'meum–tuum' of bourgeois marriage. That is almost the whole truth. Occasionally, Fram gives me an offering he has come across from my past: my christening mug or my leaflet of Cardinal Newman's *Dream of Gerontius* that I bought for six old pennies at McNaughtan's second-hand bookshop in Leith Walk in Edinburgh before I went away to school in England. I carry it in my handbag. He can't give me big things because where would they go now I'm a mobile mother? And do I actually want the things themselves? I want the continuity, the unbrokenness, the dream not woken from.

Which is like the burglar crying aloud for the uneased, unbroken window. Worse, like the roiling thug weeping over the grief and bodily harm he has inflicted. The things tell a more whole story under that happy roof than under any I might offer them.

After about one night and a bad morning when I even broke my own artificial taboo and went up on to the floor of the house where Fram and Claudia's bedroom is and where you can see the crowns of trees and be among the church bells even higher, I decided to face the fact that I could either shut up and keep all this to myself or just move my suitcase to another pitch and get on with moaning, and I was running out of places to be. The reason I tell Fram and Claudia about the sadness's shape is because they understand the metaphorical terms I, unconsciously but thoroughly, use, and that is more important to me than practically any other intimacy, the sense of swift mutual understanding. Even I could see that it was unjust to punish them for their pre-eminence among my loved ones.

So, there was a morning of me racing around trying ever more closely to define my understanding of the lostness which was of course like sewing hems with smoke. Then I settled down to their life, her taking him breakfast, and bringing it to me too, which seemed like far too much kindness, their trips to London for meetings, libraries, theatre, her book plans, her reviewing, her columns, her cousins and siblings and their babies, his going to college and returning exhausted and then working till three or four in the morning, her seeing friends, dealing with the animals, with family, the coming and going of Joanna the ironing lady who had been for ten years a steady soothant in the children's lives under our roof, and whom somewhere along the way I loosed my bond with, like so much else that had been treasured and familiar.

Who would grudge anyone that? Anyone whom they love?

And I do not.

I have, however, and it's quite an achievement, managed to empty my own life to the extent where I have made it a cell. Not St Jerome's calm study, but a prison. I haven't made a charming minimalist environment for the contemplation of the good, I have fixed up a metal cave. I think I did it with drink first and with a good disinfecting blast of high-pressure shame after that. Then I went blind.

It is easy to forget how to live. I did it. Getting back up is not easy. Getting back on, I am trying now, but the laps are faster and faster that the carousel is making, and those who are thrown off it or throw themselves or fall off it – why hadn't I noticed this at the Dutch amusement park I so hated as a child, the Bedriegertjes? – never get back on if they are tentative. You have to leap and then be rock steady. You have to leap into the centre of the awful spinning thing to find any stillness; the edge will throw you off.

.

Chapter 9: Two Instances of Spring

The darkness brought down by my closed eyes is a new way of being shut out. Since that darkness is my circumstance, unless this operation which I am awaiting works, it is surely the right thing to turn that darkness into a new way to be alone.

The stay with Fram and Claudia over Minoo's birthday was full of things that worked, as long as I kept the past from my mind. If I ceased thinking of my own life, that I had no job, no home and no systems within which to do more than exist as an organism from day to day, beyond the sketchy membranes of prayer and washing, then it was pleasant to be part of this busy house with the comings and goings of young people, conversation, and the tenor of wit and shared myth that lies at the heart of full lives.

Fram said, I am sure truthfully and I know welcomingly, that it was a matter of indifference to him whether I stayed for two hours or two years with them, they would carry on as they do with their lives, to which I might be as much of an addition as I wished. Claudia finds me easier. I second-guess his boredom and in doing so bring it into being.

Clementine and Rose came for Minoo's birthday lunch, and Olly in the evening. At lunch, there was prosecco and a roast made by the twins' father, Toby, and Clem and Rose brought presents wrapped in sparkly paper that left granular silver dust on our hands. Both girls had silvered their eyes like fish scales. Claudia's son Xavier was there, and they shared a cake sent by Cousin Audrey in Edinburgh. The garden was sunny and early flowers were through in Fram's newly made garden, scented paperwhites and wintersweet with its strong scent of milky Earl Grey tea. Clem likes Fram's gardening and enjoyed the thin squeaky-stemmed fragrant narcissi. I was glad for her that the vase and the cutlery, the napery and some of the plates were familiar to her.

I loved it that she enjoyed the ironed flowered napkins that reminded her of Fram's mother, who had chosen and hemmed them. Fram's parents were fond of my older two children.

At tea that day, there arrived Claudia's cousin Alexander with his family. He crowned the day by telling Clem and Rose that he and Claudia are their cousins. This gave plurality and wreathing life to the already happy day, so far is Alexander Waugh from the dead hand of genealogy and self-importance, unlike those satiating moments when Marcel notices how often he hears the word 'cousin' in the world of the Faubourg Saint-Germain.

Minoo became twenty, his siblings and coevals celebrated, several of his parent figures rejoiced, and his parents spent the week roughly under the same roof.

It was a blossomy time when I was in Oxford, a forward part of the country. Colonsay is slower to come into bower, so I've had two springs this year.

Claudia was establishing a new outlet for a small independent publishing house during that week, so she was busy in the most congenial of ways to a blind onlooker. Fram showed towards her the mock-exasperated mixture of pretend scepticism and actual loyalty that is his braced and bracing form of support. Their days went forward in separateness together, that state praised by Fram's friend and colleague John Bayley in his book *Iris*.

Claudia introduced me to a friend of hers who does massage. I am struck among some of her friends by their attention to the state of their own health. I might have done well to take account of the rules by which they are defending and monitoring their bodily lives, but at their age and younger, I would have thought it narcissistic to be so in touch with the body; my mistake, my very Scottish mistake. I think mean old baglike thoughts about their comparative youthful being and my own blown body and disability.

This woman however did something unlike any other massage I had undergone. There were no words, oils or embarrassing wavy or whaley soundtracks.

She used wordless intuition to make me breathe so slowly and deeply that my thoughts ceased for a time to race and repeat themselves. Her discipline has been learned over decades; she is not a proselytiser. Something really works. Regrettably, she lives on a beach with sharks in its sea at the very top of northern Queensland, but this spring I met her as often as possible before she and I went to our separate homes on islands of very different size. She has done more than most to see off the incessant internal instructions I give myself. You can attempt to defy what she does by pulling tension and acid into your mind, but she feels what you are doing and makes minutely inflected pressures that force you to release the knots and poisons. She leaves your organs with nowhere to hide. Meanwhile, you are fully clothed and forgetful of self. The sense afterwards is that you may, after all, have another chance, that you may have the equipment remaining within you with which to love.

Chapter 10: Silver Wadding and the Smell of Remorse

I became conscious of death as a thing that trembled around us, my parents and me, in the air, as soon as I came to the sort of conscious thought that I can recall, so around three or four years old. Death sent its messengers, as it does to small children: among them dead animals in gutters, flat mice, soggy poisoned rats in the area, the hopeless nestlings my mother rescued, the shrew in her cardigan pocket that she could not revive, with its nose like a tube, dying rabbits on country walks, the shocking deaths of the zoo animals for which my mother felt so misshapenly, inappropriately, much.

The wallpaper in my nursery held in its pattern the family whom I called the Cauliflowers who brought death with them. They bulked into the nightmares that seemed to reach me from day into sleep as I lay trying to construe its pattern.

Burglars came into the house and left you dead, the life sucked from you into them through their faces that were masked but for the mouth. I saw burglars very clearly in my mind as silent monochromatic breachers of safety. I felt about them as some people feel about cats, that they understood only their own advantage and moved selfishly in silence around and through the world they wanted to deprecate; the words 'cat burglar' and 'footpad' confirmed this fear.

I cannot remember when I didn't know that my father was liable to fall down dead at any point from his dicey heart. I first met him when he was twenty-seven, thin, prone to a racking cough, a heavy smoker; I cannot recall at any time in our interrupted acquaintance (I love him deeply to this day, more than twenty years after his death, but we had the most formal of contact) not being anxious for my father. I listened for his breath, which was loud yet erratic in his thin chest, especially when he was writing, drawing or smoking. Mostly he was doing at least two of those at once.

I knew very early on that I would myself die. I was hoping that I could buy life for at least one of my parents, by getting my own dying over with; I had this concept caught by the age of five, when, I'm ashamed to say, because it is blasphemous, vainglorious and self-dramatising, I dreamed I redeemed my parents through crucifixion on the wall bars of the school gym. I certainly wasn't cut out for any more conventional wall bar exercises.

My mother also felt to me imperilled. This was to do with her closeness to me and her failure to hide things from me, for which I am grateful to her. She told me for example, that she loved my father. That she told me this on the day before she was no more does not empty it of a meaning that I can utilise to reflect back into the marriage, although memory also suggests that, while it wasn't a very happy marriage, they knew great happiness at some point in and with one another.

I do not think that happiness came into it much at that time. There were other things that life was for. Certainly, you did not set out to find happiness. I don't think that that was untypical. The explicit tracking down of happiness through marriage or indeed otherwise was not so much to the fore. Satisfaction, achievement, things seen or heard or done, rooms warmed, socks darned, were proper aims. I suspect that my mother had an almost overmastering capacity for happiness that unsettled people and made her electric, both attractive and repellent. My father not. Or rather, not with my mother, not on our watch. I think he was happy in his second family and marriage.

My father, unlike my mother, was not a soul completed by an emotion or a mood. He was completed by a thing well done or a passage of visual or auditory proportion. He closed himself off against mood, which may be why my mother thought him distant and so glamorous, at once drawn by this sealedness and unknowingly encouraging him to evaporate into thought or execution.

I thought that she was going to die because I liked her so much. Then she did. I'm not sure if that left me thinking that love from me might be fatal.

Can I really never have had that thought until this moment, when I type it blind, released into these paragraphs of truth-telling by two things in the night here on Colonsay? I shall come to them, as I must try not to flinch politely away from whatever dark moth it is I am circling with my net around the prone form of my mother, on her front in a knitted green day-dress on my bed in my mushroom-grey brocade wallpapered nursery.

My mother attracted moths and butterflies. If she did not literally do so, there were more of them around in those days, and she drew my attention to them unerringly. I think of my mother with her long hair held back in a scarf or with cat's eye sunglasses, holding out a brown and orange butterfly to let it go back to land as we crossed over on the ferry to the Isle of Arran. I think of her saving gold heavy-bodied dusty moths from hot light bulbs at night, lamenting the moths' short lives.

She did her hair at the open window of their bedroom and butterflies came to her sticky newly lacquered fair fine hair and danced around her head in its staticky mist. I can see her as a healer of racehorses or an animal shrink, or an unemployed white witch. For sure, she drew familiars to herself. She was a hopeless teacher because she did things almost entirely by instinct, while my father was a splendid one, having clarity of intellect and fully trained consciousness of how our, and several other languages, had come about and what differentiated line. She would have been a marvellous . . . well . . .

My experience of her indicates that what she would have been pre-eminently, whatever job she took, is a marvellous mother. As in, a mother who provides marvels and who transmits the marvel in things.

I was reviewing her talents and atmosphere as I wrote, and it came to me without words, the sense of her kitchen and her small garden in our street, of the entertaining that she did with not much more than a cauliflower and some cheese and her stapled blue and white china bowls from junk shops. What she had was the presiding touch. Not much confidence, and less of it as her marriage progressed and she failed to live up to her mother-in-law, or to get jobs in shops, which as I recall is what she felt qualified to apply for.

Not much confidence, no, but many wasted gifts that did not yet at that time have a name, and not at all in the conventional Edinburgh of her short married life. She might be surprised to see that people pay nowadays for the things she did by nature: listening, amusing, seeing to the heart, making rooms feel whole, tracking down and reviving unloved objects, creatures, people.

My mother made jars of pink jelly that shone gold at their centre from the tart orange fruit of the rowans by the railway sidings along from the dog-racing stadium. She labelled the rowan-jelly jars with drawings of the Scottish kings (the rowan tree is the royal badge of Scotland). She made elderflower cordial with the powdery blossoms from the cemetery, after she had shaken them over muslin to spare the small flies therein a sugary death. My mother did two things or more at once and took account of other things all along, so that her life was in ribbons, but they were bright, if, by the end, pale.

It might have been enough for her to have been a wife, had her husband been at home, had he been a farmer or a farrier or something other than a man resident within his mind or else out of the house. She should have had a practical world to inhabit. Instead, and fortunes have in our time been built on such a thing (think of Cath Kidston), she made a fantasy of domesticity that was probably not to the taste of her husband, though it is a frail but vividly living thing for her daughter to handle in prose, when it would be best in transmission through re-enactment. It beats me where she got it from, this bee-loud domestic engine, as her mother could not endure anything that was unlike the neighbours' way of life for fear, I suppose, that her origins be revealed, and her father liked his experience unvarying from day to day, shares, golf, more shares, meals, no talk, televised boxing.

Well, that is where she got it from, naturally. She was reflexive.

My mother, were the thought not transgressive, I think is the fashionable term, might have been a good wife to such a man as my first husband. I was awfully aware, when we married, that she would have been jealous of me, marrying a handsome man who understood horses, shared many of her inborn traits such as instinctive conservatism and innate faith, and who would have sheltered her gifts with pride. She would have adorned his world and been a good charity committee person, painting and gardening and sitting on the bench, mixing her magical attributes with her commonsensical ones, enjoying his authoritative capacities. My father would not exert authority unless he was forced to. His socialism and his classicism were each so pure that he simply could not allow for human weakness; he thought that in an ideal world people were likely to behave well, which meant modestly, unselfishly, according to principle and proportion. My mother's humours did not accord with this conviction, requiring attention and explanation, in for which he did not go. It was his fortune later on to marry someone whose own disciplined upbringing supported him. I can offer to my mother's shade the certainty that in his older daughter my first husband shelters aspects of her grandmother, my mother. Her way of being is in part in harbour now.

It comes to me that amid the stuttering mental pain of her last months, she did go frequently to organise things for the Scottish Society for the Prevention of Cruelty to Children. I was baffled by this because she would dash to her friend Kitty's house, where the meetings took place, or to Mrs Ross-Skinner, and I would catch the drift of her errand as her basket and her scarf and her scent flew ahead of me down the windy street – that she was on her way to do 'cruelty to children'.

I could have believed it, with the bit of me that she slapped and shouted at, but I didn't, since, though I did fear her temper, I far more feared my father's, that held in it distaste. And I knew that I was an abnormally fearful child and that this was not a popular way to be and made me suspect among certain of my friends' parents.

I can't remember whether I approached death with the same sidling fascination as I approached the sexual. My own relationship with death was almost consoling. It was part of me, not something against which I made myself. That is, I was afraid of it, but I was used to being afraid of it, and when it came it was in each case not welcome, not a relief, but a thing that in that particular instance could never quite be repeated, each death being congruent in nothing but its nothingness – but peremptorily different in shape of loss.

❖

The two events of the rainy night in Colonsay are as follows. I dined with my not-brother Alexander and his family, his wife and son of fourteen, daughter of twelve. The willowy young people sat at the table, as some of the adults present wrangled noisily about the pre-existence of mind. The twelve-year-old retired to bed. The fourteen-year-old sat quietly, listened, took the shouty opinions, considered them, analysed them, cut them down to size and presented them back to us all, well groomed, but not thornless. He held his own soberly over the happily vinous table for about ten pleasurable minutes in the candlelight. It is particularly happy to watch the face of someone whom you have seen since babyhood and of whose parents you are fond. I held my forehead right up throughout the evening in order to watch the two children and their mother and father.

At four o'clock this morning, a helicopter took that boy to a cardiac unit on the Scottish mainland, where he presently is with his mother, while his father and sister are here on the island in the stair-rod rain. Nobody is over-reacting. The mode of this family in crisis is decidedly calm. But, while this had been going on, I was lying in bed thinking about all our ends, almost conversationally, while my cheap pink CD player relayed in the hush the speaking voice of a friend, reading his most recent book, that is, among other things a disquisition upon mortality.

> 'Whenever the moon and stars are set,
> Whenever the wind is high,
> All night long in the dark and wet,
> A man goes riding by'

the rain was saying, completely reassuringly.

> 'Late in the night when the fires are out,
> Why does he gallop and gallop about,
> Whenever the trees are crying aloud,
> And ships are tossed at sea',

said the rain and the wind against my bedroom shutters, while I listened to my friend's voice and was for a good part of the night less afraid than I have been for weeks, on account of the reassuring family supper; two of whose protagonists were during those same hours in another part of the house, praying for regularity to return to a beloved, faltering, human heart.

The last lines of Robert Louis Stevenson's poem, which has been one of my lifelong sleep-charms, read first to me by a parent, brings something more frightening into focus. The lovely hoofed clatter of the lines returns insistently as a firmer knock altogether. Is the night rider someone more threatening than a highwayman?

> By, on the highway, low and loud,
> By at the gallop goes he.
> By at the gallop he goes, and then,
> By he comes back at the gallop again.

Deacon Brodie was the famous Edinburgh highwayman, a minister by day and a robber by night, robbing the rich to succour his poor. He died on a gibbet of his own devising. Miss Jean Brodie is, as she explains, his descendant. Each of them is meting out a certain sort of justice and living out that famous Scottish doubledness, in order to shake things up. The pub named for the Deacon, on the Royal Mile in Edinburgh, had a sign that used to haunt me when I was small, and that has supplied one face of my fears to this day. The deacon is masked, up close, his eyes seen through holes in a tight band of cloth.

With one of the earliest book tokens I was given aged about six, I bought, on my own, operating under some compulsion to look at what struck fear into me, an American paperback of *A Journal of the Plague Year* by Daniel Defoe, precisely because its cover bore a depiction of a face looking through a white mask of cloth. It was a good read for the child I was too, as it happens, full of herbs and philtres against death.

Aged ten, I read both Aldous Huxley's *The Devils of Loudun* and a sort of shocker called *The Nun of Monza*, because they had covers that featured burning eyes staring through holes in otherwise anonymous masks of cloth. I cannot suppress fear at such spirit-extinguishing masks and my dreams employ extras in the tall pointed headwear of Ku Klux Klan or of Inquisition, hoods down over faces like snuffers over candle flames. I cannot bear large groups, in film or in life, of undifferentiated beings without faces. Orcs are perhaps are the worst, but wasps are bad, though I was ashamed to learn from the diaries of Simon Gray that wasps have specific jobs and roles in the wasp world and establish committed domestic loyalties. He learned this when he and his wife called in the pest control officer, who was a fond amateur of the creatures he was paid to exterminate, a relationship gamekeepers will find familiar.

Nothing more undoing to the tender heart than a glimpse of the exterminee's home life.

Or so you might have hoped had people themselves, once the numbers are large enough, not disproved this.

———◆◆◆———

The sky in the Western Isles moves from dark to light to dark with flashy effect upon mood. It's as enlivening as strobe lights, disconcerting, choppy, dashing. The sun is forever stripping right down to pure light and then bundling all its grey shawls on again. Today has delivered three dousings of rain from a black sky, several seemingly tented interludes of white sun from a white sky, and one golden bolt out of the blue that came down to earth with a pennant of tight respective strips of rainbow, only loosening into pallid pink green blue violet rayed haze when the next rain, as it had to, came. I feel the weather on my back as I work by the open window and I feel it over my own shawled eyelids.

In one of these gaps of light over dark, Alexander has set off in his little aeroplane towards the mainland with his daughter. He's taken a packed lunch on the plane for when they all meet up in hospital in Glasgow. He gets into the air, and sometimes, if things are jaunty and he feels like it, he tips his wing at whichever members of his family he's leaving behind.

I never saw this gesture in war, of course, but have seen it in countless films. It is hard not to get a lump in the throat, the tall man and the small machine.

Two writer friends, Janice Galloway and Julian Barnes, have recently written autobiographical works that stressed they were not autobiographies, each emphasising in its title a word of negation, even, denial. It's the intelligent way. It's the only remotely truthful way; all ambiguity in that phrase fully loaded and intentional. Her *This Is Not About Me* and his *Nothing to Be Frightened Of* both deployed to the full their very different powers of negative capability. Her book was nicotinous with slanted, smoking recall, the underskirt under the skirt, while his boned out to its full pit-haunted beauty the typical cleverness of that title. You cannot deflect his eye from the heart of his matter.

It is indeed nothing itself of which we should be frightened.

This book is among his most imaginative work. Apparently conversational, certainly lively, it is nevertheless made of prose so very clean, so deadly serious in intent, that it should hold out longer than bronze, prose that, its author knows, will, naturally, not so last.

These books are under-books, if I may make up a term for the works that form first as clouds then distil then fall during the life of a writer, who is making, or thinks he or she is making, quite other works. They are what else is going on.

The trouble with writing any book at all, though, is that it will produce its under-book, so the process is, by definition, an endless one. During the writing of fiction, this can be a beneficent, even invigorating, force. The shape of the next book consolidates beneath the one you are extracting from the waters. Reasonable enough to object that I can't have much experience of this, as I've not written a novel for so long, but that does not mean they haven't been circling me, and showing their backs up through the deep.

As a by-product of a memoir already written, the notion of the under-book leads to the sort of puzzle that is by turns a charming and a terrifying idea, one that first took hold in me when I saw in a doll's house a doll's house that contained a doll's house. I think that this realisation of infinite contained diminution comes to every child in one collapsed flash at around the age of three. It then returns, complicating and developing itself, over all the coming years as they pull themselves out of what looked like just the one vessel, but is actually a telescope, diminishing but not terminating – until it does.

My experience of Russian dolls was later, when I was about four, and somehow less interesting, because so well defined, the big capacious hollow doll on the outside, the little solid doll in one piece at the end of the, not actually in detail identical, row. The idea of the infinitude of entities fills the mind much more crammingly than its embodiment in wood and varnish dolls.

I saw the idea animated out at sea off the northernmost point of Colonsay. I mentioned the sight before in my spoken memoir, and round it has come again; it is what lies beneath, coming up each time from further below.

In engravings of sea battles, you may sometimes see in the corner, near the compass rose or churning against a fleet in order of battle, big-mouthed fish swallowing fish swallowing fish swallowing fish right down to sprats, and, it may be imagined, to fish too small to be drawn, smaller than a water drop, a single egg this size.

We were mackerel fishing in a clinker-built boat, adults and children, dipping and shaking darrows with metal and rubber lures at intervals along the simple line. The sea was neatly choppy, then stood still like setting jelly.

A breath was taken, somewhere. There began a sequence too remorseless to have been organised by anything but nature. From the sea dimpled a cloud of million upon million tiny fish the size of escaped swarming semicolons from this page, full-stop eyes and transparent comma tail. Next came the fish the length of little sentences, strips in the air, many more. Behind them and pulling some sea up with them came the flock of good-sized pollock, about a paperback long, soft and floppy and innumerable, followed by the vigorous black-printed hard-backed spines of the mackerel themselves, purposeful, rigid, silvery in flight, determined to avoid whatever it was by leaving their element. Some even fell into the boat they braved in their great print-run of collaborative fright.

In its own time, the basking shark surfaced, voluminous, dark, impossible to read, never seen entire until finished, forming and pressing aside the waters from its back, as slow as the last word, holding time up; as the small fry before it had splintered time into fraught literal quickness.

Our own amateur dipping into that sea for a few fish to clean and split, to dip in oatmeal and place in butter in a pan, was shown up as the interruption we humans are to what is actually always going on.

◆◆◆◆◆

After that easier time in February of this year staying with Fram and Claudia in Oxford, I understood that habituation was what I must use to drive out habit, and that, were I to be confronted with the reality of their life together, I would not be able to cleave so dearly to some trapping notion of their life's perfected surface. Not that their life is any less happy than I imagine it, but instead of being as far from it as I can arrange to be and thinking of nothing but it, I can try although I am blind, to see it in truth.

It is not so dreadful not to be loved as it is not to feel able to give love: 'Let the more loving one be me.' It was the thing I could do, and somehow I have so scared myself as to feel that even the love I give, that came so easily, to my children, has been chilled by my shutting myself out in the cold.

I'm running out of things to lose and therefore find myself, to my shame, with rather less to give. It happened more suddenly than I had reckoned with. I think that it must be like that for everybody. It's always too soon.

The weekend after I had spent quite a time in Oxford with them, Claudia invited me to stay again. Toby again cooked a roast with vegetables from his allotment and an aunt of Claudia's was staying. Claudia has many aunts. There are many parts for women in her family drama.

The oven hadn't been cleaned for a bit, so there was a smell of cooking. Fram is exigent about smells; they lighten or darken his mood. He was once angry when I made popcorn before Steven Runciman came to lunch at our flat in Oxford. The great student of the patriarchate of Constantinople was then in his late nineties. The air in the flat where we lived was blue with popped kernels and burnt corn oil, a seedy sort of hecatomb. Why did popcorn suggest itself as an appropriate snack?

That Friday evening in Oxford decades later by now in our own lives, Fram was scratchy, though the supper was delicious. I wondered whether it was all a put-up job, Claudia being so considerate of my feelings that she arranged to rile Fram to show me that their relationship isn't perfect. Or the two of them setting it up, with Toby, spreading carbonised fat on the innards of the stove. Or . . . these are the tergiversations of my obsession in all its banality.

The evening passed happily, robustly, confidentially. I didn't cry that much in bed after we had said goodnight and I managed to do what I do so that I will not howl like a dog, which is to have Proust ready in CD form on the turntable of the CD machine I take with me and put on the pillow next to me if I'm in a double bed. I hold another pillow and lie and listen.

Sometimes I wake up in the night and remember that I am I and what has gone before and I burn. My eyes stare open at these times, but what's the point? They aren't open, like water to light, for reading. They look at the carnage and they sting from the carbon of the burnt-up days and hopes. I burn with remorse. Its name, Remorse, suggests it is a practice form of death, 'mors', though its root is not death but the bite that it holds on the spirit.

No professional associated with the so-called 'psychological approach' to my blepharospasm had taken seriously the idea of remorse by this point. Every one of them flinched from any term that implied moral judgement or any system beyond the pragmatic, what you might call, even, the self-centred. How swiftly self has replaced even the sense of social responsibility. There is a free-market psychiatric bias in the establishment.

Perhaps the most rapacious free marketeer so far has been the hypnotist, famous and by all accounts highly effective, whom I visited just once in the New Year of this year. Her secretary took my credit card number. The waiting room offered the usual macabre trailer for what is to come. As has become familiar to me, magazines are laid out with exaggerated care as though they were learned journals, and loose-leaf files of before-and-after shots of plastic surgery procedures are helpfully disposed on a side table near the artificial flowers, that are periodically refreshed with scented spray by outside contractors. In the winter months, there may be a replacement flower arrangement in carmine and spruce. At Christmas the tree will be equipped with shiny empty presents hanging from the plastic-needled boughs.

I entered the studio (too creative in arrangement to be called a consulting room) of the renowned hypnotist, and she addressed me, looking at my woven leather handbag that I'd bought from a hippie outlet online. She spoke one word, which will be familiar to fancy shoppers.

'Bottega?' (Bottega Veneta is a, very expensive, Italian fashion house.)

No, I said, my bag wasn't from there.

She interrogated any of my clothes that were susceptible of such a nakedly undeserved upgrade, and, when I wouldn't play, she laid me low on a long leather lounger with a sticky bolster for my head. There was an almost fresh towel over it.

She encouraged me to think of a beach, on which I was lying, maybe in company, 'feeling great about myself'. I took a beach from my extensive collection, a good cold beach, with pebbles and reeking seaweed. I added litter. I am made itchy by the idea of the hot palm-fringed beaches of the brochures, so in a way I was selecting a more relaxing setting in which to become porous to her trickling syrup.

She told me that I was right under now and that men preferred blonde to grey hair, so I might think of getting my hair highlighted. I was there because I couldn't see, not because I was looking for Mr Anyone at All. Her own hair, I could not help having noticed, was what advertisers believe all men adore to run their craggy yet strangely sensitive fingers through, teased, red, and full of product. She encouraged me, in a special swooping, supercaring voice that sometimes left her grammar in trouble, to find a secret place within myself where I was 'very very calm'.

I'd rather have been reading a book.

When she started talking in a normal, coarse, 'real life' voice again, I sat up and hoped that I could disappear for good.

'It says on your paperwork you are a writer,' she began. 'I've written a book. Would you mind casting an eye over it? It's going to be called *I'm Alright, so Fuck You.*'

The extraordinary thing is that I didn't say, 'I came to you because I cannot see and it is driving me mad.' I said, 'Oh, how very interesting. Is it about self-esteem issues?'

'You are very sympathetic, Candida,' she said. 'You could be in my line of work.'

So now I know. I could talk rubbish to desperate people and be paid for it.

I cancelled the next two sessions (you had to book in batches, such was the demand). The secretary explained in a soothing voice that they would have to keep my deposit for the missed sessions. A hundred per cent. It may indeed be my path on life's winding yet rewarding journey to utilise my prodigious empathic powers to print money with the sad press of others' credulity. The book, over which no eye of mine had been cast, emerged, and is a big seller. That's most likely because I went nowhere near it. Unsympathetic magic.

The worst of the remorseful nights have been in hospital, where you are more alone for not being alone. You cannot weep. It would be cruel and selfish, among the sick and dying. And if you start to weep, you may start to howl, and call down the shape that is lying in wait for us all in the dark, coming back at the gallop (or jig, or silent tread) again. Always coming back for more.

The next day, in Oxford after the smoky roast, Fram asked me how to clean an oven. I told him and he bought the materials. Because no one else in the household bothers, he did it, and took pleasure in it. I offered to do it, and with some patience he resisted the temptation to say, 'You silly bitch, your willingness to clean the ovens of others blind while they pick flowers has got you where you are today.'

While he cleaned the oven, wearing gloves, with bicarbonate of soda, I cleaned the silver, much of it his parents', that had lived so tidy – though not tidy enough – a life with us, but a tidy life that had let it down. It was now rubbing along with all kinds of impurities and no one was bleeding.

I reunited forks with forks, knives with knives, rubbed with silver-polish-impregnated wool, and realised that I was achieving nothing but the temporary cleaning of some silver, and that it was not a metaphor for anything at all.

If I was cleaning silver, it was just so that the silver might be clean. I had lived my life trying to implement the beautiful ideal of Fram's subject of study, George Herbert, 'Who sweeps a room, as for Thy laws, Makes that, and the action, fine', but I had confused the terms of life and art. I was cleaning a lot of forks that would get dirty again as they should in the ordinary process of life.

◀•✦•▶

I must not place myself in the category of one whose life is not real, since it is the life that I have.

I cleaned the bath, here on Colonsay, doing it by feel, with gloves, and a pungent wholesale chemical scouring ointment that suited just fine. It is dangerous to live wholly through others if there is anything at all impure in your nature. I must put myself out into the warm and light, that I am convinced I do not deserve. I lie cold and burning in the drawer where I have stowed myself away like an old knife, blackening and growing self-sharpening as remorse grinds at me, burning away like this in the cold.

This pain is not even useful.

I think that I've seen it off every time, this shameful pain.

But it returns.

It is the sense that I earned my blindness by every lovely thing I saw and my unhappiness by every moment in my life that was good that galls and imprisons me. It is so trite, so dull, so inutile.

It is cold and the doves are roosting in the garden on this island. Soon it will be dark, or the light that passes for the dark in the North in spring.

Chapter 11: Pollen and Soot and the Family in the Cupboard

It is a perfect drying day, blowy, bright. The deep trees and giant rhododendrons over the terraced lawn at the back of the house make coloured walls that swim and fill up all the windows, which are wide open. Although it is Saturday, not a washday, I have washed the sheets and shirts and hung them out.

Many visitors to Colonsay are keen birdwatchers. The chough with its red beak and legs can be seen up close as a soldier in a sentry box, with just that gap for interspecies respect. The probe-beaked oyster-catcher investigates the strand between Colonsay and Oransay with its prying disdainful notation of the polished tidal sand.

Last night, sitting in the sun that brought out the Mediterranean smell of the fennel foaming in Katie's raised herb bed, we heard the scrawp of the corncrake, *Crex crex*, its Latin name remaking its call, from the field beyond the white rose hedge, '*Blanc Double de Coubert*', that smells of vanilla, which she made with cuttings from a hedge at a farm in the north of the island.

On my desk is a withering newspaper cutting. In last week's *Oban Times* the regular SermonAudio.com display advertisement carries as its text, 'Like a bird that strays from its nest is a man who strays from his home.' As if this were not striking enough to a sinner, or to anyone feeling faintly sad or guilty, the last words of this boxed item are, as they are every week, 'YOU ARE KNOWN UNTO GOD!'

God, whose search engine is ineluctable. Can I have been the only consumer (I can hardly say proper reader) of the *Oban Times* who felt discovered, found out, by these words? Is that the point of these texts in newspapers? Their applicability to everyone vulnerable, much like horoscopes, which are designed to touch all who breathe or love or doubt.

As soon as sun is reliable, and the wind is low, there is the chance that midges will arrive. So they came. You can hardly see them, even if you can see. The first sign is that you start to twitch like a dog, and flip your paws at your ears and ankles. Midges are nanotechnologists. They reach places that you could not devise for pertinacity, the base of an eyelash, the shadow of a hair, the inner circle of a bra, the far spiral in the secret ear, the tender meat that would be an oyster or the Pope's nose if you were a cooked chicken.

Inside the farmhouse, itself still used to being cold after many winter months, Katie lit the stove with kindling, put in logs cut by William from the dark windbreak pines he is steadily thinning, and closed its small iron doors over the flames in the bright daylit room. You grow used to many kinds of weather in one day, in one house. Sometimes there are several weathers at the one time, a different squall or new sunbeam for each face of a house. Weather claps soon against itself, so that an unmixed day of sun or unvarying rain seems to last longer than other days.

At nine o'clock yesterday evening, I was back at my desk in the big house, which is also table-of-all-work and dining surface, in the old nursery that is now a sitting room. Two hours of light to go, at least. Two arms of yellow dwarf azalea were dying in a dull brass vase with a smell like leaf mast and honey, too good to get rid of, though the flowers are falling in little yellow dabs and flecks down on to the table, where they stick because they are so full of nectar.

Two of the petals of Meconopsis, the blue Himalayan poppy that loves the island soil and that Katie grew from seed, have fallen from the single plant with its one four-petalled flower that she has given me in its plain pot to have beside me while I work. The fluffy pistil sticks out beyond the ring of stamens whose anthers are golden yellow with pollen, not the sooty ring of black dusty anthers at the centre of most of the poppy family's flowers.

Like all blue flowers, it looks like an idea. Speedwell, forget-me-not,

411

the blue poppy, the Scottish bluebell (also known as the harebell), chicory, gentian, plumbago; they recall bits of fallen sky.

The sky that is, we are told, not itself actually blue. Perhaps that is why these flowers are like abstractions.

As well as being a great novel, *The Blue Flower* by Penelope Fitzgerald has a most suited and suggestive title, evoking, as it does, the short life and foreshortened love of a philosopher from a northern country, Novalis. A blue flower is the plant badge or emblem of the kind of otherness, natural unattainability, sought in some areas of German Romantic thought.

All flowers summon a sense of their transience that intensifies their effect upon those susceptible to their spell, plump double flowers or the fleshy hard-wearing flowers to some of us proportionately less so.

Blue flowers seem ineffably more transient and frail. Fragile is too strong and consonantally pegged down a word for it; these flowers are frail like faded worn cloth or like those patches of sky. They are remote, as though glimpsed. They are slips of things, a hint, like very young people in the one summer when they know they are lovely but do not know the effect of it, or the sea around the next bend, or fresh water between mouth and thirsty throat. They are half-seen. Once you have lived for a certain time, a blue flower makes you at once satisfied and sad.

You can't keep it. Even the seemingly robust hyacinth is an emblem of vanished masculine beauty, for the drowned curls of young heroes. If you press a blue flower in your prayer book, its petals turn purple unless your prayers are acid-free.

The poem 'Vergissmeinnicht' by Keith Douglas, who was killed at twenty-four in the Second World War, flowers across borders of notional nationhood with its description of the words in the note-book of a dead young man, in his Gothic German script, telling his girl, Steffi, not to forget him. The myosotis around the door of the church at Balbec are what the enraged Charlus upbraids Marcel for failing to recognise – *'Ne m'oubliez pas!'*

When I looked out through the flawed glass of the windows in the evening of Friday, as well as through my own already flawed gaze, I saw the shadow of the house thrown out on to the waving, shimmering leaves of the big trees. Three chimneys measured themselves along those wide trees, and the long line of the roof offered its shadow along the lawn and the lower reaches of the trees whose individual leaves were still holding sparkling doses of light.

It is unusual to see a solid thing made insubstantial against a moving surface, but shadow had its say. Nothing lasts. There are as many ways of looking as there are of seeing. Do not think you have seen it all, just because your own sight is changing. The new leaves of the copper beech were almost transparent to the late sun, rippling, moving at a different rate from the leaves on the smaller more susceptible trees, the beech's leaves rhubarb green and pink under the plain blue sky.

At three floors, the house is lower than the trees. The trees and the house have different rhythms of regeneration; that is all. The lengths of their watches differ. The trees measure by the life of their leaves and fruit, the house measures by the years between the birth of one human generation and another. Between the trees and the house, pups lollop then dash into dogdom, go grey, stiffen, settle, stay by the stove to dream of dash and lollop and at last die, each taking a human childhood to make their life's full circle.

On the mainland, Angus's heart is beating itself better, under observation.

———◆◆◆———

Why lead my life if someone else can do it better?

Most of my experience of the last ten years is not undergone but envisioned, prefigured, particularly so, and I say this without regret, since I came up here to the island to separate myself from my own various forms of incapacity made worse by blindness. My experience has been not precisely second-hand, but often vicarious.

What is the opposite of a stalker? I do not mean the one who is stalked. I mean the one who seeks to be consumed by the fire in the lives of others, the one who is made more shadowy by others' lightness, as opposed to one made more real by their glaring lack of substance.

It is all too many of us, since this unholy loss of self and rampaging, insecure, hunting down of reasons to be unhappy is probably what makes people buy magazines.

Yet Fram and Claudia, unlike film stars, whose sway and revenues depend upon it, do not want to be lived through. They live through one another.

The magaziney vicariousness is a decadent state in which to wish away a life. On the weekend in Oxford when I cleaned the silver and Fram cleaned the oven, I thought that something was repairing itself, or, perhaps better, something new was knitting itself.

You could interpret what happened next as the necessary consequence of thinking too much in terms of metaphors. Claudia had a quiet friend staying, I'll call her Antonia.

Our son had two friends for dinner. They both had dead fathers and mixed backgrounds: American, Russian, Israeli, British, Chinese, Filipino. They had the unforgiving beauty of the very young, but the company was good and I hardly felt odd. Minoo was enjoying his 'two mothers, one father, one father's girlfriend's twins' father' caperings. I thought I was taking things pretty lightly and not coming over humourless at the scene. The happy table stretched, as it does, to embrace whoever comes.

Everyone over thirty was quite tired. Fram and Claudia had been working all day. I am always tired. Living with my hot big not quite mended leg and half-cut eyes tires me out.

But everything was going well. I hoped Minoo's friends were enjoying their look at his family.

At one point Fram said, with the weight of a gnat, not even of a gadfly, 'If Claudia dies, I will marry Antonia.'

It was just a sally. I saw then that he really is free of me. The thought that he is married, in fact, to someone else didn't occur to him.

Not a feather fell from the dove I felt had been taken by a hawk not five feet above our heads at the table. No one noticed a thing, nor thought it. Only I, and I had best get over it.

There was no reaction save within me. They were modern youth and we were modern adults. There was nothing to notice. But I collected it and swelled inside from the allergic reaction, the anaphylactic shock, of the midge-bite that I took as hawk-strike.

That's it. I have it. Anaphylactic shock is what I go into when there is talk of marriage, of husband or wife. I carry a syringeful of Adrenalin to restart my heart in case of being stung by a wasp, but it is quite as important to carry a syringe of thought within my mind for these occasions that will go on for the rest of my life, when marriage or something relating to it comes up.

By the time everyone went, I was red inside and swollen and finding it hard to breathe. When I spoke to Fram, trying to implement a new version of myself, one who spoke up when trodden on, he was angry and bored by what I had to say and said that it had been meaningless, that the terms had no weight and he was tired and wasn't thinking, least of all about that old stuff, that had no meaning. None of it meant a thing. It was very late, he had been working on papers till four the morning before and was exhausted.

All fair and reasonable.

I took myself to my bed in Minoo's room among the memorabilia of his parents and grandparents and settled with Proust and the machine that makes him possible.

Claudia said, 'Don't present him with despair he can do nothing about. It is horrible for him.' She is good at him like some people are good at croquet or, more seriously, chess. It is difficult in every dimension, but those who love it rise to the difficulty and wish only for more dimensions through which to engage with this completely absorbing game of systems, traditions, feints, tactics, glamour of thought and an infinitude of reciprocities, as many as those grains of rice my mother-in-law once told me would fill the world if you factored them up on the squares of one single chessboard, moving by a certain mathematical sequence that I now forget, or was it she who never knew, and each grain inscribed countless times itself with the name of the beloved, like the rice grain she was allowed to look at as a child in a dark family house in Bombay, the grain taken from its precious casket kept in a cabinet, a single white grain that bore, she was assured, the thousand thousand names of God written upon it with a diamond nib; and how could she ever know that this was not so?

It decided matters that the grain was small, white, much like any other grain, yet it looked, in its silver-hinged, leather, velvet-lined case, taken from the cabinet, in the dark room in the big dim house in the enormous city of Bombay, to the small girl, like no other rice grain at all in the history of the world, being alone, and, in contrast to all about it, so very small, so very white, so intensely only itself and apart from all other grains of rice ever.

So what is to be my syringe against the sting and swell when I try to contemplate my state with clear eyes? How to make a net with plenty of holes and quite a dearth of string?

It has to be words, after all and not the mathematical equation I was struggling for in Hampshire when grounded by my leg. I love the idea of mathematics, but I can't seem to carry arithmetic with me, so that I relearn principles again and again and fail to make them part of my equipment.

I need a short formula of words for topical application, when the shocks, as they will, come, and then, after I have stuck the jag into the vein, I can retire from panic into calm and listen to, or maybe even read, the longer reaches of words that lie in books and keep on seeking the way best to live.

It is Sunday now. The necessary words may have been there all along.

Cymbeline is an odd late play made of parts that fit together but roughly, some sophisticated, some simple. It contains lines to which people return because sadness has never been so consolingly expressed in spite of the dislocating oddness of the actual scene in which the lines are spoken.

> 'Fear no more the heat o' the sun,
> Nor the furious winter's rages,
> Thou thy worldly task hast done,
> Home art gone, and ta'en thy wages.'

The refrain brings pollen, soot, dust to life as the atoms to which we all come. It begins with sun and ends in dust; it is astral physics in poetic form, in a couplet. Two lines of English verse then tell us we are children of the sun, and made, all of us, of sun and dust. That black chimney where the sweeps work is where we are caught in life, even golden lads and girls. There is a view of the sun from the constraining dusty black. Some few are for a time out in the sun. All come to dust.

> 'Golden lads and girls all must,
> As chimney sweepers, come to dust.'

But it's not those lines that I have been keeping by me, against such a demand as I'm presently making for a prophylactic line, so much as those mysterious words,

> 'Hang there like fruit, my soul,
> Till the tree die.'

I have loved them for years, and do not know what they mean.

Or, they may be made to mean a number of things. They are not imprecise. They speak whereof most of us had best not try to speak or it will be wind and piss. The impression they make breathes out from within them like sea from inside a chambered shell. They express a great perhaps. These were Rabelais's, almost too perfectly conclusive, last words: 'I am in search of a great perhaps.'

The circumstances in which this line and a half is spoken, by Posthumus to his estranged wife Imogen, are not, nor can ever be, comparable to what has happened between Fram and myself. For us there is no return to what was before. Neither present truth nor passed time permit. Our separation may have been based upon a misunderstanding, but the misunderstanding was all mine.

I wish that these lines, which I have kept by me for years in case of emergency, were not spoken in circumstances like this, if it gives any impression that I dream that reconciliation of this sort may be brought about. I do not. Another sort of reconciliation, yes, but not the reconciliation of the child awaking from nightmare 'as though it had never been'. That is for dreams, romances and plays, places where time means what the dreamer or the playwright says and not what time itself, in our reality, comes to mean. I would like to take the words out of their situational context, if I may.

Anaphylactic shock, when you break the word down, means that you are without a guard against the shock. Prophylactic means that something works as a guard. *Phylax* means guard.

The mysterious, literally almost pregnant, line and a half from *Cymbeline* slips to its stilled reader the imperative to remain living until there is no life. It is a line that is hard to break down, but by no means obscure. In logical terms, it is easy to take exception to the suggestion that fruit can be longer-lived than a tree, though that is unnecessarily literal, since what is being spoken of is not a fruit but a soul. Posthumus may be addressing his wife, or his own soul, or she may be his soul; surely all of this is intended to be within the reach of the words. The ambiguities are smoky in a play that splices ancient Britain with Renaissance Italy. The line and a bit are hard to catch. They are, like blue flowers, glimpses.

This line fumes with the negative capability that shows us what can happen when certain full notes are struck, one after another. The rock cracks and a seed is set.

What is the 'tree', here? Is it Posthumus, the husband, himself, addressing the wife who is clinging to him in their reunion? Is it Posthumus himself, bearer of his own soul? Is it the body? Is it life? In my prophylactic application of the line, I think that it is necessary to take the step of saying that, for my purpose, the tree might have been Fram, but it must now be the impersonal stand that is my span of life, from which I hang, perhaps as passive as a fruit but full of something even if it is only an extract from the tree. Fruit may offer consequences, from wisdom, the apple, to hospitality, the pineapple, or a periodic sentence to hell, the pomegranate.

I have to be my own tree.

Since living here on Colonsay, William has learned how to cut down a tree safely. When a tree falls, you must have the closest possible idea as to where and how it will fall. If it falls into another tree, you can only with difficulty reduce it to logs, whereas if you cut it so that it falls into a space you have already cleared, it is ready to cut up. There is also the matter of safety. A tree falls down bringing a ton weight headlong. A man working alone can be pinned and killed by a tree that will crush his ribs like those of a bird. Legislation on chainsaw work attempts to avoid this, but the chief safety is prevention. All is established by the precision of the sink-cut that must go in at forty-five degrees at the base of the chosen tree at precisely the point opposite to the direction in which you want the tree to fall.

My friend Trevor, whom I have known and respected for a generation and who is a woodsman to the ends of his branches, says that in parts of Hampshire the sink-cut is called the gob-cut. Trevor listens with such attention to trees that he would rather drive towards them than away from them. He means that he would rather be in the country than the town. In spite of this, he has sat with me in London hospital waiting rooms waiting for doctors to come and see to my various fellings. Trevor has seen it all, and his conclusion is that he would rather be outside among trees than anywhere else. He likes to read about trees. Recently, his power saw was stolen, and his toolbox. What use can those tools be to someone else? He had had that saw for twenty years and he and it had grown used to one another. He had wanted to hand that saw to his son.

This year was a big bluebell year in the woods where Trevor works. He can't remember a year as good for bluebells. He thinks that the bluebell woods get better every year because the number of bluebell years may be melting for us all at the age we are. He does not pretend that we haven't seen our youth away.

A tree, when it falls, brings all manner of tenants down with it. There may be birds' nests in its branches, a marten nest in its bole, a squirrel drey in its heart, an ant city under its bark at the root, thousands of grey slaters or woodlice pouring from it, moths in chipping millions coming out like stars or dust.

***

If I think of my life as a tree, it is clear that I have taken, or given to myself, the gob-cut. But no one but myself is trying to fell me and I want for as long as they wish it to offer shade to my children. When I delivered that sink-cut to Fram thirteen Aprils ago, it smote him, but his roots were too strong to let go their hold and he has grown well beyond the cut and up into the canopy from where the view is clearer. His heartwood has strengthened. Arrows and longbow taken from his seasoned aim and reach hit home.

It is the last evening of the last day I am allowing myself for these eleven chapters about the year since I spoke the first part of this memoir. I intended to look clearly at why it happened, and I think I perceive two answers, one reductive and deadly and the other more open to some kind of remedial use.

I am very blind as I type this, twisting my head around in the search for sight. It does not escape me that I am twisting away, too, from the subject. In spite of being one who loves family, home, and the detail that comes with settling, what I have done is cut and run when I can extract no answer that does not involve confrontation or change. I am anxious to staunch this reaction, as I hope to curtail the delusion of self-comfort by means of suicide, in order to protect the next generation.

The way that I can see to staunch it is to see, or to try to see, and certainly to name, only what is true about it all, and not to rush from hurt into harm, or from pain into damage, since harm and damage affect those others, whom I live not to hurt or pain.

It is easier by far, I am afraid, to come to these serene-sounding conclusions living alone on an island, where little is required of me save the capacity to earn enough to pay for my keep. I need not see here, nor walk, nor have social contact, all of which are beyond me. I keep clean and live retracted like a claw within a paw.

At least I need not insist on pressing upon the thorn in the paw. At some point I may allow it to work its way out. I must not define myself around it.

Young thrush are everywhere in the garden this evening. They are slighter than their parents, no speckled waistcoat yet. They sing their hearts out in the long grass under the soft-leaved flowering sorbus that line the drive of this much adapted house in which I first found refuge over forty years ago.

It was pale strawberry-ice pink then, with white sills and window frames. Its wings wore, as they still do, mock windows that need painting in, like eyes on a blank face, like those eyes in the front of a boat I mentioned at the start of this memoir. Now the house is pale cream, its sills a pigeon grey. Or is it yellow? It depends on the rain. At its skirt where it meets the gravel of the drive along its two embracing arms and surprised central block, are still ranged hundreds of green glass floats and two cannons. At the back the house rises from a sea of planting, mainly blue flowers, agapanthus, blue poppy, aquilegia, cerinthe, iris. A magnolia and creamy roses clothe its walls.

Downstairs the bigger rooms are shuttered and cool. They are seldom in use till summer is higher, as they used to be when there were two parents and six children and me here.

The dining room and the drawing room smell of wood polish and damp, the flagged hall of stone and coal, the billiard room of leather from the brown eighteenth-century books that sit around the old half-sized table. The cues are in their clipped rack, the stained ivory balls arranged in patterns by the last children who played there. Even if you didn't know, you would be able to tell that it was little girls rather than small boys. The colours are arranged in patterns along the cushioned table-edge, to look pretty. It's not set up for a game, nor are the balls all scattered on the green. Girls have been here.

Or someone who has the fiction writer's habit of making patterns out of anything at all that comes to hand.

The curving corridor-room that leads from the hall to the drawing room has changed least. It has lost the stuffed bison head and a tally of bird-sightings that used to be kept beside the wind-up telephone over the window seat. The wind-up telephone has gone and there is one that our children now think of as old fashioned as we thought the wind-up one with its separate mouthpiece shaped like the chained drinking cup from the wishing well halfway up the old drive, that has chased around its rim, DRINK YOUR FILL THEN WISH YOUR WILL. The window seat is curved, like all the fitted furniture in the embracing wooden room. The window looks out on to a lawn at whose centre rises an enormous member of the lily family that looks like a palm tree.

Under the old lairds, the McNeills, that part of the garden was laid out to look like a Victoria Cross. Things in the shape of other things, that British passion. Now the borders around the lawn are soft in the revived cottage fashion, taking advantage of the pocket of botanical shelter and comparatively hospitable soil that lies around this house. The corridor-room is rayed in its curved ribs of bookshelves with many hundreds of clothbound books set in order by various sometimes contradictory understandings of sequence. History used comfortably to crop up everywhere, while gardening took up twenty or more densely plotted and embedded shelves, the books tucked in as tight as alpines. There were rather few novels, except for Wilkie Collins and C.S. Forester. Lawrence Durrell made a flashy showing in a lower shelf. He seems for now to have made off with the gardening books. They will be coming to an arrangement in one or another bird-wallpapered bedroom in the house. Walter Scott meanwhile has settled in the billiard room.

In the shelves of the corridor-room, the spines of the cloth bindings have succumbed to the light of the Hebrides; bright hues have quietened down so that the shelves now show the muted upstanding ranks of the field of lupins, purple and cream and dim yellow and soft pink bars of opacity ranking the length of one long curve, taller than a man, measured in batons of soft colour all along the tight arrays of shelving opposite the big window.

This evening there is no one in the bigger rooms, and even were Alexander and his family here, the rooms would most likely be empty, though not devoid of living things.

The drawing room has two tall windows that look out at the same lawn as the corridor-room window, a curvaceous triple window in the vaulting Regency idiom out to the front of the house, and a double door out to the long glass-roofed loggia that is full of scented plants and surrendering wicker furniture, and a tired cushioned swing on a rusting white-painted iron frame, with a rotting canvas jalousie. There is a ceramic sink on the loggia, for washing glasses and picnic plates or cleaning flowerpots or garden shears. When you turn the tap on, the water trembles within the pipe that is conducting it long before it condescends to arrive. The pipe softly clanks. The bolts holding it to the side of the house loosen minutely.

Growing up through a window seat in the first tall window as you enter the drawing room is a tall glaucous-leaved tree poppy, romneya, with petals white like a kerchief in a portrait of a lady by Romney himself. The romneya asserts its spindly but persistent life annually through the house's painted pebbledash skim, through its brick, through its floorboards, and into the habitual place it achieves, determinedly driven by the imperative to reproduce itself, clipped between the shutter and the cushioned window seat, on which piles of green photograph albums, recording equivalent human struggles and bloomings, lie and soften in the damp efflorescent air.

In the cupboard opposite the loggia door, drinks are kept, and an oval tray of the old silver Madeira cups that came out on the Sundays when we listened to long-playing records on the wind-powered record player, also stationery and some outlived toys. In this cupboard one recent spring, a mallard raised her brood among the envelopes and sticky labels. Did she have an accomplice, who let her out to fetch grubs for her ducklings? Did she feed off the spiders and mites and woodlice who would conquer the drawing room in a sleeping beauty's rest time, if they weren't shooed away from time to time? Were those ducklings raised on correspondence cards and flat Schweppes mixers?

Any precise answer rests with that duck mother and her children, so the answer will be, as it is to many things, a dry quack and no more.

We cannot always see the whole picture, after all.

It may be as well to keep a door in the mind open to whatever may alight among the paper and strong drink and forgotten toys.

Afterword

It is now mid-September. Mr Foss operated on my right leg and both eyes on 30 June. He took out the tendons from behind my knee and sewed them in beneath the skin, stitching up my eyelids to my brows, pegging my brows from stitches above them in the 'blank' area of my forehead, so that there is a system of artificial tension that counteracts the blepharospasm's continual downward force and in so doing offers sight. My forehead hurts. It feels as though it is cork, with drawing pins, six of them, set circumflexwise above each eye. There are six points of pain, connected by unhappy but essential tension.

The effect is at once of wound and freeze, vulnerability and a harder surface than the subtly changing thin-skinned area around a human eye usually offers. My eyes are fat-looking, peering piggily through swollen yet not smooth crevices. They feel bruised and stiff, both the eyes themselves, weirdly, and the lids. But – I can see.

I can see.

I look broken and I look mended. I have a bodged face. I'm not complaining. I'm attempting to define. There is no eyelid and there are no fluttering delicate surfaces for another person to read. I'm unclear as to how my face is legible to anyone who sees it. Most people say reflexively that I look the same. I haven't asked them, the same as what? There is no need for them to say that; it's a nervous reaction, like saying one looks well when one has suddenly got fatter. The most sensible description was from a friend who said that I looked as though I'd been stitched up after a fight. Sometimes I feel as though my face has been pegged up like washing, on metal pegs, then hung, heavy, and been frozen like a dishcloth in a cold snap. My soft old face depends loosely from its new circumflexed stitches.

But I can mostly see out from it, out of it, this face on pegs. This return to a world where I can read is an unlooked-for relief, a blessing that I had not imagined would come my way. I had believed that, since blepharospasm rarely goes into remission, I was shut in the dark for good.

Sometimes, if I am tired or frightened, or if the light is bright, I clamp blind again, so I still carry my foldable white stick, though not, of course, on to aeroplanes, since it would make a plausible weapon and is therefore not allowed. I have learned that, as I'm a nervous traveller, I do tend still to go blind at railway stations and airports.

Mr Foss said that my tendons are of notably poor quality and he had to reinforce them with some synthetic strings called something like 'Plastron'. He says that you can improve the quality of tendons by regular running. He says that running is 'hell at the time'. It is clear he cannot lie. I still love trying to guess what he will say next.

Mr Foss said that it was 'a pig of an operation'.

His own sport, I've discovered, is high-level competitive fencing.

Mr Foss is slight, and only ever to the point.

Things had got quite bad by the time I went to the hospital for this last operation. Nottingham has several hospitals including the Queen's Medical Centre, the largest in Europe. I arrived in the morning at the small hospital on the Mansfield Road where Mr Foss had stripped out my eyelid muscles in January, having come down from Colonsay the day before. It was a journey that would not have been responsibly possible on my own, I was so blind by then, yet not an adept, since not a reconciled, nor, thanks to Mr Foss's operation, a resigned, blind person, and was also still lame from my broken leg. William came with me on the boat to Oban and handed me to his daughter Flora at Glasgow.

She had come up that morning from Euston in order to accompany me to Nottingham. We had a number of train-changes between Glasgow and Nottingham. Flora participated in a Virgin Trains hot-meal survey. Asked to choose between Lancashire Hotpot and

Chicken Curry (it was a conspicuously warm day), she asked to try both, otherwise how could it be a survey? She's skinny and always hungry. She received a thimbleful of hummus and two small red 'presentation tomatoes', together with a press release more substantial than the snack itself, about moving forward into a future where the customer came first. You can see why Mediterranean travellers are baffled in Great Britain.

We crossed a lavishly green part of England after the always for me too sudden loss of Scotland.

By the time I was in the hospital, I wanted anaesthesia of thought and condition, and was, I now see, inexcusably unprofessional (is being a patient a profession?) in speaking to both Mr Foss and the anaesthetist the way I did. I asked them if they wouldn't just let me go to sleep for good.

It was a bad thing to say. I was exhausted by my condition. Nonetheless, it was ugly. When I think of it now, I see – I see! – how things had grown in. Like ingrowing toenails, I had ingrowing eyeballs, or, more precisely, an ingrowing brain. I was doing time with my sadness, it is true, but at least I *had* the time to do.

Mr Foss, when I asked him, said that our lives are not ours to take, nor are those of others, and that the doors you do not, ever, open are cruelty and madness. He could have said much more.

He did not tell me what follows, but I found out later, and by accident. His great-grandfather Sigismund Stanislaw Voss, a Latvian engineer who spoke six languages, who had converted when he married his Lutheran wife, Wally, had survived the Russians but was lost to the Third Reich, which took him from his post at Massey Engineering in France and to the concentration camp at Drancy. There is no record of his fate.

The anaesthetist, when I asked if he couldn't just knock me out, said that if anything happened to my life, his wouldn't be worth living. Later I learned that he had recently had a heart attack and spent many weeks in hospital.

After the operation, he wrote me a detailed thoughtful response to my telling him that I had at some point been 'aware' during the operation. This is when the patient can hear what is going on and can think, but is unable to move (or they believe this to be so). As you will imagine, this state has a lot in common with certain nightmares of powerlessness and muffledness, when you know and see but cannot utter no matter how you strive. He questioned me closely, and sent me a number of articles on the subject. His guess was that my odd feeling might relate to my size and to my being an alcoholic. He managed to put both things tactfully. The sort of tact that must have been in demand at the Tudor court.

He said that I must warn any anaesthetist who was about to put me under at any time in the future of this incidence of 'awareness' (it's a medically identified phenomenon), and he or she would increase the dose of one of the drugs involved to make sure that my brain as well as my body slept.

My sons and Fram came up for the night after the operation. I was bandaged and couldn't see them. I am told that I annoyed them by asking about their journeys. They felt that I should be telling them my news. I didn't really have any. I hadn't arrived anywhere yet. I felt a bit useless. Olly had come all the way up just to see some bandaged ghoul on a gantry, probably identifiable as his mother by its bulk. He was having to go to America early the next day.

◆◆◆◆

I am writing this in the beginning of autumn on a balcony beside an Italian lake, like some civilian idea of a real writer. The air is cool. There has been a Shelleyan squall. From where I am writing I can see – already the sentence is too rich in meaning to bear that meaning without my giving it an intrusive interjection for support, like the stitches holding up my stripped eyes – from where I am writing I can *see* a headland with growing upward out of it one quite small cypress, that seems to be gathering itself slimly for dive or flight. Its poise and pose remind me of a painted diver – the Tufa – on a wall at Paestum, in another part of this country that makes more sense to me than most.

The water is green and choppy tonight, the air just pink. Behind the headland, two long mountains meet in layers of blue. The sky is fumed with dusk as though the light weren't going, just fainting away. On the opposite shore, the small yellow town of Bellagio disposes itself. Two campanili stand out white and will later be lit up. I know this because we have been here long enough for habits and rhythms to have laid themselves down. We shall have been here for six nights tonight.

Not only can I see, but I am recommencing to see in steady planes and charges of colour, not just the juddery reception I had when I lifted my eyes with my hands. The sort of vision that I think I have lost, unless habit makes it return, is my sharp peripheral vision that used continually to be collecting. To an irksomely upbeat degree, for one so stuck on metaphor, I can only look forward – unless I swivel my head, which aches a lot of the time, I think from the tension it generates when pushing internally against the blepharospasm that waits inside it.

Quentin arranged that we might all be together in this place at the end of the summer. It is the first summer holiday that all four of the children have ever been on together. My three haven't been together in the summer like this for more than thirteen years.

The villa is reached by 184 steps down the sheer cliff from the swerving lakeside road. There was no such road when a group of four young Englishmen, calling themselves 'the Lizards', cleared the site they had clubbed together to buy in 1891 for a hundred pounds. They built a jetty, made the tall arcaded villa, established a garden and a little harbour. One of them kept a diary, which is downstairs. From it you gather the struggle and devotion required to plant and establish just one wisteria, the physical effort involved in creating this idyll on the edge of a moody body of water at the bottom of a cliff at the other side of the Simplon Pass which had not been open for that long. It's curious, this nineteenth-century English tendency to choose to domesticate the intractable.

I feel a connection between Colonsay and this house and its situation, the close relationship with weather, the dependence upon boats, the choice of rising to physical challenge and natural beauty over other forms of indulgence, made by men of the privileged class with the world at their feet at the height of Empire and on the verge of irreversible change.

These are the last redoubts where a man could feel himself master. It is a sort of play, though it could not be further from the drawing room. It is a way of addressing otherness by not having to read or talk about it, while draining off animal spirits through considerable physical exertion. The pioneer character favours natural beauty over the created kind.

The demands made by beauty upon this house are visible through its windows and from its several balconies. All the beauty asks is that one absorb the light, which is changing all the time, dim and pearly yet full of sharp attentive spills that fall on the mountains, showing up here a grey rock, here a white church, or on the water, reaching down into it to show a lake trout hanging there in a column of revealed green, or to catch a dragonfly clipped in the air for its moment, the same size, apparently, as a single scull lying on the water moving with the smooth unbroken rhythm that looks like stillness.

In 1910 the villa was burgled. Finding it empty, the thief spent the night. He left a note, '*Cantate anche per me*' ('Pray for me, too').

The older children have come from their work for the weekend. There is so much to see just now that I am staying at home at the villa.

Everyone goes out in the boat to look at things. I stay at home and see things. I've lots of work and am still lame over distances and bad at stairs. The pearls I wear always, that Quentin gave me twenty-seven years ago and that need restringing every year or so on knotted cotton, now have the sort of fastening that is made for blind pearl-wearers, a magnetic clasp. It collects safety pins and paperclips while I sleep.

I work here for ten or so hours a day and meet the family at meal-times and when they visit my balcony. I go rather slowly in order not to choke on my new experience of sight. It is hard to ration sight, but I am trying; I cannot yet avoid the superstitious sense that the consequence of seeing too much will be again to have my credit of sight-time withdrawn.

------◆◆◆◆------

This July after my second operation, Fram discovered, after a lot of enquiries and effort, a priest who was also a psychiatrist whom I made an appointment to go and see. There had been some suggestion that I might start taking lithium for anxiety. Lithium is a drug whose reputation is at present enjoying a degree of rehabilitation after being thought of as quite controversial. A helpful doctor friend had identified what she called an ingrained habit of what she called 'depersonalisation' in me; she was right, if it means, as I think it does, a coping system of saying to oneself that nothing bad matters if it's happening to oneself. Or, that nothing matters, since it's happening to oneself.

She also told me that she believed more strongly every day that one never knows what is going on inside other people. It's a sense upon which my life has been built, and which is a premise of, or a challenge to, much interesting fiction, but you seldom hear a doctor say it. Isn't that odd?

I was willing to do almost anything to find some sort of dry land to rest on.

Most days, I walked to the chemist's to buy new dressings and show my wound to the pharmacist. I put a gauze dressing on and then a creamy elastic long bandage that I wound round and round my thick right leg and pinned with little toothed clasps. My legs were thicker than ever, thick as waists at the knee, spongy and blue-red. Fram worried that the wound wasn't healing and badgered me to do something more assertive. I didn't.

The stitches were taken out of my leg. The scar was wet and about five inches long. The stitches had been neat. The stitches in my face came out in Nottingham, ten days after the operation, on 11 July. Fram took me. He and Mr Foss seemed to like each other; they were intrigued by one another's take and speed. They had that never-questioned high-functioning intelligence in common. I turn dozy in such company but it's the sort I like. I'm not bored; I'm listening. It's like listening to music, not eavesdropping.

On 17 July, I went to Nottingham alone, a treat. I was already going blind again. Mr Foss had warned of this. He said that after the second operation there is often a honeymoon of twenty-four hours when the patient feels as though everything has righted itself. This honeymoon, he warned me, is misleading. I visited Mr Foss to have the first go of Botox injections which I will now have every three months for the rest of my life, if I want to see.

'If' I want to see? Do some people actually decide that they want to remain in the dark? Apparently, the answer to this, in any intelligent terms, is yes. We'll come to that.

Mr Foss gave me four injections at specific points around each eye, eight featherlight poison darts in all. Any comparison with fencing is perfectly apt. He handles a syringe more lightly, more precisely, than anyone who has so far injected my eyes. Some people hurt. In their hands the needle feels wide and thick, unconfident. He was, as he always is, quick. He gave me the tiny jar of poison to take away, in case I needed topping up.

My deadly poison is still in Fram and Claudia's freezer. How like a fairy tale. The poison that makes me see is in the coldest part of their warm home.

❖

Minoo and I went to Edinburgh for the Book Festival for ten days. Every other day, I visited a surgery, to see about my leg, which had not healed properly, and which had put me back in the hospital for a time in Oxford. The flat we had rented was up many stone stairs.

Everything got better in Edinburgh. I was surprised by what happened to me at the Book Festival. I had felt I was there as a visitor, more than an author. Then someone got hold of the human story, the story that makes out of my whole recent experience something soppy; the 'I once was blind, but now can see'. Which is far too simple and not true, so it will probably be what is remembered.

I hope not, though.

It is a human story. It is also a story about words. If I hadn't been asked to write about going functionally blind for the *Scottish Review of Books*, *The Times* would not have reprinted the piece. Marion Bailey would not have read the piece nor so generously got in touch with me and told me about Mr Foss. I owe my present new-made sight to many, but directly to the *Scottish Review of Books*, *The Times*, John and Marion Bailey, and Alexander Foss.

The fight inside my head will not disappear, but the curtains may be lifted so that it may look outwards from its internal drama.

In there in my brain, decisions have been taken to shut my eyes down, taking much else with them.

Out there in the world, someone was imaginative enough to know what it might be like to be able to see and not to be able to see, and clever and knowledgeable and courageous enough to know that it might be done, and how.

433

Now it was the paper that owns the *Scottish Review of Books* that broke my little story. A few others went with it. The general tone was 'Triumph over Tragedy'. Not so, of course. One interviewer, from *The Times*, asked very shrewd questions. In each case he hit the spot. He asked, 'But has your condition gone or is it just held off?' And he asked, 'What has happened to your idea of yourself?'

My condition, or 'the' condition, so that it knows I'm not hugging it possessively to me, hasn't gone. It is held off. That must be good enough for me. It fights back day and night and I feel it punching from within my head. I have a sore head and tense eyes most of the time. But I am not shut in in the dark alone as I was.

You, having read this book, will have some idea of the answer to the second question. I worry that I will look ugly in my children's wedding pictures. I do look peculiar. I often don't recognise myself. I realise that I did rely, to an extent I did not understand, on how I looked. But I never knew that I was, sometimes, beautiful. I didn't feel it. Sometimes I see it now, in a photograph, and I think, 'You fool, you didn't do it right at all. When you looked like that, you felt as though you looked like this. You had it coming to you.'

So much for vanity. I have to meet new people with my self and not my face. People who knew me before are sometimes shocked. Often they don't recognise me. Sometimes I feel cross then relieved about this because I knew they were creeps all along and I can add it to my dossier on them and walk on, at others I feel sad but sad as one feels in an afternoon alone when one has just missed a telephone call; sad, but fairly sure that life is like that and that it might equally well have been a caller you didn't want to hear, a wrong number, or some unreal win on a non-existent lottery for which you haven't signed up.

———◆———

To some degree at the age I am, one is composed of loss, and here is a loss I have behind me, the loss of a beauty that wasn't a safe gift for me. Loss is the new beauty after a certain age, a matter for refining and sharing. I didn't ever admire the sort of looks I had. I looked a bit thick, where thick overlaps with apparently sexy. A bad mix for a sardonic introvert.

As to the less superficial stuff. My identity is shot to bits, I cannot pretend it is not. But I have some chance of finding it and maybe even changing it a little or patching it up where it was wearing out or set stubbornly in the wrong direction, frozen by habit.

What, if not writing, will be the home of any self I can build from the bits I finding lying around me as I look about after these years when I came to naught and thought that this was it?

Why write?

The tree isn't dead yet.

I want to pass it on, to pass the shiver that comes when we read and know for a time what it is to live, think, feel and be inside the mind of another.

———◆••◆———

There are phrases that stick. We can't probably be lucky enough to write one –

'And still she wished for company'

'Quoth the false knight upon the road'

'The Scots Lords at his feet'

– but we can recognise one, and pass it to a friend, a baton in the dark.

I write because the work is real. It involves concentration and a study of life, which is all we have. I write because I want to help my parents out of their graves, she wherever she is, and he in the wall of Scottish heroes. I write because I cannot often express things face to face, being at once (or I was; we'll see about that) performative and shy. I write because I don't think most of my children are interested at the moment in what may interest them after I am dead, the half of themselves that will have been buried with their mother, but that lives in them. I write because I want to write more well. And better. And better. I write because I read, and they are my patriotisms and loyalties, reading and writing. I write because it is the act of glorification and gratitude to which I am most suited to take up my apprenticeship. I write in order to keep abreast of the swim of words and to hold the world – whose glory is, with its sadness, that it will not be held.

I write because I wake up, I fall short, I sleep, I wake.

I write because the world and all I love in it is forcing itself upon my attention and to pay attention is everything.

I write because words change one another when they lie together. Because words change things. They make people see.

Words can mend what is broken, or render it more interesting than mended. They can make people attend to one another.

They are what we have that cannot be taken from us and what we have that we can give to other people without feeling stolen from.

Also plain words are always under threat. The languages of severely systematised untruth and imprecision, that exactly mean what they don't say, don't say what they mean, rejig it how you will, are used to sell everything from systems of government to hair gloss. Readers are mistrusted by those in power and not encouraged to keep their side of the bargain, which is to partake in the work themselves. If you wait for everything to be signalled, in a work of fiction, you lose connection with man and stars because you are listening to the satnav. A good writer has put in the invisible turnings, the neglected hedgerows, the boarded-up shops and dead men within the shadows or environs of his story, so that the reader may feel the wind in his mind, smell the wild rose, hear the rats, smell the deep pond, as he passes them. Do not underestimate the silences or breaks in a line.

I write because I'm not dead yet. And I seem to want not to be.

———◆•••◆———

I flew back with my older son and his girlfriend from Italy. The queue to get back into this country at Gatwick was long. I took my place in it. Oliver and his girlfriend went ahead, into the exit channel that was for identification by the irises of their young eyes. Their lives move at another speed, the speed of sight. Over the entrance to their route back into this country was a graphic of an eye. Eyes are everywhere, if you look. I want to attest to the goodness of life and I want to share something. If it isn't a life – well, then, let it be a sentence.

Acknowledgements

I used to have a life connected by many strands and anchors. It is less so now, considerably. Not all of them were more than notional. Several of them have been worn and loosened by time. Many have strengthened in spite of removal, change or death.

It will be evident that I owe boundless gratitude to those named within this book, my family and families. There are others without whom my life is hard to imagine and whom I would like to thank. They are Clare Alexander, Dan Franklin, Hannah Ross, John and Marion Bailey, Julian Barnes, Edward Behrens, Rupert Christiansen, Jamie Fergusson, Joe and Helen Fernandez, Flora Fraser, the late Anthea Gibson and all her family, Marianne Hinton, Arthur Hobhouse, Niall Hobhouse, Alan Hollinghurst, Flora Joll, Amanda Mackenzie Stuart, Sophie-Caroline de Margerie, Adam Mars-Jones, Trevor Messenger, Peter Parker, Frances Powell, Michael Sandberg, Nicola Shulman, Liv Stones and Ellis Woodman. They have, with my family and others named in the book or sealed in my heart, been my eyes at the worst of it and my connection to life at the best of it.

Now that I've had the good fortune to arrive in the United States in paper-and-thought form (possibly more actual than my flesh-and-blood self), I would like to thank Jennifer Barth and Jason Sack at HarperCollins for their response, their detailed grip, their openness to jokes, and their scrupulousness. That they judged that certain forms of repeated pain might not entertainingly be inflicted on their/my American readership and made their own surgeries is a matter for which you the reader may well wish to thank them also.

To the place and the people of the island of Colonsay, it is to a degree my life I owe as well as my love. I opened my eyes upon Scotland and it is upon Scotland that I hope to close them.

Alexander Foss has the burden of my articulated admiration to bear, a paper umbrella where he, a fencer, might have preferred a swordstick. He turns away from it, fearing hubris. He read this book in anticipation of finding in it the words of Milton upon his deceased wife, with which I shall cut its last tether to me, the words that cut to the quick, and to the dead:

'I wak'd, she fled, and day brought back my night.'

About the Author

Candia McWilliam was born in Edinburgh. She is the author of *A Case of Knives* (1988), which won a Betty Trask Prize; *A Little Stranger* (1989); *Debatable Land* (1994), which was awarded the *Guardian* Fiction Prize and the Premio Grinzane Cavour in its Italian translation for the best foreign novel of the year; and a collection of stories, *Wait Till I Tell You* (1997). In 2006 she began to suffer from the effects of blepharospasm and became functionally blind as a result. In 2009 she underwent an operation to partially reverse the condition. *What to Look for in Winter* won the South Bank Sky Arts Award for literature, the Spear's Book Award for memoir, the Hawthornden Prize, and was shortlisted for the Mind Book of the Year Award and the Duff Cooper Prize.